FORGED IN AMERICA

# THE GOLDSTEIN-GOREN SERIES IN AMERICAN JEWISH HISTORY

General editor: Hasia R. Diner

*Is Diss a System?: A Milt Gross Comic Reader*
Edited by Ari Y. Kelman

*We Remember with Reverence and Love: American Jews and the Myth of Silence after the Holocaust, 1945–1962*
Hasia R. Diner

*Jewish Radicals: A Documentary Reader*
Edited by Tony Michels

*An Unusual Relationship: Evangelical Christians and Jews*
Yaakov Ariel

*All Together Different: Yiddish Socialists, Garment Workers, and the Labor Roots of Multiculturalism*
Daniel Katz

*1929: Mapping the Jewish World*
Edited by Hasia R. Diner and Gennady Estraikh

*Hanukkah in America: A History*
Dianne Ashton

*Unclean Lips: Obscenity, Jews, and American Culture*
Josh Lambert

*Jews and Booze: Becoming American in the Age of Prohibition*
Marni Davis

*The Rag Race: How Jews Sewed Their Way to Success in America and the British Empire*
Adam D. Mendelsohn

*Hollywood's Spies: The Undercover Surveillance of Nazis in Los Angeles*
Laura B. Rosenzweig

*Cotton Capitalists: American Jewish Entrepreneurship in the Reconstruction Era*
Michael R. Cohen

*Jewish Radical Feminism: Voices from the Women's Liberation Movement*
Joyce Antler

*A Rosenberg by Any Other Name: A History of Jewish Name Changing in America*
Kirsten Fermaglich

*A Mortuary of Books: The Rescue of Jewish Culture after the Holocaust*
Elisabeth Gallas

*Dust to Dust: A History of Jewish Death and Burial in New York*
Allan Amanik

*Jews Across the Americas: 1492–Present*
Edited by Adriana M. Brodsky and Laura Arnold Leibman

*Forged in America: How Irish-Jewish Encounters Shaped a Nation*
Edited by Hasia R. Diner and Miriam Nyhan Grey

# Forged in America

*How Irish-Jewish Encounters Shaped a Nation*

*Edited by*
Hasia R. Diner *and* Miriam Nyhan Grey

NEW YORK UNIVERSITY PRESS
New York

NEW YORK UNIVERSITY PRESS
New York
www.nyupress.org

© 2023 by New York University
All rights reserved

Please contact the Library of Congress for Cataloging-in-Publication data.
ISBN: 9781479826063 (hardback)
ISBN: 9781479826070 (paperback)
ISBN: 9781479826100 (library ebook)
ISBN: 9781479826094 (consumer ebook)

This book is printed on acid-free paper, and its binding materials are chosen for strength and durability. We strive to use environmentally responsible suppliers and materials to the greatest extent possible in publishing our books.

Manufactured in the United States of America

10 9 8 7 6 5 4 3 2 1

Also available as an ebook

*To Loretta and Lew*

*"Talk about a combination"*

CONTENTS

*Foreword: A Good Place to Meet*     ix
    Kevin Kenny

Introduction: Forged in America     1
    Hasia R. Diner and Miriam Nyhan Grey

1. A Singular Encounter: Irish and Jews in Their American Home     9
    Hasia R. Diner

2. The Right to Choose: The Public Health and Birth Control Movements of Lillian Wald and Margaret Sanger     32
    Hannah Zaves-Greene

3. "Tammany's Chosen People": How the Irish Courted the Jewish Vote in Progressive-Era New York     56
    Terry Golway

4. Jews, Paul O'Dwyer, and a New York Life     67
    Robert W. Snyder

5. Defending Literary Genius: James Joyce's *Ulysses* on Trial     89
    Brett Gary

6. Laughter and Love between the Irish and the Jews     115
    James R. Barrett

7. Irish-Jewish Couples in American Film and Television     127
    Lawrence Baron

8. Playing the Nation: Constructing Cultural Revivals in the Irish and the Jewish Diaspora     149
    Dan Lainer-Vos

9. The Irish, the Jews, and Wilson's "Self-Determination"     167
    Marion R. Casey

10. A Tradition of Acceptance: Jews and Their Basketball Players
at an Irish Catholic College  184
*Jeffrey S. Gurock*

*Acknowledgments*  203

*Notes*  205

*About the Editors*  255

*About the Contributors*  257

*Index*  259

FOREWORD

*A Good Place to Meet*

KEVIN KENNY

As you walk down Fifth Avenue toward Washington Square, you may notice an elegant two-story red-brick building on your left, just before the Arch. Many pedestrians take a quick look at this building and the small garden in front as they pass by. Some take note of the plaque to the left of the door: Glucksman Ireland House. Inside is NYU's interdisciplinary center for the study of Ireland, Irish America, and the Irish diaspora. A welcoming home for everyone with an interest in things Irish, the center was created by one of New York's great Jewish-Irish couples, Lew Glucksman and Loretta Brennan Glucksman.

*Forged in America: How Irish-Jewish Encounters Shaped a Nation* originated as a public lecture series in Glucksman Ireland House organized by Professor Hasia R. Diner and Dr. Miriam Nyhan Grey. This lively collection of historical essays examines how the Irish and the Jews interacted in the United States, in ways they or their ancestors never would have done in Europe. The union of Loretta Brennan Glucksman and Lew Glucksman, and their creation of Ireland House, emerged from one such encounter. So too did the stewardship of the House in 2017–18 by Professor Diner, a renowned historian of the Jewish experience who has published influential studies of Irish American history as well. In its own distinctive way, Glucksman Ireland House embodies the unlikely meeting between the Irish and the Jews in the United States. It embodies, too, a distinctively cosmopolitan approach to Irish history and culture, captured in the scholarship and public programming of Dr. Grey.

Migration threw Irish and Jewish people together in the new and unexpected setting of urban America. They would not have come together otherwise. Jewish immigrants in the United States encountered people from backgrounds they had long been familiar with—German, Polish, and Russian—in ways that sometimes reproduced long-standing tensions and animosities. But with the Irish there was no prehistory. There was a small but significant Jewish community in Ireland, to be sure, but for the most part the Irish and the Jews met for the first time in the United States. The encounter happened by force of circumstances, and the story needs to be told if we are to understand the history of either group.

Jewish-Irish encounters in America featured tension, conflict, and bigotry, but also creative, open-minded, and mutually beneficial interaction. Irish American gangs were unusually aggressive in controlling their patches of urban territory against Jews and other immigrants, often with the tacit support of Irish-dominated police forces and political machines. In the 1930s, the radio priest Father Charles Coughlin reached over forty million listeners a week in his vicious anti-Semitic broadcasts. Conversely, historians have documented how some Jewish Americans looked down on the Irish for their lack of education, rough manners, abuse of alcohol, and other undesirable traits. But as Hasia R. Diner and James Barrett emphasize in their contributions to this volume—and as all the essays abundantly demonstrate—there was a lot more to the interaction than tension and conflict. Without denying the uglier sides of the story, this book proposes an interpretation that is both more optimistic and more nuanced and complicated.

The simplest facts in history are often the most powerful but also the easiest to overlook. The Irish were the first non-Protestant group to arrive in the United States in large numbers and their ability to speak English gave them a significant advantage over nearly all immigrants at the time and later. This was true both of those who came during the Great Famine of the 1840s and those who arrived simultaneously with Jewish immigrants in the late nineteenth and early twentieth centuries. Although 25 percent of the Famine immigrants could speak the Irish language, the great majority of these Irish speakers were bilingual. Ironically, even as many Jews retained or even discovered their languages in America, Irish immigrants had a significant—if quite unintended—advantage because they had learned English, often compulsorily, in Ireland.

Having established themselves as an ethnic group by the mid-nineteenth century, the American Irish served as gatekeepers for immigrants in the Ellis Island era, setting a template for Jewish, Italian, and other immigrants. In a series of practical ways, they taught subsequent generations of immigrants what it meant to be American. When Jews in New York or Chicago looked for models of immigrant adjustment and success, they found everyday models in the Irish example. This was true of life on the streets and in the tenements, in the labor movement, in politics, in education, and in popular culture. Irish and Jewish immigrants, after all, did not simply become American: they became either Irish-American or Jewish-American. Acquiring an ethnic identity was a precondition for becoming American, not an impediment; the hyphen operated as a means toward assimilation rather than an obstacle. Refusing to renounce their heritage in the United States, especially when it came to religion, Irish immigrants in the nineteenth century laid down a model of cultural pluralism, insisting that being Irish was perfectly compatible with being American. Immigrants in the Ellis Island era followed the path the Irish had opened.

In their interactions in the early twentieth century, Jewish and Irish Americans expanded upon and enriched this model of cultural pluralism. Just as the nineteenth-century Irish began with no preconceived ideology when insisting on their right to be American on their own terms, immigrants in the Ellis Island era were not seeking to apply some abstract theoretical framework to society. On the contrary, the Irish and the Jews interacted because they had to, once they found themselves living together in the unique and unanticipated conditions of urban, immigrant America. Neither side wanted to break down all the social, cultural, and religious boundaries between them, as these boundaries defined their communities (and, to varying degrees, created stratifications and divisions within those communities). But by coming together as they did, maintaining difference through interaction, both sides had something to gain. *Forged in America: How Irish-Jewish Encounters Shaped a Nation* illustrates the mutually enriching aspects of this Jewish-Irish interaction—in public health movements and reproductive rights; in local, national, and international politics; in fine arts, film, literature, and popular culture; and in education and sports.

Hannah Zaves-Greene examines the careers of two progressive reformers: Margaret Sanger (1879–1966), a pioneer of women's health and reproductive rights, and Lillian Wald (1887–1940), a proponent of "public health nursing" for all Americans. The Wald and Sanger families came to the United States in the mid-nineteenth century. Wald's parents and grandparents left from elite positions in Central Europe, where the family included rabbis, scholars, merchants, and professionals. They settled in Rochester, New York, and did well. Sanger's Catholic parents, by contrast, fled from County Cork during the Great Famine of the 1840s and lived in a working-class community in Corning, New York. Wald was raised in middle-class comfort, Sanger in poverty as one of eleven children. Yet both women emerged as progressive reformers, influenced by socialism and deeply committed to public health—especially women's health—in urban America. Their lives intersected only briefly, but they catered to the same working-class immigrants in turn-of-the-century New York City. A study in contrasts as well as comparisons, Zaves-Greene's essay examines their separate yet complementary approaches, as Wald pioneered the field of public health nursing and Sanger became famous, indeed infamous, for her advocacy of birth control.

The American Irish, unusually, acquired urban political dominance before economic success. Even as immigrants and their children struggled to find good jobs and lagged behind on most measures of social mobility, the Irish took over Tammany Hall in 1871 with the ascension of "Honest John" Kelly as boss. As the machine controlling Manhattan's Democratic Party, Tammany ran the political life of the city and eventually exercised a decisive influence on state politics as well. To preserve its power in the early twentieth century, however, Tammany needed the support of other immigrant and ethnic groups. The machine wanted votes; Jews and Italians wanted help getting settled and finding jobs. To that extent, the relationship was symmetrical. But Tammany walked a fine line between supporting Jews and other non-Irish immigrants, on the one hand, and exposing the limits of its patronage resources on the other. The machine provided jobs, financial support, and emergency relief in an era before the welfare state. Yet it could not help everyone. The Irish had priority when it came to political positions and jobs in the police and fire departments, public transit, and the public school system. Assistance to other groups was sometimes tangible (supporting businessmen, newspapers, and community organizations) but often symbolic (attending funerals, endorsing candidates for local office). The bubble burst in 1933 when Fiorello La Guardia (1882–1947), the son of Italian immigrants, put together a pan-ethnic coalition to displace the Irish and was elected mayor of New York City.

By that time, however, Irish Americans were well on the way to prominence in state and national politics. As Terry Golway shows in his essay, their cooperation with Jewish reformers, politicians, and policy-makers in New York was the catalyst. This interethnic political alliance had several points of origin: the admission of Jewish members to Tammany Hall; support for the election of Jewish officeholders; pressure on Albany by left-wing Jewish activists, most prominently Rose Schneiderman (1882–1972) after the Triangle Shirtwaist Factory fire of 1911; and the response to that tragedy by two prominent products of the machine—Alfred E. Smith (1873–1944), the grandson of an Irish immigrant, and Robert Wagner (1877–1953), a German immigrant. Smith went on to serve four terms as governor of New York, with a progressive agenda that anticipated the New Deal. His three closest advisers as he pursued his reformist agenda, Golway notes, were Belle Moskowitz (1877–1933), Robert Moses (1888–1981), and Joseph Proskauer (1877–1971).

Robert Snyder's essay focuses on another prominent Irish political figure, Paul O'Dwyer (1907–1998), and his connections with Jewish individuals and organizations. Born in County Mayo, Ireland, in 1907, O'Dwyer moved to Brooklyn when he was eighteen. The American Irish were ascending to national political prominence at just this time, but losing their control over New York City. O'Dwyer went on to become a prominent lawyer, politician, and Irish nationalist. In the cosmopolitan setting of New York City, he developed a sense of universal justice and a commitment to ethnic and racial diversity. Snyder traces O'Dwyer's political thinking through his interactions with Jewish New Yorkers—from the students he knew at St. John's University to his colleagues at the law firm O'Dwyer and Bernstien; his support for the Bergson Group—a set of Zionist political action committees organized by Hillel Kook, under the name Peter Bergson, in response to World War II and the Holocaust; his work with Jewish activists as president of the National Lawyers Guild in the 1940s; his involvement with Jewish Reform Democrats during the 1960s; and his campaigns for elected office against Jewish candidates, most notably Jacob Javits (1984–86). Through one individual's life story, Snyder demonstrates how closely Jewish and Irish New York were intertwined. Neither one makes sense without the other.

Brett Gary's essay examines how Morris Leopold Ernst (1888–1975), a Jewish American trial lawyer in New York City, liberated Ireland's most famous novel, *Ulysses*, from America's obscenity laws. The son of a Jewish immigrant father from Pilsen, Bohemia, and a second-generation Jewish American mother, Ernst was born in Alabama and grew up in comfortable middle-class surroundings in New York City. He worked in the family shirt-making business while attending the New York Law School at night—a common practice at this time, driven partly by financial concerns and partly by the discrimination that excluded Jews from prestigious schools and law firms. Through his affiliation with the ACLU, Ernst connected free speech with sexual censorship. He became a prominent opponent of American laws restricting materials deemed lewd, indecent, or scurrilous—a wide net that readily captured Joyce's novel. Even if many readers struggled to read or understand *Ulysses*, the book was notorious for its treatment of bodily functions and especially sexuality. Freeing it from censorship would be a great victory in the battle against the obscenity laws. Ernst accomplished just that goal in a famous case in 1933, though his subsequent embrace of anticommunism tended to overshadow his earlier work in the cause of free speech.

If Irish Americans and Jewish Americans interacted in the rarefied world of the high arts, their encounters in popular culture were widespread and dynamic. Vaudeville theater, with its mix of burlesque comedy, song, and dance, its urban tenement settings, and its concern with ethnic and racial interaction, was the quintessential art form of immigrant America at the turn of the twentieth century. The Irish, having arrived before other immigrant groups, played a dominant role in urban musical theater, gaining renown for their impersonations of other ethnic groups. By the turn of the twentieth century, as James Barrett's essay demonstrates, Jewish and African American actors had joined the Irish in performing these multiple roles. It would be anachronistic, Barrett observes, to dismiss these performances as instances of "cultural appropriation." On the contrary, historians tend to see vaudeville as a dynamic engagement with the newfound complexities of race and ethnicity in immigrant America, as different groups came to terms with one another through a mixture of parody and mutual appreciation. Emerging alongside vaudeville, Tin Pan Alley songs—named for the stretch of Twenty-Eighth Street between Fifth and Sixth Avenues where numerous songwriters and musical publishing firms were based—also carried a heavy Irish inflection. Tin Pan Alley often featured second-generation Irish American ethnics looking back nostalgically on a country they had never known. But the theme of nostalgia appealed to all immigrants and, as Barrett notes, Jewish businessmen dominated the industry.

One central theme in vaudeville and Tin Pan Alley was intermarriage, especially between Irish and Jewish couples. Lawrence Baron traces the history of Irish-Jewish unions in American film and television, from the era of silent movies to the present. Early caricatures of immigrant parents who opposed intermarriage, he demonstrates, gave way in the 1920s to positive portrayals of Americanized immigrants and ethnics transcending their backgrounds through cross-ethnic unions. Ethnic animosity and anti-Semitism stood in uneasy tension with toleration for most of the mid-twentieth century, however, and films and television programs celebrating intermarriage emerged into their own only in the 1960s and 1970s. These portrayals were not without their Jewish critics, who raised concerns about the corrosive effects of intermarriage on Jewish American identity. In the multicultural context of the last thirty years, however, the emphasis has been on celebrating intermarriages that do not require the spouses to abandon their heritages.

As well as creating new lives in the United States, Irish and Jewish Americans built or retained links with their homelands. Dan Lainer-Vos's essay examines how both groups negotiated between their emerging American identities, on the one hand, and their attachment to the new nation-states their people formed in Ireland and Israel respectively. He focuses on the Gaelic Athletic Association (GAA) in New York from 1904 to 1916 and Massad, a Jewish American summer camp that operated in the Pocono Mountains of Pennsylvania from 1941 to 1981. Both organizations were devoted to fostering and revitalizing a sense of national culture through play and recreation, creating a sense of belonging and camaraderie among members of diverse backgrounds with varying understandings of what it meant to be a member of a nation.

Lainer-Vos applies the tools of the sociologist to the formation of ethnic and national identity, which he sees as a set of organizational challenges rather than an abstract cultural question. The GAA addressed differences between Irishmen from different counties by bringing them together in competition, creating a space where they could celebrate a national culture in ways that were strenuous, fun, and exciting. At the same time, to foster competition and talent, the league created a two-tier structure that allowed the traditionally strongest counties to play one another. A generation later, a group of American Zionists established Massad (literally "foundation"), a nondenominational summer camp based on three organizational principles: using Hebrew in everyday life, modeling the camp physically on Israeli geography, and fusing elements of American Jewish and Israeli culture. Like the GAA, Massad faced organizational challenges, including a lack of Hebrew-speaking counselors and differences between American Jewish and Israeli campers. But these challenges, Lainer-Vos demonstrates, did not impede the process of creating a national culture; on the contrary, they served as the building blocks of that process. In portraying their camp as "a miniature Israel," the educators at Massad were not suggesting that it was really like Israel. Nor were they seeking to deny the real tensions between American and Israeli Jews. But bringing diverse constituencies together in a model community produced an organized space where differences could be negotiated in a creative and playful performance of national and diasporic identity.

Zionists in the United States drew inspiration from the organizational skill of Irish American nationalists. Immigrants and ethnics often participate politically in the affairs of their homeland, and the oldest, best organized, and most successful movements were those of the American Irish. Marion R. Casey's essay explores the nationalist activism of Irish and Jewish Americans in the aftermath of World War I. President Woodrow Wilson promised that the aspirations of small nations would be considered in the postwar settlement, but his inspirational rhetoric did nothing to advance Irish or Jewish aspirations at the Paris Peace Conference, where the British representatives preempted self-determination. This marriage between British imperialism and American pragmatism meant that both the "Jewish problem" and the "Irish question" remained unresolved. In the decades that followed, Jewish and Irish diaspora nationalists continued to object, respectively, to the formation of Mandatory Palestine and the Irish Free State. Conflicts over sovereignty and borders, as Casey shows, remained prominent legacies of British rule throughout the twentieth century.

Back in the United States, meanwhile, significant numbers of Jewish Americans attended Irish-dominated colleges and universities, at a time when most elite universities continued to discriminate against Jews. Many Jewish college students and law students, as Jeffrey S. Gurock's essay reveals, matriculated at St. John's University in Brooklyn. During the period between the two world wars, when relations between New York City's Irish and Jews were often tense, St. John's provided a welcoming home for Jewish students. Those who showed outstanding abilities could enter the law school after two years and graduate with two degrees. Jewish students seem to have integrated well with the predominantly Irish Catholic student body, and those who were recruited to play on the St. John's basketball team received the warmest welcome. Gurock tells the remarkable story of the "Wonder Five," four Jewish players and one Catholic who composed the starting five on the St. John's basketball team, regarded as one of the greatest of all college teams. Jews at this time were regarded as perfect basketball players—an ethnic stereotype, as Gurock reveals, that had both a positive dimension (quick-wittedness, imagination, and subtlety) and a negative one (suitability for a game that supposedly rewarded trickery and scheming). The coaching staff at St. John's recruited Jewish stars who led the team to a 23–2 record in 1928–29, 23–1 in 1929–30, and 21–1 in 1930–31, when the team won national attention. Although the star players were eventually barred from competing for the college after playing for money—something that many students did at this time of economic crisis—the legendary accomplishments of the Wonder Five inspired more Jewish basketball players to come to St. John's over the next generation. The African American players who dominate the sport today, Gurock notes, endure some of the same stereotypes, both positive and negative, that the Jewish players on the Wonder Five experienced.

*Forged in America: How Irish-Jewish Encounters Shaped a Nation* examines an intriguing set of interactions and connections in American history. It does not claim to be exhaustive or definitive. Many topics remain unexplored and await further attention. To take one example: Irish and Jewish immigrants had among the lowest rates of return migration among all immigrant groups in the United States in the early twentieth century. Even when they could afford to, members of neither group wanted to return to the lands they had left. At the same time, both groups were known for their sense of exile—the Irish because so many of them interpreted their departure as imposed by the British, the Jews because of persecution in Eastern Europe. In both cases, return would have negated their sense of exile. About half of all Italians in the Ellis Island era, by contrast, came to America as "birds of passage," migrating with the intention of returning after four or five years' work. Accordingly, Italian rates of naturalization—and hence of political participation—were initially low whereas Jewish and Irish rates were very high. Here is a subject ripe for comparative analysis.

The best recent scholarship on American immigration and ethnic history moves beyond studying any given group on its own, as though its history unfolded in a vacuum. Immigrants interacted with and shaped their host society; they also interacted with other immigrant groups. Studying the Irish and the Jews together is therefore a timely approach, especially as it has not been done before in the way presented here. In this respect, *Forged in America: How Irish-Jewish Encounters Shaped a Nation* provides a model for studying US immigration history more generally, and it does so in a lively, accessible style. The book beautifully captures the atmosphere in Glucksman Ireland House on a typical, bustling, prepandemic Thursday evening.

    Kevin Kenny
    Glucksman Ireland House
    April 2022

# Introduction

*Forged in America*

HASIA R. DINER AND MIRIAM NYHAN GREY

This book of essays brings two fields into conversation with each other and by doing so, we hope that it will transform them both and, furthermore, leave its mark on the larger subject of American ethnic history. For the most part, the histories of the many groups that make up the American mosaic have been told separately, one from the other. Each history stands in a kind of splendid isolation from any other, as all the books and articles detail the specifics of conditions in the many places of origin, the separate moments of arrival, the group-by-group processes of settlement in the United States, their work histories, how they formed their communal institutions, and the trajectories of integration, cultural and political, of this population or that. Certainly, each one of these histories deserved to have been told and historians have amassed the relevant primary sources, built archives, and produced robust literatures.

But in all of these works that constitute the field of American ethnic history, the women and men who are not members of the group, outsiders, others, have no role. They do not factor in as coimmigrants in steerage, as neighbors, shopkeepers, role models, employers, teachers, coworkers, competitors for political favors, or collaborators in common undertakings. If they make occasional cameo appearances, they do so mostly as antagonists of the group being examined.

Yet we know from many carefully plotted urban histories that immigrants rarely lived in spaces only with others from the same place of origin, speakers of their same languages, or adherents to the same religious traditions. Instead, cheek-by-jowl immigrants and their children lived near and had ample opportunity to intersect with people unlike themselves, people whom they might never have met had they not immigrated to the United States. American life, its cities in particular but also rural areas, threw people together with seemingly little in common, in a multiplicity of settings, and playing a range of roles that their histories intertwined.

That intertwining has heretofore played little role in the scholarship, and we hope that this volume will stand as something of an exemplar of how to essentially tell two histories at once, with neither occupying center stage. The fullest history possible requires both players to be on stage simultaneously and in constant conversation with each other.

The Irish-Jewish entanglement is neither unique nor the only one that can highlight the multiethnic nature of American society and the ways in which American circumstances affected the experiences of people from abroad, regardless of where they came from. So many other pairings could serve the same purposes and indeed histories could be written about multiple groups, not just two, pivoting around each other as a result of shared spaces and common quests.

We hope that this volume will nudge American Jewish historians to contemplate that the history of the three million or so Jews who immigrated to the United States in the long nineteenth century took its shape in part as a by-product of the Jews' encounter with the Irish. While scholars of American Jewish history have been hard at work since the 1890s chronicling the Jewish presence since the seventeenth century in what would become the United States, they have mostly presented Jews as authors of their own experiences. They arrived, took advantage of American political and economic realities, defended themselves, went about the business of forging new institutional forms, and maintained their global ties to Jews in other lands. In the many scholarly discussions of Jews in politics, in the labor movement, in education, and more, Jews acted on their own, and even if not successful in achieving what they wanted, they did what they could, voting, lobbying with government officials, joining unions, going to school, and more. By dint of their visions, energy, and resources they shaped their American experiences, and did so by themselves, alone.

The scholars who have shaped the field never pondered that every one of those activities depended upon others, in this case Irish women and men who had been in the United States longer, in greater numbers, and who for a range of reasons helped construct the history of America's

Jews. Heretofore they have had no place in American Jewish historical narratives, other than as occasional anti-Semites who did what they could to embitter the lives of Jews in the America, making America indeed more like the Europe that the Jews left.

Similarly, we hope that this collection will prompt scholars of the American Irish experience to revisit the ways in which they have described the trajectories of the Irish in the United States. Too often, and for good reason given the large and extended demographic impact of the migration, commentators on the Irish have viewed this experience in an ethnic and racial vacuum. No more than American Jews, the American Irish did not live their lives divorced from contacts, collaboration, and conflict with other ethnic and Black Americans. Yet the historiography largely continues to bely the more integrated on-the-ground lived experience. Too often the social, political, and economic patterns of Irish migrants are "explained, intentionally or unintentionally, in terms of their *Irishness*, as though this constitutes a homogeneous, coherent, and constant phenomenon."[1]

Given the significance of New York City as hubs of Jewish and Irish migration, it will come as little surprise that many of the interventions in this collection center that location. New York City boasts expansive footprints of Irish and Jewish migration and both groups, in different ways, are integral to the history of the city in the past 150 years. As such, the essays to follow here serve as microhistories of New York that draw on the intersection of Irish and Jewish New Yorkers and allow us to extrapolate as to Irish-Jewish interactions in other places, and they also raise important questions about the groups in relation to other migration groups in other places and times. Important immigrant cities like New York and London, for example, brought Jewish and Irish migrants together into encounters that were new to both groups, and it is enlightening to see the myriad ways in which they made sense of their new locations by engaging with each other and often learning from the other group.

The coupling here also underscores the significance of timing. Demographically, the heyday of Irish immigration comes earlier in urban America and in that sense the American Irish had a blank ethnic canvas on which to carve out spaces that would frame later encounters. Are we to imagine that the intense anti-Catholicism of the nineteenth century did not influence how Irish immigrants engaged with their ethnoreligious sensibilities? And what did that mean when they would come into contact with Jewish immigrants who did not fit into the Catholic-Protestant binary of the homeland? In other words, how was the cultural baggage of Europe shaped in urban America by these groups? And to what extent was the American Irish experience drawn upon by American Jews as they worked to carve out a space for their group in an American context? More generally, what do these groups, by their example, tell us about proximity in the migrant experience? In other words, by being proximate to one another Irish and Jewish immigrants significantly shaped one another and added more nuance to the American ethnic experience in the process.

The essays here turn the historical trope that pits Irish and Jewish American against one another on its head, and in doing so, we envision that they will usher in a newer, more accurate, and more expansive tradition in the writing of this history. The pieces included in this volume not only do some intellectual work by pushing American Jewish and Irish American history closer to each other, setting up a dialogue, but they also bear witness to a moment in time.

The intellectual origins and rationale for this collection grow out of a particular Irish-Jewish entanglement, one that transpired on the campus of New York University, which has fundamentally shaped Irish Studies in the United States and beyond: the founding of Glucksman Ireland House. Understanding the history of this New York hub for the study of Ireland and the Irish diaspora provides vital context to many of the themes of this collection.

In the late 1980s a couple, he Jewish American, she Irish American, generous philanthropists in New York and actively involved in New York University, spotted a lacuna in the life of the institution that mattered to them. Among the various international houses attached to NYU, Ireland was absent. The Greenwich Village neighborhood, through the aegis of the university, boasted La Maison Français, Casa Italiana, and Deutsches Haus. Not only did Ireland not have a physical presence, a house that carried its name, but no place existed for students at the undergraduate and graduate level to learn about Ireland, its language, literature, and history.

Surely there had to be room for an "Ireland House"? Surely students at NYU might benefit from learning about James Joyce, William Butler

Yeats, the Rising of 1916, the Irish emigration to America that had made New York a global center for the far-reaching Irish diaspora, giving the city an Irish tone for more than a century of its history?

Loretta Brennan Glucksman had a familial connection to Ireland by way of Allentown, Pennsylvania, growing up as the granddaughter of four Irish immigrants who left from Donegal and Leitrim for the United States in the latter half of the nineteenth century. Lew Glucksman, a Jewish New Yorker whose parents had come to the United States from Hungary, had fallen in love with Ireland during a furlough from the US navy during World War II. Smitten by that journey across the Irish Sea, Lew, who then came home, studied at NYU, and plunged into the world of Wall Street, never forgot that experience. In the course of his immensely successful business career, NYU recruited him to its Board of Trustees where he served with dedication.

In 1987, Lew—remembering the tremendous impression that Ireland had made upon him—brought Loretta to Ireland for the first time. Ironically, or in a twist of history whose contours this book explores, this son of Jewish immigrants from Central Europe reconnected the granddaughter of Irish immigrants with her roots, the place from which her forebears had come. The trip made a tremendous impression upon her, kindling a connection to a place once seemingly lost in her consciousness. Lew and Loretta, together then, began to use their philanthropic largesse for projects in Ireland that spoke to them. The Glucksmans played a significant role in the founding of the University of Limerick, and their contributions to other Irish universities are manifest with University College Cork's Glucksman Gallery and Trinity College Dublin's Glucksman Map Library.

They then turned their attention to a place closer to home, New York City, and indeed even closer, New York University, Lew's alma mater and the institution on whose board he served. In 1993, after a couple of years of planning, Glucksman Ireland House opened its doors on Fifth Avenue, just north of the grand arch that sits at the head of Washington Square Park.

Their vision exerted a profound impact on the campus, the city, and on matters Irish around the globe. Never narrow, in either national or ethnic terms, Ireland House always positioned itself about connections between Ireland and the Irish and other peoples. In 1997, for example, when Ireland House, under its then director Robert Scally organized an international conference on the 150th anniversary of the Great Famine in Ireland in the 1840s, it included speakers such as Irish president Mary Robinson, who contemplated famines in many other places and how they too transformed their populations. The second director, Joe Lee, has written extensively on famine in Irish history. The current director, Kevin Kenny, has written one of the best books available on the concept of diaspora, a matter of importance well beyond the Irish story but one that helps deepen understanding of the Irish people and their worldwide communities. In 2017, on an interim basis, Hasia Diner, one of the co-editors of this book and a contributor, assumed the interim directorship of Glucksman Ireland House. A scholar primarily of American Jewish history and a faculty member in the Skirball Department of Hebrew and Judaic Studies, she had also written about Irish American women, which gave her some bona fides in this temporary position. More importantly, though, her involvement with Ireland House bore witness to the breadth of its mission, its constantly expanding inclusiveness, and its understanding that the history of one people perforce needs to be understood as touched by the histories of others.

The history of Glucksman Ireland House, the vision behind it, and the expansiveness of its understanding of the complexities of the Irish experience serve as the ground from which this book emerged. Particularly in the United States, as this book exemplifies, people of diverse backgrounds had to meet. They had no choice, but in those multiple meetings they changed and changed each other.

Loretta and Lew exemplified so many of the themes of this volume. New York City's intellectual engagement with Ireland and the Irish experience would surely have been so much less interesting without the collaboration of Brennan and Glucksman. They embodied in their public works the reality—in the United States, and New York in particular—of people who, had their ancestors stayed at home be it in Ireland or Hungary, would never have encountered each other. But America and New York gave them the opportunity to do so, and in that process, they made history.

Part of that history involves the production of new ideas about history, and with the twenty-fifth anniversary of Glucksman Ireland House on the horizon, and the coincidence of Hasia Diner's service as interim director, faculty at Ireland House decided that programs dedicated to the interconnectedness of the Irish and Jewish American experiences would be highly appropriate and would generate new ways of thinking about the American, Irish, and Jewish pasts. The programs have made a worthy intellectual commitment, one we expect will generate more scholarship and programming in the future while also serving as an homage to the vision of the founders. Because, to quote William Jerome and Jean Schwartz's 1912 song on Irish and Jewish Americans, "Talk about a combination."

1

A Singular Encounter

*Irish and Jews in Their American Home*

HASIA R. DINER

The histories of the Irish and the Jews converged in the United States. Their American histories entwined with each other, taking their shape from the national and global forces that sent them as immigrants to the United States, making them neighbors and collaborators in urban America starting in the latter decades of the nineteenth century. While incidents of communal antagonism punctuated their interactions, those moments did not define the ways in which Irish and Jews hovered around each other's orbit. Rather, the Irish who had arrived in the United States earlier by several decades and in substantially larger numbers than the Jews served as models, mentors, and mediators for the Jewish newcomers from Europe.[1]

Both underwent distinctive encounters with their new home, in their immigrant generations and among their American-born descendants, as they went about the process of forming communal institutions, building new identities, navigating the larger, often uninviting, American society, and reconstructing transnational ties. Both played an outsized role in American entertainment at the same time that both protested the unflattering stereotypes that abounded on the stage. They embarked on these projects in the same way, often making some very different decisions.[2]

But the Irish and the Jews had no choice but to carve out places for themselves in America and engage in group defense, as both understood that as permanent immigrants to the United States, their futures depended on these. They recognized the fact of their outsider status in the Anglo-Protestant nation, which saw them as alien and unassimilable.

Both groups left their marks on the social, political, and economic developments of the United States. They did so differently, but American realities threw together these two populations who literally would have never met had they not decided that life in their places of origin, Ireland for the one and the European continent stretching from Alsace in the west to Ukraine in the east for the other, held out too few prospects for making a living.

Having arrived in the United States—the Irish first, beginning in large numbers starting in the 1840s and continuing for decades, followed by the onset of the Jews' great migration from Europe as of the 1870s, curtailed only by the immigration restrictions of the 1920s—they continuously collided with each other. They met in a range of settings, including schools, union halls, the backrooms of political organizations, the hallways of apartment buildings, and just on the streets where ordinary people had no choice but to interact. Romance and marriage between typically Irish women and Jewish men, while not widespread, took place. The experiences they had in America mutually affected each other.

For the most part scholars have had little to say about this historic meeting, reflecting a tendency among historians to study one group or another, each in an analytic silo, relatively oblivious to the reality that in the United States, lyrically depicted as a "nation of immigrants," the social, political, economic, and cultural experiences of no one group took place isolated from those of others. Certainly some Central Europeans and Scandinavians set off to form relatively homogeneous enclaves in farming regions. Some immigrant religious communities, like the Mennonites, sought isolated spaces far from other people in expectation of recreating the structures of the homes they had left.[3]

But most newcomers and their children settled in ethnically complicated neighborhoods, labored in mixed workforces, and by dint of quotidian circumstances negotiated American realities in conjunction with other newcomers and their offspring. Whether dealing with merchants, police, teachers, or neighbors, the world of most immigrants revolved around constant interactions with strangers, many themselves relatively recent arrivals as well.[4]

Rudolf Glanz, a Jewish refugee from Nazi-infested Vienna, stands out as an exception. He published *Jew and Irish* in 1966, something of a companion to his earlier works "Jew and Chinese in America," *Jew and Mormon*, and then *Jew and Italian*. Quirky pieces of writing, packed with many snippets of materials gleaned from newspapers, sundry reports, memoirs, and fiction, these lacked real analysis or any kind of central interpretative framework. But Glanz did hit upon a crucial fact, something he gleaned from his arrival in New York and his extensive travels around his new country.[5]

Jewish immigrants to the United States alighted onto the shores of a place peopled by women and men of backgrounds and religions, as in the case of the Mormons, utterly unknown to them back home. Millions of these, like the Jews, had arrived in recent generations from elsewhere, and they, like the Jews, grappled with the issues that sprang from being, in biblical parlance, "strangers in a strange land."

In their new home—the world's largest immigrant magnet, which drew in newcomers from more places than any other—Jews rubbed shoulders with and had to come to some modus vivendi with people, some of whom they did not know, to whom they had no point of reference, might never have even heard of, and whose histories had never intersected with their own. Likewise neither the Chinese, Irish, nor Italian newcomers to America would have ever met a Jew or known anything of Jewish practice or culture.

Jews lived in Italy but in small numbers and concentrated in a few cities, primarily the large centers in the north, and therefore had nearly no presence in the regions—Sicily and the south—that sent out the masses of rural Italians to the United States starting in the 1890s. Minuscule Jewish enclaves in China, in Shanghai and Harbin, made up primarily of Sephardic merchants, could not have made any impress upon the immigrants who hailed mostly from Guangzhou, then called Canton.

And as for Ireland, the fewer than three thousand Lithuanian Jews who immigrated to it in the later decades of the nineteenth century did so just as many of their sisters and brothers were moving to the United States. They peddled in the countryside and kept shops in Dublin, Limerick, and Cork, after the bulk of the Irish exodus to the United States had thinned out. Hence most, or even all, the Irish immigrants who came to America arrived with no previous experience with or knowledge of Jews. Conversely, the millions of Jews who immigrated to the United States may well have never even heard the words Ireland or Irish, and if so, only through newspaper accounts.[6]

The three nationality groups whom Glanz chose made sense and provide a handy way to start thinking about the singularity of the Jewish-

Irish meeting in America. The Irish, like the Italians and the Chinese, represented an American novelty for Jewish immigrants, and conversely Jews must have appeared to them as people previously unknown and distinctive to the American scene. The interactions between Jews and these three groups offered Glanz much to think about, differently in each case.

This simple premise helps center the idea that in the context of American Jewish history, the Jews' interaction with the Irish proved particularly transformative. Unlike the Italians, the Irish predated the Jews and constituted a substantial, visible, and settled immigrant population when the Jews arrived. The Italian migration started up in earnest a decade or two after the Jewish one; as such they did not serve as models or guides for Jewish ethnic integration. The Chinese immigration from its onset labored under the burden of racially inspired legal discrimination. The first substantial decade of Jewish immigration from Eastern Europe overlapped with the passage of the Chinese Exclusion Act, and as men, for the most part, with no rights of naturalization and acquisition of citizenship, Chinese *residents* of the United States could not offer Jews any assistance in navigating American politics nor ally with them to circumvent a common foe, namely the white Protestant native-born elite. Additionally, both Italian and Chinese immigrations had been decidedly male in their composition, while Irish and Jewish women swelled the ranks of the immigrants. In all of this the Irish and the Jews resembled each other in some crucial ways more than either resembled the Chinese or the Italians, which affected both their integration and the relationships that developed between them.

The Irish-Jewish encounter can be understood in the context of what made this American meeting so different from the ones that took place between the Jews and other immigrants and between the Irish and other immigrants.

Most of the other immigrants, Italians excepted, who came in large numbers at the same time as the Jews and who lived near them may be rightly thought of as the Jews' old neighbors from back home. Jews and non-Jews emigrated at the same time from German-speaking lands, where Jews had lived for centuries. Jews in small towns and cities lived throughout the lands that would in 1870 become a unified Germany. They also had long made homes in substantial numbers in many of the regions of the Austro-Hungarian Empire, such as Bohemia, Moravia, and Galicia. Both Jews and Christians left Romania. And as for the Christians who came to America from Lithuania, Ukraine, and Belarus, the Jewish heartlands of the Russian Empire—or in other words, the Pale of Settlement—Jews knew those non-Jews and the non-Jews knew them.

In all those places, the Christian majorities recognized Jews as real people, whether as peddlers, tavern keepers, market stall owners, cattle dealers, land agents, and other kinds of middlemen who affected local life. Across religious lines they spoke the same languages, and Christians throughout Central and Eastern Europe had some familiarity with Jewish customs. The Jews in many of those places had, in order to survive, learned to live among and between a multiplicity of groups, whether French and German speakers in Alsace, Czech and German speakers in Bohemia and Moravia, as well as Christians who defined themselves as Polish, Ukrainian, Lithuanian, and Russian, living in the polyglot, multiethnic spaces where Jews lived. The consummate outsiders everyplace they lived, Jews had little experience connecting with non-Jews as equals or jostling with other marginalized peoples with whom they could make common cause.

Many of the immigrants from Europe, coming to the United States, would have witnessed, maybe participated in, acts of violence perpetrated against local Jews and their communities. Talk about Jews, real and imaginary, swirled around everyday life. The question of the place of the Jews figured into local and national politics, and activists in the movements for national self-determination—in Poland, for instance—debated what should be the role of Jews in their yearned-for, but not yet achieved, independent homelands. For the most part, in those lands Jews lived as more or less a tolerated minority, defined as occupying a different status than the legitimate denizens of the place. The Jews had to go through the process of emancipation, which dragged on over many decades.[7]

The Irish who chose the United States showed up with little actual exposure to ethnic diversity before migration and few, if any, opportunities to navigate lived differences in language and national origins when interacting with neighbors, employers, employees, shopkeepers, or customers. Religious difference—Protestantism, practiced primarily through the Church of Ireland, versus the Roman Catholicism of the masses—provided the basic cleavage in Irish life. English landowners and administrators operated in Ireland. But as the Englishwomen and men present in Ireland represented a ruling class, interactions perforce rendered their relationships with the majority population unequal in terms of privilege, status, and power. Some few thousand French-speaking Huguenots had fled to the northern counties in the seventeenth century, simultaneous with the flight of a few thousand Protestants from the German Palatinate, both encouraged by the English crown eager to expand the non-Catholic population of the island.

These hardly represented the kind of on-the-ground ethnic diversity that would characterize the Irish immigrants' lives in America. For the most part the daughters and sons of Ireland came to America from monoethnic communities devoid of differences in language, customs, social patterns, or group memory. They neither had to accommodate to others nor did they establish any kind of power base that others had to learn to navigate. In the United States, as one example, while the Irish faced a white Protestant elite that looked down on them, they also established in the large cities, within a few decades of their arrival, a near monopoly on such jobs as police officer. From that position, they wielded power over the newer immigrants who came after them.

Life in America proved different for both the Jews and the Irish as they entered into a world made up of a jumble of people from a vast array of backgrounds, so many of whom also had emigrated from somewhere else, or if not they themselves, then their parents had. All had to negotiate American novelties, including how to participate and advance their interests in a multiethnic democratic society, where white people, regardless of where they came from, could choose from a range of options as they navigated American public life, whether in terms of economic, political, religious, or cultural possibilities.

By dint of geographic circumstance, Jewish and Irish Americans engaged with all the peoples around them. Such encounters—Irish and Italian, Jewish and Italian, Jewish and German, Irish and French Canadian, Polish and Jewish—and so on, a kaleidoscope of pairings, offer rich possibilities for analysis; all deserve study.[8] So too the histories of Irish and Jews with those Americans defined as nonwhite, and therefore subjected to laws and state actions that deprived them of rights, reveal much about the United States and about these two immigrant populations.

But the relationship between Jews and Irish can be seen as singular among all the others. Their relationship took shape from the fact that they had little reason to compete with each other. Occupying such different religious institutions obviated any chance of conflicts over institutional power. Catholics made up a hefty majority of the post–1870s and 1880s immigrants. They confronted in America a church shaped and dominated by the Irish, who since their arrival in the 1840s had defined church practices and set priorities for the still-reviled minority faith community in Protestant America. They held the reins of American Catholicism, making up the majority of the clergy and the prelates; other Catholic groups had to pivot around them. Italians, Poles, Lithuanians, French Canadians, and other Catholic immigrants battled the Catholic, that is, the Irish, establishment for the right to have priests who spoke their language. They had to find ways to allow for festivals, saints, and rituals associated with their places of origin to be enshrined in America, often against the orders of the local, Irish, hierarchy. In some cases renegade factions broke away to be liberated from Irish control, asserting their cultural prerogatives. Robert Orsi showed this in his classic study *The Madonna of 115th Street*. Immigrants from Genoa who settled in New York's East Harlem wanted to recreate a beloved devotional pageant dedicated to their patron saint, but faced a recalcitrant Irish hierarchy in New York that considered the street festival primitive and embarrassing. To get the festival, they had to negotiate with Irish church leaders.[9]

Jews and Irish also entered quite different sectors of the American economy. They labored separately, with no need to view the other suspiciously as challengers or as threats who would drive down the wage scale. Jews gravitated almost exclusively to two sectors of the American economy. For many immigrant Jews, small business, starting at the bottom as peddlers and graduating to shopkeepers specializing in clothing and dry goods, offered them a distinctive niche and an elevator to the middle class.[10] Many more, in New York and in lesser numbers in Chicago, Philadelphia, Boston, and elsewhere, gravitated to the garment trade, hundreds of thousands as laborers and others as employers.[11] While Irish men and women also had made a living in the needle trades, they never provided them with the core of their American work lives as they did for Jews. Those Irish immigrants who had sewed for a living did so as skilled tailors and seamstresses rather than sweatshop laborers. By the time the Jews arrived in large numbers, Irish employment in garment shops had dwindled. Compared to the Jews, the Irish dominated a much larger range of occupations and were involved in many more industries.

Likewise, by the 1880s and 1890s Irish male immigrants and their sons had moved up into skilled labor in work sites where Jews did not go. The kinds of enterprises that saw Irish entrepreneurship, construction for example, did not attract Jewish workers, who mostly worked for other Jews in garment making.

Additionally, in the always gender-segmented labor force, Jewish women and Irish women got their toeholds in the economy in quite different places, meaning that competition with each other did not frame their work lives. For Irish women, domestic service provided the gateway occupation. Its drudgery and the demeaning snobbery evinced by employers aside, Irish women household workers, universally referred to as "Bridget," found the job a stepping stone to acquiring both middle-class standards of comportment and economic resources. Most Irish domestics lived in with their employers. Unlike other poor women in the workforce, domestic servants in their years of labor could save and invest resources for their futures. Certainly Irish women who came with families did find jobs in sewing, but domestic service offered employment for most.[12] Jewish women, the daughters of male immigrants who brought their older children with them to America as the avantgarde of the family transplantation, found work in garment making, whether sweatshops or by the 1910s, factories. Even the single women who migrated by themselves or with female friends or relatives eschewed domestic service and headed for clothing manufactories owned by Jewish employers, and labor conflict did not pit Jew against Irish or vice versa.[13]

Their separateness in these two areas, religion and employment, prevented them from clashing over sacred space or economic security. It allowed them instead to work together, literally or figuratively, in some crucial matters that immigration and the process of integration entailed for them. Those similarities began with several demographic aspects of their respective transplantations to the United States.

The permanent bases of these two migrations shaped a formative demographic reality. Women participated in the movement of these peoples. Many other immigrants, particularly after the 1880s, yearned to go home with cash in their pockets, and nothing compelled them to bring along women—wives, daughters, or sisters—in equal numbers. Those migrating to work in heavy industry opted for the kinds of places where few jobs existed for women, whether unmarried daughters or wives.[14]

Both the Irish and the Jewish communities were marked by women's strong participation in the labor force. These two immigrant populations, for example, produced the largest numbers of organized women workers, both in the rank and file and in the leadership. Leonora Barry, Kate Mullaney, Agnes Nestor, Mary Kenny O'Sullivan, and Leonora O'Reilly on the one side and Rose Schneiderman, Pauline Newman, Fania Cohen, and Bessie Abramowitz on the other dedicated their lives to advancing the cause of unionization, particularly of women workers. Among the white women who emerged as key figures in the labor movement, Irish women and Jewish women predominated.[15]

Their lives as breadwinners, as women who commanded little respect from either the male union leaders, many of them men from their own community, or from the employers, drove home the point. Women had to organize themselves. These women did not direct their efforts solely toward women of their own group but recognized the reality that all women in industry, regardless of ethnic origins, needed the protection of a union, and that a broad appeal on the basis of gender mattered more than narrowly focusing on those just like themselves.[16]

That Irish women and Jewish women came to this realization meant in fact that they allied with each other to accomplish their goals. Because Irish women's organizing went back to the days of the Knights of Labor in the 1870s, reaching its zenith in the 1880s, they came on the labor scene before Jewish women entered the American labor force. When Jewish women starting at the turn of the century developed their consciousness, they found, in these Irish women veterans, eager teachers, mentors, and guides for how to navigate the world of organizing. Leonora O'Reilly, for example, brokered the stormy relationship between the elite women who supported the Women's Trade Union League and the Jewish women who constituted the majority of the strikers during the 1909 Uprising of the 20,000 in New York's garment industry.[17]

While Jewish male labor leaders, including individuals like Sidney Hillman, also sought out Irish guides shaped by earlier labor wars—such as John Fitzpatrick, leader of the Chicago Federation of Labor—the women's side of this Irish-Jewish encounter demonstrated more sharply the nature of the relationship, a blending of allyship with mentorship.

Here timing mattered in structuring the Irish-Jewish encounter. The numbers of Irish immigrants had crested by the time the mass Jewish immigration commenced. While Jews had lived in the United States long before the 1880s and Irish immigrants continued to make their way to America after that, for the most part the two immigrations did not overlap. That meant the United States, and its cities specifically, teemed with Irish immigrants and their first American-born generation with decades of experience under their belts that affected the Jews.

One example especially highlights the Jewish-Irish meeting in America. American Jews generally, and historians of the American Jewish experience as well, have made much about the role of public education in launching Jewish children into the American middle class. In their narrative about success they have posited a direct line by which Jewish boys and girls streamed from the steerage section of their immigrant ships into the classrooms of America, in the Lower East Side in particular.[18] The communal narrative of mobility through education swells with pride about the legions of American Jews who grew up in families where parents labored in sweatshops and factories, or struggled to earn their livings as pushcart peddlers and operators of shabby and derelict shops, and who went on to become doctors, lawyers, accountants, schoolteachers, and more.

Whether overstated or not, at this moment in historical time, these Jewish immigrant children in the public school found themselves sitting behind desks looking at female teachers whose mothers and fathers had been born in Ireland. By the latter part of the nineteenth century, Irish American women formed the backbone of the public school teaching force. As early as 1870 over 20 percent of New York's teachers were Irish women, and in the next few decades the percentages rose. They tended to concentrate as educators in the immigrant enclaves.

The job offered steady employment, clean working conditions, reasonable pay for a woman, and tended to be unscathed by the constant ups and downs of the capitalist economy. In the big cities public schools operated under a ward system and the political machine, dominated by Irish men, dispensed these jobs, often as rewards to its operatives and loyal constituents. A sought-after job by Irish women, teaching tapped into parental, particularly maternal, aspirations for respectability and middle-class comfort. The constant arrival of new immigrants necessitated the constant hiring of new teachers to keep up with the growing number of children.[19]

This had particular significance for Jews and the forging of the Irish-Jewish synergy. Children made up a much larger proportion of the Jewish immigration than they did of the Italian one, for example. About 25 percent of all Jewish immigrants during the peak decades fell under the age of fourteen, and while many went right to the factories and sweatshops, most went to school. The fact that Jewish women and men migrated in roughly equal numbers meant that they produced crops of children, American-born youngsters, who streamed into the public schools for relatively long periods of time, many going on to high school.[20]

By 1920 school teaching had become the fifth most common occupation of first-generation, American-born Irish women. These teachers played a key role in acclimatizing the newly arrived Jewish immigrant children, showing them through dress, speech, and comportment the ideal of American middle-class standards. They may indeed have been the only native-born middle-class Americans whom Jewish immigrant children knew. Even more so, they embodied America, its non-Jewish majority.

It mattered little that these Irish teachers may have, as most did, come from working-class homes, that their mothers had once been domestic servants and their fathers manual laborers. To the immigrant children, and from what the spotty historical record indicates, their awestruck parents who knew no English, these women functioned as the standard-bearers of American culture. None of the historical scholarship that has mined the records of Jewish life on the Lower East Side or on Chicago's West Side, with its hefty number of Irish American women teaching Jewish students, points to conflict between parents and teachers. The record offers no complaints by Jewish immigrant parents that these teachers demeaned the students, or that the newly arrived Jews evinced any complaints that the Irish American teachers misunderstood their children or belittled their culture.

When Jewish parents rose up and mounted campaigns against school policies, they turned their anger on the administration, made up mostly of white Protestants, not on the teachers. For example, in 1914 they directed their ire at those in the central administration who wanted to impose the Gary Plan, an anti-Tammany effort at school reform that Jewish parents thought would relegate their children to vocational education. They did not define the teachers, the Irish women, as the problem.[21]

Rather, as Irving Howe described it in his magnum opus of 1976, *World of Our Fathers*, "the bulk of the memoirs dealing with East Side childhood contain warm, sometimes remarkably tender descriptions of the years in school." Howe then mused with his readers, "Were there no petty tyrants, no mean-spirited bigots teaching school in the immigrant Jewish neighborhoods?" Answering his own query, Howe concluded: "very few if one goes by the pupils' remembrances."[22]

Rather, those memoirs related how these teachers led the Jewish children in the Pledge of Allegiance, sung with them the nation's patriotic hymns, informing them about Thanksgiving, Lincoln's birthday, Washington's birthday, and so on, as well as drilling them in spelling, reading, math, social studies, science, and the like. These Irish American women served on the front lines of integration, as new Jewish immigrant children entered their classrooms with no English at their command but expected by their parents to master the skills of American life.

Jews at the time, the leaders, writers, communal activists, as well as the ordinary women and men on the Jewish street, placed great stock in education as the vehicle to propel mobility and transform immigrant children into Americans able to take advantage of the economic, cultural, and political opportunities. They expressly did not create an alternative system of education in which Jewish immigrant children would have learned by themselves from Jewish teachers, achieving proficiency in Judaic texts. Instead they entrusted Irish women to shepherd their children into citizenship.

The story of Myra Kelly illustrates how the role of the Irish in American society benefited the Jews in the crucial immigrant decades. Born in Dublin, she came to the United States with her father, a physician who established a practice on the Lower East Side. Graduating from Teachers College, Columbia University, in 1899, Kelly took a teaching job at Public School 147 in the heart of the Jewish immigrant enclave, remaining there until 1901.

Myra Kelly's story has survived, unlike those of most of the teachers, because she turned to writing short stories that she published in magazines, transforming her classroom experiences into literature. She then bundled these works together into a number of books that garnered something of a readership. With apt titles such as *Little Citizens* (1904), *Wards of Liberty* (1907), and *Little Aliens* (1910), these works described her interactions with the Jewish immigrant children. Her main character, Constance Bailey, teaches Irish and Russian Jewish immigrant children the intricacies and puzzles of American life. While a minor theme of Kelly's books concerns the changing ethnic character of the neighborhood and the displacement of Irish families as the Jewish immigrants arrive, her sweet tales offer a small window into a large and important historical phenomenon: the encounter between the well-placed Irish Americans, as teachers, and young Jews who learned from them as new immigrants.

The small window opened by Kelly's writing opens a bit wider in the second collection, *Wards of Liberty*. Published by the respected, progressive-leaning McClure's, this book appeared with a foreword by President Theodore Roosevelt. Written as a letter to Kelly from his home in Oyster Bay, Long Island, the introductory remarks connected the fictional classroom to the larger reading public. Roosevelt began by thanking her for the stories and how they made him recall his years as New York City's police commissioner. He shared with readers across the country how, during those years, "I quite often went to the Houston Street public school and was immediately interested and impressed by what I saw there. I thought there were a good many Miss Baileys there, and the work they were doing among their scholars (who were so largely of Russian Jewish parentage, like the children you write of) was very much like what your Miss Bailey has done."[23]

Roosevelt's words, and this short-story collection in general, reveal several strands of the Irish-Jewish encounter in America, pointing to the predominance of Irish women as schoolteachers who guided the first American steps of "Morris Mogilewsky, Sadie Gonorowsky, and their associates" living in "the Ghetto." The book offers an example of how Irish women served as interpreters, whether accurate or not, of the lives of these children and their parents, presenting them to the larger American public. Kelly's volume with the president's laudatory words also appeared at a fraught moment for Jews, as issues of immigration restriction loomed large, anti-Semitism reared its head in America, scientific racists had much to say about the Jews' inherently negative traits, and the persecution of Jews in the Russian Empire raged, involving the United States diplomatically.

By the 1920s the daughters of many Jewish immigrants in New York sought teaching jobs in the public schools, many enrolling in the Maxwell Training School, which had opened in 1907. Here they met Irish American women who by this time made up the majority of its faculty. One anecdote offers a tempting insight into this encounter. In an oral history of retired Jewish women teachers, an informant reflected on the start of her long career as a classroom teacher in New York and vividly recalled how most of her own teachers had been Irish, most of them daughters of immigrant women who had first been domestic servants in some of the city's "finest homes." She recalled how the Maxwell educators had learned from their mothers, the onetime Irish servant girls, "oh-so-proper manners [and] they tried to teach us the same. In the spirit of noblesse oblige," they "forever invited us to their genteel tea parties. . . . We who drank tea from a glass at home, trying to lift our pinkies like our teachers." These teachers tried to show that "to be a teacher meant one was a lady" and "we should learn how to be ladies by emulating them . . . implying that we Jewish women had no idea what being a lady meant and needed their help in this way."[24]

Whether the Jewish girls had alternative ideas about "being a lady" or not, the Irish had, in schoolteaching and other endeavors, shown up first, chosen places in the society and the economy that worked for them, and then recognized by the late nineteenth century that the new immigrants, Jews included, would soon overwhelm them numerically. Hence they, the Irish, could retain their influence and maintain visibility by harnessing the power of the newcomers and their numbers to serve Irish ends.

Nothing demonstrated this more vividly than the role of the Irish in municipal politics, with their equally firm control of municipal services. The relatively quick integration of Jewish men into American, especially New York, politics and the Irish role in engineering it reflected the demographics of Jewish migration. Jews transplanted themselves to the United States as permanent immigrants. Many of the other European immigrants, particularly those who arrived simultaneously with the Jews, returned home after a number of years in the United States. Even for those Italians, Poles, and others from the Slavic lands who did not go back, the idea of doing so and the circumstances of their families back home played a role in increasing the number of years before naturalization, acquisition of citizenship, and immersion in local politics.[25]

That less than 10 percent of Jews went back, mostly in the 1880s, only demonstrates the larger point that Jews had no interest in doing so. As permanent white immigrants in the United States, Jews, like the Irish before them who migrated to stay for good, recognized the advantages that came from being involved in local politics.[26] Seeing how the goals of their migration required political participation in the broadest sense of the word, their rates of naturalization, becoming citizens, voting, and participating in politics to advance their own interests show little lag time from their first American steps.

This meant that for the Jews, the Irish, who had arrived earlier in substantially larger numbers and had mastered the political sphere for their own good, served as gatekeepers, allies, and mentors. Both groups clustered in the largest cities, New York in particular. Jewish men entered into an urban world in which Irish men dominated politics, from the street corner and on up.

The history of skillful Irish involvement in the machinery of American urban politics has been told elsewhere in great detail. The path they opened up for themselves paved an important path for all white male immigrants, not just Jews. For Jews, however, this proved novel and decisive.[27]

Jews for the most part arrived in America with little or no experience of the political dance of being wooed, courted, and appealed to by non-Jews, men with power and influence, for the not so simple purpose of getting Jewish men to vote for this or that party, or support this or that candidate, Jews being no more and no less crucial to such outcomes than anyone else. They had not emigrated from democratic societies where votes were always up for grabs and those with political clout distributed favors in exchange for ballot-box loyalty.

In every city Jews went to they encountered Irish politicians, from the ward captains on the street level and then up the ladder to those with greater clout, who wanted the Jews' votes and coveted their electoral loyalties. Every vote counted and their Jewishness proved no barrier to Irish political outreach to them.

Irish political operatives showed up at Jewish weddings, funerals, *b'nai mitzvah*, synagogue dedications, meetings of B'nai B'rith lodges and of *landsmanshaften*, the very popular hometown societies, and other Jewish gathering places. Here they demonstrated and often stated how much they liked, cared about, valued, and needed the new Jewish voters. In the 1890s Tammany money helped launch a Yiddish newspaper, and when local, regional, and global incidents of anti-Semitism flared, someone from the machine would offer words of support for the Jews. As one commentator noted about Tammany Hall in 1893, "Tammany knows no race or creed when it is a question of acquiring or preserving political power. Some of its election captains are Jews."[28] Over time, more and more Jewish men found themselves swept into the machine, garnering positions of influence in it and in city government.

No reflection of an ideology of cultural pluralism or a profound belief in cross-ethnic solidarity, such behavior on the part of Tammany and its counterparts in Boston, Chicago, and elsewhere reflected hard-nosed political canniness. Jewish men, as citizens or about to become citizens, had votes, and it served the interests of the Irish politicians whether they represented a single machine like Tammany or one of a number of factions, all led by someone of Irish background. It worked for them to appoint Jews to visible positions in the party's apparatus, offering them jobs in city government, slotting them to run for office, helping them secure municipal contracts, on a personal level helping individual Jews in times of acute need, speaking out for them on their issues, the machine always thinking about the next election day.

Martin Lomasney, a child of immigrants from Fermoy, Ireland, a Boston political operative having served at various times as a state senator, state representative, and alderman, achieved his renown as the boss of the West End neighborhood. Nicknamed "the Mahatma" for his uncanny ability to deliver votes for his preferred candidates, Lomasney controlled Ward Eight, later renumbered Ward Five, then Ward Three due to redistricting, and wielded considerable influence in city and state politics for over forty years. Looking back on his life in politics, Lomasney noted about Boston in the 1890s: "The population in Ward Eight was not static. It became a way-station in the continuous migration of Boston's transient nationalities. The Jews began to move in by the 1890s and in fifteen years had become the dominant group. For them the West End was the proving ground of social and financial ambitions." The child of Fermoy immigrants realized that he could retain his "Mahatma" status in the increasingly Jewish ward only by including the Jews. So too many of his local Boston Irish rivals and colleagues, such as James Michael Curley, Patrick Kennedy, or John "Honey" Fitzgerald, drew Jewish men into their orbit to keep power for themselves.[29]

Boston's Curley and New York's Alfred Smith, the first Catholic to run for president, moved far beyond ward-level trading of votes for benefits with Jewish constituents. Both at the state level paid attention to Jewish legislative lobbying on a range of issues, and on the national scene they championed the fight against immigration restrictions, something Jews cared about deeply, while in the 1930s they emerged as foes of Nazism, demanding a firm US response to the menace of German anti-Semitism. Smith, Curley, along with Judge Jeremiah Mahoney worked assiduously but failed to get the American Athletic Union to boycott the 1936 Berlin Olympics.[30]

That the politicians, coming from and metaphorically representing Irish America, had something to gain from their outreach and advocacy for Jews does not diminish the services they performed. So too a number of key Irish American writers and journalists spoke out for Jews, at home and abroad, to the larger public, in part to show their own liberal credentials and humanitarian instincts.

A collaborative relationship between the poet, editor of Boston's Catholic newspaper *The Pilot*, and Irish nationalist leader John Boyle O'Reilly, a recognized figure in the Fenian movement, and Boston's Rabbi Solomon Schindler offers one such instance. In 1881 Schindler asked O'Reilly to contribute a poem to his *Illustrated Hebrew Almanac for the Year 5641*, both in recognition of the quality of his poetry and in thanks for the many articles that appeared in *The Pilot* attacking anti-Semitism. *The Pilot*, both under O'Reilly's editorship and that of his successor, the Queens County, Ireland–born James Jeffrey Roche, devoted space to ferreting out and lambasting actions against Jews, whether in

Europe or at home in Boston. Both editors spared no words in exposing instances of discrimination against Jews by the local, Protestant, "Brahmin" elite, which had little love for the Irish as well.[31]

(Decades later, in 1913, O'Reilly's daughter Mary, a journalist, would publish several articles based on her exclusive interviews with the chief rabbi of Kiev during the harrowing years of the Beilis Affair. Mendel Beilis had been charged, arrested, and put on trial in the Ukrainian city for having allegedly killed a Christian child to use his blood for matzah, the unleavened bread Jews eat on Passover. O'Reilly's stories not only evinced a deep sympathy for the clearly innocent Beilis but included specific information on the history of the blood libel among European Christians in their centuries-long attacks on Jews.)[32]

To American Jews, the Irish seemed to be well connected, politically sophisticated, and able to command wide audiences for their words. They did not hesitate to turn to individual Irish and Irish Americans to defend them in public against attacks from the outside. Those outside attacks became particularly alarming by the 1890s as political anti-Semitism emerged as a visible force in France, elsewhere in Europe, and the United States. In 1893 a prominent group of white-Protestant-elite Americans in Boston banded together to found the Immigration Restriction League, focused on pushing the United States, through legislation, to curtail immigration with regard to numbers and quality, that is, by legislating some immigrants as worthy of admission and others as not worthy by means of a eugenicist national categorization by race.

The year before a number of notable American Jews, either themselves immigrants from Central Europe or the children of those who had left the German-speaking lands earlier in the nineteenth century, established the American Jewish Historical Society. They and their counterparts in Europe turned to history as a means to parry assaults against their people, including claims that Jews, as unassimilable foreigners, contributed nothing and had no loyalty to the lands where they now lived. The society's journal featured articles noting how long Jews had been present in North America, going back indeed to the seventeenth century; the depth and breadth of their contribution to the war efforts and well-being of their adopted home, the United States; and the support they had received from notable Americans like George Washington.

The writings of Charles P. Daly, born in County Galway, Ireland, and by then the chief justice of the New York Court of Common Pleas, buttressed the Jews' self-defense. In 1893 he wrote a book-length history, the first ever, of America's Jews. It enjoyed a particular distinction in that, unlike the articles in the American Jewish Historical Society's publications, it had been written by an obvious outsider with no personal self-interest in the campaign for Jewish respectability and acceptance.

Published by the American Hebrew, a company known for its respected monthly magazine, Daly's book *The Settlement of the Jews in North America* was a rousing tribute to the Jews, who, he pointed out, had first arrived in America in the 1650s and were hardly newcomers or alien to American life. They had always taken care of their own, he noted, a not insignificant matter since just a decade earlier, in 1882, Congress had passed an Immigration Act that blocked the admission of any person likely to become a public charge.

Ten years earlier Daly had published a smaller book on *The Jews of New York* that took the same tack, focusing on the city itself as the emerging epicenter of Jewish life in the United States. Like the larger-scale study, it appeared under the publishing imprimatur of Philip Cowan, the editor and publisher of *The American Hebrew*. *The Jews of New York* is a paean to the Jews and a chronicle of their good deeds. Daly notes, for example, that the first piece of evidence of Jewish presence in North America involved "an act of benevolence on the part of a Jew to a friendless Christian stranger and certainly the history of no people in any place can begin with an incident more creditable to them than the exercise of that charity which is limited to no sector or creed."

Daly had a history with New York's Jews that began before the 1883 publication of this book. Daly, a well-respected member of the New York political elite and loyal son of Tammany Hall, served as vice president of the Democratic Republican Young Men of the City and County of New York and recording secretary of the New York Workingmen's Democratic Republic Association. An activist in Irish communal affairs, he presided over the St. Patrick's Society and chaired the Committee for the Relief of Ireland. Daly had counted himself among the friends of the Jews and had been a spokesman for their causes since the 1870s. In 1872 he gave the keynote address at the jubilee assembly of the Hebrew Benevolent Society of New York. He then expanded the talk and in 1883 delivered it at the laying of the cornerstone of the Hebrew Orphan Asylum.

In all these presentations, Daly, the invited, honored Irish guest, emphasized Jewish service and beneficence. He stressed that, rather than burdening American society, the Jews kept their own people off the public rolls, assisting them to become useful and productive Americans.

At the request of lawyer Max Kohler, a Jewish communal activist and defender of immigration for Jews and others, Daly agreed to the reissue of his two books. In his introductory remarks, Kohler made clear the genesis and import of Daly's research, and why the American Jewish elite, like Kohler himself or Cowen, so wanted to see these books disseminated. According to Kohler, Daly directly challenged the assertions of anti-Semites like Goldwin Smith, the British historian and journalist, who claimed that since the days of Rome the Jews had been parasites who only pursued money and gain for themselves. Smith offered no less scurrilous words, though in a different vein, about the Irish, whereas Daly, Kohler wrote, exposed "the arrogance and effrontery to characterize the Jews in America as parasites."

Upon Daly's death, Kohler published a tribute to him in *The American Hebrew*, reprinted also in pamphlet form. He lionized him as one who "chose to espouse so zealously the Jewish cause and so conspicuously enriched our communal life and thought by means of important contributions to Jewish history, to the extinction of anti-Semitic prejudice and the elevation and amelioration of American Jewish life." Not a Jew himself, Daly's words could never be dismissed as special pleading, and as a luminary in New York's Irish community he revealed, as the Jews saw it, the good deeds of the Jews to an influential segment of the city's political elites.[33]

Just a few years later the American Jewish leadership again turned to an Irish person, one with a substantial American following, to defend the Jews and get their case heard. Michael Davitt's *Within the Pale: The True Story of Anti-Semitic Persecution in Russia* offered the American reading public an eyewitness account of the aftermath of the bloody attack on the Jews of Kishinev. The only English-language book on the subject by a non-Jew, *Within the Pale* described the events that flared in the Moldavian city on April 19 and 20, Easter 1903, using eyewitness accounts and interviews. The book graphically described how the mob had fallen on the Jewish community of Kishinev, killed some fifty souls and injured many, raped women, wreaked extensive property damage, destroyed Jewish homes and shops, and essentially brought the word "pogrom" into the consciousness of the American public.[34]

Davitt, an Irish nationalist leader of great renown who earned a living as a journalist, had arrived in Kishinev at the behest of the Hearst newspapers to report back on what he saw, whom he interviewed, and to offer some assessments of the Jewish future there. His articles appeared in British and American newspapers, and almost immediately upon his return from Kishinev the Jewish Publication Society of America, which aimed to foster Jewish culture and defend the Jews worldwide, asked Davitt to arrange his articles as a book, one that extended beyond the reportage in the press. Other publishers in Britain and the United States also brought out the book, but the initiative of the Jewish Publication Society provided an important example of the Irish-Jewish connection in America, reflecting both the Jews' agenda and that of Irish nationalists as represented by Davitt.[35]

Davitt's book did not spare the details. He reported on the sights and sounds of the Jewish quarter in shambles. He talked to victims. He garnered evidence from Jews and Christians, both ordinary people and clergy, as well as medical personnel, bearing witness to the "revolting deeds of mediaeval savagery in our day."[36]

Davitt, the Irish nationalist, linked his larger political project to Kishinev. Telling the history of the Jews in Russia in the context of the pogrom offered him a chance to take on his foe, England. Throughout the book he found opportunities, despite his obvious sympathy for the Jews, to show how even despotic Russia actually did more for its people than England did. Davitt, whose rural County Mayo family had been in arrears to the landlord for the rent, had migrated to Lancashire with its "dark Satanic mills." At age nine, Michael had gone to work in a cotton mill and lost an arm in a machine. In *Within the Pale* he asserted that "Russia, unlike England, recognises the national danger of physical degeneracy through overcrowded cities. Knowing how the prospect of better wages in these centres attracts workers of the soil to the employment of mills and factories, she sets herself the task of encouraging the growth of such counter-industries as will tend to minimise the extent of this movement."[37]

Davitt fused the Irish and the Jewish causes in other ways. As an advocate for land reform and home rule in Ireland, he pointed to the Russian Jews' need for a home of their own. That is, he, like many Jews around the world at the time, considered the lesson of Kishinev to be the imperative of Zionism, a newly formed but already potent movement that advocated Jewish reclamation and return to the land of their ancestors.

Davitt made a linguistic usage that also bound together the Jewish and Irish experiences. While he was not the first to use the English word "pale" to refer to the swath of land to which the czarist state had restricted the Jews since 1791, the term gained greater traction with his book. As a word it derived from Irish history. Referring to that area of Ireland, near Dublin, that first came under direct English rule in the fourteenth century, "the Pale" essentially connoted Irish loss, their alienation from their own land at the hands of what they defined as a hostile colonial power.

As for the Jews, what did they hope to gain from enlisting Davitt to help tell their story? The explanations lie in the fraught moment when the pogrom erupted. Immigration restrictions loomed on the political horizon in both the United States and Britain. In the latter, those favoring restrictions focused in particular on the specter of Russian Jews arriving in droves, while in the former, Jews from Eastern Europe, along with so many others, were seen as undesirable by those committed to preventing the mass entry of so many people seen as so different from "real" Americans. In the 1903 Immigration Act the US Congress consolidated its power to restrict immigration, and while the act's particulars did not pose any new threat to the Jewish influx, apart from the addition of political beliefs as a basis for exclusion, those watching the creeping growth of restrictions, coupled with the violence in Moldavia, shuddered in fear.

In 1903 the British parliament, press, and public engaged in an intense debate over what would become in 1905 the Aliens Act. As a piece of immigration legislation, the Aliens Act contained a clause that Jews in both Britain and America, while concerned about any restriction, could see as potentially lifesaving: the act being discussed in Parliament allowed for the entry of those fleeing persecution, something US legislation never included.

By enlisting Davitt to report on the horrors of Kishinev, by labeling the events of that city a case of persecution, a term that assumed state-based action against a group of people as opposed to mob violence by nonstate actors, and by broadly and widely disseminating Davitt's book, the Jewish Publication Society and its political allies hoped to slow down the move toward restrictions in general and to ease it for Jews. Kishinev, the events surrounding it in the United States, and notably Davitt's book cannot be dissociated from the ongoing American Jewish campaign to keep America open to Jewish immigration, particularly for those from the Pale.

That these American Jews—Cowan and Kohler in cooperation with Daly, and the members of the Jewish Publication Society in cooperation with Davitt—turned to Irish and Irish American activists, political figures, and individuals associated with Irish communal life offers a compelling example of how American Jews saw their Irish neighbors as politically savvy and well-connected players in American society who could help them in their projects. In a world where American Jews quite rightly believed they had few friends, in the Irish they found individuals willing to work for and with them.

In the other direction, the Irish partners in this two-way relationship also had something to gain from their association with Jews. It offered Davitt, Daly, and before them Roche and John Boyle O'Reilly a chance to face the Protestant, native-born, self-described Anglo-Saxon elite and claim the mantle of liberalism and humanitarianism, brimming with sensitivity to the plight of the oppressed. In an American culture steeped in anti-Catholicism, deeply built into the hostile reaction toward the Irish, Irish Americans could demonstrate openness to others and tolerance, qualities that critics claimed Catholicism lacked.

That role involved for the most part a set of crucial lessons that Irish immigrants and their daughters and sons taught Jews. Those lessons, as given and received, grew out of a singular relationship forged in America that served both peoples. Based not on an ideology of pluralism or of similarity in outlook, it functioned well as the two groups recognized the services they could mutually provide. A deeply American phenomenon, it reflected the particular dynamics of American life. Indeed the Irish-Jewish encounter, with its important learning experiences provided to Jews by Irish Americans, differed from any other encounter experienced by Jews before or after. And as for the Irish, their ability and willingness to cooperate with Jews worked well for them.

# 2

## The Right to Choose

*The Public Health and Birth Control Movements of Lillian Wald and Margaret Sanger*

HANNAH ZAVES-GREENE

On February 25, 1929, Margaret Sanger received a note from her former employer Lillian Wald. Sanger had asked Wald for permission to use her name as a patron of a dinner to benefit the Birth Control and Research Clinic, adding the caveat that "the use of [Wald's] name [did] not entail any further obligation."[1] Wald complied, but asked Sanger to "please have that as a personal matter—not as a Henry Street Settlement one,"[2] intentionally dissociating the settlement house she had established on Manhattan's Lower East Side from Sanger's controversial birth control campaign. Wald, the pioneer of public health nursing, and Sanger, the founder of the birth control movement, both emerged as boundary-breaking healthcare reformers during the Progressive Era. Though their paths crossed but briefly, each of these first-generation American women made unprecedented practical and ideological strides in public health, based significantly on their work with immigrant families in New York City. Simultaneously, they negotiated their own immigrant histories and complex relationships with their religioethnic communities of origin. Wald remained reluctant to embrace her own Jewishness, while she garnered considerable financial aid and social cachet from uptown acculturated Jews. Sanger's experiences growing up in a working-class Irish Catholic family informed her dedication to birth control, and sharpened her antipathy to the Catholic Church's anti-birth control stance. Wald and Sanger shaped and influenced American healthcare ideologies, practices, and policies for decades to come, propelling a vibrant national conversation about public and maternal health in the United States.

The Wald and Sanger families both immigrated to the United States during the mid-nineteenth century. Wald's Jewish parents and grandparents left elite positions in Central Europe, where they had been rabbis, scholars, merchants, and professionals. Once they arrived in the United States, they successfully integrated into the middle class of Rochester, New York.[3] Sanger's Catholic parents fled from the Famine in County Cork, and lived in a heavily working-class community in Corning, New York. Unlike Wald's comfortable middle-class upbringing, Sanger's girlhood taught her the privations of poverty and the pressures of providing for a family of eleven children. Though her father rejected the teachings of the Catholic Church, her mother remained a devout Catholic, which Sanger associated with her near-perpetual pregnancies that contributed to her untimely death. Sanger witnessed firsthand the toll that these pregnancies took on her mother, leading to her ire against the church for its opposition to birth control.[4] Wald's and Sanger's navigation of their religious and ethnic backgrounds, starting at an early age, helped structure the course each took as she chose to pursue a professional life.

Despite their divergent upbringings, experiences, and religiocultural milieus, Wald and Sanger inaugurated new fields that not only influenced American healthcare itself, but how government and society conceived of it. Influenced by socialism, these women viewed health and healthcare as a public and social, not strictly individual, matter. Wald coined the term "public health nursing" to describe the method of comprehensive healthcare she cultivated and wished to offer to all Americans, regardless of class, race, ethnicity, or sex. Sanger originated the phrase "birth control" to refer to the personal and economic liberation she desired to make accessible to women by giving them authority over their reproductive systems. They maintained their disparate focuses and strategies throughout the early twentieth century, on occasion benefiting from each other's labor, while pursuing their individual public health reforms predominantly with the same immigrant and working-class populations.

Wald's girlhood in Rochester showed her that a religious and ethnic group could integrate into the American civic polity and offered a model for how to do it. Her girlhood as a daughter of a middle-class Jewish family in Rochester showed her a gendered means of surmounting difference that stayed with her throughout her medical career. Aspiring middle-class Jewish women and men followed the gendered economic patterns of their American neighbors, in which men became breadwinners and women nurturers and moral guardians of the home. These acculturating Jewish women and men capitalized upon the privatization of religion, downplaying Jewish distinctiveness while emphasizing parity between mainstream middle-class American and Jewish conceptions of gender differences. Wald's family did not hold themselves apart as Jewish. They joined a Reform synagogue that welcomed intermarriage, and took advantage of Rochester's fluid class and ethnic demarcations thanks to industrialization and the liberalism that Christian revivalism had inspired. Wald's father and uncles became successful garment manufacturers, while her mother and aunts pursued philanthropy and social reform. Women counteracted the masculine sphere of business and politics, serving as voices of virtue and religiocultural custodians within the home and community.[5]

The charitable world of women intensely influenced the young Wald. Premised on the concept of maternalism, Wald's female relatives—like other Jewish women of their class—began to step into the public sphere.[6] Maternalism opened doors to these women. They supposedly possessed an innate capacity to nurture and care, and could and should harness that natural instinct to check industrial capitalism's encroachment and exploitation of workers, immigrants, and the poor. This essentialist conceptualization of femininity paved the way for women to undertake new educational and professional opportunities without losing respectability.[7] Wald remained a staunch devotee of maternalism throughout her life, simultaneously utilizing and subverting traditional understandings of gender division that allocated fixed roles and behavioral styles to women and men, thereby allowing her to push against the boundaries of that which middle-class American society deemed woman's place.

After meeting the nurse who attended at her older sister's childbirth, Wald decided that she too wished to pursue the "womanly, congenial" work of nursing, for which she felt she had a "natural aptitude."[8] One of the few professions then open to women, nursing offered a way to earn a living and an alternative to the normative course of home, husband, and children. It enabled women to immerse themselves in a homosocial female-centric environment where technical skills and professional attainments defined them instead of marriage.⁹ As advances in bacteriology and medical specialization began to coalesce by the last decade of the nineteenth century, leaders in the field started to standardize nursing education, thereby enhancing its respectability.¹⁰ Both Wald and Sanger availed themselves of this relatively new opportunity, though Sanger chose to become a nurse out of economic necessity while Wald did so because of the passion she discovered she had for the work.

Wald became one of the four Jewish women who graduated from Bellevue Hospital and the New York Hospital Training School for Nurses between 1875 and 1920. Though American Jewish women generally disapproved of nursing as a profession in the latter half of the nineteenth century, perceiving it as Christian and ungenteel,¹¹ Wald saw nursing as closely connected with her womanhood—even as her professional aspiration indicated her resistance to the limitations imposed upon middle-class women. Her letter of application revealed the extent to which she viewed her family as successfully integrated into middle-class America, while it offered her the rhetoric of gender that facilitated her admission. "My life hitherto has been," she asserted, "a type of modern American young womanhood." Discontented with "society, study, and house keeping duties," she felt compelled to undertake some "serious definite work."¹² More than just one occupational possibility among a handful of alternatives, Wald understood nursing "as an extension of women's moral duty to heal,"¹³ and one that particularly appealed to her. For Wald, gender, rather than Jewishness, functioned as her most personally salient marker of identity. Gender legitimated her professional work as a nurse and opened her path to healthcare reform.¹⁴

Wald's professional ambitions, then, lay squarely within her conception of what was appropriate for and becoming of women, even while she elasticized the definition of what those ambitions could entail. Nursing represented Wald's first exposure to women's professional and political work.¹⁵ Although she emphasized that women continued to possess a natural inclination for caregiving, she maintained that the times required them to seek the educational qualifications necessary for adjusting their intrinsic skills to the needs of society.¹⁶ With the correct training, they could apply their reverence for life to the problems and inequities within their communities and countries. Just as women could heal the physical body, they could heal the social body. Nursing gave Wald the knowledge and tools to do so. As she later reflected in her *House on Henry Street*, based on a compilation of articles that the editors of the *Atlantic Monthly* urged her to publish as a book in 1915,[17] "I had little more than an inspiration to be of use in some way or somehow, and going to the hospital seemed the readiest means of realizing my desire."[18]

After completing her nursing degree in 1891, Wald worked briefly at the New York Juvenile Asylum. The asylum inculcated in her an enduring aversion to institutionalism that determined her to seek additional training at New York City's Women's Medical College with the idea of becoming a doctor,[19] and primed her eventual establishment of public health nursing. During her student days Wald encountered urban tenement life for the first time. While she was teaching home nursing to Jewish immigrant women from the Lower East Side tenements, a young girl sought Wald's aid to tend to her hemorrhaging mother who had just given birth. Shocked and appalled by the insalubrious conditions in which the family lived, Wald underwent an epiphany that she later dubbed her "baptism of fire."[20] Revisiting the moment in retrospect, she declared that

> to my inexperience it seemed certain that conditions such as these were allowed because people did not *know*, and for me there was a challenge to know and to tell. When early morning found me still awake, my naïve conviction remained that, if people knew things—and "things" meant everything implied in the condition of this family,—such horrors would cease to exist, and I rejoiced that I had had a training in the care of the sick that in itself would give me an organic relationship to the neighborhood in which this awakening had come.[21]

Wald's first contact with the formidable challenges of tenement life stood as a watershed moment in her life and career. It spurred her to assist the sick poor and become an ambassador for them, raising awareness of the conditions in which they lived. Her insistence that the lack of public notice and knowledge of the urban poor's struggles directly contributed to their dire working and living circumstances remained a recurrent refrain throughout her professional life.

She isolated physical conditions from moral judgments, averring that "it would have been some solace if by any conviction of the moral unworthiness of the family I could have defended myself as part of a society which permitted such conditions to exist."[22] Wald charged society, not the poor, for producing and failing to address the problems of poverty, and stressed that "care and prevention" afforded a better mode of amending social injustices than "police power and punishment."[23] The occasion and severity of disease frequently originated in unsafe living and working conditions over which the sufferers had no control.[24] Prompting her to leave school and move to the Lower East Side to determine how she could best help the working women, men, and children who lived there, this epoch marked the first stage in her development of the field of public health nursing.

Wald referred to this occasion in Christian-inflected language as a "call,"[25] indicating that, at least as she presented herself publicly, her Jewishness did not act as her primary muse. She spoke to a generalized form of religious mission in the spirit of the Social Gospel that invoked human relationships as the religious center of progressive reform.[26] Her work became her source of spiritual expression rather than either Judaism or Jewishness, imbuing her nursing and efforts to combat poverty with sacred significance in her eyes. "From the root of the old gospel," she wrote, "another branch has grown, a realization that the call to the nurse is not only for the bedside care of the sick, but to help in seeking out the deep-lying basic causes of illness and misery, that in future there may be less sickness to nurse and to cure."[27] Nurses had to do more than dispense reparative or palliative care. They needed to discern the basis of disease and uproot it. As she discussed in a letter from 1908, she understood religion as premised upon "the good will, the humanitarianism, the very strong desire to achieve justice and equality of opportunities, to eliminate from the lives of men [sic] women and children the sordid conditions that drag them down spiritually, to lessen the greed of people, to place the highest value upon tolerance, kindness, and love."[28] None of these attributes depended upon any given religion or required adherence to any specific denomination. This type of rhetoric allowed Wald to distance her public persona from her Jewishness, as she consistently endeavored to do. It also meant that particularities of belief and praxis did not have to preclude anyone from participating in or benefiting from the medical care she felt herself called to provide.

The Progressive Era activism in which Wald found a home encompassed a variegated assortment of social amelioration efforts between roughly 1890 and 1920. These reformers summoned previous ideas about the roles and intersections of government, charity, and gender, to meet developing social needs and conditions as a result of urbanization and industrialization. They urged government to correct the devastation that the free market and increasingly mechanized economy inflicted on society's most vulnerable. In the interim, they intervened directly to provide immediate aid, modeled after their biases toward white, middle-class, Protestant Americanism, and frequently accompanied by their devaluation of the cultural traditions and ideologies that incoming immigrants brought to the United States.[29]

Throughout this period, middle-class women fashioned new ways to engage in the public sphere. They built their entry points upon conceptions of domesticity, which permitted them to participate in social reform work in the form of philanthropic clubs, political organization, and settlement houses.[30] Citing the ideology of maternalism, these women drew upon motherhood as their ticket outside of the home. Instead of orienting their lives exclusively around their families, they now applied the same concern to the welfare of society. Numerous Jewish women reformers invoked maternalism because it linked middle-class American and Jewish ideals of motherhood as the apex of womanhood, simply redefining the extent of what motherhood entailed.[31] For them, their performance and experience of gender and Jewishness formed an interlocking and mutually sustaining whole. Wald took a different track, privileging her gender over her Jewishness to highlight her assumed role as a caregiver over her religioethnic background.[32] She joined myriad other middle-class women who wanted an alternative to the conventional route of heterosexual matrimony, and accordingly sought opportunities that enabled them at once to pursue their professional goals and live in the company of other women, independently of men.[33]

Despite Wald's aversion to identifying publicly as Jewish, her Jewishness played a notable part in making her healthcare reform and advocacy possible. It first brought her to the Lower East Side, when she assented to a request that she teach nursing to working-class Jewish women because of her Jewish background. Upon encountering the hazardous working and living conditions that these women experienced on a daily basis, Wald left medical school and moved to the neighborhood with one of her colleagues. She did not want a top-down approach, in which she dispensed charity and then returned to a home isolated from the community that she served. Inspired by the settlement-house movement, in which middle-class women and occasionally men moved into impoverished urban enclaves to live and pursue social reform, Wald desired to work, live, and socialize in the same neighborhood, "and, in brief, contribute to it [her] citizenship."[34]

Wald's status within the New York Jewish community led to her introduction to the Jewish businessman and philanthropist Jacob Schiff, who funded the eleemosynary Henry Street. With his financial support, she opened the Henry Street Settlement House in 1893. Much as Wald's reform work served as a source of her spiritual expression, Schiff based his philanthropy on biblical injunctions to help the poor. He befriended and mentored Wald, and his economic aid helped preserve Henry Street's nonsectarianism. Similar to Wald, he regarded Henry Street as an institution where members of various ethnic and religious groups could unite beyond differences of identity, and as such—though he advocated the importance of sustaining Jewish continuity—he concurred with Wald that Henry Street should not come across as distinctively Jewish.[35]

Wald's Jewishness emerged most strongly in her personal and professional networks that sustained Henry Street. Jews across the religious and political spectrum, from the Yiddish intelligentsia to Stephen Wise and the Free Synagogue,[36] supported her work with immigrants and working-class families. Though most Americans did not associate her with Jewish communal or institutional organizations, within the Jewish community Wald maintained her status as one of the Central European Jewish elite. Positioned opposite the poor and immigrant Jews with whom Wald worked, these established Jews possessed elite socioeconomic standing and sought to integrate Jewish newcomers into the United States in a pattern after themselves.[37]

Henry Street's strict nonsectarianism separated it from prior nursing services. Wald did not publicize her Jewishness, and even refused inclusion in a book about prominent American Jewish women because she did not want to associate Jewishness with her reform work. She preferred to portray herself as "a universal representative of all of the urban poor."[38] Paralleling her liminal status as an American Jewish woman, Wald viewed public health nurses as translators and interpreters who could mediate between their frequently foreign-born patients and middle- and upper-class Americans.[39] Henry Street and the Visiting Nurse Service she subsequently founded provided care to all women, men, and children, regardless of ethnicity, religion, race, class, or gender, and employed staff across religious, ethnic, and racial lines.[40] Unusual among her white colleagues, Wald hired Black nurses. Though they could not attend white families or attain supervisory positions, they received equal payment and professional courtesies.[41] Derived in part from her family's success in acculturating and entering Rochester's middle class, Wald held that descent should not define a person's life course or group association. As such, she viewed religion as a personal matter and encouraged residents to maintain the religious practices and traditions that they found most meaningful, if they wished to observe organized religion at all.[42]

However, suiting her views of the intermediary role that public health nurses should play in representing the interests of the disadvantaged to society, Wald deployed her uptown Jewish station to rally support for her neighbors and patients. The National Council of Jewish Women, an organization founded in 1893 by a group of acculturated American Jewish women primarily of Central European descent,[43] invited her to give an address on working-class poverty at their first national meeting in 1896.[44] However, wealthy Jews' financial and social endorsement of Wald's work also granted them leverage to criticize Henry Street as insufficiently Jewish. Their economic contributions served as the basis for their claiming Wald as their own, and hence imposing more Jewishness upon her than she liked, although never enough to alter Henry Street's nonsectarianism. Traditionally observant Jews voiced concern about Henry Street's lack of Jewishness because they feared the erosion of Judaism in the United States, while some Jewish immigrants worried that Henry Street would convert them to Christianity. That said, the fact that Wald received donations and free positive press from Jewish individuals, communal notables, and organizations indicates that most American Jews eagerly embraced both her and her work.

The monetary backing that Wald received from Jewish benefactors enabled her to embrace the Progressive Era settlement model that animated Henry Street. She steered clear of "the institutional form of philanthropic work" so that residents would "preserve their identity as individuals."[45] Henry Street would counteract the damage that male-dominated and impersonal capitalism wrought on workers, reflecting Wald's views of women's and men's social roles. Its underlying philosophy embodied her critique of socioeconomic disparity. Instead of solely curing disease and remedying immediate ills, Wald contended that nurses could enhance human welfare writ large[46] but that any such grand aims had to commence at the local level.[47]

Working in a population significantly composed of Eastern European Jewish immigrants, Wald commented on the "undreamed-of opportunities" that settlement life granted "for widening [her] knowledge and extending [her] human relationships."[48] She stressed that "from what we call the settlement point of view we believe that the patients should know the nurse as a social being rather than as an official visitor."[49] Distinguishing Henry Street from other nursing programs, Wald advocated cultivating mutual relationships and treating patients individually, taking into account their "entire environment[s],"[50] rather than applying a generic one-size-fits-all model.[51] In keeping with settlement philosophy, Wald invoked "the life possible through making our home among the people in a simple, informal way,"[52] recognizing patients as neighbors and fellow citizens rather than as diseased bodies or ridden with vice. No aspect of her patients' lives, whether labor, leisure, or living conditions, was too minute. She treated them as people, not cases.

Wald's approach to human relationships characterized the paradigm of nursing that she developed to tend the sick poor in their homes. She designated it "public health nursing" to indicate both holistic concern for her patients' overall quality of life, and that its practitioners cooperated with private and public organizations to promote a just and inclusive society.[53] Unhappy with the current state of visiting nursing, in which only well-to-do families could afford private nurses and the charity nurses who attended the poor signaled their destitution to their neighbors, Wald sought "to create a service on terms most considerate of the dignity and independence of the patients."[54] Inspired by the preexisting method of private nursing, she designed a system such that public health nurses could develop bonds with their patients and be available to them at a moment's notice without the intercession of bureaucracy or the mediation of a doctor. Families paid according to their means, based upon a sliding-scale fee. As Wald saw it, lack of funds should not mean lack of superior medical care, and patients and their families should maintain agency and self-respect throughout. Modeled after hospital wards, Wald divided the city below 125th street into districts and assigned nurses to each, where they cared for all residents of their districts irrespective of class, religion, ethnicity, and race, to promote equitable and accessible healthcare among working-class New Yorkers.[55]

Henry Street and its Visiting Nurse Service combined the intimacy of private visiting nursing with the administrative thoroughness of a hospital. Wald wrote in 1905 that "I have long felt that the home nursing deserved to be considered by committees in a large way, as a legitimate branch of the whole care of the public health, and as a logical correlation of the work of the hospital."[56] Public health nurses offered detailed care on par with hospitals, but at a fraction of the expense and space, a boon in the highly populated metropolis of New York City. Each district functioned like a hospital department, maintaining comparable record systems and treatment protocols, and with their own allocated staffs able to address a range of conditions.[57] Between her nurses' rigorous training and her introduction of meticulous medical documentation, Wald aimed to care for the 90 percent of the urban poor she stated could not or, at any rate, did not avail themselves of public hospitals.[58] She did not compete with hospitals, but acknowledged that many immigrants, whether out of concern for observing Jewish dietary laws, fear of proselytizing, distaste for institutionalism, inability to get there, or unwillingness to accept the social stigma of poverty associated with public hospitals, remained at home. The standardization she fostered benefited both patients and nurses, who were "gratified that the former casual and almost sentimental attitude of the public toward them and their work has been replaced by a demand for standards of efficiency."[59]

Although the settlement movement inspired Wald's work, she shaped it according to her own vision. Public health, as she defined it, incorporated all aspects of her patients' lives, considering wellness to stem from a constellation of interlocking factors. Wald affirmed that "our nursing work is the 'raison d'etre' of our existence, from which all our other activities have had their natural and unforced growth."[60] Henry Street devoted special attention to maternal health and pediatric medicine, in addition to treatment and prevention of tuberculosis. Combining what would eventually emerge as professional social work, activism, and healthcare, public health included educating families about hygiene, instituting the office of school nurse, lobbying to accommodate children with disabilities in classrooms, staffing safe-milk stations,[61] supplying free school lunches, running social clubs and activities, providing education to women, offering vocational training, hosting theater performances, and more. Befitting Wald's proclivity toward universalism, public health both took a programmatic approach to individuals' welfare and embraced people of diverse backgrounds under its auspices.

In contrast to Wald's all-encompassing approach to healthcare, Margaret Sanger opted for a significantly more targeted focus in her work, though with comparably ambitious goals. Inspired by her medical background, including as a visiting nurse at Wald's Henry Street settlement house, she founded the birth control movement to promote women's access to and knowledge of contraception. Like Wald, though much more drastically, she personally dissociated herself from her religious heritage. However, where Wald expressed ambivalence toward her own Jewishness and maintained close connections with other Jews, Sanger estranged herself completely from the Catholic Church and vehemently resisted the obstacles it placed in the way of birth control. The daughter of an apostate father and devout mother, Sanger's fraught relationship with Catholicism began in her girlhood, eventually contributing to her decision to marry a Jewish man and culminating in her fervent anti-Catholicism as she waged war with Catholic clergy and laypeople over contraception.[62]

Sanger joined the cohort of women then beginning to pursue higher education, frustrated with the systemic limitations women faced. Similar to Wald, she initially hoped to become a doctor. Her family's precarious finances forced her to leave school early to earn an additional income to support them, until her mother's tuberculosis brought her back home full-time as nurse and to assume her mother's domestic responsibilities. Following her mother's death in 1900 and refusing to return to her hated teaching job, Sanger started nursing school at White Plains Hospital, where she ultimately headed its small women's ward. She studied the nascent field of gynecology, although the 1873 Comstock Act that forbade the dissemination of "obscene" material through the mail meant that her textbooks could not include information about abortion or contraception.[63] Nursing had a formative impact on Sanger's approach to the women with whom she would eventually work in her birth control clinic. She retrospectively avowed in 1940 that nursing "removes from . . . consciousness the prejudices of race, creeds and sex, enabling [the nurse] to administer and to give service to old and young, black and white, Jew and Gentile. . . . She is taught to observe not only the dust in corners, but the pupils of the patients' eyes."[64]

After a hiatus from nursing because of her whirlwind courtship, secret marriage, pregnancies, and chronic tuberculosis that she had contracted from caring for her mother, Sanger returned to nursing in 1910 to help support her family. She worked part-time as a Henry Street visiting nurse specializing in obstetrics.[65] Unwilling to remain solely a wife and mother, Sanger yearned to be an active participant in life, and threw herself into social and political causes from socialism to bohemianism. These, however, did not satisfy her, particularly once she experienced sharp class divisions through the lens of her work, when most of her medical cases shifted from young professionals to impoverished families on the Lower East Side. The disparate conditions she encountered shocked her into action. Not only did her work with these families reveal to her what historian Ellen Chesler termed "the social pathos of a poverty hauntingly familiar to her from her own youth and its victimization of women and children,"[66] it awoke in her a fierce determination to rectify the socioeconomic inequalities that she believed caused her patients' extreme suffering. Speaking to Henry Street's holistic outlook, Sanger averred that "my concern for my patients was now quite different from my earlier hospital attitude. I could see that much was wrong with them which did not appear in the physiological or medical diagnosis. A woman in childbirth was not merely a woman in childbirth. My expanded outlook included a view of her background, her potentialities as a human being, the kind of children she was bearing, and what was going to happen to them."[67]

She witnessed her patients' near-constant pregnancies and recourse to dangerous and illegal abortions, combined with the desperation of exhausting work hours and minimal educational opportunities. These together made them old before their time and forced their children prematurely into the labor force or to abandon their families in the hopes of better lives for themselves. Sanger diagnosed the disease plaguing these women as "destitution linked with excessive childbearing,"[68] a gradual realization that set in motion her transition from revolutionary fervor to emphasizing the value of science and education to improve their lives.[69]

Sanger told the story of her awakening to women's need for safe and reliable birth control in her autobiography. While a thriving market for black-market contraception had long existed, and women of different class backgrounds used it to varying degrees of success, both the risks associated with it and its lack of regulation posed considerable challenges.[70] In 1912, she wrote, she had been called to nurse the "madonna-like"[71] Sadie Sachs, a woman suffering from an infection caused by a botched abortion. Sadie[72] begged the doctor to tell her how to avoid having more children, fearful that another pregnancy would kill her. The doctor scoffed in response. Some months later, Sanger's story went, she returned to the same home only to witness Sadie's death from septicemia after another failed abortion. She left the Sachs home distraught, haunted by specters of "women writhing in travail to bring forth little babies; the babies themselves naked and hungry, wrapped in newspapers to keep them from the cold; six-year-old children with pinched, pale, wrinkled faces, old in concentrated wretchedness . . . white coffins, black coffins, coffins, coffins interminably passing in never-ending succession."[73] Determined that she "could not go back merely to keeping people alive,"[74] Sanger decided that she must instead "seek out the root of evil . . . do something to change the destiny of mothers whose miseries were vast as the sky."[75] Nursing taught her how to treat the symptoms of indigence and disempowerment. Sanger wanted to treat the cause.

This epiphany, like Wald's, signified a turning point in more respects than one for Sanger. By this point, she had experienced her mother's illness and death hastened by the bodily fatigue of numerous pregnancies, her own arduous deliveries, and the dogged shadow of her tuberculosis. Upon recognizing the unsafe conditions in which immigrants lived on the Lower East Side, she built upon her devotion to progressive and radical causes to organize women to fight for their bodily autonomy and consequently socioeconomic liberation.[76] Whereas Wald came to socialism through public health, Sanger came to birth control through socialism. In contrast to Wald's maternalism, Sanger fought against the idea of separate spheres and argued "that the price women pay for achieving equality should not be their sexuality or personal fulfillment."[77] She left nursing, realizing that she could not accomplish the radical overhaul of women's reproductive freedom that she desired within the male-imposed restrictions on the profession.[78] Just as Wald held that all people possessed the right to healthcare, Sanger held that women possessed the right to control their own bodies and reproduction. Giving women the ability to regulate their reproduction would benefit workers as well, since it would reduce birthrates and as such labor supply, pushing employers to pay their workers better.[79] She sought to bring contraception to poor women like those who lived on the Lower East Side,[80] but struggled to find relevant information because of the Comstock Act's censorship. In time, she endeavored to establish a network of clinics that would distribute all manner of birth control devices, family planning, and sex education, particularly for working-class women and those who wanted the option of women-centric care instead of male doctors.[81]

Together with friends and colleagues, Sanger coined the term "birth control" to denote the liberation she wanted to bring to women by offering them the necessary tools and knowledge to exert control over their reproduction and sexuality. Birth control, in Sanger's eyes, offered a viable antidote to the flood of either seemingly interminable births, or risky and illicit abortions—which she approved only when all else failed—that poor women attempted annually in the United States.[82] She combated the widespread false belief that synthetic contraception caused prostitution, licentiousness, infertility, and insanity among women.[83] Prostitution, for Sanger, was an economic issue rather than a moral one, and she argued that birth control use among married couples would stop it in its tracks.[84] She began publishing *The Woman Rebel* in March 1914, the first American magazine of its kind intended for working women. Proclaiming as its motto "Working women, build up within yourselves a conscious fighting character against all things that enslave you," it encouraged working-class women to band together and upend their "biological subservience to man"[85] that restrained them from independence and advancement. Birth control formed the first step on their path of socioeconomic emancipation, although Sanger could not legally disseminate information on how to use it because of the Comstock legislation. *The Woman Rebel*'s first issue laid down the law, declaring the societal wrongs inflicted upon women and that they must "revolt"[86] to unfetter themselves from their bondage to "the world machine . . . sex conventions . . . motherhood and its present necessary child-rearing . . . wage-slavery . . . middle-class morality . . . customs, laws, and superstitions."[87] Sanger knew well from her mother's early death that prolific childbearing could destroy women's health and strength, in addition to keeping them from financial security and taking risks for fear that they would not be able to feed their families. Nor, she argued, was it healthy or beneficial for the children thus conceived. Sanger declared that "the basis of Feminism might be the right to be a mother regardless of church or state,"[88] contending that without control over their own bodies, women could not become emancipated from the other forces that enslaved them.[89]

*The Woman Rebel* reached approximately two hundred subscribers, despite the fact that Sanger self-published it under the threat of legal action. Preaching "the right of the individual" with the slogan "No Gods, No Masters," Sanger emphasized that "I wanted that word [Gods] to go beyond religion and also stop turning idols, heroes, leaders into gods."[90] She asserted that women had a duty "to look the world in the face with a go-to-hell look in the eyes; to have an idea; to speak and act in defiance of convention."[91] She exemplified her own goal, openly sharing information about the taboo topics of sex, sexuality, and human reproductive systems as foundational to "her vision of preventive medicine,"[92] and urged mothers to do the same with their children. Rape too fell under her jurisdiction, as she insisted that it required attention as a woman's issue, one treacherous to ignore and for which women should not be impugned.[93]

Here again the Comstock Act reared its head. It classified birth control as pornography, resulting in Sanger's arrest for violating the law by circulating literature that discussed birth control through the postal system. In October 1914, Sanger confronted a dilemma as to her best course of action.[94] *The Women Rebel* had hit upon an urgent demand for authoritative educational materials about contraception, compelling Sanger to publish covertly a pamphlet entitled *Family Limitation* that provided explicit instructions for how to use birth control devices and illustrations of the female reproductive system. Since she maintained that what she saw as her right to publicize information about the birth control movement was intertwined with the freedoms of speech and press, Sanger did not want to go to trial and potentially jail for the wrong case. She fled to Europe so that her friends and colleagues could continue to print *Family Limitation* while she studied sexuality, sexology, and neo-Malthusianism abroad to develop her ideas about birth control and a plan to overturn the Comstock laws. Her fourteen years of nursing and cognizance of the wretched conditions of poverty, compounded by her outrage that wealthy women could pay their way to birth control while poor women could not, fired her dedication to the cause. Railing against the Comstock Act as, in her view, the latest manifestation of Christian religious domination, Sanger polemicized that "the Church, not daring to come out and to interfere with moral or religious principle openly, hides behind the closed doors of the 'Suppression of Vice Society,' and works its poisonous way through the Government *via* [emphasis in original] its special agent, Comstock."[95] She asserted that Christian hegemony, government, and moneyed interests worked hand in hand to ensure the perpetuation of a cheap labor force consisting of women and children, and called for women's knowledge of birth control as a means to end child labor.

A year after she returned to the United States because of the publicity surrounding her husband's trial for distributing *Family Limitation*, Sanger established America's first birth control clinic in Brownsville, Brooklyn, where she provided birth control but not abortion. Although intended for working-class and immigrant women, women across the socioeconomic and ethnic spectrum welcomed Sanger's clinic. Undergirded by what Sanger later called the "right to voluntary motherhood," she viewed her mission as "protect[ing] women from ill health as the result of excessive child-bearing and, equally important . . . giv[ing] them the right to control their own destinies."[96] Reminiscent of the preventive care that Wald offered via Henry Street, Sanger maintained that women deserved access to birth control to prevent the necessity of either perilous abortions or unplanned children whom they could not support.

Wald too favored birth control, but not as an official Henry Street policy. Contrary to Sanger's position that all women were entitled to birth control, Wald initially inclined to the belief that only legally married women should be allowed to use it under the guidance of a reputable physician.[97] She later explained that doctors should be allowed to share information about contraception with their patients, so that bodily autonomy extended beyond the exclusive province of the wealthy.[98] She evidently permitted her nurses to disseminate such information, indicating in a letter that nurses who wished to do so should be aware of an arrest made on the charge of violating the Comstock Act. While, she added, the arrest resulted in a dismissal and "it seemed to be a ridiculous attempt to molest her, but nevertheless it shows that the police will take authority,"[99] she took care to ensure that her nurses understood that such an outcome could occur. When Sanger faced public trial in 1916 for distributing information about birth control, she included Wald among the friends to whom she appealed for support.[100] Wald privately gave money and lent her political support to Sanger's birth control revolution, but took care to keep her actions separate from Henry Street.[101]

Sanger exercised no such caution as Wald. Arrested again for running her Brownsville clinic, she came to trial in January 1917. To applause from the women in the courtroom, Sanger proclaimed her refusal "to obey a law [she did] not respect."[102] The case ended in her imprisonment, for which Sanger blamed the local Catholic church. From prison, she educated inmates about contraception and strategized the next steps of her movement, desirous to carry her case to the highest court she could.[103] A year later the New York Court of Appeals sustained Sanger's conviction, but provided her with the legal basis to establish her network of physician-staffed birth control clinics when it reinterpreted the Comstock Act to allow doctors to disseminate birth control to married patients for health reasons.[104]

Although the 1918 ruling marked a victory for Sanger, it would hardly be the last time she would confront resistance about birth control. Contrary to the Jewish community's embrace of Wald, Sanger encountered strident opposition from the American Catholic Church, including from the women who formed its lay backbone.[105] Sanger, already critical of Catholicism, became increasingly antagonistic toward it as she encountered the opposition of church leaders and major American Catholic institutions toward birth control. The National Catholic Welfare Conference and Catholic Charities Appeal, both established in the interwar period, contributed substantial sums of money to anti–birth control efforts, and condemned Sanger for corrupting women and benefiting financially from birth control. In 1919 a cohort of American bishops published a letter forbidding the use of contraception as indulgent, unnatural, and undutiful.[106] Father John Ryan, who soon became the leader of the National Catholic Welfare Conference's social action department, published *Family Limitation and the Church and Birth Control* to outline the Catholic Church's stance. His pamphlet stated in no uncertain terms that "all positive methods of birth prevention (abortion and all the so-called contraceptives) are condemned by the Church as grievous sins" since "all these devices constitute the immoral perversion of a human faculty" by curtailing procreation.[107] Urban Catholics, who became a key element of the Roosevelt coalition, in the coming years would mobilize to shut out birth control from the New Deal.

The 1921 Town Hall raid in New York City functioned as a milestone in Sanger's battle with the church. On the final night of the First American Birth Control Conference, which Sanger had planned throughout the year to generate a national conversation about birth control from medical, sociological, economic, legal, eugenic, and settlement perspectives,[108] she had intended to announce the founding of the American Birth Control League.[109] By this time Sanger had shifted from feminist to eugenic rhetoric, then considered a creditable and respectable science, to bolster her birth control efforts. Organizations to study and enact eugenics proliferated during the 1910s and 1920s, granting Sanger a new platform to frame and communicate her ideas in favor of birth control.[110] She deployed the language of eugenics to point out a national need she asserted she was specifically qualified to fill, by virtue of concurrently tapping into American racism, ableism, and xenophobia, and offering a solution in the form of contraception.[111] The conference functioned as a platform to discuss "medical and social aspect[s] of Birth Control and its relation to National Health"[112] that strategically preceded the bicentennial anniversary of the American Health Association, garnering national attention for her movement.[113] Issuing a pamphlet entitled *One Hundred Years of Birth Control: An Outline of Its History*, the conference sought to legitimate birth control as a procedure of long standing, proclaiming that "in its ethical, social, and hygienic aspects, the idea of Birth Control is a mature, tested, and practical solution to the great fundamental national and international problems demanding solutions today."[114] Birth control, in other words, would serve as a mechanism of social engineering that enabled the hegemonic status quo to maintain its authority.

At the Town Hall meeting, Sanger capitalized upon the increasingly popular field of eugenics to build a coalition of supporters. During the 1920s, interest in eugenics burgeoned among elite American men, since it offered them ostensible scientific evidence to support their claims of preeminence and a cohesive framework to help them maintain their dominant positions. Sanger found in eugenics a useful tool to attract adherents to her cause and communicate her arguments in favor of birth control in a way that professional and intellectual white men could appreciate. She explained that birth control would accomplish at least two aims. It would safeguard the health of the American population by limiting the birthrate of the "unfit"—in other words, nonwhite people, poor people, and people with disabilities. Meanwhile, it would strengthen the American economy by reducing the number of people who would eventually depend upon public institutions.[115]

To illustrate her points, she divided society into three groups based on class and assumed correlated extent of personal responsibility. The wealthy could afford and used birth control to limit their family sizes. Many in the middle and lower classes wished to regulate their family sizes, but lacked the resources. The third group, she averred, the "irresponsible and reckless," many of whom were "diseased, feeble-minded, and . . . of the pauper element,"[116] either did not care about the impact of their decisions or chose not to limit their family sizes for religious reasons. Sanger asserted that "there is no doubt in the minds of all thinking people that the procreation of this group should be stopped. For if they are not able to support and care for themselves, they should certainly not be allowed to bring offspring into this world for others to look after. We do not believe that filling the earth with misery, poverty, and disease is moral."[117] Explicating that morality meant the improvement of the social body grounded in science and modern medicine, rather than Christian or other religious teaching, Sanger stressed that birth control would prevent society's diseased parts from progressing for the benefit of the whole.

The last evening of the meeting did not proceed as Sanger had intended. Police burst in and interrupted the proceedings, shutting the conference down and carting Sanger off under the charge of disorderly conduct. The *New York Times* claimed that Archbishop Patrick Hayes of St. Patrick's Cathedral had ordered the raid. Hayes's representative who attended the conference informed the reporter that "the attitude of the

Catholic Church is well known, through pamphlets and brochures made public when this matter came up before . . . written by eminent theologians, who set forth the age-old doctrine of the Church, explaining fully that the Roman Catholic Church could have no sympathy with this so-called movement, so similar as it is to a practice which is against the law of every civilized country."[118] A subsequent inquiry could not directly link Hayes with the raid, but the New York Archdiocese certainly did not approve of Sanger's birth control activities.[119]

Sanger seized the moment to respond to the American Catholic Church leadership's opposition to birth control. She saw Catholicism as standing for blind faith and authoritarianism, especially with respect to women's minds and bodies, in direct contrast to the liberation of women that she fostered. Marshaling her resources, Sanger took aim at the church in full view of the public. As the executive secretary of the American Birth Control League wrote to Wald, "the seeming calamity of the Town Hall meeting being closed has resulted in a great victory for the Cause. The press and the public have been more widely educated to the dignity and the fundamental necessity of Birth Control. The indifferent and inert believer has been galvanized into permanent activity."[120] Framing her argument in terms of women's and children's rights, Sanger proclaimed that not only did women have the rights to their own bodies and to voluntary motherhood, not only did children have the right "to be desired" and "conceived in love" with "a heritage of sound health," so too "every mother in this country, either sick or well, has the right to the best, the safest, the most scientific information . . . disseminated directly to [them] through clinics by members of the medical profession, registered nurses and registered midwives."[121] Indicting the church's obstruction of birth control, she asserted that it had historically countered

> the progress of woman on the ground that her freedom would lead to immorality. We ask the church to have more confidence in women. We ask the opponents of this movement to reverse the methods of the church, which aims to keep women moral by keeping them in fear and ignorance, and to inculcate into them a higher and truer morality based upon knowledge. And ours is the morality of knowledge. If we cannot trust woman with the knowledge of her own body, then I claim that two thousand years of Christian teaching has proved to be a failure.[122]

Criticizing the church for what she described as its oppression of women, Sanger linked its rejection of birth control with its opposition to women's suffrage.[123] She conceived of birth control as moral because its usage implied "increasing forethought for others, even for those yet unborn"—albeit from a troubling eugenics perspective that premised birth control's morality in part upon its improvement of "the level and the standards of the human race."[124]

Her success in associating the birth control movement with the social elite, many of whom were eugenicists, won her favorable press coverage in major New York newspapers that denounced the Town Hall raid. Meanwhile, it further intensified her already tense relationship with the Catholic Church. She had been scheduled to speak in the substantially Catholic cities of Albany, Syracuse, and Boston, but after the raid community figures either canceled or disturbed her presentations. American Catholic notables banded together to combat birth control at the institutional and political level, rather than locally as they had done before. In 1919 American bishops published an anti–birth control letter that prohibited Catholics from using it, asserting that doing so was a sinful abrogation of "the responsibility of bringing children into the world." A postwar Catholic Charities appeal landed money in Catholic coffers to fund their fight against birth control, while the newly established National Catholic Welfare Conference (NCWC) condemned birth control for debasing marriage, atrophying self-discipline, and promoting indulgence. The *Catholic Encyclopedia Supplement* proclaimed that women who used birth control were equivalent to prostitutes and that it caused everything from cancer to divorce, while the Pennsylvanian *Catholic Light* disparaged Sanger "and her 'pals'" for "'profiting' from birth control business."[125] Sanger responded in kind via letters and her *Birth Control Review*, deriding Catholic officials as hypocritical and on the wrong side of history. The matter traveled all the way to Rome, when Pope Pius XI issued *Casti connubii* in 1930, rejecting contraception as sinful and counter to divine law, since it dissociated sexual intercourse from the procreation of children.[126]

Sanger's battle with the church reached a new height in the 1930s, when American Catholic leaders harnessed their political organizing power to halt federal birth control reform. She termed her 1931 birth control bill a "Mother's Bill of Rights" and testified on its behalf before the Judiciary Committee.[127] The support that Sanger had obtained from friends including Wald,[128] which she sought as well for subsequent efforts to pass birth control legislation,[129] could not sustain the bill. The next year she attempted again, and again the bill failed in the face of the combined opposition of the Council of Catholic Women, Knights of Columbus, and International Federation of Catholic Alumni. Even in the face of the bill's defeat twice over, the NCWC stepped up its hostility to birth control, alleging that it was a "national menace."[130] Catholic publications poured negative editorials into the press, laypeople swamped their representatives with letters against birth control, and birth control supporters and providers faced intensified browbeating. Sanger tried once more during Roosevelt's administration, holding a conference that urged the legalization of birth control as a component of public health and social welfare programs, and obtaining favorable testimony from Protestant and Jewish clergy. The bill almost passed in 1934, but stopped short once the Irish Catholic anticommunist senator Pat McCarran demanded a recall to unanimous agreement in the Senate.[131] Sanger thought that persistent Catholic resistance represented a last gasp of the church's influence on familial and social life, and erroneously believed that the church would ultimately be forced to concede.[132] As time passed, already predisposed to regard Catholicism and the church with antipathy, her clashes with the church over birth control led her to become increasingly and vociferously anti-Catholic as the chasm broadened between them.[133]

 Lillian Wald and Margaret Sanger left indelible marks on public health and birth control in America. Both of these daughters of immigrants spoke of their awakenings upon witnessing inequities that particularly targeted poor women and families, many of whom were themselves immigrants or first-generation Americans. Where Wald spoke of universalism and maternalism, Sanger invoked women's liberation. Wald and Sanger emphasized that reformers had to attend to the physical needs of those whom they aspired to help, ensuring that they had access to quality and wide-ranging healthcare that treated patients as human beings as Wald underscored, or bolstering women's ability to regulate and control their bodies for the sake of health and independence as Sanger stressed. Though they distanced themselves from their own religioethnic backgrounds to varying extents, they each took these backgrounds into account as they concentrated on the hardships that the poor and immigrants faced. While they navigated the relationship between their work and their own bifurcated identities, Wald and Sanger discussed their public health reforms as part of a broader political project. Wald described the obligations and development of citizenship,[134] while Sanger focused on woman's "right . . . over her own body."[135] Writing of immigrants' children's needs, Wald asserted that "they carry on their shoulders our hopes of a finer, more democratic America, when the worthy things they bring to us shall be recognized, and the good in their old-world traditions and culture shall be mingled with the best that lies within our new-world ideas."[136] Sanger pointedly included the "immigrant with a vision . . . who had courage to leave the certain old for the uncertain new"[137] and her children in her vision of women's bodily and socioeconomic freedom, emphasizing that these newcomers could infuse life and energy into the nation's health. Though both women wrestled with their immigrant backgrounds, they nonetheless recognized the strengths that immigrants brought to the United States, and how immigrants forced mainstream American culture and society to question its accepted premises and choose new alternatives. Conscious from their families' immigrant histories of the role that choice played in fashioning their own identities, professional ambitions, and selected communities, Wald and Sanger asserted that offering all American families this option of choice—whether of comprehensive healthcare, or whether to become parents—constituted necessary steps toward a more just society.

3

"Tammany's Chosen People"

*How the Irish Courted the Jewish Vote in Progressive-Era New York*

TERRY GOLWAY

At the height of its power a century ago, Tammany Hall was not only the most famous political machine in the United States but arguably one of the most powerful Irish organizations in the world. Indeed, so large did it loom in the Irish imagination on both sides of the Atlantic that both Michael Collins and Harry Boland made references to Tammany's ways and means, not all of them flattering, during debates in Dáil Éireann over the Anglo-Irish Treaty in 1921.[1]

The Irish takeover of Tammany, fully achieved with the ascension of Honest John Kelly as boss in 1871, led to New York becoming, in the words of Daniel Patrick Moynihan, "perhaps the first great city in history to be ruled by men of the people . . . as a persisting, established pattern." Maintaining power from the bottom up in the early twentieth century required Tammany's Irish leaders to cement alliances with the newcomers with whom they shared the sidewalks of New York. And broadly speaking, that meant the city's burgeoning Jewish community.[2]

Tammany rather famously (or infamously, depending upon how one views its actions and the motives behind them) cultivated the city's immigrant community and often, although not nearly always, reaped the benefits on election day. The Jewish community offered a particularly bountiful harvest as the nineteenth century faded—according to one analysis (of many), the Jewish population of New York grew from about half a million in the beginning of the twentieth Century to a million and a half by 1920.[3]

Tammany, then under the leadership of the unjustly forgotten Charles Francis Murphy, regularly supported Jewish candidates for local offices and promoted the son of Russian Jewish immigrants, Aaron Levy, to the post of majority leader in the State Assembly in 1913. Murphy mobilized the Tammany machine on behalf of these newcomers from Eastern Europe in much the same way that his predecessors served Murphy's own father, a Famine immigrant, and hundreds of thousands of other Irish immigrants in the mid-nineteenth century. To start with, the machine welcomed them (again, not entirely out of the goodness of its heart) and withheld moral judgment about their customs, culture, and character. Those attitudes contrasted with the outright nativism of the old Whig Party in the 1850s and the more refined prejudices of elite progressives in the early twentieth century.[4]

Secondly, Tammany mobilized its extensive network of operatives and clubhouses to serve as a shadow government, providing connections to rudimentary social services, to jobs, and to the criminal justice system at a time when there was neither a safety net nor the sort of professional outreach from government that has become the norm in the twenty-first century.

"Thousands of new citizens and soon-to-be citizens found an impersonal government translated and interpreted here by the personal touch," wrote Tammany operative Louis Eisenstein, whose mostly Jewish neighbors were introduced to New York culture and politics in the clubhouse of the John F. Ahearn Association (named for and run by a popular district leader and state senator) on Grand Street and East Broadway on the Lower East Side. "The harshness of life in an unfamiliar New World was cushioned for newcomers who could not fill out citizenship papers or meet excessive rent payments and for those in need of jobs or peddlers' licenses."[5]

The relationship between Tammany's Irish leaders and New York's Jewish community surely was rooted in these kinds of pragmatic considerations: immigrants were looking for help and guidance; Tammany was looking for votes.

But there was something deeper to this relationship than a mere (albeit important) transaction. The Tammany Irish were, by and large, Catholics; one important exception to that rule was Richard Croker, the Irish Protestant immigrant who ran the machine from 1886 to 1902. They and their Jewish constituents were cultural outsiders in a city whose unelected power structure remained self-consciously Protestant, at a time when these religious distinctions carried with them markers not only of class but of true Americanism. Indeed, it was Franklin Roosevelt—and not, say, a member of the Know Nothings—who asserted that the United States was "a Protestant country, and the Catholics and the Jews are here on sufferance." And he said that in 1942, when Catholics and Jews were fighting in Europe and the Pacific against racist and exclusionary regimes.[6]

The shared sense of alienation from the cultural mainstream, and the fears those feelings produced, surely played a key role in the Tammany-Jewish alliance. That was evident not long after the Irish takeover of Tammany was complete during the Gilded Age and the machine prepared to test its power at the ballot box by nominating one of its own, an Irish Catholic immigrant, for the city's highest elective office in 1880.

William Russell Grace fled the Famine in 1847 as a teenager and made a fortune in the shipping industry. Tammany nominated him for mayor in 1880, threatening the Anglo-Protestant monopoly on City Hall. The city's newspapers, Protestant ministers, and distinguished citizens were horrified—no Catholic, no Irish immigrant, had ever been elected mayor. Elihu Root, a future Nobel Peace Prize winner, told an audience in Cooper Union that if Grace were elected, the "fundamental principle of our republic that Church and State shall be separate" would be threatened. The *New York Tribune* raised the possibility that Grace was not actually a citizen of the United States, condemning Tammany for running a candidate "about whom old and well-informed residents ask whether he is even a citizen." And the *New York Herald* anticipated Franklin Roosevelt's argument by sixty-two years, declaring, "This is a Protestant country and the American people are a Protestant people."[7]

On the Sunday before election day, parishioners gathered in Central Methodist Episcopal Church near Union Square, including former president Ulysses S. Grant, heard the Reverend John Newman declare that they ought to oppose "the Democratic candidate for Mayor," leading the congregation to burst into applause.[8]

The city's Jewish community understood that the campaign against Grace was driven by Anglo-Protestant presumptions about power, culture, and narrative in what was even then a diverse, multicultural city. The bigotry preached from editorial columns and pulpits was aimed at a Catholic, but the same forces would pounce, no doubt with greater force, on a Jew. So just a few hours after the Reverend Newman's anti-Grace homily, several hundred Jews gathered in a hall on the Lower East Side to condemn the bigotry and hatred that had overtaken the campaign for mayor. Among the speakers was Albert Cardozo, father of future US Supreme Court justice Benjamin Cardozo. He and others warned that if the city's highest office were denied Grace simply because of his religion, the city's Jews could expect similar treatment. The attacks on Grace, Cardozo said, were "contrary to the spirit of this country and its institutions."[9]

Grace won, although he went to bed on election night thinking he had lost. His margin of victory was a mere three thousand votes, a shockingly narrow victory for a candidate with Tammany's backing. (Tammany's previous winning candidate, William Wickham, won election as mayor in 1874 by nearly thirty-five thousand votes.) Whether or not the Jewish rally on the Lower East Side helped Grace is hard to determine. But it surely didn't hurt.

The Irish who ran Tammany beginning in the Gilded Age had a greater appreciation for mass democracy and, as Moynihan noted above, the notion of bottom-up leadership than their opponents in the city's reform movement did. Broadly speaking, reformers in New York in the late nineteenth century tended to regard the spectacle of campaigns and the drudge work of elections as vulgar exercises and impediments to efficient government. Just a few years before Grace's election, the city's reform movement got behind an effort to disenfranchise the poor in local elections in order to ensure more favorable outcomes. One of the measure's supporters, Yale University president Theodore Dwight Woolsey, argued that "none who do not own property should vote for representatives who lay taxes on property." The proposal had the support of the city's newspapers, one of which expressed the hope that restrictions on the vote would purge the city of "tipsy statesman" who "discuss politics over their gin and bitters."[10]

Tammany's leaders mobilized their constituents to beat back this challenge to universal male suffrage, and the "tipsy statesmen" who practiced street-corner politics continued to build bridges to the city's new arrivals—and, in marked contrast to New York's reformers, they encouraged them to vote. Preferably early—voters in Charles F. Murphy's Assembly district on the Lower East Side received handwritten notes if they didn't turn up at the polls by mid-afternoon.[11]

As defenders of suffrage rights, the Tammany Irish understood the power of mobilized numbers. Their outreach to Jewish newcomers was, in its basest form, a pragmatic reaction to the city's changing demographics. But it also nurtured ties between Irish politicians and Jewish voters, leading inevitably to the admission of Jewish members to the Society of St. Tammany (the private organization that controlled Manhattan's Democratic Party), the election of Jewish officeholders, and the promotion of those officeholders to leadership positions.

At the close of the nineteenth century, the roster of Tammany-supported state legislators certainly didn't lack for conspicuously Irish names, but also included Assembly members Emanuel Cahn, Milton Goldsmith, and Julius Rosen. The Board of Aldermen in the early twentieth century included Tammany-supported Moritz Tolk, Leopold Harburger, and Philip Harnischfeger. The Society of St. Tammany inducted six new members in early 1897; five of them were named Simon H. Stern, Edgar Levy, Nathan Straus, Randolph Guggenheimer, and Herbert Merzbach.[12]

The integration of Jews into Irish-controlled Tammany was a bottom-up enterprise, starting at the clubhouse level. Tammany's vaunted network of clubs was the source of its grassroots strength, for in these proverbial smoke-filled (and, to be sure, male-dominant) rooms, the organization's "tipsy statesmen" met for hours with residents who required assistance, a favor, an intervention.

The Ahearn Association, mentioned above, became the crossroads for this interethnic exchange in the early twentieth century, for its clubhouse was on Grand Street near East Broadway, a largely Jewish neighborhood in the shadow of the brand-new Williamsburg Bridge. The association's leader and namesake, John Ahearn, was famously tolerant on matters spiritual: the Tammany leader George Washington Plunkitt once said that Ahearn ate "corned beef and kosher meat with equal nonchalance" and was as likely to be found in the district's synagogues as he was in his own Catholic parish.[13]

That sort of outreach was welcomed, even if Tammany's critics dismissed it all as so much pandering. "At the turn of the century . . . who else offered aid?" asked Eisenstein. "Certainly not the stiff, aloof Republicans, [while] the Socialists were too busy preparing for the brave new world of the future to bother with the immediate needs of the present."

Eisenstein, who witnessed the Ahearn operation as a child and young adult, went on to become a precinct captain for Tammany on the Lower East Side from the 1920s to the 1950s.[14]

Eisenstein's dismissal of starry-eyed socialists may have reflected his own, lived experiences as a child of the Lower East Side, but broadly speaking, the relationship between Tammany's Irish and left-wing Jewish activists in New York was not necessarily either/or. That became especially evident after the Triangle Shirtwaist Factory fire in 1911 as Jewish labor activists, most prominently Rose Schniederman, demanded not simply better sprinkler systems and fire escapes, but systemic changes in the industrial order.[15]

The story of Tammany's response to the fire, which killed more than 140 people, most of them young Jewish and Italian women, generally focuses on two young products of the machine, Alfred E. Smith and Robert Wagner. They astounded reformers by leading a years-long investigation into industrial practices throughout New York State and guided reforms through the legislature. The Triangle investigation marked a turn to the left for Tammany, culminating in Smith's progressive agenda as governor in the 1920s, which, in turn, anticipated the New Deal.

That story, however, misses the impact of socialists and left-wing activists, many of them Jewish, on Tammany's response to the Triangle outrage. Schneiderman emerged as the face and voice of the movement for reform, and with her was the International Ladies' Garment Workers Union, with its strong Jewish membership. The union showed off its political strength in 1914 when it mobilized behind the candidacy of a Russian-born Jewish socialist, Meyer London, who shocked Tammany's Henry Goldfogle to win a seat in Congress from the Lower East Side. Three years later another Russian-born Jewish socialist, Morris Hillquit, won nearly a quarter of the vote in that year's mayoral election, nearly foiling Tammany's campaign to replace John Purroy Mitchel with a one-time transit worker, John Hylan. And in 1920, five socialists from New York were elected to the State Assembly, including the Yiddish-speaking Gus Claessens, labor lawyer Louis Waldman, Polish immigrant Louis Orr, and Charles Solomon, who represented a heavily Jewish and Italian district in Brooklyn.

Coincidentally or not (probably not, though there is no way to say for sure), Tammany's Irish leadership adopted and passed a raft of social welfare reforms as many Jewish voters began turning to Socialist Party candidates for local office. Between the Triangle fire and Smith's fourth and last term as governor ending in 1928, Tammany supported measures such as improved workers' compensation, pensions for widows and orphans, the beginnings of a minimum wage, college scholarships for poor children, prison reform, pay increases for teachers, slum clearance, creation of open space and parks, and greater workplace safety regulations.

Some of this, to be sure, was the result of a new generation of Irish American politicians imbued with a sense of social justice, some of it rooted in Pope Leo XIII's landmark encyclical, *Rerum Novarum* (Of New Things), which argued that people in "exceeding distress" should be helped "by public aid." One of the young Tammany leaders of the 1920s, Jeremiah T. Mahoney, said that the encyclical had a "marvelous" effect on Irish Catholic politicians and political activists.[16]

Still, it is impossible to avoid the correlation between Tammany's leftward drift in the second and third decades of the twentieth century and the rise of left-wing Jewish activism—and, more to the point, voting patterns—at the same time. If, as Hasia R. Diner has argued, Irish "ward bosses and block captains" helped teach successive waves of new immigrants how to be Americans, perhaps it could be said that Jewish immigrants helped to teach those bosses and captains how to be reformers.[17]

Immigrant Jews and their children and grandchildren were able to wield power over Irish-dominated Tammany because they, like the Irish before them, recognized the power of the ballot box. They availed themselves of the franchise, something the Irish who ran Tammany respected. Historian Steven Erie observed that New York's Jewish community had become "Tammany's chosen people" by the 1920s.[18]

The alliance between Tammany and New York's Jews was best personified by Al Smith, grandson of an Irish immigrant, four-term governor of New York, and the Democratic Party's nominee for president in 1928. Smith lived on the Lower East Side from his birth in 1873 until he moved uptown in the 1920s, so he saw the neighborhood's transformation as it became one of the most celebrated centers of the Jewish diaspora. Although he is often described as parochial in his attitudes and politics, Smith in fact was as prepared as any political leader in the

Roaring Twenties for the new heterogeneous America that was emerging in the streets of the nation's great cities thanks to the years he spent amid the ethnic mosaic of the Lower East Side. Not coincidentally, his three closest advisers were all Jews: Belle Moskowitz, Robert Moses, and Joseph Proskauer. And they were as loyal to him as any of Tammany's Irish district leaders and block captains.[19]

Moses and Moskowitz were part of a generation of reformers attracted to municipal government during the administration of John Purroy Mitchel, an Irish Catholic opponent of Tammany who won election as mayor in 1913. Mitchel was the grandchild of John Mitchel, the Young Ireland rebel of the 1840s who went on to become a noted journalist and author in the United States, where he landed in 1853 after escaping from the British prison colony in Van Diemen's Land.

John Purroy Mitchel, just thirty-four when he took over City Hall, brought policy experts like Moses and social reformers like Moskowitz into an administration that emphasized progressive ideals over retail politics. High hopes soon gave way to bitter recriminations as Mitchel declined to engage the larger electorate, leading to protests over issues like school reform. His reelection campaign in 1917, months after the United States entered World War I, was an acrimonious mess as he questioned the loyalty of future US senator Robert Wagner, a German immigrant, and all but accused his opponent, John Hylan, of German sympathies.[20]

For Mitchel's allies, his failed administration offered lessons about practical politics, consensus building, and the value of compromise. Moses and Moskowitz came to see Smith as a leader who shared most if not all of their reform instincts but who also understood how to turn ideals into legislation. Moskowitz never had an official role in the governor's office under Smith, who served from 1919 to 1920, and then again from 1923 to 1928. But she was regarded as his top political adviser, especially after Tammany boss Murphy died in April 1924.[21]

Moses, a public policy intellectual with a PhD from Oxford University, bonded with Smith during long walks through the Lower East Side during the two years the governor spent out of office in 1921 and '22. When Smith was returned as governor in 1923, he and Moses turned their discussions into (literally) concrete achievements as Moses began his controversial career as New York's master builder.

Joseph Proskauer, a Jew from Alabama, served as an adviser, political operative, and speechwriter for Smith through the 1920s, eventually becoming a prominent judge. Smith turned to Proskauer in 1927 when, in what became a literary sensation, a well-known lawyer named Charles Marshall argued in the *Atlantic Monthly* that Smith's Catholicism should bar him (or any other Catholic) from the presidency. Smith confessed that he had never heard of the church documents that Marshall cited in making his case, so he asked Proskauer to draft a reply. Proskauer was quick to note the irony: "A Protestant lawyer challenges a Catholic candidate on his religion, and the challenge is answered by a Jewish judge," he quipped.[22]

Only in New York.

Smith's reliance on three non-Tammany Jews certainly did speak to his open-mindedness and tolerance, but it is fair to say that not all of his Irish allies were so ecumenical. According to Robert Caro in his biography of Robert Moses, some resentful Tammany stalwarts composed a ditty about the influence of these perceived outsiders: *Moskie and Proskie / Are the brains of Tammany Hall*.[23]

They had no choice but to accept their leader's inclusive spirit. Those Jewish brains—Moskowitz, Proskauer, and Moses—propelled Smith to a presidential nomination in 1928 and helped to make Smith exactly what his Tammany mentor, Charles F. Murphy, hoped he would be: a respectable representative of the Irish machine in New York.[24]

Smith's eight-year tenure as governor remains one of the most significant political milestones in New York history. He energized Tammany's traditional Irish base and expanded it to include New York City's Jews, leading to historic achievements in prison reform, school construction, park development, and social welfare programs that were implemented during a rightward turn in national politics. During the Smith years, New York saw a marriage of progressive idealism and real-life pragmatism, a union arranged by the Irishman Al Smith and his three Jewish advisers.

The relationship between the Tammany Irish and New York's Jews was never the same after Smith left Albany following his failed bid for the presidency in 1928. Then again, Tammany was never quite the same, either. The machine became embroiled in a series of scandals in New York City, leading to the election of a Yiddish-speaking son of Italian immigrants, Fiorello La Guardia, as mayor in 1933. The charismatic La Guardia formed a coalition of African Americans, Puerto Ricans, Jews, Italians, and elite reformers to put an end to Irish Tammany's decades of dominance.

Even as Tammany declined, though, a remnant of the old days and the old alliance continued to build bridges between New York's Jews and Irish. Edward J. Flynn, a Fordham-educated lawyer and son of Irish immigrants, was a protégé of Tammany boss Charles Murphy and, at Murphy's request, took control of the Democratic Party's county organization in the Bronx in 1922. Flynn went on to become a close adviser to Franklin Roosevelt and Harry Truman, served as chairman of the Democratic National Committee in the early 1940s, and was at FDR's side at the Yalta conference. Through it all, he retained control of the Democratic machine in the Bronx until he died during a trip to Ireland in 1953.[25]

Flynn became a strong advocate for Jewish interests as the Bronx, particularly his home neighborhood of Riverdale, became more Jewish and less Irish in the immediate postwar years. He was a staunch supporter of Zionism and was among those who helped to persuade Harry Truman to recognize the state of Israel in 1948.

While Tammany politicians—like any politicians, including reformers—could be accused of pandering rather than acting out of principle in their relations with organized interests or constituent groups, there is evidence that Flynn's outreach to New York's Jews and other groups was based on something other than mere political calculation. At the height of World War II, Flynn dispatched a letter to Eleanor Roosevelt, with whom he was very friendly, condemning ideologies and racial prejudice that had stained the American experiment.

"It seems to me that we can never have a complete settlement of world conditions until the Anglo-Saxon begins to realize that he is not of a superior race but that all races are equal," Flynn wrote. "Certainly, we are today fighting against the ideology of Hitler in which he sets forth the Aryans as superior people to all others. We do not seem to be consistent when we fight against this doctrine and on the other hand do nothing to try to bring about a better understanding" of racial and ethnic differences at home.[26]

The story of the Tammany Irish and New York's Jews is, of course, not entirely one of cooperation and mutual aid. But through the first quarter of the twentieth century, the machine's Irish leaders came to see the city's Jews not only as voters to be courted but as partners in writing a new social compact for New York, a compact that helped serve as a model for the New Deal.

That is a legacy worthy of interrogation, and perhaps even of celebration.

4

## Jews, Paul O'Dwyer, and a New York Life

ROBERT W. SNYDER

In 1980, in an oral history interview for the American Jewish Committee, Paul O'Dwyer reflected on what would happen to New York City if all its Jews left. "Ghost town," he said. The interviewer, Jill Levine, repeated the phrase. "Yes," O'Dwyer replied. "The arts and the sciences and nobody to argue with."[1]

O'Dwyer's observation, delivered more than fifty years after he arrived in New York City as an eighteen-year-old immigrant from Ireland, illuminated not just the importance of Jews in New York City, but the significance of Jews in O'Dwyer's own story. O'Dwyer was thoroughly Irish and devoted his life to the cause of Irish republicanism, but his embrace of his adopted city was large enough to take in more than his own ethnic group. If his upbringing in Ireland amid the struggle for Irish freedom made him sympathetic to underdogs, his engagement with the ethnic and racial diversity of New York City fostered in him a cosmopolitan commitment to universal justice. He was indelibly Irish and a Democrat, but his spirit always overflowed the boundaries of his ethnic group and political party. He opposed anti-Semitism when it appeared in the Irish community and timidity when it surfaced among Democrats. In a party defined by the tension between reformers and regulars, he was forever an insurgent—even going so far as to support a third party, the American Labor Party, in the 1940s when it appeared to be an alternative to the Democrats.

Yet there was one constant in the many causes that O'Dwyer embraced. In every stage of his New York life—from his early days as an immigrant waterfront worker to the *New York Times* obituary that described him as "New York's Liberal Battler For Underdogs and Outsiders"—Jews were an important presence. His most important legal partner, the gunrunners he represented in the years of Israel's founding, many of the radicals he defended in court, his comrades in the civil rights and anti–Vietnam War movements, and his great political rival—the liberal Republican Jacob Javits—were all Jews.

The story of O'Dwyer's engagement with New York's Jews is much more than the tale of a man with a generous spirit, firm principles, and deep loyalties. O'Dwyer's ties with Jews were the product of not only his personal traits, but the broader social and political currents of his time. Indeed, a full understanding of O'Dwyer and the Jews illuminates a wide range of topics: how immigrants learn in and from the city; the labor movement and radicalism in the mid-twentieth century; the place of Israel in Jewish American politics; the evolution of Democratic Party liberalism in New York City; the importance of third parties in New York politics; and the changing political alignments of New York's Irish and Jewish communities in the second half of the twentieth century.

The irony of O'Dwyer's political life—which reached from the radicalism of the 1930s to the conservative turn of the 1970s—is that it offered him grist for many good fights but few opportunities for political security. (He ran for state or citywide office in nine political seasons but was victorious only twice.) He played a robust part in two decades of radicalism—the 1930s and 1960s—yet in both he was more liberal than many members of New York's Irish community. And as much as his devotion to the cause of Ireland won him the admiration of Irish Americans of varying political persuasions, in the latter years of his career the Irish population in New York was so divided and diminished that it no longer offered him a firm political base. More than a narrow ethnic politician, O'Dwyer looked around for friends and allies. Over the course of his life, whether he was pleading a client's case in court or addressing a rally, there were likely to be Jews at his side. Yet there was no sign of this when he was born in the village of Lismirrane in the parish of Bohola in County Mayo, Ireland, in 1907.[2]

Bohola, as O'Dwyer recalled it, was a parish of small farmers who pulled together a living by going to England or Scotland to labor as agricultural workers. His parents were teachers a generation removed from farm life, and O'Dwyer grew up as one of eleven children. Bohola was almost entirely Catholic, but young O'Dwyer grew up with a skepticism about religious authority that eased his exchanges with people of many faiths for the rest of his life. The armed conflicts that followed the Easter Rising of 1916 came to remote Bohola slowly, but when they arrived they left an enduring stamp on O'Dwyer's life. The Irish War of Independence, followed by the Irish Civil War, cemented young O'Dwyer's faith in Irish republicanism and made him a lifelong friend of the Irish Republican Army. O'Dwyer was too young to be a soldier, but at the age of eleven he tacked up messages of support for Sinn Féin, the Irish nationalist party, in the elections of 1918. Later he watched the marauding of the Black and Tans with anger. During the Irish Civil War, the opponents of the partition of Ireland who refused to accept the truncated Irish Free State found refuge in the O'Dwyer home. So did explosives, which for a time were stored in such quantities that O'Dwyer thought they could blow up "half of Ireland."[3]

Although a Jewish peddler might pass through Bohola occasionally, no Jews lived there. O'Dwyer met a Jew only in his studies, when he read Shakespeare's *The Merchant of Venice* and encountered Shylock, the moneylender whose effort to turn a profit on a loan goes awry. By the end of the play Shylock's daughter has abandoned him and converted to Christianity, while Shylock himself is impoverished and forced to convert. Scholars and critics have debated whether the character of Shylock is a figment of anti-Semitism, but for young O'Dwyer "he was a moneylender and a usurer."[4]

O'Dwyer's lasting introduction to living Jews came with his immigration to the United States. When he steamed into New York Harbor on April 21, 1925, he disembarked in a city that was defined by an array of European immigrants—prominent among them Irish, Germans, Jews, and Italians—and a growing African American community.

O'Dwyer settled into a boardinghouse at 103rd Street and Columbus Avenue with his brothers Jack and Frank. With help from his brother Bill, who was more settled in New York and embarked on a life that would lead him from hod carrier shouldering bricks on construction sites to police officer to district attorney to mayor, he found short-lived jobs as a stock clerk, elevator operator, and (for one day) a stable hand. In his daily experiences, he acquired a practical education in the ways of the city and its ethnic pecking order that left him with "conflicting feelings," as he put it in his memoir. "I found myself clinging to my Irish identity because it gave me an edge over an Italian, and to my Catholic identity because it gave me a favored position over a Jew. I was aware that being white put me in a class in which I was, even as a noncitizen, ahead of a black American citizen of long standing."[5]

O'Dwyer had ambition and a desire for education, and by September, with help on tuition from his brothers Frank and Jim, he was working by day and taking law courses at night at Fordham University. To the American-born students of Irish ancestry, O'Dwyer was a greenhorn with an accent. Jews, however, were more welcoming. The Jewish students he met there, all immigrants or the children of immigrants, "did not create any distinction between an Irishman born in New York and an Irishman born anywhere else." Equally memorable to O'Dwyer was a Jewish professor at Fordham by the name of Shames who helped him with his speech and pronunciations.[6]

Fordham turned out to be a brief passage in O'Dwyer's life. Soon after he finished his first year of night classes, Fordham tightened its requirements for continued enrollment. "We had no recourse but to accept the verdict," O'Dwyer wrote in his memoir. "Some who were exceptionally well connected with the Church were given a spot. The rest of us had to forage for ourselves."[7]

O'Dwyer's foraging led him to St. John's University, a Catholic university that offered law courses in downtown Brooklyn. St. John's Law School, as O'Dwyer recalled it, did well by educating "the raft of young Jewish students, the children of East Side immigrants who had crossed the East River into Brooklyn and who were hungering for legal education." O'Dwyer remembered his law school class at St. John's as 85 percent Jewish, along with some Irish and Italian Americans. They studied in a modest building at 50 Court Street that had "few pretensions" but offered, "for those whose options were limited, some hope of entering the professional life of the city."[8]

To cover his costs of room, board, and tuition O'Dwyer—with help from his brother Bill, who as a police officer had patrolled the Brooklyn waterfront—found a job on the docks as a checker, supervising the stowing and unloading of shipments of cargo from around the world, and joined the International Longshoremen's Association. He left the "Irish environment" of his boardinghouse on 103rd Street in Manhattan and found a furnished room in Brooklyn with a Scandinavian family, close by the waterfront and a half hour from law school. Working alongside "an assortment of gangsters, toughs and the most kindly, loyal and gentle people," and going to sea in the summer when classes were not in session, he learned about his adopted city, labor, unions, the nativist antiradicalism that struck his Italian coworkers during the Sacco and Vanzetti case, and the gap between American ideals and realities. On the docks, he recalled, he "became a New Yorker years before I became an American citizen."[9]

If the waterfront introduced O'Dwyer to labor and unions in a setting where Italians were a strong presence, law school at St. John's introduced him to law and politics in the company of Jews. When a study group with Irish classmates considered becoming a fraternity—with the stipulation that no Jews would be admitted—O'Dwyer declined. (As he said later, "It sounded too much like 'No Irish Need Apply.'") Instead, he began to study with some Jewish friends. When one of them proposed joining a Democratic club, O'Dwyer casually agreed to become a member of the Kings County Young Democratic Club. His first lesson in practical politics (and the American penchant for exclusion) came at a club meeting where a member proposed limiting membership to American citizens. When O'Dwyer pointed out that this would have excluded him, the motion was revised to admit those, like O'Dwyer, who had begun the naturalization process. O'Dwyer went on to learn something about the limits of ethnic politics when he ran for club treasurer against Irwin Bronstein of Coney Island in a club of thirty-five Jews and one Irishman. "I beat him by two votes," O'Dwyer recalled, "so the ethnic voting didn't work."[10]

Students at St. John's, working-class in origins and immigrants or New Yorkers of immigrant stock, learned from one another as they made their way toward professional life. Significantly for the course of his own life, O'Dwyer learned that Jews and Irish both had histories of suffering and persecution. Modestly, O'Dwyer thought that he learned more from his classmates than they learned from him. In conversations with Jewish students at St. John's, O'Dwyer learned to speak Yiddish, a skill—like his knowledge of the waterfront—that would serve him well later in his life.[11]

Graduating from law school in 1929, O'Dwyer soon confronted the crisis of the Depression. Despite his law degree, he was not yet a citizen and could not take the bar exam. His brother Bill, by now an attorney, and State Senator Philip Kleinfeld petitioned Judge Benjamin Cardozo on the New York State Court of Appeals for a solution. Judge Cardozo issued an order allowing O'Dwyer to take the exam, but even after he passed he had to wait two years to be admitted to the bar. In the meantime, O'Dwyer worked at the law firm of Cohen and Lieberman "serving summonses, typing complaints, and conducting investigations." He was eventually admitted to the bar in 1931, but unsatisfied with his work, faced with the Depression, and eager to see the world, he went back to sea.[12]

For O'Dwyer, as for the city and country around him, the 1930s were a time of transformation. Despite his legal training, as the decade began O'Dwyer was as much a worker as he was a lawyer. Politically he was a Democrat, but he was a member of a party at the brink of great changes that would shape his life and work. By 1940 he was a labor lawyer, a political activist, and on the cutting edge of efforts to create a national labor party to complement the political changes wrought by the election of President Franklin D. Roosevelt and the rise of the New Deal. As in his earlier evolution from immigrant laborer to Brooklyn lawyer, Jews played central parts.

Foremost among them—as employer, mentor, and ultimately law partner—was Oscar Bernstien, the Russian-born son of a student of Talmud who made his way to New York and pursued a legal career. As in other episodes in his life, O'Dwyer followed a road paved by his brother Bill, who worked with Bernstien in the firm of Holmes & Bernstien at 26 Court Street in Brooklyn. O'Dwyer went to work with them, chafed at the role of younger brother, left, and then returned. In working with Bernstien, Paul found not just a legal partner and a guide to the wider world. Bernstien was not a trial lawyer, but he excelled at research, writing briefs, and preparing cases. O'Dwyer described him as "a man of great culture, a devotee of literature, theater, science and math." His wife Rebecca Drucker, another immigrant from Russia, had the more public-facing career: first in journalism as a staffer at *The American Magazine*, where she met John Reed and Ida Tarbell, and later at the *New York Tribune*, where she was a reporter and an assistant to the columnist Heywood Broun. By the 1930s she was working as a theatrical publicist and consumer activist.[13]

Radical insurgencies and the Roosevelt presidency brought new levels of energy and conflict to politics that echoed into Bernstien and Drucker's home. When O'Dwyer attended gatherings in their apartment at 121 Madison Avenue, he met people like Broun, United Mine Workers president John L. Lewis, and Jack Fahy and Charlie Keith—veterans of the Abraham Lincoln Brigade in the Spanish Civil War. Conversations in what O'Dwyer called "Oscar and Becky's living room" crackled with talk of the Depression, discrimination, anti-Semitism, the Scottsboro case, Soviet communism, the rise of Hitler, fascist tendencies in the United States, and WPA theatrical productions. O'Dwyer's brother Bill, an occasional participant in these gatherings, encouraged him to think about the world beyond the Irish community. Over time, O'Dwyer recognized that "Ireland was not alone in its struggle for freedom." Out of that realization came O'Dwyer's commitment to a spirit of universal justice that energized his life in the 1930s and lasted for the rest of his days. Jews would be his comrades in many of those fights, and he did not hesitate to take on fellow Irishmen if they trafficked in anti-Semitism.[14]

In the 1930s, New York City was gripped by the Great Depression but animated by a political energy that veered to the left of center. Mayor Fiorello La Guardia was closely allied with the New Deal, and the city hummed with public works projects, labor actions, and radical politics. But New York was hardly a place of political consensus. As La Guardia brought Jews and Italians into city government, some Irish—long accustomed to political strength in the city—felt displaced and resentful. This bitterness, along with the hardship of the Depression, led some Irish New Yorkers to embrace the politics of Father Charles Coughlin, a radio priest whose broadcasts were laced with anti-Semitism, and even more reactionary groups like the Christian Front and Christian Mobilizers.[15]

By 1935 O'Dwyer was married and living in Brooklyn, an attorney for unions of hod carriers, grain workers, and warehouse workers, and the founder of one of the Brooklyn divisions of the Ancient Order of Hibernians, an Irish American organization. His friend Mike Quill, a former IRA man who was friendly to the Communist Party, was founder and leader of the Transport Workers Union. But as O'Dwyer's work as a lawyer pulled him into the orbit of the left, his moral and political loyalties put him at odds with a portion of Brooklyn's Irish community.[16]

At a meeting of the Ancient Order of Hibernians, two motions were raised that struck at O'Dwyer's principles and loyalties. One was to condemn Quill for being a communist, and another addressed the Coughlin phenomenon. O'Dwyer was one of two members present to support Quill and the only member present to condemn Coughlin. Seeing how he had become a minority in his own community, O'Dwyer and his wife Kathleen sold their Brooklyn home and moved to Manhattan. Looking back on the episode, he described the final act as an "emancipation."[17]

Moving to Manhattan inaugurated a long phase in O'Dwyer's life, lasting through the 1930s and 1940s, that would define him for the rest of his days as a lawyer who proudly defended radicals, an activist in a variety of causes on the leftward end of the Democratic Party, and an Irish republican who was firmly committed to his ethnic community but always ready to dissent from its conservative members. O'Dwyer also rose in professional prominence when, with the death of Frank Holmes in 1939, the law firm where he worked became O'Dwyer & Bernstien. Jews would play important roles as colleagues, comrades, and defendants in this drama.[18]

The first act took place during 1940 in the trial of the leadership of the communist International Fur and Leather Workers Union, most prominently its president, Ben Gold, on charges of violating the Sherman Anti-Trust Act (because union activities allegedly restricted trade) and of obstruction of justice. The trial had deep roots in both the factional politics of the garment workers unions, which fiercely pit socialists against communists, and the gangster-ridden underbelly of the garment industry, where unions and employers both used violence to enforce their will on competitors. Jews, with their strong presence in the garment and fur industries, were to be found among workers, unionists, gangsters, and business proprietors. In this context, the furriers' union under Gold was notable for the communist ideology of its leadership, the good contracts that it delivered for its workers, and the union *shtarkers* (Yiddish for tough guys) who fought gangsters on their own terms.[19]

The 1940 trial was rooted in an earlier and unsuccessful federal attempt to prosecute unions, individuals, and businesses for running what allegedly amounted to a fur trust, and the courtroom proceedings illuminated both racketeering and high questions of antitrust law. O'Dwyer was invited onto the defense team by Louis Boudin, an immigrant labor lawyer born in Russia who was the author of books on both Karl Marx and the Supreme Court, and an officer of the American Organization for Rehabilitation through Training (an international Jewish organization for vocational education). Also on the defense team was Samuel Leibowitz, the prominent defense attorney who, although no radical, had won fame for defending the Scottsboro Boys. Initially, prosecutors convicted Gold and others of violating the Sherman Anti-Trust Act, but that conviction was later overturned by an appellate court on the grounds that the act had been too broadly applied. The same trial also produced charges of obstruction of justice, and although prosecutors won some convictions Gold was acquitted of the charge.[20]

In defending members of a communist union dominated by Jews, O'Dwyer was a lawyer serving the cutting edge of radical unionism. (He later learned that his service on the case attracted the attention of J. Edgar Hoover of the Federal Bureau of Investigation.) The experience put him in the orbit of politically engaged lawyers on the left, and colleagues on the defense team invited him to join the National Lawyers Guild, which one of its founders, the Detroit labor lawyer Maurice Sugar, described as a "national organization of progressive, liberal and radical attorneys." The guild held its first convention in February 1937, when Franklin Roosevelt had recently been reelected in a landslide that was a referendum on the New Deal, and the Communist Party was in its short-lived but influential Popular Front period when it sought an alliance with liberals against fascism abroad and reactionaries in the United States. At the guild, O'Dwyer served as president of the New York Chapter in 1947, and from 1948 to 1951 on the national board of directors. The mixture of liberals and radicals was both heady and fractious.[21]

The founding generation of the National Lawyers Guild defined itself against the American Bar Association and strongly supported the CIO and civil rights. Before long, however, the guild was rocked by debates over the Soviet Union, Roosevelt's approach to the Supreme Court, the proper role of professional organizations, and freedom of political expression. As in other Popular Front organizations, energetic communists exercised an influence beyond their numbers, leading to charges that the guild was nothing more than a communist front. The guild was more than that, but the internal fights and external pressures that emerged quickly—and heightened in the Cold War—could obscure the strengths of its heterogeneous origins.[22]

O'Dwyer was more than an intermediary between progressives, liberals, and radicals. Indeed, he had something of each in him: a radical's fighting spirit, a liberal's faith in law and justice, a progressive commitment to underdogs that both could share, and a desire to expand the political possibilities of American democracy rather than abandon it. If membership in the National Lawyers Guild was O'Dwyer's first effort at building an organization that would provide a proper home for his complex political identity, the other would be his work with the American Labor Party.

O'Dwyer's service on the furriers' trial, like his membership in the National Lawyers Guild and his work with the American Labor Party, put him at close quarters with leftist Jews. This was partly a testament to the overrepresentation of Jews on the left but also to O'Dwyer's breadth of vision: as Irish as he was, he was also capable of empathy for Jews, African Americans, workers, and others who were downtrodden.

The American Labor Party was born in 1936 of both local and national circumstances, when leaders of New York's heavily Jewish garment unions—which had socialist roots and a communist presence—organized to create a political voice for a broad bloc of labor activists, socialists and communists, and urban reformers. If their largest goal was to create a party of the left, in New York—bolstered by a state law that allowed candidates to run with more than one party's endorsement—they sought to provide a home for voters who supported the New Deal but were queasy about voting for Democrats (like President Roosevelt) when they ran as candidates of a party that included Jim Crow white supremacists in the South and urban machines in the North. In 1937 the party provided a line for Fiorello La Guardia when he ran for the mayoralty as a Republican; it provided a line for Mike Quill, O'Dwyer's friend and leader of Local 100 of the Transport Workers Union, when he successfully ran for the City Council in 1937 and again in the 1940s until 1949. Quill shared O'Dwyer's progressive politics, Irish republicanism, and opposition to racism and anti-Semitism.[23]

As in the National Lawyers Guild, the mixture of communists, socialistsm, and liberals in the American Labor Party was combustible. The Hitler-Stalin Pact of 1939 diminished the cooperative spirit of the

Popular Front, and although communists would become enthusiastic supporters of the war against Nazi Germany after the Soviet Union was invaded in June 1941, prewar amity between communists and liberals could never be entirely reestablished. Liberal and socialist members left the American Labor Party to found the Liberal Party in 1944, but the ALP did not expire until 1956. In New York, where the ALP and the Liberal Party differed more on the Soviet Union than they did on domestic policies, the ALP line retained value for both convenience and progressive principles until the most heated days of the Cold War. Bill O'Dwyer successfully ran for mayor on the ALP and Democratic lines in 1945, and his brother Paul did the same running for Congress in 1948. Moreover, despite real differences between the ALP and the Liberal Party on Stalin and Soviet Jewry, cultural and ideological commitments ran deep in the varied sectors of the Jewish left, and Jews could be found in both the American Labor Party and the Liberal Party.[24]

The full impact of these splits would not register on O'Dwyer's life until after World War II, however. During the war, O'Dwyer—married, a father, and already in his mid-thirties—joined the National Guard after he was rejected in attempts to join Naval Intelligence and the Coast Guard. He was on the verge of being called up through the Selective Service, but the army reduced the oldest age for induction, leaving O'Dwyer too old for the draft. He remained in the United States, where he represented clients who included American IRA men who—if they were inducted into the American military—did not want to be drafted to serve alongside troops of the British Empire.[25] On this issue, O'Dwyer's Irish and Jewish interests did not align perfectly. To most Jews, Britain was the opponent of Nazi Germany and an ally to be supported.

Nevertheless, in the middle and late 1940s, O'Dwyer took on a task that went beyond what many Jews did to support the establishment of Israel: he ran guns to Palestine to arm Jewish forces. In this effort he worked with the American League for a Free Palestine, an organization fiercely committed to establishing a Jewish nation, and the Irgun Zvai Leumi, a right-wing underground moment in Israel aligned with the strongly nationalist Revisionist movement. His partners in this effort were Ben Hecht, an author and screenwriter, and Peter Bergson (born Hillel Kook,) a Lithuanian Jew who immigrated to Palestine. Hecht and Bergson worked through small but committed organizations to passionately focus attention on the plight of Jews during and after the Holocaust. The league, and its allies in the Revisionist Zionist movement in the United States and Palestine, were frustrated that the United States did not act more aggressively to save Jews during the war, convinced that mainstream Jewish organizations were too timid and reluctant to offend American authorities, and willing to combat both British forces occupying Palestine and Arabs to hasten the establishment of Israel.[26]

The plight of European Jewry surely fired O'Dwyer's instinctive anger against oppression and sympathy for the suffering, and support for a Jewish state was widespread among American Jews of all ideological stripes. (Ben Gold, his former client and communist leader of the Fur and Leather Workers Union, in 1948 was grand marshal of ten thousand demonstrators who marched through pouring rain carrying signs like "Save the Jewish State" and "Arm the Haganah.") Although, as a liberal who bordered on being a leftist, O'Dwyer had little in common politically with the conservative Revisionist Zionists, who sought a Jewish state on both banks of the Jordan, the internal politics of Zionism was not his issue. He was also, like many liberals and leftists living in the aftermath of the Holocaust, inclined to see the founding of Israel as an issue of justice and Jewish safety, and not concerned with the fate of the Arab peoples of Palestine. There were aspects of the Irgun's spirit that he admired, however. The American League for a Free Palestine compared the struggle for a Jewish state to the Irish struggle for freedom. In the negotiations that Jews held with the British authorities that governed Mandatory Palestine during World War II and its aftermath, O'Dwyer sensed a Middle Eastern version of Ireland's long struggle with the British Empire to establish independence. And in Irgun raids on British forces in Palestine, O'Dwyer saw reflections of his own cherished IRA.[27]

Within the league, O'Dwyer's Irishness lent a fresh dimension to fundraising efforts as he worked to get more dollars from people who had already donated to Jewish causes. He spoke in public about the urgency of the Jews' plight in Europe and Palestine. When arms were shipped to Palestine, his old waterfront experience came in handy. He even put to use his IRA connections. He visited Dublin and lobbied Mayor Robert Briscoe—a former IRA man and a Jew—to help the Irgun with printing and the movement of volunteers to Palestine. When he needed to stash money for arms (in this case for the Haganah, the main Jewish paramilitary organization in Palestine that eventually evolved into the Israel Defense Forces), he used the New York office of Sean Keating, an old IRA man who worked in city government.[28]

When Joseph Untermeyer, nineteen, the son of a former judge and poet, was arrested in a Manhattan loft as he packed guns for shipment, O'Dwyer represented him and a codefendant in court, arguing that the charges were unjust and amounted to prosecuting men for being freedom fighters. The judge dismissed O'Dwyer's points about freedom fighters but ruled in the defendants' favor on the more technical point that they did not have exclusive possession of the weapons.[29]

As much as there was broad support among New York Jews for the establishment of Israel, and for the Labor Zionists who dominated the country in its early years, there was less acclaim for the Revisionists, the Irgunists, and their leader Menachem Begin. That mattered little to O'Dwyer. When Begin visited New York in 1948 O'Dwyer welcomed him, dismissing criticism from both establishment and leftist Jews who considered him a right-wing terrorist. In response to such criticism, O'Dwyer responded: "The Irgunists are good boys, and they did a very intelligent job of chasing the British out of Israel." He continued, "To ask me to turn my back on the Irgunists would be like asking me to denounce the Irish Republican Army." Although he remained a strong supporter of Israel, he did not pursue further involvement in issues inside Israel. "The battle was won," he wrote, "and much as I admired the daring Irgunists and the courage of their leader, I did not share their philosophy. My interest was in Israel and not in a particular party."[30]

O'Dwyer's service running guns to a nascent Israel earned him enduring affection from Jews, an affection that received close attention when O'Dwyer made his first bid for public office. In 1948 O'Dwyer ran for Congress in a race in a district that included the Washington Heights and Inwood sections of Northern Manhattan, areas with large Irish and Jewish populations. His opponent was Jacob Javits, a son of Jewish immigrants raised on the Lower East Side, who ran as a progressive Republican and a Liberal (reflecting the split in the American Labor Party over communist involvement that led to the founding of the Liberal Party) and represented his party's liberal wing. O'Dwyer ran on the Democratic and American Labor Party lines, a strategy that his brother Bill had used to win the mayoralty in 1945.[31]

The contest between Javits and O'Dwyer was colored by complex tensions and rivalries. In the 1930s and 1940s, Washington Heights and Inwood were the scene of anti-Semitic attacks on Jews and Jewish institutions; the perpetrators of these attacks were typically young Irish Catholics. The Christian Front and Christian Mobilizers were also present in the area. The emotions behind such actions surfaced in street-corner rallies when Javits was heckled. Right-wing elements in Inwood also called him soft on communism.[32]

Yet the same people who railed against Javits for being insufficiently anticommunist attacked O'Dwyer for his own association with communists in the American Labor Party. And when O'Dwyer pointed out that he had raised his children as Roman Catholics, offered references from priests who could testify to his character—and his supporters printed up leaflets attesting to the same—Republicans attacked him. "I was attacked by the Irish for being a Communist, the same label was applied to me by the Liberals, Christian Mobilizers and Catholic War Veterans, while in Jewish sections of the district I was accused of running a campaign catering to the very crypto-Nazis who were the most active workers against me."[33]

O'Dwyer's efforts to defuse the situation began with a successful interview with *Aufbau*, a German-language newspaper that served the community of German Jewish refugees in upper Manhattan. In the interview he stressed his progressive views and described how Jewish struggles for freedom reminded him of Irish struggles for freedom. In closing, he affirmed that he had taken part in many Jewish actions and had earned the trust of Jewish fighters—a subtle reference to his recent work with the American League for a Free Palestine and the Irgun. In subsequent days he visited neighborhood synagogues, debated Javits, and publicly stated that he was not a communist—but defended the rights of communists and dissenters on constitutional grounds.[34]

On election night, early returns favored O'Dwyer. Over the course of the night, however, Javits won by a narrow margin, gaining 66,455 votes to O'Dwyer's 64,297. O'Dwyer would not run for office again for fifteen years.[35]

As the 1940s gave way to the 1950s, O'Dwyer's life was marked by changes and continuities. As a lawyer and a political man, he was ever a crusading liberal. He remained involved in Irish issues, and he worked as a labor lawyer, defended clients against charges of being communist subversives, and fought for the integration of Stuyvesant Town, a large Manhattan housing complex created by the Metropolitan Life Insurance Company. He took on more show-business clients, though, and in his memoir *Counsel for the Defense* described the years 1951–58 as something of a "'leave of absence'" from politics.[36]

The political world that nurtured him was changing. The American Labor Party, under attack for its ties to communists, died in 1956. The National Lawyers Guild lost members as it, too, was attacked on similar grounds.

O'Dwyer quietly resigned from the guild, but for reasons that had nothing to do with red-baiting. He quit the organization because, for all its Jewish and leftist members, it would not openly oppose the Slansky case—a show trial laced with anti-Semitism, conducted in 1952 in communist Czechoslovakia, that sent eleven men to the gallows and sentenced three to life imprisonment. O'Dwyer, working in private, tried to persuade the guild's leadership to denounce the proceedings. When he failed, he left the guild quietly to avoid the appearance of being an informer (an anathema to an Irishman like O'Dwyer) and because he did not want to find himself questioned in public over the affair by the anticommunists of the House Un-American Activities Committee.[37]

Over the course of the 1950s, O'Dwyer's political terrain narrowed. The anticommunist Liberal Party emerged as New York's main third party. Over the years it would provide a convenient home for liberal Republicans who wanted to gain Democratic votes—a strategy that would never be open to O'Dwyer. The mayoralty of Paul's brother Bill ended in allegations of corruption, and the new energy in the Democratic Party—at least in New York City—seemed to be with reformers who were inspired by the venerable Eleanor Roosevelt, former New York State governor and senator Herbert Lehman, and the cerebral but unsuccessful presidential candidacies of Adlai Stevenson.[38]

As O'Dwyer recognized, what excited him in politics was the liberalism of the New Deal years. He carried that spirit forward in a broad way for a long time—equally at home with Democrats, dissenters and radicals further left. In 1961 he defended Martin Popper, another member of the National Lawyers Guild and a Jew, when Popper refused to tell the House Un-American Activities Committee whether he had been a communist. Popper thought it was an improper question on First Amendment grounds and was indicted on a charge of contempt of Congress. Popper lost in court, but the conviction was set aside at the appellate level.[39]

Decades later, Popper, who held O'Dwyer in deep affection, argued in a short essay that the guild was built and sustained by two kinds of people: "those who believed in the need for a fundamental transformation of our social and economic system and the creation of a socialist society" and "those who, though they were critical of the inequalities and injustices in our society, nevertheless believed that the needed changes could be achieved within the present system." Each group needed the other to succeed, Popper concluded.[40]

O'Dwyer lived comfortably in that mix. He was no communist, but starting out in the 1930s he developed an ability to work with radicals without ever breaking with the Democratic Party. He took this tendency forward into the insurgencies of the 1960s, the next surge in political activism to engage his energies, when he made common cause with a new generation of radicals and liberals who supported civil rights for African Americans and opposed the Vietnam War.[41]

The Democratic Reform Movement that O'Dwyer participated in during the 1960s and 1970s had roots in the 1950s. At every level from the Eisenhower presidency to state politics in New York, the Democrats appeared to be a weak party. In New York City Mayor Robert Wagner governed, but the Tammany organization that had once reared generations of Democrats—including Wagner himself—was wounded by charges of corruption and in decline. After Democratic candidates were badly beaten statewide in 1958, a coalition of young and old Democrats, among them Eleanor Roosevelt, came together with the goal of invigorating the Democratic Party in New York State.[42]

Reform movements are an enduring phenomenon in New York City politics, but as Herbert Kaufman and Wallace Sayre observed in their book *Governing New York City: Politics in the Metropolis* (published in 1960, as the reform movement began to flower), the purposes of the city's reform movements have varied over time. In the late nineteenth century, for example, reformers tended to be Republicans who sought to curb the powers and spending of city government. From the era of the New Deal down to the 1960s, however, reformers were more likely to be

Democrats who sought to gain power for the city—especially its mayor. They might share an antipathy to corruption that distinguished earlier generations of reformers, but coming up in the shadow of the New Deal they had an expansive vision of what city government, in partnership with federal government, could accomplish. And even though phlegmatic Mayor Wagner governed the city in the tradition of the New Deal, and even left behind party regulars to embrace the rising reformers, most who went into the reform movement yearned for a mayor with more vigor. Indeed, the differences between reformers and regulars were to a degree differences of political style, with regulars stressing party loyalty, hierarchy, order, and pragmatism while reformers emphasized issues, independence (to the point of fractiousness), and principles.[43]

Although New York's Democratic Party has been described as a collection of Irish and Italian regulars and Jewish and Protestant reformers, the party was always a bit more complex. (There were plenty of Jewish and African American regulars, for example.) And O'Dwyer, in his own way, bridged the differences between these camps. He was older than most reformers, and was shaped not by postwar prosperity but by the Great Depression and World War II. His style had much in common with Irish Democrats of the past, especially the common touch that defined many Tammany men. Excelling at face-to-face politics, O'Dwyer had a warm, easy way with greetings and handshakes and a good memory for family details. His time in the ALP and the National Lawyers Guild gave him a passionate grasp of issues and causes that were the domain of reformers, and a familiarity with the kind of Jewish activists who were prominent in reform circles—some of whom were former communists. And even though he maintained friendly relations with mainstream Democrats, like other reformers he was more concerned with upholding principles than with gaining expedient victories.[44]

By the early 1960s, during Mayor Wagner's third term, it was clear that New York City was entering a period of wrenching changes. The seaport industrial economy that had sustained it during World War II was declining; the suburbs were luring a growing number of whites; Black and Puerto Rican migrants to the city faced discrimination in jobs, housing, and schools; and crime was rising. Nevertheless, when O'Dwyer ran for city councilman at large in 1963, in a campaign managed by a Jewish reformer, Victor Kovner, Mayor Wagner praised O'Dwyer as a man with a distinguished past who was right for the times. O'Dwyer, he said, "has been and remains today the champion of the underdog, the advocate of labor, the spokesman for minority groups, for the exploited, the unrepresented, the poorly paid and forgotten." Wagner argued also that O'Dwyer was "a lovable man" and "a fighting man" who "fights with charm and wit, as well as with passion." Conceding that some reformers found O'Dwyer "soft on the old guard" and that some of the "old guard" found him "starry-eyed," Wagner concluded that O'Dwyer was above all "an independent."[45]

O'Dwyer went on to win the post of city councilman at large, but it was not to be the first of a string of victories. From his first bid for office in 1948 to his last in 1977, O'Dwyer would run in primary contests and general elections—for the House of Representatives, for the US Senate, for city councilman at large, for mayor of the city of New York, and for city council president. He won only twice in general elections, in his bid for city councilman at large in 1963 and in his race for city council president in 1973. He served a total of six years in office.[46]

He once told a journalist that his vocation was less the nuts and bolts of elective office than the "politics of attitudes." He worked to change minds on subjects as varied as civil rights, racism, anti-Semitism, dissent, the First Amendment, the rights of workers, and—perhaps most successfully—the Vietnam War. In 1968 he supported the "Dump Johnson" movement and Eugene McCarthy's bid for the Democratic presidential nomination. In a fiery year, his presence matched the moment. "When he came into a room you knew he was there," said his friend and political associate Sarah Kovner. Lowry Hemphill, who saw O'Dwyer from a distance while she working for Allard Lowenstein's congressional campaign in 1968, called him a candidate with "star power." Even in the subdued setting of a television appearance, his bushy eyebrows and mane of swept-back white hair gave him the appearance of a man perpetually standing on a windswept podium, sailing forward to confront the forces of history.[47] In what was perhaps his most consequential race he ran for the US Senate in 1968, facing his old opponent Senator Javits. If his problem in Democratic primaries was finding a way to win in a crowded field, his race against Javits brought him up against an incumbent with relatively liberal views for a Republican and a slot on the Liberal Party line. O'Dwyer could draw on goodwill built up in his advocacy for African Americans, Israel, and ending the Vietnam War, but he lost by one million votes in a race where six million votes were cast. Looking back on it later, he took satisfaction from his conviction that "we were taking a country engrossed in an immoral war, and we were changing this nation, and we made it feel ashamed."[48]

With the prominent exception of Ed Koch, who soured on O'Dwyer over his support for the IRA, and backstage critics who found him less than a strong presence in the fiscal crisis, O'Dwyer retained affection from an exceptional array of public figures. Reformers praised him for his causes, while regulars—such as members of the Beame administration in 1976, during the fiscal crisis—valued him as a steadying presence with a quick mind and a capacity for talking to adversaries.[49]

In victories and defeats he remained himself, especially with his Jewish connections. He stuck with old friends like the Kovners, and his 1968 Senate race featured a folk music fundraiser where one of the featured performers was Theodore Bikel, an actor and folksinger who began his career with the Habimah Theater in Tel Aviv. In December 1973, as City Council president, he went to the Soviet Union with Manhattan Borough President Percy Sutton, then the highest-ranking African American official in New York City government, to investigate the plight of Soviet Jews; they submitted a report on their trip to the Greater New York Conference on Soviet Jewry and called for US action on behalf of Jews in the USSR. O'Dwyer remained a strong supporter of Israel. When he toured the country and visited the Knesset, he witnessed the arguing and humor among the legislators and thought to himself, "It's like a West Side reform club."[50]

Fittingly, in his last successful campaign, a race for City Council president in 1973, his campaign manager was Charlie Keith—a son of Jewish immigrants who became a communist and merchant seaman, fought in the Spanish Civil War with the Abraham Lincoln Brigade, was captured and imprisoned, then came home to serve again as merchant seaman in World War II. (O'Dwyer first met him at the Bernstien home.) After the war Keith was evicted from the Communist Party in an internal dispute, then rousted from the National Maritime Union when he refused to turn around and blacklist communist mariners. Barred from going to sea, he settled into working as a housepainter. Eventually he went into real estate and amassed considerable wealth. He was, as the newspaper columnist Murray Kempton put it in an obituary, a "noble itinerant."[51]

The same could be said for O'Dwyer, who more than once found himself in competition with candidates who shared his fervor for change. In 1976 he ran in a five-way field seeking the Democratic nomination for US Senate that pit him against both the more conservative Democrat Daniel Patrick Moynihan and an old Jewish comrade from the National Lawyers Guild, Bella Abzug. (Moynihan won, narrowly besting Abzug, and O'Dwyer came in a distant fourth.) In 1977, four years after winning a seat as City Council president, O'Dwyer was defeated in a Democratic primary runoff by State Senator Carol Bellamy, a feminist who valued her reputation for independence and had been active in the movement against the Vietnam War. During the race and afterward she and O'Dwyer had praised each other as worthy candidates, but Bellamy argued that O'Dwyer had become passive in office. On the morning after he lost their primary runoff, O'Dwyer consoled himself by saying that he had fallen to the very forces of change and reform that he had helped to launch.[52]

He never again held elected office, but he remained true to his familiar causes and commitments. Soon after the race for City Council president, he took up the case of David Horowitz, a Jewish journalist and friend from O'Dwyer's days as an Irgun supporter. Horowitz was the target of a libel suit brought by Ferenc Koreh, who argued that Horowitz had libelously depicted him as a Nazi. (Koreh, a Hungarian fascist who immigrated to the United States and settled in New Jersey, had disseminated pro-Nazi propaganda that paved the way for the slaughter of Hungarian Jewry.) O'Dwyer took the case. Koreh settled out of court on libel, but ultimately acknowledged his work as an anti-Semitic propagandist and was stripped of his citizenship.[53]

In city government, O'Dwyer served in appointed positions—first as Manhattan Borough Historian and then as commissioner for the United Nations and Consular Corps. In both cases he was appointed by his old friend David Dinkins, who was Manhattan Borough President and later the city's first African American mayor. O'Dwyer stepped down from the UN post in less than two years, explaining that the position made it impossible for him to speak his mind on issues such as Haitian refugees and the plight of Iraqi Kurds.[54]

In politics, O'Dwyer remained active in Irish affairs and welcomed Sinn Fein leader Gerry Adams to the United States in 1994. Although a friend of the IRA, he encouraged Irish republicans to reach out to Unionists to achieve peace in Northern Ireland. In his eighties, he lobbied President Bill Clinton to name a peace envoy to Northern Ireland, which the president eventually did over British opposition.[55]

When O'Dwyer died in 1998 at ninety, his funeral was an occasion for a gathering of New York City's political elite and for remembering a lifetime of battles lost, battles won, and unyielding principles. Obituaries recalled his support for the Irgun in Palestine, striking flight attendants, and civil rights workers in the United States.

In New York, a city where ethnic boundaries can be sharp, O'Dwyer made a life out of building bridges, finding allies, and taking on uphill battles. He was indelibly Irish, but his experiences with oppression and inequality in Ireland made him an egalitarian warrior for justice in New York. Instead of seeing ethnic differences as eternal barriers, he knew how to see the inner Irishman in a Jewish freedom fighter or an African American civil rights worker. At the same time, thanks to Jewish law students at St. John's University who fanned the flames of study and intellect that burned inside O'Dwyer, and to many years of work and mentorship with Oscar Bernstien, he discovered something of a Jew inside himself.

O'Dwyer's coffin was draped in the Irish tricolor, but his sense of justice and his sense of empathy gave him a unique breadth. Percy Sutton, O'Dwyer's African American political colleague who traveled with him to the USSR on behalf of Soviet Jewry, explained O'Dwyer well. "Paul O'Dwyer was not just Irish," said Sutton. "Paul O'Dwyer was Italian. Paul O'Dwyer was Jewish. Paul O'Dwyer was Greek. He was Polish. Paul O'Dwyer was also African-American. In his involvement in the causes that were not necessarily his, Paul O'Dwyer was us."[56]

In making the causes of the downtrodden his own, the first group that O'Dwyer embraced, in a way that marked him for the rest of his life, was the Jews. But in New York, where politics is deeply influenced by ethnic factions and ethnic rivalries, neither his Irish ancestry nor his many Jewish friends and allies ensured political victories in elected office. The evolution of his own political life, and the changing currents of politics in New York and the nation, intersected awkwardly and to O'Dwyer's disadvantage.

He arrived in New York City in the 1920s, when Irish political power had already crested and Jews and Italians were on the rise. His political views and his Jewish connections, which he maintained with integrity, set him off from many Irish Americans. (The only Irish figure of stature in mid-twentieth-century New York who matched O'Dwyer in this respect was Mike Quill of the Transport Workers Union, with his IRA history, leftist politics, Jewish allies, and Jewish second wife.)[57]

Yet O'Dwyer's Jewish connections did not carry him to higher office. He came close to winning a congressional seat when he narrowly lost to Jacob Javits in 1948, but the increasingly conservative political climate of the 1950s doomed his political chances thereafter for more than a decade. His second race against Javits, in 1968 for the US Senate in the heat of the Vietnam War, was an even bigger defeat—a loss enlarged by Javits's ability to win votes on both the Liberal Party line and the Republican line. There was no third-party option for O'Dwyer because his ALP past distanced him from the Liberal Party. If early in his career the liberal nature of New York politics left him fighting for recognition, in his later years the conservative turn in his state and city—wrought by backlash politics, the fiscal crisis, and the GOP ascendancy nationally—left him out of step with his times. By 1977, when O'Dwyer was defeated in a runoff for City Council president, Jewish politics in New York—and New York City politics in general—was being moved in a more conservative direction with the mayoral victory of Ed Koch. Politics gave O'Dwyer a place to fight for justice, but it did not give him a permanent home.

Instead, his home was the city of New York, where experience made him a street-smart cosmopolitan who won acclaim not by winning office, but by sticking to his principles. At his funeral Mass on the Upper West Side, his niece Joan O'Dwyer Savarese suggested that if your life really does flash before you at the moment of death, then her uncle witnessed quite a show. And whether he saw himself cracking the books in law school, arguing a case in court, or inspiring a political rally, Jews were certainly at his side.[58]

5

# Defending Literary Genius

*James Joyce's* Ulysses *on Trial*

BRETT GARY

No work of modern literature more fully embodied the experiments in literary form intrinsic to modernism than James Joyce's *Ulysses*. Critics agreed it was *the* masterpiece of the age, placing Joyce in the company of Chaucer, Shakespeare, Balzac, Rabelais, and Flaubert, and alongside his contemporaries Freud and Einstein. The book's official status as an "obscene" work offended and galvanized the literary world. Malcolm Cowley, editor of *The New Republic*, affirmed his enlistment in the plan to fight its censorship, declaring that "James Joyce's position in literature is almost as important as that of Einstein in science. Preventing American authors from reading him is about as stupid as it would be to place an embargo on the theory of relativity."[1]

Two Jewish New York City lawyers, Morris Ernst and Alexander Lindey, planned the battle to free *Ulysses* from the clutches of the censors, making the story of Joyce's protagonist Leopold Bloom, a Dubliner of Irish and Jewish parentage, available for all the world to read. In August 1931, more than two years before they would finally bring the book to trial in a federal courtroom in New York City, Lindey reminded his senior partner Ernst of the stakes of their incipient legal campaign when he wrote, "I still feel very keenly that this would be the grandest obscenity case in the history of law and literature, and I am ready to do anything in the world to get it started."[2] Lindey was right—it would be.

Freeing the Irishman James Joyce's masterwork would require prodigious dedication and aplomb.[3] Ernst, who grew up in an immigrant family where education was prized, and acquaintance with art and literature were signs of intellectual achievement, had no truck with censorship and the Protestant underpinnings of the American obscenity laws. His and

Lindey's efforts on behalf of Joyce's great tale of his Irish-Jewish protagonist's mental and physical journeys through Dublin certainly brought *Ulysses* to the attention of American audiences beyond the literati, and their victory on its behalf became a great symbol of liberal Americans' opposition to censorship in American culture and politics. Indeed, Ernst connected the victory to FDR's own political victories, declaring, "The New Deal in the law of letters is here."[4]

*Ulysses* had been legally banned in the English-speaking countries since its publication in 1922, and was nearly as reviled as it was revered. Even its most ardent advocates had to admit to its many "Rabelaisian" moments, reveling in what Edmund Wilson described as "this gross body—the body of humanity."[5] While the fact that *Ulysses* was still censored a decade after its 1922 publication struck denizens of the literary world as absurd, Joyce insistently transgressed literary and moral categories and *Ulysses* was profane, scatological, and salacious. As literary historian Paul Vanderham asserts, the obscenity in Joyce's work "is more than a Victorian fantasy."[6]

The nineteenth-century US obscenity laws, known as the Comstock Laws, contained strict prohibitions on materials lewd, immoral, and indecent—and all the other synonyms used to define obscenity. Named after Anthony Comstock, the nineteenth-century antivice crusader and author of the federal obscenity laws, the Comstock Laws were used to enforce restrictions on birth control information, sex education materials, and erotic literature.[7] Those moral-purity laws were routinely deployed by prosecutors and upheld by judges, and because Joyce's novel was rife with passages that could be construed as immoral, scurrilous, and indecent, a successful challenge to its official status in the United States as an obscene work was not at all guaranteed, despite its monumental standing among literary moderns.

Records show that Lindey and Ernst had *Ulysses* in their sights well before they had a publisher who would take the risks of financing a potentially losing case, and also that defending the notorious work was a logical but risky extension of their systematic campaign against the US obscenity laws and their enforcement.[8] While their success on behalf of Joyce's *Ulysses* and their client, the New York publisher Random House, made Ernst famous in his day, it was part of a larger battle. Ernst and Lindey targeted the extensive, widely used federal and state obscenity laws that facilitated the suppression of literary works, sex education materials, and virtually anything having to do with birth control or abortion: Joyce's *Ulysses* stood out as a symbol of the problems with that suppression, and taking up its defense would bring greater attention to the cause, and potentially transform the censorship of serious literary works.

The nineteenth-century US obscenity laws were vigorously enforced into the 1930s (and well beyond into the early 1960s), cutting a broad swath through all materials related to sexuality. When, in 1927, Ernst became aware of the extensive censorship powers the obscenity laws granted federal and state authorities, he undertook a study of Anglo-American censorship practices, published in book form as *To the Pure* (1928). This primer laid the intellectual groundwork for a strategic attack on censorship and the obscenity laws that made it possible.[9] He was greatly aided by Lindey, who joined the Greenbaum, Wolff & Ernst law firm in 1925, a successful all-purpose firm Ernst had formed in 1915 with other Jewish lawyers—the brothers Eddie and Laurence Greenbaum, and Herbert Wolff. While Ernst and Lindey were the firm's chief defenders of literary and sexual modernism in the US courts, other talented young Jewish lawyers including Harriet Pilpel, Samuel Schur, Newsome Levy, Benjamin Kaplan, and Nancy Weschler sought employment in the firm, and also took on obscenity-law battles on behalf of publishers, including G. P. Putnam's Sons, Covici-Friede, Simon & Schuster, and also on behalf of the birth control movement, sex educators, novelists, bookstore clerks arrested in police raids, and burlesque-theater owners.[10]

Ernst and Lindey's defense of *Ulysses* needs to be situated in the context of their larger pursuit of what Ernst called "rational sex laws," and their campaign against what Ernst would describe as the "necessity for hypocrisy and circumlocution in literature."[11] The decision to find an American publisher for, and pursue the defense of *Ulysses* followed directly on a series of favorable verdicts in the federal courts challenging both US Postal and US Customs practices. Their defense of the birth control pioneer and sex education pamphleteer Mary Ware Dennett (in *US v. Dennett*) and of the British birth control advocate and sex educator Marie Stopes (in the cases of *US v. Married Love* and *US v. Contraception*) were landmark legal precedents that made it even conceivable to mount a challenge to *Ulysses*'s banned status.¹² Those cases also illustrate the far-reaching purview of the obscenity laws, from Dennett's sex education pamphlet, to Stopes's marital health manual, to the work of Margaret Sanger's birth control clinic.

Additionally, victories in New York State courts against the prosecutions initiated by the New York Society for the Suppression of Vice—the primary censorship agency in New York City—also gave Ernst and Lindey legal momentum and confidence in their strategy for defending literary works, and evidence that some judges at least were amenable to bringing nineteenth-century obscenity laws in closer concert with the tastes and needs of the twentieth-century public. Plus, those cases brought them excellent publicity in New York City and national publications, and many valuable allies as well. Heading into the *Ulysses* case they knew that the writers, critics, editors, scholars, and publishers with whom they had already built alliances could be counted upon to support the liberation of *Ulysses*, the suppression of which was the most notorious symbol of American "Comstockery" gone awry.¹³ They knew how to build a legal argument, work the courts, compile testimonies about the value of literary and sexology works, and create publicity for their efforts. They and their eventual client Random House knew their defense would produce considerable publicity for and public interest in Joyce's great work. The *Ulysses* case also gave Ernst near-celebrity status in the New York City literary world, as well as in the nation's civil liberties circles. At mid-century he was still recognized as one of the most important civil libertarians in the United States.¹⁴

A 1938 profile of Ernst in *Scribner's* magazine, and another in 1944 in *Life* magazine, trumpeted the lawyer's accomplishments in the realm of sexual and literary free speech.¹⁵ Both the *Scribner's* piece and the *Life* profile sketched quick biographies, telling readers how he went from being a son of a German-speaking Jewish immigrant from Pilsen, Bohemia (then part of the Habsburg Empire) who initially settled in Alabama, where Ernst was born, to working in the family shirt-manufacturing business in Brooklyn while also attending the New York Law School at night. (Ernst studied on the train, reading Blackstone's *Commentaries* while commuting to and from work and school.) Both profiles focused on Ernst's remarkable string of victories in his sexual-censorship cases, his openness about matters sexual, and his propensity for self-promotion. *Life*'s Fred Rodell ascribed Ernst's success to his abundant energy, his alert eyes and athletic strength, and to his "exhibitionism." (Although Ernst routinely described himself as an exhibitionist, Rodell's use of the term made Ernst seem superficial, and his overall tone irked Ernst.) Rodell, also a Jewish lawyer, implied Ernst's Jewishness by describing him as "a smallish, darkish man whose birdlike eyes and manner belied his seeming physical solidity . . . and a general air of being about to take off."[16]

Both profiles reported that defense of *Ulysses* earned Ernst the reputation of being "preeminent among lawyers crusading against censorship,"[17] and also explained that the case was one in a series of censorship battles he and his partners had taken on. Both asserted he was justly famous because he had transformed how censorship laws were enforced. As the *Scribner's* piece noted, "Before Ernst came along the vice crusaders used to scare booksellers into pleas of guilty and light fines by promising to get the case over quickly, and without publicity." But by waging "almost continuous warfare against Federal, State, local, private, and ecclesiastic censorship bodies," he had changed that dynamic.[18] As the *Life* profile observed (while taking a dig at him), Ernst could "crow, with pardonable pride" that "no book published by a regular publisher, or reviewed by a regular critic, no book published honestly and without surreption, is in any danger of suppression."[19]

A 2019 *New York Review of Books* essay by the novelist Michael Chabon celebrating Ernst's defense of *Ulysses* describes him as "erudite, polished" and a "well-connected New York hustler" who "conspired" with publisher Bennett Cerf to free James Joyce's notorious *Ulysses*. Chabon alludes to Ernst's broader body of work, writing that he was "known, and much sought-after, as a gifted, skilled, and cagey courtroom attorney with a discerning eye for the kinds of cases that could change the law if you won them." Chabon celebrated Ernst's skill, proclaiming that he had "brought as much artistry and erudition and sly, masterful skill to defending one book, called *Ulysses*, as its author had brought to its creation."[20] That's high praise indeed.

Who was this once-famous now largely forgotten figure, and how did he and his long-forgotten colleague Alexander Lindey become the lawyers who "freed" the Irishman Joyce's great masterpiece from its status as a banned book?

## Family and Law-Firm Background

Son of a German-speaking Jewish immigrant from Pilsen on his father's side, and a second-generation German Jewish immigrant on his mother's side, Ernst grew up in New York City, in homes filled with books, musical instruments, and immigrant aspirations for education and economic security. Ernst was born in Alabama in 1888, where his father and uncle first lived when they arrived in the United States. On a business trip to New York, his father "went to where the immigrants were," as Ernst recalled later in life, where he met, courted, and soon married an "educated, literate, and cultured" New York City woman. His mother had graduated from Hunter College, and music, theater, and intellectual attainment were key values to her. When Ernst was two years old the family moved to New York City so that he and his siblings would have better educational opportunities. His father also valued education, Ernst said, "like all immigrants."[21]

Being a second-generation immigrant who was not rooted in a sense of ancestry or place shaped Ernst's sense of self. He reflected in a late-in-life interview that he had "no ancestors," "had no past." Asked to explain, he said he had "no great grandfather, no rootedness," and no sense of belonging to a longer stream. By comparison his second wife, Margaret Samuels, from a well-established Jewish family in New Orleans, "had security, I had none." Margaret, he said, was "one of the few secure people I've ever known. I'm not secure." He continued, "I'm a ham. I like publicity."[22]

Ernst's immigrant sensibility and the attendant insecurity come across potently in this interview. He did not discuss his Jewishness per se, other than calling himself a "non-worshipping Jew," but clearly the values and aspirations of Jewish immigrants were central to his identity as a Jew. Perhaps he did not discuss his Jewish identity much because it made him feel vulnerable. Matthew Silverman explains that later in his life Ernst "recalled how he was mocked during his formative years for his appearance. 'I had been brought up to believe that I was ugly. . . . I had uncles who always kidded me about my big Jewish nose which did my ego no good.'" He also recalled being "told that I was Jewish, and for that reason, inferior."[23]

Ernst internalized the financial precariousness of immigrants, too. His father made (and occasionally lost) money in the real estate business, so his family had difficult periods, and his mother was frequently ill with tuberculosis, so he would live with relatives, away from his siblings. While his father had enough financial success that he could send Morris to the prestigious Horace Mann School for high school, and then to Williams College in western Massachusetts, he was aware of how his Jewishness (and small physical stature) marked him off. At Williams he was one of the few Jewish students. But he was gregarious, a successful debater, and fit in well enough to be accepted into a Jewish fraternity and gained confidence in his talents. Upon graduation he returned to New York City and, as noted, worked in the family shirt-making business (established by his father and uncle) while at night attending the New York Law School, where other immigrants and Jews (like Alexander Lindey) took their legal education, both for financial reasons (so they could work by day) and because bigotry in the legal profession kept them out of more prestigious schools, and the white-shoe law firms, when they graduated.

Ernst was always self-deprecating about his legal education. He repeatedly described himself as a "half-trained lawyer" who had "no legal background."[24] The fact that he went to law school at night, while he worked in the family business by day, left him feeling only "partially trained" as a lawyer (but also gave him room as an improviser who thus did not venerate legal traditions). Night schools were not unusual for immigrants who got their legal training in East Coast cities during the first half of the twentieth century, although this route deepened his sense of insecurity. He also described himself as a "dilettante," as consequences of being "ancestorless" and only "partially trained." ("Dilettante" was, in fact, not an inaccurate description of the latter decades of his career, in which he'd dash from one issue to the next, and hurriedly "scribble" the twenty books he wrote or cowrote. But he was decidedly not a dilettante in that phase of his career when he focused on obscenity-law issues.)

Jerold Auerbach describes the obstacles confronting Jewish lawyers especially in the era prior to World War I, when a "deep bigotry announced by those at the top of the profession" kept Jewish students out of the top schools and out of the most prestigious law firms. This was the moment Ernst was earning his law degree and getting his career started, and his sense of being half-trained was no doubt reinforced by the intense, voluble criticism by law school deans and judges of the immigrant and Jewish lawyers who obtained their law degrees in the night schools. Their narrative of inadequately trained and "foreign" types was used to "explain" both the inferiority of and the refusal to hire those Jewish lawyers trained in night schools, rather than at institutions like Harvard, Yale, Columbia, Wisconsin, or Pennsylvania (or Fordham and Georgetown for Catholic lawyers).[25]

When Ernst formed his practice with Eddie and Laurence Greenbaum and Herbert Wolff, also Jewish graduates of Williams College, they built a successful firm known for expertise in corporate law and real estate law. Their work in these fields provided considerable financial security for the partners and gave them latitude to provide their legal services pro bono, as Ernst and Lindey did in many of their obscenity-law cases.[26]

Ernst came to anticensorship issues by way of other progressive causes and affiliations. By the mid-1920s he had distinguished himself enough in New York City's progressive legal circles to become part of the national leadership of the American Civil Liberties Union (ACLU). He became a member of the ACLU's Executive Board in 1927, where he worked with the ACLU's founding generation including Roger Baldwin, Clarence Darrow, Norman Thomas, Elizabeth Gurley Flynn, Scott Nearing, and John Dewey.[27] He served as the ACLU's co–general counsel with Arthur Garfield Hays from 1929 to 1954.[28]

These affiliations shaped his focus on censorship and free speech issues. Virtually everyone who played a leading role in expanding free speech and press ideals in the decades between World War I and World War II was affiliated with the ACLU, in part because the free speech violations during World War I were so disastrous, and the ACLU became the organization most committed to fighting for the free speech and free association cause.[29] As historian Leigh Ann Wheeler's work shows, the ACLU was also the organization that took on the longer-term project of "making sex a civil liberty."[30]

Ernst was instrumental in this project, and many of his cases were promoted by the ACLU. His focus on obscenity-law issues was basically a parallel sexual free speech movement to the free speech battles on behalf of political radicals and labor unions taken up by his ACLU colleagues. He was committed to an unfettered "marketplace of thought," a principle he adopted from the work of the first Jewish Supreme Court justice Louis Brandeis, Ernst's idol from whom he developed a core principle about the necessity of public access to a diverse marketplace of ideas.[31] (He hung a large framed portrait of Justice Brandeis behind his office desk.) The First Amendment, he believed, was premised upon and should guarantee such a marketplace, and he thought this ought to extend to artistic expression and other areas, like sexual information, where the public needed scientifically dependable, up-to-date information that would make their lives better and less filled with the hazards of ill-informed notions gained from inadequate sources.[32]

When Ernst, Lindey, and others took up battle against obscenity laws and "Comstockery" as a cultural and legal force, they also took up battles with John Saxton Sumner, who succeeded Comstock in 1915 as the executive secretary of the New York Society for the Suppression of Vice. Sumner maintained Comstock's vigilant enthusiasm for keeping smut at bay. (He was the official who sought the arrest of the bookstore owner who sold the *Little Review* issue carrying Joyce's "Nausicaa" episode in 1920.) Sumner was Ernst's primary foil in the press as the symbol of American censorship, and he fought Sumner in the press and in the courts. But federal and state courts' enforcement of the obscenity laws was the core legal problem.[33] The federal courts consistently upheld their constitutionality, and judges were unwilling to hear them challenged on First Amendment grounds. (Late nineteenth-century Supreme Court decisions upheld the constitutionality of obscenity laws, and twentieth-century judges relied on those precedents, refusing to accept the idea that they were unconstitutional.) Moreover, powerful federal bureaucracies (i.e., the Post Office and the Customs Bureau) administered the obscenity laws almost unchallenged, and powerful moral guardians like Sumner, who patrolled the New York–based publishing industry with a vengeance, used their considerable power to enforce reticence regarding human sexuality, whether it was scientific, medical, artistic, educational, or theatrical.

In short, federal and state obscenity laws were capacious, covered a broad range of materials, were buttressed by extensive legal precedent, and enforced by administrators and police agents who had largely unchecked authority. When Ernst and his colleagues took aim at the obscenity laws, they knew they had to selectively pick away at them. The courts were not going to overturn the laws; rather they would assess, on a case-by-case basis, whether an individual work was obscene. So Ernst and his partners had to choose their cases (and clients) carefully on behalf of materials that had obvious scientific or artistic merit with demonstrable value to the public. But because both popular and intellectual culture were out of sync with the laws and their enforcement, Ernst and his team could count on plenty of allies in New York City, home to the nation's most important publishers and a city filled with sexual and artistic moderns.

If there was a place and time to take on these laws and wage censorship battles, it was New York City in the 1920s and 1930s. John Sumner was a perfect foil for Ernst; his humorless mien and book-burning image were at dramatic variance with New York's Jazz Age cosmopolitanism. New York City's burgeoning media and publishing industries, and heterogeneity, made it a prime battleground to challenge laws aimed at maintaining a homogeneous, Protestant-inflected nineteenth-century moral order. Federal postal and customs officials, Vice Society agents, and politically ambitious (frequently Roman Catholic) prosecutors who tried to enforce the moral order by raiding bookstores, magazine stands, and closing down burlesque theaters were going to face challenges in Jazz Age New York City. The city teemed with people interested in the new and the modern, and was home to a literary and artistic avant-garde who insisted on opening up their canvases to a far broader range of human experience than permitted by the Comstock laws. Ernst and his colleagues took up their battles in a city filled with potential allies, and could count on plenty of supporters as they developed their legal strategies.

And they were strategic at all stages. They sought reputable (as distinct from seedy) clients and chose only works that could be plausibly defended as having value to readers or users, whether literary, scientific, medical, or educational. A brief résumé of their cases prior to *Ulysses* illustrates their choices and the body of precedents accrued. In 1929 Ernst and Lindey won a federal circuit-court appeal reversing a lower federal-court conviction of a sex education pamphlet by Mary Ware Dennett entitled *The Sex Side of Life*. The *Dennett* decision facilitated other challenges to postal and customs administrative decisions, including on behalf of Marie Stopes's books *Married Love* and *Contraception*. They also successfully defended Radclyffe Hall's lesbian-themed novel, *The Well of Loneliness*, and Arthur Schnitzler's ribald novel, *Casanova's Homecoming*, about the decline of the once great lover. These cases helped them develop a template for the defense of literary works and a body of valuable precedents, making it a reasonable gamble for Random House's Bennett Cerf to arrange a publication deal with Joyce and his agents and to finance Ernst and Lindey's legal challenge.[34]

### Ulysses: The *Little Review* Cases and Early Legal Travails

When Ernst and Lindey took up the defense of *Ulysses*, they inherited its troubling legal record in the United States, a history that might make their job more difficult. That history began in the World War I era when Margaret Anderson and Jane Heap, publishers of the American literary magazine *The Little Review*, first published *Ulysses* in episodic form from 1918 to 1920, as Joyce was completing his novel as a whole. As scholars Paul Vanderham, Kevin Birmingham, and others have made clear, *Ulysses* transgressed many cultural fault lines in the era at the tail end of World War I—political, religious, aesthetic, and moral.[35] Vanderham explains that Joyce "not only rejected" but also intentionally "attacked" Victorian moral opposition to discussions of erotic desire and pleasure.[36] Beginning with the January 1919 issue, US Postal officials banned four separate issues of *The Little Review* carrying Joyce's episodes. The New York Vice Society's John Sumner brought charges against Anderson and Heap in New York State courts in 1921 for publishing and distributing the "Nausicaa" episode.

Anderson and Heap—just as willing as Joyce to attack conventional morality—were also trying to increase subscriptions to their magazine when they sent unsolicited copies of the "Nausicaa" issue through the mail, one landing in the hands of a prominent New York lawyer's daughter.[37] She complained to her father, who complained to the Manhattan district attorney, who complained to Sumner and sought his help bringing legal action against the publication.[38] Sumner found the issue for sale at a Washington Square bookstore and filed an obscenity complaint against the owner of the store, along with Anderson and Heap.[39] (The bookstore owner was dropped from the ensuing prosecution.)

As law professor Stephen Gillers and Paul Vanderham both point out, Anderson and Heap's unsolicited mailing of the "Nausicaa" episode in

*The Little Review* to an adolescent girl exemplified precisely what Sumner and the obscenity laws were trying to prevent: sexually provocative materials falling into the hands of young, vulnerable female readers. Moreover, Joyce's "Nausicaa" episode clearly burlesqued the whole notion of the "vulnerable" and innocent young female. Gerty McDowell, leaning backward on the beach, knew exactly what was going on in Leopold Bloom's britches as he masturbated while watching her reveal her bloomers to him. The reader learns that Gerty already knew of "men like that," and nevertheless offers up more of herself for his viewing:[40] "She leaned back she caught her knee in her hands so as not to fall back looking up and there was no one to see only him and her when she revealed all her graceful beautifully shaped legs like that, supply soft and delicately rounded, and she seemed to hear the panting of his heart his hoarse breathing, because she knew about the passion of men like that..."[41]

And the fact that the young-woman reader who complained to her father understood what was going on proved Joyce's satirical point about Victorian female innocence.

The magistrate-court judge also figured out what Bloom was doing and declared the book obscene. He ordered Anderson and Heap to stand for criminal trial in the New York Court of Special Sessions.[42] That three-judge panel also found the episode obscene and convicted the publishers Anderson and Heap. Their lawyer, John Quinn, who was also one of Joyce's primary financial benefactors, did not pursue an appeal.[43]

After the convictions, Quinn could not interest American publishers in the book. Sylvia Beach, owner of the Parisian bookshop Shakespeare & Co., published it in English (in France) in 1922, and for the next decade plus, *Ulysses* was contraband in the English-speaking world, a status reinforced by the 1928 US Customs Court *Heymoolen* ruling (discussed later in the chapter). Sylvia Beach continued as the only authorized English-language publisher, US Customs authorities continued seizing shipments, US booksellers had to hide their stockpiles, and travelers to Paris routinely made pilgrimages to Beach's bookstore filling extra suitcases with the book to sell and give to friends upon their return to the United States.

The book's relatively widespread, albeit illegal distribution—including to public and college libraries as well as to scholars and critics—greatly assisted Ernst and Lindey's defense of the book because they could draw upon a decade's worth of critical appraisal and scholarly exegesis to illustrate its value to the literary world. The growing body of critical work contributed to the consensus that it was the literary monument of its age.

While the World War I–era fears of the book's political and aesthetic anarchism virtually disappeared from its opponents' worries, concerns about its sexual licentiousness only deepened with the addition of its final "Penelope" episode, Molly Bloom's ribald soliloquy. This shocking chapter reinforced the fears about *Ulysses*'s sexual anarchy, potentially undermining Ernst and Lindey's arguments that the book was not obscene. When the reader finally encounters Molly Bloom's half-awake erotic reveries, they learn that Leopold Bloom's cuckolding wife loved sex, thought about sex, and thought about exactly the kinds of sexual activities and pleasures most societies deemed immoral, unnatural, perverse, illegal, and that had no place in respectable literature: she ruminated about her lover's penis size and the frequency of their intercourse, of taking penises in her mouth, of her anal pleasures, of wiping ejaculate off her buttocks, and more. What's more, she had no "shame" about any of this.[44] Molly, far more than young Gerty, was the fully embodied, shamelessly sexualized woman that the Anglo-American obscenity laws had been deployed to silence.

The work's entire legal record in the United States posed an obstacle to Ernst and Lindey's efforts. And yet, they were thrilled by and confident about the prospects of defending Joyce's masterpiece. Their series of wins in other obscenity-law cases had established the scaffolding for defending it, making it plausible to take on *Ulysses*, especially if they could bring the case before a discerning jurist open to the intrinsic value of literary experimentation.

## Securing a Publisher and Acquiring Expert Testimonials

Ernst and Lindey began working to find an American publisher for *Ulysses* in the summer of 1931. Editors Ben Huebsch at Viking Press and Bennett Cerf at Random House both considered getting *Ulysses* under contract. Ernst and Lindey met with them, trying to determine who would bankroll the legal defense.[45] In December 1931 Cerf told Ernst he was interested in "talk[ing] further about *Ulysses*," and by early March

1932 the thirty-three-year-old Cerf and his partner Donald Klopfer agreed to a contract, with the lawyers collecting 5 percent of royalties, a deal that would significantly contribute to Ernst's wealth over time.[46]

Cerf and Lindey immediately went to work obtaining readers' testimonials and other materials surrounding the book's distribution and uses.[47] Because other writers were sympathetic to Joyce's victimization by literary pirates—who were selling and making money from unlicensed versions of his book, while he was earning nothing from those sales—the lawyers correctly assumed they would get widespread support for the action from the literary world, beyond the matter of the book's literary value.[48] Lindey and Ernst knew how to obtain support from potential experts and simultaneously work the publicity front, building expectations for their case. They also knew in this instance that they needed to understand and explain the monumentally complex work. This would require extensive groundwork and study of the book and its critical commentary, a job Lindey took on.

Lindey and Cerf sent out requests for testimonials from writers and critics, constructed surveys to send to the nation's librarians, and sought evidence that it was already being taught in American universities despite its status as a banned book.[49] Within days they began receiving enthusiastic letters from leading literary figures, including the editor of *The New Republic* Malcolm Cowley, the novelist Theodore Dreiser (author of *Sister Carrie* and *An American Tragedy*), and F. Scott Fitzgerald; these offered resolute opposition to censorship and unanimity in their estimation of the book's genius. They, like many others, averred that Joyce was to literature what Freud and Einstein were to the mind and science. They acknowledged the work's bawdiness, but were appalled that it was still literary contraband.

Theodore Dreiser, who was in perpetual warfare with censors over his own works, wrote, "I have always regarded the attempted censorship of any book as one of the most absurd of all unintelligent human actions." But *Ulysses* occupied a different plane altogether: "To read it is to spend a day inside a seeking and profoundly observant human mind, to learn its mysterious wanderings and secret paths. And because it is what it is, some things enter into it which are not generally recorded. But, and for precisely this reason, these things add to its value as an amazing, if not unique, social and literary document."[50]

For the writers who weighed in, *Ulysses*'s censorship provided unequivocal proof that the moralists empowered to police the mails, surveille customs' ports of entry, raid bookstores, and monitor publishers' lists were egregiously out of touch with contemporary sensibilities, especially learned opinion.

Lindey and Ernst promiscuously used the dozens upon dozens of letters they received, quoting them in the legal memoranda they submitted to the courts, and built their formal "Testimonial" appendices around them. Moreover, the letters helped them identify and clarify key defense arguments, especially the nearly automatic assumption that "obscenity" connoted masturbatory purposes. As F. Scott Fitzgerald wrote, the "people who have the patience to read *Ulysses* are not the kind who will slobber over a few little Rabelaisian passages."[51] And as many of Joyce's defenders routinely noted, given the other "obscene" materials obtainable in booksellers' stalls and through the mails, no one would read *Ulysses* to aid their masturbation. As Cerf told Lindey, those who might think it would serve those purposes would "certainly throw down the book in hopeless disgust after trying to wade through the first two chapters."[52]

There was also a general consensus that its staggering complexity would benefit the defense. Lindey began studying the literature so he and Ernst could explain to judges the book's formal elements—particularly its stream-of-consciousness experiments (a technique that added to its occasional baffling indecipherability). Because the courts understood the purposes of obscenity law as protecting vulnerable readers, they could also explain that the book's technical difficulties posed insuperable obstacles to young readers or those in search of smut. Lindey drew especially from a 1929 review by literary critic Edmund Wilson in *The New Republic*.[53] Wilson's long essay downplays—indeed barely mentions—the book's notorious sexual passages. When, deep into his essay, he finally addresses them he quickly asserts that these moments are actually Joyce's best writing in the book. Lindey chose a similar tactic in barely treating these passages in his and Lindey's formal legal memoranda (although he certainly could not risk suggesting these were the book's best-written segments).

Wilson placed Joyce's small oeuvre in the stream of Continental literary experimentation, and explained the elaborate correspondence between Joyce's *Ulysses* and Homer's *Odyssey*. This explained Leopold Bloom's single day's odyssey through Dublin's streets, pubs, and brothels looking for his lost "son" Telemachus (Stephen Dedalus), while also worrying about his own Penelope (Molly), who was not nearly as true as Odysseus's had been. Wilson wrote:

> Joyce's Ulysses is a Dublin Jew, an advertisement canvasser named Bloom. Like Stephen, he dwells among aliens; a Jew, son of a Hungarian father, he is still something of a foreigner among the Irish; a man of genuine, though mediocre, intelligence and sensibility, he has little in common with the other inhabitants of the lower middle-class world in which he lives. He has been married for many years to an Irishwoman, the buxom daughter of an army officer, a professional singer, of prodigious sexual appetite, who has been continually and indiscriminately unfaithful to him. . . . He is Ulysses with no Telemachus and cut off from Penelope.[54]

Wilson's essay provided the backbone for Lindey's formal memoranda. Both Wilson and Lindey essentially refused to say that there was anything in the book akin to obscenity, with that concept's whole chain of associations like dirt, smut, or pornography.

## Customs' Seizure and US Attorneys' Cooperation

On May 1, 1932, Paul Leon, Joyce's agent in France, cabled Bennett Cerf informing him that a copy of *Ulysses* had set sail on the *U.S. Bremen* and was due in New York Harbor on May 3. Lindey immediately contacted the New York Customs House, apprising them of the book's imminent arrival. He tried to persuade customs officials to allow the book entry, giving customs a brief primer on recent obscenity decisions.[55] Ten days later Assistant Collector of Customs H. C. Stewart informed Lindey that *Ulysses* had been formally detained as an obscene book, in violation of Section 305 of the Tariff Act. *Ulysses*, he explained, was still banned under the ruling from a 1928 customs-court decision, *A. Heymoolen v. United States*.[56]

Lindey and Ernst anticipated this result and worked to cultivate a cooperative relationship with the US attorneys for the Southern District of New York, Samuel C. Coleman in particular, as well as his boss,

George M. Medalie, to whom customs forwarded the book. They had recently worked with these federal prosecutors in bringing Marie Stopes's books directly before Judge John M. Woolsey, thereby avoiding a jury. Ernst's team and the US attorneys enjoyed mutual respect and goodwill through the entire process of determining *Ulysses*'s fate.

Lindey checked in with Coleman a month after the US attorneys received the book, wondering about the prospects for dismissing the obscenity libel.[57] Coleman told Lindey he wasn't sure what to do about the book and did not want to be the one responsible for "starting proceedings" against *Ulysses*, so he sent the matter up the chain to his superior, US Attorney Medalie.[58] Medalie finished reading the book two months later in August 1932. He acknowledged it was "a very important book" but reported that he would "have to proceed with the case." He tried to reassure Ernst and Lindey by saying that he was "pretty sure we can arrange to have it brought before Judge Woolsey," who had ruled favorably on both *Married Love* and *Contraception* by Marie Stopes. Medalie added he hoped Woolsey would "dispose of it by motion."[59] Later Medalie told the Ernst firm he was especially "worried about the latter part of the book, particularly as to the musings of the wife," and this was why his office needed to proceed with the libel claim.[60] Importantly, Coleman and Medalie were not antagonists: Medalie agreed the book would not be a threat to minors, and he let Ernst's office know he was interested in seeing all the expert testimony Lindey and Cerf had compiled.[61] Moreover, when another assistant US attorney, Nicholas Atlas, joined Coleman as part of the prosecution, the US Attorney's office actually added a devoted reader of *Ulysses* to their mix.

Turning *Ulysses* into a Classic

While awaiting a decision from the US attorneys and room on Judge Woolsey's docket, Alexander Lindey made a brilliant tactical move, challenging the 1928 *Heymoolen* ruling officially designating *Ulysses* an obscene work. In 1930 Congress had amended Section 305 of the Tariff Act, allowing individual collectors to import works deemed "classics."[62] Ernst and Lindey were keen to test this new provision, and getting *Ulysses* formally declared a "classic" prior to trial in the US District Court could only redound to their client's benefit.[63]

Lindey had Joyce's agent Paul Leon ship another copy to him, and petitioned customs to admit the book as a classic under the revised Tariff Act.[64] This gave him an excellent chance to make use of the hundreds of testimonies he had collected and to rehearse his legal arguments. As he explained to customs, Joyce had achieved an "undisputed reputation" as a writer "of first-rate importance," and *Ulysses* had earned "worldwide acclaim . . . as the foremost prose masterpiece of the twentieth century."[65] "One might be inclined to look askance on such extravagant praise," he added, "were it not for the enclosed exhibits which appear to justify the claims made for the book and its author." He also attached an extensive bibliography he described as the "vast critical library" that had grown up around the book. These materials provided, he wrote, a "trustworthy mirror of all the literate elements in the community."[66]

Lindey succeeded. In June 1933 the Treasury Department ruled that *Ulysses* had standing as "a classic." This essentially meant it would be available for importation by individual recipients, although not for commercial sale by US booksellers; while the ruling designated the book a "classic" it still did not address its status as an obscene book, so this matter had to be resolved in the US District Court in New York. However, the 1928 *Heymoolen* decision would no longer be the latest customs-court ruling on the book's status.[67]

Ernst and Lindey immediately let the press know these results, and promoted the upcoming action on the book's behalf.[68] While Sam Coleman was irked to find out about Lindey's petition from the newspapers, he also suggested it might mean that the "libel proceedings will be dropped and *Ulysses* cleared . . . without a court fight."[69] Coleman was not the only prosecutor who did not want such a fight.

US Attorney Nicholas Atlas was a part-time English lecturer and loved *Ulysses*. Atlas had graduated from Fordham Law School in 1924 and "practiced occasional law," but he also "taught English at City College, and worked as a literary critic at the *Brooklyn Daily Eagle*." Atlas had lived in the bohemian precincts of New York's Greenwich Village in the 1920s, and "*Ulysses* had come to him, as it had come to many of his generation, with the force of a liberating revelation; he could hardly be expected seriously to move the Court to confiscate and destroy it."[70]

No one in the US Attorney's Office for the Southern District of Manhattan was committed to finding the book obscene. But they all thought a decision of this magnitude needed to be made by a federal judge, not by their office.⁷¹ But getting an actual hearing scheduled on Judge Woolsey's calendar would require patience; once they got on his calendar, they did not want to lose him.⁷² When told it might take Judge Woolsey six weeks to read the book, Ernst told his younger associate Jonas Shapiro, "We don't care how long he wants to read the book."⁷³

## Defending *Ulysses*: Lindey's Legal Brief

While he was reading it, Lindey and Ernst sent Judge Woolsey their trove of testimonials, guides to the book, and Lindey's brilliant legal brief, his "Preliminary Memorandum."⁷⁴ Lindey would expand his arguments in the formal brief he submitted in October 1933, but previewed his arguments for Woolsey as he was reading the book and attendant commentary.⁷⁵

Lindey focused on a particular topic of Joyce criticism—the work's technical difficulty—thus refuting worries about how the "vulnerable reader" might be corrupted. Additionally, Lindey drew clear distinctions between Joyce's novel as a celebrated work attended by hullabaloo, and Joyce's own austere life and seriousness as a literary craftsman. His rigorous education had built the foundations to produce literary art at the highest levels, Lindey explained, and although his works were "few in number," Joyce was nevertheless "the most important figure in world literature today."⁷⁶

He was not a purveyor of cheap, commercial trash—the usual fare of obscenity rulings. Indeed, Joyce had "led a monastic existence" in the seven years it took him to write the book. Nor had Joyce attempted to profit from his achievement. He was anticommercial: "He has delivered no lectures, given no interviews, posed for no newsreels . . . issued no manifestos, written no magazine articles which might have yielded him easy harvest." In fact, much to the chagrin of the Random House editors, he would not even attach "explanatory prefaces to his works" to make reading his complicated masterpiece easier. Joyce had eschewed the marketplace, spending his life in a proverbial tower.⁷⁷

Lindey explained Joyce's stream-of-consciousness technique.⁷⁸ Using a quote from the English writer Louis Golding, he explained that Joyce's wanderings into "the red chambers of the flesh" were inextricable from the novel's experimental technique.⁷⁹ Every time a character's thoughts moved toward the bawdy or the body, the discerning reader knew it was because that was where the unpredictable flow of the character's consciousness led. The characters had pasts that inexorably infringed on the present: Leopold Bloom's masturbation at the sight of Gerty's bloomers was not separable from his inability to consummate his marriage to Molly over the previous ten years; Gerty leaning back to give Bloom a better look could not be separated from her fancy for romance novels and fantasies of being rescued by inscrutable foreign men; and Molly's ruminations about her sexual pleasures with her lover Blazes Boylan were indelibly tied to Leopold's own sexual failures in their marital bed.

Lindey then developed a series of arguments about the book's alleged obscenity. A core argument was that cultural standards, and what was considered shocking, were sure to vary over time.⁸⁰ Lindey's favorite, oft-used example was women's bathing suits: "In 1900 any female who appeared on a bathing beach without sleeves and a long skirt would have been jailed. . . . A few years ago the one-piece bathing suit came into its own; and today the so-called sunsuits leave very little of the human form concealed."⁸¹

As to the idea that *Ulysses* might be shocking in that era's print-culture marketplace, Lindey averred, "Our tabloids carry stories of passion and lust, of crime and perversion, told with a degree of vividness and frankness unheard of a generation ago. Every man, woman and child in the community has easy access to the complete details of torch-murders, of marital infidelities, of boudoir intimacies, kidnappings and abnormalities."⁸²

And perhaps most effectively, he suggested that the courts had essentially reduced the question of whether an artifact was obscene to a simple biological matter: Did it produce sexual arousal to the point of lust? He couldn't state it, but the implicit question was, did it induce masturbation? He led Judge Woolsey through the case law, asserting that the issue of arousing lust was the sole test agreed upon by the courts.

Although *Ulysses* dealt with sexual matters in certain moments, Lindey pointed out it had none of those features "almost invariably present in a work of pornography" such as graphic illustrations and anonymity of authorship. Moreover, it would be "tedious and bewildering" for those in search of the pornographic. It was "a prodigious work of 732 closely-printed pages" and it was difficult reading, "even for the mature and the intelligent." Someone reading it simply for its sex scenes "would not get beyond the first dozen pages."[83] Pornographic works were understandable, easily ascertainable. *Ulysses* was neither.

Likewise, the book's "Extrinsic Circumstances"—the literary reputation of the author, the opinions of critics, the attitudes of librarians, its networks of sale and distribution, its acceptance within the community, its uses in university classrooms—all negated claims of obscenity. Moreover, Joyce had a reputation and stature as "a supreme literary artist."[84]

Finally, they ended their brief with an argument they had rehearsed elsewhere, one that had become well accepted in the New York magistrate courts and was gaining momentum in the higher state and federal courts: that Joyce's novel had to be judged as a whole. Obscenity, they asserted, is "a question of entirety" and this book's questionable sections made up a "negligible" fraction of the work as a whole.[85] As for those questionable sections, they needed to be understood as Joyce's unflinching exploration of this "gross ill-drained body of humanity," to quote Edmund Wilson. The book was, they wrote, a "torch of truth": "It is only by such exposure that we can hope to banish darkness and taint. Joyce's penetration and courage deserve praise, not condemnation."[86]

## The Government's Case

Judge Woolsey never requested submission of formal legal memoranda and Coleman and Atlas never submitted one. They essentially allowed the defense to define the history of obscenity law, to discuss recent cases, and to present all of the evidence and expert opinion about *Ulysses*. While Coleman offered a few assertions during the formal hearing that parts of the book were obscene, their internal documents evince no interest whatsoever in demonstrating its obscenity. In fact, the US attorneys began their oral argument with Coleman by asserting they were not censors.

The richest of the US attorneys' documents actually reveal Atlas's considered engagement with and fondness for Joyce's work. Atlas's erudite "James Joyce" essay reads far more like an admiring literary review than a prosecutor's brief.[87] He celebrates the book's poetry, its experimental techniques, and its status in the literary world. Vanderham writes that "by avoiding mention of the objectionable passages, [Atlas] gives the impression that the government's libel has little or no basis."[88] As for the legal history of *Ulysses*, Atlas makes a remarkable argument, essentially saying the US attorneys in his office should not be prejudiced by either its prior legal history or its notorious reputation. "On the contrary, we approach the book with great respect," especially for its experiment in literary technique.[89]

When Atlas turns to the narrative, he neither describes nor worries about the possible obscenity. Noting that Bloom "goes to a beach," he says nothing about Gerty McDowell on that same beach, and nothing about Bloom's masturbation. He is far more interested in explaining the characters, their histories, their milieu, and their minds. He says very little about Molly and her dalliances, or her monologue, only noting that Bloom "has his troubles. He is married to an Irishwoman of whom he has reason to believe—and before the day is done, of whom he is sure—that she commits adultery."[90] Atlas does not address Molly's sexual reveries. He was far more interested in celebrating the book's "rare poetry."

### The Hearing before Judge Woolsey

The oral argument finally took place on November 25, 1933, in a courtroom in midtown Manhattan.[91] According to reporters, Judge Woolsey "talked freely from the bench and from time to time told of his extremely difficult position in being required to pass on a book that for ten years had evoked the most violent denunciations and praise from all manner of learned men and women." The courtroom broke into laughter "when the judge admitted that to his 'shocking surprise'" he "'perfectly understood' the passages that had been described constituting the obscene sections of the manuscript."[92] When Woolsey reported that *Ulysses* "left him 'bothered, stirred and troubled,' Ernst replied, 'I think that is exactly the effect of *Ulysses*. You have not used the adjectives 'shocked' or 'revolted.' You have used the adjectives 'bothered,' 'troubled.'"[93]

On December 6, 1933, Judge Woolsey ruled that the government could not seize *Ulysses* as obscene. His famous decision did what Lindey and Ernst hoped, restricting the definition of obscenity as "tending to stir the sex impulses or to lead to sexually impure and lustful thoughts."[94]

Understanding that his verdict on this celebrated and notorious work would be closely scrutinized and would reverberate in subsequent obscenity-law decisions, Woolsey challenged and reworked some of the core assumptions about obscenity law. He embraced the book- and publisher-protective positions that had been evolving in the courts. He accepted the guidance of Lindey and Ernst on the essential overlapping definition of obscenity with pornography and arousal. Most famously he offered an appreciative tutorial on Joyce's work.

Woolsey used the terms "obscenity" and "pornography" interchangeably when he declared early in his decision that "if the conclusion is that the book is pornographic, that is the end of the inquiry and forfeiture must follow."[95] He averred, however, that he did not find pornographic intent, famously writing: "In *Ulysses*, in spite of its unusual frankness, I do not detect anywhere the leer of the sensualist. I hold, therefore, that it is not pornographic." Rather than worrying about the work's erotic effects on the reader, Woolsey held that it had great integrity as a work of art.[96]

Woolsey acknowledged that the courts needed to consider the potential, probable, or actual effects of such a work on its readers. But because *Ulysses* was not written "with what is commonly called pornographic intent," the effects therefore were presumably not pornographic either. However, he also understood that an author's "intention" was not wholly adequate for assessing a work's effects, and he knew that American obscenity law had long accepted the Hicklin standard's concerns to protect vulnerable readers from "depraving and corrupting" effects.

Here Woolsey initiated an important shift, gesturing toward the necessity of finding some actual readers, and some "objective measure of effects," rather than merely assuming harm or no harm to possible readers. Woolsey asserted that his sole responsibility was to determine "whether *Ulysses* is obscene within the legal definition" of the word "obscene," and then offered the idea that the standard test ought to be understood as "tending to stir the sex impulses or to lead to sexually impure and lustful thoughts."[97]

And, he added, there ought to be some "objective" test of effects on the average reader: "Whether a particular book would tend to excite such [sexual] impulses and thoughts must be tested by the court's opinion as to its effect on a person with average sex instincts—what the

French would call *l'homme moyen sensuel*—who plays, in this branch of legal inquiry, the same role of hypothetical reagent as does the 'reasonable man' in the law of torts." Woolsey's "reasonable man" was not some craven youth looking for pornography.

Woolsey reported that he ran a small experiment. He enlisted two anonymous readers (friends of his) to report to him whether or not they had been aroused to lust by reading *Ulysses*. They were reasonable men, "learned in the art" of literature, and also of "average sex instincts." They reported that the book "did not tend to excite sexual impulses or lustful thoughts," and more telling, they found it "a somewhat tragic and very powerful commentary on the inner lives of men and women."[98]

Woolsey concluded that not only did it not have the arousing effects of pornography, it in fact had more of an antierotic, sickening effect. He summed up by writing, "My considered opinion, after long reflection, is that, whilst in many places the effect of *Ulysses* on the reader undoubtedly is somewhat emetic, nowhere does it tend to be an aphrodisiac."[99]

Woolsey's decision set the stage for new obscenity-law jurisprudence when addressing significant works of literature. The distinctions Woolsey implicitly made (considering the interests of serious adult readers, taking the book as a whole, weighing literary reputation, considering the work's seriousness as art, the necessity of discerning actual effects, and recognizing the gulf between adult and youthful readers) slowly got worked out in federal courts over the next twenty-plus years. He adopted the arguments Morris Ernst and Alexander Lindey had been making, and gave them the transformative authority of his immediate classic opinion in *The United States v. One Book Called "Ulysses."*

Judge Woolsey's decision became an immediate classic, and along with Ernst's brief preface was reprinted in the edition of *Ulysses* immediately set in print by Random House following his ruling. Ernst took Woolsey's ruling and tried in his preface to the book to make the largest possible claims for its effects on the law and literature. "It would be difficult to overestimate the importance of Judge Woolsey's decision. For decades the censors have fought to emasculate literature. They have tried to set up the sensibilities of the prudery-ridden as a criterion for society, have sought to reduce the reading matter of adults to the level of adolescents and subnormal persons, and have nurtured evasions and sanctimonies. The *Ulysses* case marks a turning point. It is a body-blow for the censors."[100]

It was not quite the end-of-censorship breakthrough that Ernst and others proclaimed. It was not a constitutional challenge to obscenity law, just a challenge to its application against "One Book Called *Ulysses*." But it helped turn the tide against the censorship of serious works of literature, and more important for literature generally, freed readers to wrestle with Joyce's great modernist achievement. It certainly helped make obscenity laws less capacious, giving judges language and criteria to assess works of literature that might also have libidinous effects, as did the subsequent opinion handed down by the Federal 2nd Circuit Court of Appeals in New York upholding Woolsey's decision, with Judge Augustus Hand writing the majority opinion, signed by his cousin Judge Learned Hand. Judge Martin Thomas Manton dissented.[101]

The majority decision of the 2nd Circuit Court of Appeals embraced Woolsey's key points, and was more expansive about the "taken as a whole" argument, which it referred to as the "dominant note of the publication" test while embracing the "libidinous effect" test Woolsey had laid out. Holding that "the same immunity should apply to literature as to science, where the presentation, when viewed objectively, is sincere, and the erotic matter is not introduced to promote lust and does not furnish the dominant note of the publication," Judge Hand added, "*The question in each case is whether a publication taken as a whole has a libidinous effect*" (emphasis added).[102]

## Conclusion

The *Ulysses* case was a significant development in the long process of transforming and narrowing nineteenth-century obscenity laws in the American courts in the 1920s and 1930s. It was also a signal achievement for Ernst and Lindey, a crucial part of their anticensorship campaign and overall challenge to the nation's obscenity laws and their goal of creating more room for serious, up-to-date, scientifically accurate information about sexuality while fostering a more robust literary marketplace of books that probed the mysteries of minds and bodies, works that had far greater value to actual readers than presumed harms to possible readers. Once he and Lindey began winning their series of obscenity cases in the New York city, state, and federal courts, they recognized that defending *Ulysses* would be, as Lindey predicted in 1931, "the grandest obscenity case in the history of law and literature."[103] The transformational authority of their cases is, in many ways, their greatest legacy.

The *Ulysses* case made Morris Ernst a celebrity of sorts, at least for a time. Ernst's fame in his era, and after, for being "the man who freed *Ulysses*" was the headline of his 1976 *New York Times* obituary, over forty years later. Freeing *Ulysses* marked a vital turning point in American obscenity jurisprudence and created greater room for modernist experimentation, offered greater protection for publishers who might wish to bring forth other literary works that challenged the tastes and sensibilities of the moral guardians, and allowed generations of readers to experience Joyce's magnificent treatment of one day in the mind of a Jewish Irishman wandering the streets of Dublin. Two Jewish lawyers in New York City—Ernst the son of a German-speaking Czech immigrant, and Lindey an immigrant of Hungarian origins—mastered the law, courted the press, cultivated New York's cosmopolitan intellectuals to aid their collective anticensorship goals, and persuaded the courts that Joyce's masterpiece ought to be available to all readers who were interested in tackling its complexities and willing to endure its nearly indecipherable passages. Their work was a monumental achievement in anticensorship jurisprudence, achieved on behalf of one of the great literary monuments of the twentieth century. Had Morris Ernst passed the troubled Leopold Bloom on the street he might not have noticed him, but he surely would have understood Bloom's sexual ruminations and troubles as being inescapably human, and profoundly important for that reason alone. If asked he might have even directed Bloom to a bookshop or a newsstand where, hidden below the counter, safe from the patrolmen, Bloom might find some useful, scientifically accurate pamphlets on better marital sex, something to take home to try and rekindle things with his affectionate, willing Molly.

# 6

## Laughter and Love between the Irish and the Jews

JAMES R. BARRETT

It is not as easy to characterize relations between Irish and Jewish Americans as conventional wisdom might suggest. Given their divergent religious and cultural traditions, as well as the competition for urban space and political power, there was plenty of room for conflict. On the other hand, both were minorities with long experiences of oppression, poverty-stricken immigrant peoples coming to terms with a new urban world. One might expect them to have a lot in common.

By the time large numbers of Eastern European Jews arrived in American cities in the late nineteenth century, millions of Irish immigrants and their children had settled in. Urban streets and institutions were often dominated by the Irish, and encounters between the two groups often led to conflict. Irish street gangs were particularly aggressive, but Jews also contended with bigoted cops and well-oiled Irish American political machines. Ignoring this background of intolerance can lead to misunderstandings of the relationship, but leaving the story here is equally misleading. As is often the case with the history of relations between ethnic groups in the city, the narrative is, or should be, a bit more complicated. There was clearly also an affinity between the two groups. What I have to say here acknowledges the element of conflict in the streets and elsewhere, but emphasizes that affinity, especially on stage and in music.

### Trouble in the Streets and at the Polls

Jewish immigration led to occasional tensions in Ireland, but anti-Semitism there was rare and violence nearly nonexistent. The small Jewish population occupied an important position in the nation's economy and, eventually, in its political life. The Irish might exhibit profound ignorance of Judaism, but they showed little overt hostility toward Jews. This suggests that the animus common among many Irish Americans was more a product of the American city than the Irish countryside.[1]

In New York, Chicago, and other cities, Jewish immigrant communities often developed in close proximity to Irish American turf. With Irish gangs in control of many streets, Italians, Jews, and other recent immigrants trod warily. Most gangs were defensive, University of Chicago sociologist Frederic Thrasher observed, but Irish gangs "seemed to look for trouble."[2] The Irish, and particularly young males, showed a strong sense of ethnic territoriality. Anti-Semitic comments and physical altercations were common, and Irish-dominated police departments often sympathized with the gangs. "When the Irish won," Abraham Bisno wrote of conflict with the gangs near the Chicago Ghetto, "it was not safe to show your face on the street for almost a week."[3]

The relationship between Irish American nationalism and Jewish immigrant Zionism is a case in point. On the one hand, American Zionists found inspiration in the Irish struggle for independence and a model of sorts in the group's large, well-organized nationalist groups. Irish nationalist leaders often stressed parallels between the two groups and expressed support for a Jewish homeland. On city streets, however, Irish Americans could and did attack Zionist symbols and demonstrations.[4]

Politics represented another source of conflict between the two groups, though again the relationship was rather complex as it evolved in the early twentieth century. The Irish certainly dominated the Tammany Hall machine throughout this era, and in the era around the turn of the century and even later, they resented Jews for a strong streak of political independence and some tendency toward political radicalism. Yet particularly in the Lower East Side and other areas with large Jewish populations, Irish politicians had little choice but to court Jewish voters and gradually integrate political operatives from the community. Moreover, some Tammany politicians displayed a genuine sense of appreciation of their Jewish constituents.

Big Tim Sullivan (1862–1913), boss of the Lower East Side, was raised in a tenement in the old Irish slum of Five Points, but he never missed a beat when the region's demographics shifted. He recruited a small army of Jewish and Italian operatives, and he seemed to thrive on the remarkable diversity of the neighborhoods and the vaudeville industry where he owned a string of theaters. He often showed up for events in the Jewish community wearing a yarmulke, and his 1913 funeral brought out a remarkable array of Lower East Side denizens. "The ethnic coalition that Sullivan put together, and its curious amalgam of party regularity, social-welfare reform, and organized vice," journalist William V. Shannon observed, "typified the Irish political machines that began to emerge in the 1890s and flourished in the first forty years of the twentieth century."[5]

John F. Ahearn (1853–1920), who also built his career on the Lower East Side and became Manhattan Borough President, was what one Tammany stalwart termed a "cosmopolitan." He ate corned beef and kosher food "with equal nonchalance," Tammany philosopher George Washington Plunkitt explained, "and it's all the same to him whether he takes his hat off in church or pulls it down over his ears in the synagogue. When he died, prayers were heard in more than one synagogue for this Catholic."[6]

None of this meant that the Irish shared many of the advantages that derived from the machine system. In 1910 Sullivan's district was 85 percent Jewish and Italian and only 5 percent Irish, yet from 1908 to 1933, every Lower East Side Tammany candidate for the Board of Aldermen, the State Assembly, and the Senate was Irish. As late as 1932, three-quarters of the Tammany leaders were Irish, only one-fifth Jewish.[7] Irish machines also tended to cling to control of city jobs long after the new immigrants arrived. In 1910, when New York City's foreign-born Irish population had fallen to 15 percent, one-third of all first-, second-, and third-generation Irish worked in the public sector—on the fire and police departments, on the publicly owned subways and buses, in the waterworks and port facilities, and in the public schools. When second-generation Jews began to enter public school teaching in larger numbers during the 1920s and 1930s, this often brought conflict with aging Irish American teachers and supervisors. This failure to share the spoils of machine politics led to resentment of the Irish, an insurgency based on second-generation Italians and Jews, and eventually to Fiorello La Guardia's reform-oriented machine and the decline of Tammany. In a striking metaphor for the change of power, Tammany's mortgage on its famous "Wigwam" headquarters was sold to the progressive, Jewish-led International Ladies' Garment Workers Union.[8]

In turn, an Irish backlash against the loss of jobs and political influence in the course of the Depression contributed to anti-Semitism and Irish support for right-wing movements in the 1930s, especially in Boston and New York. Although Catholic unions, journalists, and reform groups denounced anti-Semitism and continued to support social reform, Father Coughlin and other bigots derived significant support from Irish Americans, and this activism undoubtedly placed greater strain on Irish-Jewish relations. In the context of the Cold War and a domestic turn to the political right, a new conservative icon emerged—the Irish American FBI agent.[9]

Not surprisingly, while Jewish immigrants often embraced the Irish as model "Americans," their attitudes toward the Irish were often quite critical. Jewish residents in a predominantly Irish block in Harlem at the turn of the century found their Irish neighbors "drunken," "thriftless," and "careless." Such attitudes were common enough that Jews exchanged "Irish jokes" and a derogatory Yiddish term developed to refer to the Irish.[10] It is a mistake to ignore this very real tension between the two groups. Here, I would like to focus more on their affinity for and cooperation with one another, especially in the realm of popular culture.

## Vaudeville: The Stage Irishman-Jew

In its urban tenement setting, its concern with ethnic and racial difference, its often crude characterizations of a variety of ethnic groups, and its enormous popularity among immigrants and their children, vaudeville theater stood at the very center of popular culture in the increasingly diverse American city at the turn of the century. A strong "Celtic presence" characterized the vaudeville stage, its audience, and its entrepreneurs.[11] As in other realms of urban life, the Irish were deeply entrenched in musical theater long before the newer immigrants arrived and tried to make a place for themselves in the industry. They regularly took on the personae of others and peppered their performances with a good dose of self-deprecation, a characteristic, it seemed, of Irish humor. Even when it focused on Irish American themes, vaudeville resonated across ethnic lines with the urban experience of immigrant people and their children. "Elements of city life furnished the primary source of material. . . . Racial, occupational, sexual, and regional, national, and ethnic stereotypes all abounded."[12]

By the early years of the twentieth century, Irish performers increasingly shared the stage with Jews, Blacks, and other ethnic groups, but, again, they still exercised an important influence. "In vaudeville, Irish performers created a style that was both urban and ethnic," musician Mick Moloney writes. And to the extent that they conveyed an Irish "style," this was "intimately bound up with an urban sensibility."[13] Much of early vaudeville was dominated by Irish performers with experience in minstrelsy, but its interethnic quality at the turn of the century is particularly striking. As vaudeville blossomed, there were "Dutch" (German), Jewish, Irish, Black, and Italian acts performed by artists from a bewildering array of backgrounds. In this tendency to ethnically "cross-dress," vaudeville owed a great deal to minstrelsy, and like its forerunner, it was a distinctly American art form precisely because of its preoccupation with ethnicity and race.[14]

Such humor might be intentionally crude and even insulting to the targeted group, but its popularity with immigrants themselves also suggests what Joyce Flynn has termed a "cautious cosmopolitanism" in the musical theater of the early twentieth century. Audiences were drawn to the diversity that they saw about them in their neighborhoods and their daily lives. Their efforts to grasp and negotiate this diversity were reflected on the stages of the vaudeville circuit and immigrant audiences responded with enthusiasm.[15]

Many immigrant communities sustained their own foreign language theaters, Yiddish theater being the best example. But these ventures, deeply embedded in the various ethnic enclaves, operated toward very different ends from those of vaudeville. This theater was "a primary mechanism for the expression of ethnicity . . . and for projecting aspects of the Old-World experience deemed worthy of honor and remembrance. Ethnic theater thus functioned to maintain ethnic groups through the ritual celebration of shared ethnic cultural values. It provided a sense of belonging for the disoriented and dislocated."[16] Ethnic caricatures in mainstream venues served a different function, interpreting the burgeoning ranks of the foreign-born to the native-born middle class and, later, to ethnically mixed working-class audiences. From the late nineteenth through the early twentieth century, vaudeville was filled with stage "Dagos," "Micks," and others. One trade publication referred to a "Hebrew Craze" right at the turn of the century. Irish comics, singers, and dancers were involved in just such interpreting, but vaudeville ethnic humor and song represented something different, undoubtedly perpetuating negative stereotypes in an era of widespread xenophobia.[17]

Yet there was far more going on in the ethnic skits than attacks on one or another immigrant group. Ethnic stock characters were certainly stereotypes, but they often bore some resemblance to characters that immigrants and their children were apt to encounter on the streets of the Lower East Side, Chicago's near West Side, and other immigrant neighborhoods. A critic noted "how quick patrons of vaudeville are to recognize an act that comes near to the truth."[18] And it seemed to be this perceived "authenticity" as much as any slapstick humor that gave the acts their enormous popularity with their remarkably diverse audiences.[19]

The transgression of ethnic lines was central to one of the most popular acts of early twentieth-century vaudeville, the Jewish comedy team of Weber and Fields. The two appeared in blackface but then impersonated African Americans, Germans, and Irish. Influenced by the Irish minstrel performers McIntyre and Heath, in 1889 Weber and Fields joined a company specializing in Irish two-acts, then moved into traditional vaudeville performance. "Here we are, a colored pair," they announced in heavy Yiddish accents and minstrel outfits. Then they changed their ethnic makeup and costumes to fit the next stereotype—green satin breeches, black velvet coats, green bow ties, and green derbies to signal the Irish, but they changed not a word in any of their jokes. It was less the jokes and more the spectacle of the Jewish comics dressed in Irish outfits and the sound of them singing "Acushla Gal Machree" and other Irish-language songs in their Yiddish accents that the audiences seemed to love.[20] Likewise, audiences considered an Irish comic impersonating a Jewish or Chinese immigrant in a heavy brogue hilarious.

Political scientist Michael Rogin suggests why such theatrical transgressions of racial and ethnic boundaries were popular with early twentieth-century audiences. "In the hands, disproportionately, of Irish and then of Jewish entertainers, this ethno-cultural expression served a melting-pot function. . . . Facing nativist pressure that would assign them to the dark side of the racial divide, immigrants Americanized themselves by crossing and re-crossing the racial line."[21]

Thus, in providing a venue for their "Americanization," vaudeville might also start the recent immigrants on the road to a broader white identity, a journey that the Irish pioneered, but immigrant Jews also experienced.[22] When they did not signal outright hostility toward one group or another, ethnic skits represented immigrant performers and audiences working their way toward some understanding of one another.

Irish and other immigrant groups did react against these negative caricatures on the vaudeville stage. The Ancient Order of Hibernians launched a number of protests and boycotts against "stage Irishmen" in Chicago and elsewhere at least as early as the turn of the century and by 1904 they were calling for an end to Irish comic stereotypes in cartoons and newspaper features. "It is indecent to depict any race by its lowest feature," a reader wrote to the *New York Sun*, "and to hold up to ridicule an entire people because of any poverty or faults of a small number."[23]

The Hibernians and the nationalist Clan na Gael organization were also active in the unsuccessful 1910–11 national boycott of the Abbey Theatre ensemble's performances of John M. Synge's *Playboy of the Western World*, arguing that his portrayal of their idealized Irish peasant society reflected badly on Ireland and on its women in particular. The Hibernians and the Clan drove such protests, sometimes eventuating in "theater riots" where audiences pelted the performers with epithets and flying objects. In 1927 proposed legislation in New York would have empowered the commissioner of licenses to revoke the license of any theater showing a film that "maligns, ridicules or gives offense to any racial or religious group." Though the proponents were largely Irish Catholics, the bill was also supported by representatives of the city's Jewish community. Again, Irish Americans framed their complaints in the name of universal ethnic tolerance. "We believe in liberty," a speaker for the United Irish Societies declared before a public hearing on the bill, "but we are opposed to license which openly insults any race or creed. This is a free country. Let us make it free from prejudice."[24]

The same sort of sensitivity spread to other ethnic communities, particularly Jews, and the stock ethnic caricature so characteristic of vaudeville began to decline. "Someday," a theater manager wrote the home office in 1903, "the Hebrews are going to make as big a kick as the Irish did against this sort of burlesque of their nationality."[25] He was right. When Jews later launched their own protests against the more offensive vaudeville stereotypes, they distinguished, as Irish protesters had, between ethnic humor per se and offensive caricatures in particular. They also modeled their own boycotts and agitation on the Irish protests, but they also saw a difference in the two experiences. Dr. Emil Hirsch, a founder of the Anti-Defamation League in Chicago in 1913, highlighted the difference in the depictions of Irish and Jews. "A stage Irishman is funny and not offensive because he is a good-humored caricature," Hirsch reasoned. "We wouldn't mind being laughed at in that way." Many stage caricatures of Jews, however, were more sinister. Hirsch, who considered himself an "Irishman by adoption" and was a frequent guest at Chicago's Irish Fellowship Club, noted a "strange affinity between the Irishman and the Jew." Irish priests and community leaders often supported the efforts of the new league and others meant to discourage negative ethnic and racial stereotypes.[26]

The area along West Twenty-Eighth Street between Fifth and Sixth Avenues in Lower Manhattan, home to numerous songwriters and musical publishing firms, gave its name to the popular musical industry of the early twentieth century—Tin Pan Alley. Tin Pan Alley songs emerged in tandem with vaudeville. The songs, which enjoyed huge popularity in the decade before the First World War and through the 1920s, were often based on traditional Irish melodies and themes and invoked nostalgia for an idealized Ireland for which Irish American urbanites pined. But nostalgia for the Old World was not peculiar to the Irish, and immigrants and particularly the second generation in other ethnic communities responded. To the extent that the Irish were moving up, it was precisely this distance from their roots that produced such nostalgia in the second and third generations.

But Tin Pan Alley lyrics also reflected the diversity of the cities that provided both their settings and their audiences. The Irish remained as creators and subjects, but Jews increasingly dominated the industry. These and other groups were often in dialogue with one another across ethnic and racial lines. In the vaudeville song "The Kellys," a young immigrant from Cork encounters both the ubiquitous and upwardly mobile Irish and their diverse neighbors:

> I went to the directory me uncle for to find,
> But I found so many Kellys that I nearly lost me mind.
> So, I went to ask directions from a friendly German Jew,

But he says please excuse me but me name is Kelly too.
Dan Kelly runs the railroads, John Kelly runs the seas,
Kate Kelly runs the suffragettes and she looks right good to me.
Well I went and asked directions from a naturalized Chinese
But he says please excuse me but me name it is Kell Lee.[27]

Such lyrics were less the products of the immigrants themselves than of a second generation probing its place in American society in relation to other ethnic groups. Many songs reflected increasingly close relations between the Irish and other ethnic groups in diverse city neighborhoods. Intermarriage was one common theme with Irish men marrying or courting Indian, Hawaiian, or Arab women. By far the most common romantic pairing, however, was the Irish-Jewish match, as in "My Yiddisha Colleen" and "It's Tough When Izzy Rosenstein Loves Genevieve Malone." The humor tended to be more at the expense of the Jews than the Irish, yet it displayed a clear affinity between the two groups. In some degree it might also have reflected developing political alliances. "If It Wasn't for the Irish and the Jews," the creation of an Irish-Jewish team, Jerome (William Flannery) and Schwartz, suggests both of these traits:

> Talk about a combination,
> Hear my words and make a note,
> On St. Patrick's Day Rosinsky,
> Pins a shamrock on his coat.
> There's a sympathetic feeling,
> Between the Blooms and McAdoos,
> Why Tammany would surely fall,
> There'd really be no hall at all,
> If it wasn't for the Irish and the Jews.[28]

## The Irish and the Jews in Love: *Abie's Irish Rose*

Interethnic love and marriage was a theme in vaudeville and then in film at least as early as the 1912 silent *Becky Gets a Husband*, but this trope matured on stage and screen with the second generation in Irish and other immigrant communities. In the early 1920s the movie, play, and novel *Abie's Irish Rose* captured the imagination of a wide segment of the US public by sympathetically depicting the love between a second-generation Jewish immigrant man and a second-generation Irish American woman. Rose's father, Patrick Murphy, a contractor from County Kerry, represented one possible response to the ethnic and racial other, while his priest represents another. Patrick is full of ethnic humor and stories about youthful Jewish-Irish fights in the streets of New York. Objecting to the proposed marriage on the basis of stereotypes, Patrick is confronted on his racism and anti-Semitism by a remarkable Irish priest. Wildly successful, despite some hostile reviews, the play ran for over 2,300 performances on Broadway and then toured the United States for several months. It spawned two separate film adaptations, a weekly radio show through the early 1940s, and was revived twice on Broadway.[29]

*Abie's Irish Rose* was representative of a much broader cultural phenomenon that featured Irish-Jewish romances in scores of ragtime songs, in other stage productions, and in twenty-one other films between 1921 and 1930.[30] Jewish-Irish comic pairings were a staple on the vaudeville stage and sports fans followed the antics of Jewish and Irish roommates and teammates on the New York Giants and the Chicago White Sox. By the twenties, if not earlier, rabbis and other representatives of the Jewish community often spoke at St. Patrick's Day celebrations.[31] The theme clearly resonated widely and had a deep meaning for its audiences. What was going on here?

Such films and plays were largely intended for and viewed by second-generation ethnic audiences, including large numbers of Irish Americans and Jews, especially in large cities like New York and Chicago. Negotiating their own sense of ethnic identity, such audiences were drawn on the one hand to older stock ethnic characters, like Abie's and Rose's parents, who helped them to label and distance themselves from the first generation in their own communities. As "Americans," they were leaving the old-fashioned values and prejudices behind. On the other hand, they were drawn to characters like Abie and Rose who, like themselves, were working out their attitudes toward the second generation in other ethnic communities. Vaudeville's ethnic cross-dressing reappears in these films with young Jewish and Irish Catholic characters assuming one another's ethnic backgrounds in an effort to reassure or deceive their families.

Songs, plays, and movies continued to depict the Irish American woman as a vehicle for both comedy and the assimilation of new immigrants. "If the melting pot existed, it was in the cultural imagination of the 1920s."[32]

Yet ethnic intermarriage, though rare in the first generation, increased from that point on in New York and elsewhere—between the Irish, the Jews, and young people from various other ethnic backgrounds. Like other ethnic groups, the Irish were more likely to marry within their own community and even in the second generation, more likely to marry with other Catholic ethnic groups. Still, Irish American women were viewed as more eligible, and, in fact, did intermarry more often than women from other immigrant groups and far more often than Irish American men. One explanation for this was that women outnumbered men among Irish immigrants, especially from the late nineteenth century on, a rare situation among more recent immigrant groups in the same era. Thus, Irish women were more available partners for single immigrant men. Earlier intermarriage between Irish women and African and Chinese American men in the nineteenth century may have enhanced their reputation as eligible partners (even as it contributed to fears of "racial amalgamation"). Also, since intermarriage was more common in the second and third generation, the Irish, as one of the earliest large immigrant groups, were already turning this corner by the early twentieth century. Jews were particularly endogamous, especially in the first and to some extent in the second generation, so Irish-Jewish intermarriage might have been more imagined than real, but it was not unknown.[33]

Thus, another possible explanation for the ubiquity of this theme is less optimistic—a considerable level of anxiety over the whole issue of intermarriage as the ultimate test case for interethnic relations. Like the fictional one in *Abie's Irish Rose*, mixed marriages generally were relationships in which tension continued: Would the Irish and new immigrants mix and if so, on what basis? Given the strength of ethnic cultures in the immigrant generation, many were concerned about what identities the children of such "mixed marriages" would carry. In *Abie's Irish Rose*, Rosemary Murphy and Abraham Levy symbolically sidestep the looming conflict by marrying before neither a priest nor a rabbi, but a Methodist minister.

Yet many of the Irish-Jewish plays and films seemed genuinely concerned with using these interethnic love affairs to display an affinity between the two communities. At their best, these productions conveyed a sense of ethnic and racial tolerance. Given the strength of ethnic and religious prejudice in these years, it would be a mistake to read too much into such images, but the extreme popularity of these plays and films suggests a longing for interethnic tolerance in a large part of the second-generation immigrant population.[34]

Relations between the Irish and the Jews in American cities suggest the full range of possibilities—from violent confrontations in the street to political competition and cooperation, from fictional representations of one another on stage and in song to romantic love and intermarriage. Such relations, like those among other ethnic groups in the American city, were neither stable nor simple. In their complexity and uneven qualities, they helped to shape a new urban culture that was the creation not of one group or another but, rather, the product of the interactions among them all.

7

# Irish-Jewish Couples in American Film and Television

LAWRENCE BARON

When the short silent film *Becky Gets a Husband* premiered in 1912, it ushered in the cinematic trope of the religiously irreconcilable, but romantically irresistible Irish-Jewish couple. Living next door to each other, Becky Cohen and Pat Casey flirted and fell in love. Although their mothers approved of the relationship, their fathers vehemently opposed it. At the wedding the fathers quarrel, sparking a brawl between the Irish and Jewish guests with each group siding with their coreligionists. Unable to restore order, an Irish and a Jewish cop call for the Fire Department to intervene and douse the flaring tempers with cold water.[1]

*Becky Gets a Husband* belonged to a trend in American silent films that highlighted the competitive, cordial, or hostile relationships among the diverse ethnic, racial, and religious groups who immigrated to the United States during the late nineteenth and early twentieth centuries until the 1920s when the Johnson-Reed Act sharply reduced the numbers of immigrants admitted to the country. These movies typically contrasted the parochialism of first-generation immigrant parents with the open-mindedness of their American-born children.[2] That recently arrived Jewish characters frequently appeared opposite their Christian counterparts in such motion pictures drew on earlier literary and stage traditions of dramatizing romances between Christians and Jews to illustrate that coupling with Jews either posed a religious, sexual, and social danger to the predominantly Christian populations of Europe and the United States or represented the fulfillment of the secular egalitarianism of liberalizing and modernizing Western societies.[3]

This chapter focuses on the evolution of Irish-Jewish love stories first in American feature films and then in television shows. The messages conveyed by these motion pictures and programs changed as the status of both groups shifted from despised immigrant outsiders to upwardly mobile insiders within the United States. Similarly, the outcomes resulting from such marriages and romances altered as the multicultural model of a heterogeneous society supplanted the melting-pot paradigm of a homogeneous one. The nature of internal censorship within the film industry and external pressure from Catholic, Jewish, and Protestant advocacy groups also influenced how Irish-Jewish love stories were conceptualized.

The transition from social interactions defined by class, ethnic, familial, or religious backgrounds to those conducted with individuals not sharing those affiliations became the grist of much Irish and Jewish American comedy, drama, film, and music in the periods when their waves of arrival in the United States overlapped. Irish and Jewish immigrants and their children played a disproportionate role in the composition, performance, and production of plays, songs, and vaudeville skits satirizing interethnic amicability and animosity. Between 1820 and 1860, two million Irish Catholics fled persecution, poverty, and hunger in their homeland to build a better life in the United States. In the ensuing sixty years, the Irish sought opportunity and refuge there in even greater numbers.[4] Around 135,000 Jews from Central Europe entered the United States in the same period as the first great wave of Irish immigration.[5] Between 1880 and 1920, two million Jews joined the influx of over twenty million people from Southern and Eastern Europe seeking American citizenship.[6] Talented members of both groups gravitated to the burgeoning field of entertainment where they faced less entrenched discrimination, permitting them to express their aspirations and experiences to fellow immigrants.

While the Irish and Jewish newcomers were segregated initially by communal affiliations, language, religious worship, and residential neighborhoods, they encountered each other in business, government, law enforcement, or schools.[7] Within the realm of popular culture, they often mocked and stereotyped each other, but Irish-Jewish comedy and songwriting teams developed as well.[8] Such teams explored the humorous incongruities between the two groups, but also the serious consequences if casual relationships blossomed into intimate ones in violation of parochial loyalties. In the years before the release of *Becky Gets a Husband*, American audiences already were listening to songs like "It's Tough When Izzy Rosenstein Loves Genevieve Malone," "My Yiddisha Colleen," and "Yiddisha Luck and Irisha Love" with its stomach-churning verse: "Corn beef and gefilte fish, mixed together, that's a dish."[9]

The early silent movies about interethnic marriages and relationships mirrored the ambivalence Americans exhibited toward the European immigrants who entered the country from the late nineteenth century until World War I. Nativists clamoring for immigration restriction perceived the immigrants, starting with Irish Catholics and the subsequent influx from southeastern Europe, as a biological threat to the white Anglo-Saxon Protestant founders of the nation and corrupters of the culture, economy, mores, and political system they had established. Proponents of immigration believed the newcomers would assimilate and lose their distinctiveness when they became citizens. Depending on one's viewpoint, interethnic romances and intermarriage could erode or enhance the American way of life.[10]

Though immigrants hailing from many countries appeared in American silent films, Irish and Jewish characters emerged as the most likely to meet each other as adoptive parents of orphans, boxers, business partners, customers, friends, and rivals in silent short films watched at penny arcades and nickelodeons by poor immigrant viewers who recognized the ethnic caricatures, relationships, and tensions being portrayed even when they could not read the English intertitles.[11] As Mari Kathleen Fielder has observed, "That the Irish and Jews were mutually alien in so many ways actually enhanced their appeal for entertainment purveyors intent on creating heightened dramatic conflict and appeasing the audience's fears about the chaotic, polyglot city."[12] Nevertheless, plotlines specifically about Irish-Jewish couples were not common until the 1920s. Only *Becky Gets a Husband* and *For the Love of Mike and Rosie* (1916) fall into this category. While love prevails in the former, the melee with which it concludes corroborates nativist perceptions of the Irish and Jews as overly contentious and emotional. The latter explicitly reinforces this impression by pitting a boxer dubbed the "Jewish Lion" against his presumed Irish rival in a boxing match for the affections of Rosie Goldfinger. Unbeknownst to the "Lion," Rosie's Irish suitor hires a ringer nicknamed the "Irish Terror" to pummel him.[13]

Since the mass emigration of Jews from Czarist Russia fleeing discrimination, pogroms, and poverty to the United States continued until the outbreak of World War I, star-crossed romances between their children and those of their persecutors appeared more frequently on screen than Irish-Jewish ones until the 1920s. Family and religious ties proved stronger than love in films set in the shtetls. In *Broken Barriers* (1919) based on a Sholem Aleichem story, the prodigal daughter Khavah renounces her marriage to a Russian peasant, repulsed by his family's abusiveness and coarseness and outraged by the edict expelling Jews from her village. She learns that her father had been right about how her marriage was doomed from its inception: "Fedka is a fine boy but Jew and Gentile—oil and water."[14] Conversely, mixed Russian and Jewish couples in the United States could overcome the historical enmity between their kinfolk there. The movie adaptation of Israel Zangwill's *The Melting Pot* (1915) paid tribute to American tolerance by not allowing bitter bygones to sever the romantic bonds between the daughter of a Russian governor who ordered the massacre of a Jewish village and the son whose parents were slaughtered by her father.[15]

From 1923 until 1928, seventeen films about Irish-Jewish couples were produced, displacing those about Russian-Jewish pairings as the most popular type of star-crossed couple.[16] Several factors account for this shift in ethnic configurations. During World War I, Thomas Edison's attempt to monopolize film production through the Motion Picture Patents Company on the East Coast was blocked by the courts, and the center of filmmaking shifted to the predominantly Jewish-owned studios located in Hollywood.[17] Edison's company tended to portray new immigrants in general and Jews in particular more negatively than the ascendant Hollywood studios.[18] Moreover, the Supreme Court ruled in 1915 that cities and states could establish censorship boards to regulate films that it classified as interstate commerce and not constitutionally protected free speech.[19]

Developments in the politics of immigration and film censorship during the 1920s also affected how Jewish and Irish characters were portrayed during that decade. The nativist campaign against unfettered immigration had gained enough momentum to pass increasingly restrictive legislation in 1921 and 1924 limiting the numbers of immigrants admitted to the country.[20] Lessening those numbers had the paradoxical effect of enhancing the suitability of earlier immigrant groups as protagonists of "melting pot" narratives. As Thomas Cripps observes, "With

Ellis Island closed, thus denying anti-Semites their bugbear—the threat of inundation of Anglo-Saxon culture by 'Mittel Europa'—Hollywood in the twenties used cinema to define Americanism as an unthreatening drift toward assimilation, a path many studio heads had already personally chosen."[21]

During the 1920s conservative Protestant organizations and powerful public figures like Henry Ford channeled the backlash against the Bolshevik Revolution, Jazz Age libertinism, organized crime, and a series of Hollywood scandals to exert pressure for federal censorship to curb the deleterious influence of movies. They attributed the medium's glorification of sex, vice, and violence to the amoral, deracinated, and greedy Jewish movie "moguls" who were foreign-born or raised by immigrant parents.[22] To avert federal censorship, the studios formed the Motion Picture Producers and Distributors of America (MPPDA) in 1922 to improve Hollywood's reputation, lobby against federal regulation, and recommend guidelines for appropriate movie content that ideally would not ridicule any nation, creed, or clergy.[23] Catholic and Jewish defense organizations differed on whether such policing should be exercised by government or internally by the industry itself, but agreed on the need to prevent defamatory depictions of their respective adherents and beliefs.[24] The threat of federal censorship and the MPPDA's input contributed to more positive cinematic images of immigrant groups including the Irish and the Jews. So did the evolution of movies from a crude form of entertainment for urban audiences comprised of immigrants and working-class Americans to fare that would appeal to their socially mobile children and middle- and upper-class Americans in both rural and urban areas.[25]

Why did the predominantly Jewish studio owners seize upon the theme of Irish-Jewish couples to symbolize the Americanization of their coreligionists and their shedding of Old World tribalism for the sake of love? While these pairings appeared on the silver screen with increasing frequency, this did not reflect any significant uptick in their numbers in real life. The intermarriage rate among Jews was under 1 percent among first-generation immigrants and less than 3.5 percent among their children.[26] The rates of intermarriage for Irish immigrants, particularly women who outnumbered Irish men, were higher than those of Jews but tended to be with American-born Christians or other ethnic Catholics.[27]

Whatever affinities existed between the Irish and the Jews did not usually translate into halcyon relations between the two groups. The Irish had arrived earlier in the United States than the surge of Eastern European Jewish immigrants at the end of the nineteenth century. By the 1920s they had carved out their occupational niches in American cities as civil servants, domestics, factory workers, firefighters, entertainers, manual laborers, police, politicians, pub owners, and schoolteachers.[28] Recent Jewish immigrants often found themselves in competition with the Irish for jobs or dependent on those who occupied positions of authority. Since the vast majority of Jews hailed from countries where they had endured persecution, they harbored bitter memories of their former tormentors that accompanied them to America. There simply weren't many who came from Ireland whose Jewish population was minuscule, rendering the Irish an unknown quantity to them.[29] Both groups had endured systemic discrimination in their homelands and considered themselves in exile.[30] Yet their cultures, lifestyles, and values clashed considerably. Residing near or within each other's enclaves, many of their youth engaged in gang battles. Overall, their relations with each other were generally marked by cloistered indifference or hostility.[31]

Disregarding the rarity of Irish-Jewish intermarriages and the tenor of their daily interactions, Hollywood filmmakers confidently dismissed the ethnic or theological distrust that divided the two groups as vestiges of the Old World mentalities that had plagued the first generation of immigrants, but no longer inhibited their children from marrying each other and hastening their integration into American society. Timothy Meagher ascribes these filmmakers' fixation on Irish-Jewish coupling to several factors. Each group possessed familiar stereotypes and traits portrayed in literature, music, prewar silent films, theater, and vaudeville. Having been in the country longer than the Eastern European Jewish immigrants, the Irish had earned the grudging respect of their fellow citizens. In the eyes of Gentile audiences, the marriages of the Americanized children of first-generation Irish and Jewish immigrants diminished the sense of foreignness associated with their parents. Matrimony between Irish and Jewish characters diluted ethnic and religious differences that the American melting-pot ideal aimed at dissolving. Simultaneously, the accents, rituals, and traits performed by the mothers and fathers of the couples featured in these films elicited feelings of ethnic continuity and nostalgia among Irish and Jewish moviegoers.[32]

The commercial impetus for why Hollywood recycled scenarios about Irish-Jewish couples in so many films during the twenties also lies in the phenomenal success of Anne Nichols's play *Abie's Irish Rose*. It broke Broadway box-office records, running for 2,327 performances from 1922 until 1927. At the height of its popularity, theaters throughout the United States and the world staged it.[33] In 1927 Nichols authored a novel based on the play.[34] The next year it was adapted into a film released in a longer silent version and a shorter sound version that featured the chanting of the kaddish and a few lines of dialogue.[35]

Though the play didn't invent the embattled Irish-Jewish lovers' plotline, it demonstrated its popular appeal and served as the template for subsequent movies revolving around the feuds between the Irish and Jewish first-generation immigrant parents and their second-generation children who intermarried. The opening of the movie testifies to the pre-1921 American hospitality toward immigrants, the grateful patriotism of its beneficiaries, and the equality afforded all citizens as visualized in footage of immigrants arriving at Ellis Island, an ethnically and racially diverse school class of children including the young Abie Levy pledging allegiance to the flag, and a segue shot of the boots of marching soldiers encapsulated by the intertitle: "So they went to that baptism of fire and thunder—Catholics, Hebrews, and Protestants alike—newsboys and college boys—aristocrats and immigrants—all classes, all creeds, all Americans."[36] Abie and Rosemary Murphy meet in France during World War I, where he had been wounded and she entertained the troops. Upon their return to the United States, they wed in a Methodist service, a compromise choice American Protestants probably deemed gratifying.

Although the fathers of the couple are middle-class, their ethnic roots manifest themselves in their ethnically coded accents, mannerisms, and sectarianism. The Irish father, however, is palpably more Americanized than the Jewish one.[37] Abie and Rosemary attempt to deceive their fathers about the true identity of their spouse. Abie introduces his wife as Rosie Murpherski to his father Solomon and agrees to being married by a rabbi to assure him that Rosie is a bona fide Jew. Relieved that Rosie isn't Irish, Solomon recounts a bad experience he once had with an Irishman. Solomon insists that the couple invite Rosie's father to the wedding. In her telegram to her father Patrick, she tells him the groom's name is Michael Magee. Entering the Levys' home, Patrick suspects the Levys are Protestants because their home is decorated with oranges, the color associated with Irish Protestants. Solomon explains that he selected this motif to make Rosie and Patrick comfortable since they were from California. Both fathers quickly see through the ruse and banish their children. The rabbi and the priest Solomon and Patrick hired to officiate Jewish and Catholic marriage ceremonies counsel the fathers to forgive their children. So does Solomon's friend Mrs. Cohen. After Rosie gives birth to twins, the fathers consent to visit their grandchildren for the first time on Christmas Eve. Their objections to the marriage fade away upon learning that the baby girl has been named after Abie's deceased mother and the baby boy after Rose's father. The priest exclaims, "Now if the Jews and the Irish would stop fighting and get together, they'd own a corner of the world!"[38]

Scholars of cinematic and literary representations of ethnicity disagree over the religious connotations of the film. Fielder contends that the celebration of Christmas by Jewish characters without a reciprocal observance of a Jewish ritual by the Irish characters implies that the majority faith prevailed in such mixed marriages.[39] Perhaps the most blatant example of this trend occurred in the earlier silent movie *The Jew's Christmas* (1913) wherein a rabbi who had cast out his daughter for marrying a Gentile eventually celebrates the holiday to endear himself to a girl living in his apartment building who turns out to be her child.[40] These films, however, never entertain conversion of either spouse as a solution. The producer of *Abie's Irish Rose* sought to be evenhanded and hired a rabbi and a priest to serve as consultants about how to stage the religious rites that were performed in it.[41] Ted Merwin argues that contemporary critics who censure the play and film for caricaturing the fathers' behaviors and beliefs to promote assimilation miss the point that the majority of Irish and Jewish audience members felt the distinctiveness and malleability of their cultures had been validated.[42]

The gender politics underlying *Abie's Irish Rose* also have stimulated much academic debate. Riv-Ellen Prell interprets the recurring trope of Jewish men marrying Gentile women in film, literature, and the theater as an assimilationist male strategy to escape the taint of anti-Semitic stereotypes that get projected onto Jewish women.[43] She notes that the rotund Mrs. Cohen dresses garishly and possesses an overbearing personality, contrasting sharply with Rosemary's American good looks, reserve, and stylish clothing.[44] Jewish men courting or marrying Jewish women, however, constituted the exception in this cycle of films as will be discussed below. Fielder asserts that the preponderance of Irish male and Jewish female pairings in these movies meant "that the Irish, not Jewish, name would be carried on and that the Irishman would rule over his Jewish wife in the American home setting."[45] Neither Abie nor Rosemary conforms to the sexual dynamics Joshua Louis Moss discerns as driving the plots of prior literary and film narratives about Anglo-Jewish love.[46] What is conspicuous about the partners in the 1920s film is that their affection for each other and their attractiveness are rendered wholesome and thus unthreatening to Protestant Americans. Christopher Shannon also cautions against generalizing from such films that Irish characters were obsessed with finding Jewish partners. He reminds readers of his book on the depiction of American Irish figures in Hollywood films that there was a spate of films about "Bowery Cinderellas," working-class Irish women who either resisted abandoning their ethnic and humble roots by marrying a rich WASP as evidenced in *Amarilly of Clothes-Line Alley* (1918) or who achieved social mobility by marrying one as happens in *Irene* (1926).[47]

Sixty percent of the Irish-Jewish couples appearing in films from the twenties were comprised of Irish men dating or marrying Jewish women. *The Cohens and the Kellys* (1926), the most successful of these, spawned six sequels set in different locales.[48] It pitted a struggling Jewish shop owner against an Irish policeman, both of whom resided in a neighborhood where "there are three races, Irish, Jewish, and innocent bystanders." Nannie Cohen and Tim Kelly fall in love and secretly marry. Meanwhile, Jacob Cohen inherits a fortune from a great-aunt and buys a mansion, but forbids Tim to visit Nannie there. Upset at the prospect of Tim dating his daughter, he berates Patrick Kelly over the phone and temporarily goes to Florida. While he is away, Nan reveals to her mother that she is married to Tim and gives birth to a baby girl. Upon his return, Jacob forbids the Kellys access to their grandchild and disavows his daughter who moves in with the Kellys. In an implausible plot twist, a Jewish lawyer reveals that Jacob's great-aunt was also related to Patrick and intended him to be the heir to her wealth. The lawyer promises not to disclose this if Jacob will split the money with him. Jacob refuses to lie and tells Patrick, who rewards him by becoming Jacob's business partner. The harmony quickly dissipates as the two men argue over whose name will be listed first on their store's sign. The plot of Irish and Jewish parents at loggerheads with their intermarried children had become so hackneyed by 1930 that a federal judge ruled against Anne Nichols in her copyright-infringement lawsuit against *The Cohens and the Kellys* on the grounds that the movie's stock ethnic characters were so clichéd that he considered them in the public domain.[49]

A second kind of Irish-Jewish romance from the 1920s minimizes ethnic and religious differences as the source of generational conflict. Instead, the vocational choices made by the American-born children of immigrants trigger family discord. The film *His People* (1925) depicts the patriarch of the Cominsky family doting on his older son Morris for becoming a lawyer while frowning upon his brother Sammy for boxing and gambling.[50] Assuming his lower-class and Eastern European Jewish background might hurt his chances in wooing the daughter of an upper-class German Jewish judge, Morris claims he is an orphan who raised himself up by his own bootstraps; whereas his brother clandestinely pursues his career as a prizefighter under the fearsome Irish moniker the "Battling Rooney." Sammy and Mamie Shannon have been sweethearts since childhood. Mamie and her mother live in the flat across the airshaft from the Cominskys' tenement flat. They are presented as the only "foreigners" in the Jewish neighborhood, and Mamie is described as "so sweet, you wouldn't know she was an Irisher." As soon as his mother and father sit down to eat, Sammy glimpses Mamie in the window of her apartment and leaves the table to chat with her. Morris rushes through the meal so he can visit his girlfriend. The scene imparts how areligious the two brothers are and how Mamie already is a de facto member of their family. The only other Irish reference in the film is when Mrs. Shannon prescribes corned beef and cabbage to hasten Mr. Cominsky's recuperation from pneumonia. The inevitable marriage of Sammy and Mamie apparently does not bother Mr. Cominsky as much as his realization that Morris cares less about his father than Sammy, who fights a highly ranked boxer to win money to pay his parents' expenses to move to a warmer climate more conducive to Mr. Cominsky's health.[51]

*The Jazz Singer* (1927) deploys a similar narrative strategy. The play and movie revolve around the conflict between a father's insistence that his son Jakie follow in his footsteps as a cantor and Jakie's desire to be a pop singer.[52] Although it is left open whether the dancer Mary Dale who promotes Jakie's musical career under the stage name Jack Robins is Irish, the casting of the Irish American actress May McEvoy lends itself to this interpretation. In the original short story on which the play and movie were based, Jack's paramour and patron is Amy Prentiss who is the daughter of a Boston lawyer. A Jewish chorus girl attracted to Jack speculates that Amy's allure is that she's a *shiksa* from a wealthy family.[53] Given the Boston connection, it is plausible that Amy hails from a "lace curtain Irish" family. Jack's engagement to Mary in tandem with his occupational preference precipitates his father's death. The movie relegates the Jewish-Gentile element of the story to a cursory exchange between Jack's mother, who fears the Mary Dale whom Jack writes to her about may be a Gentile, and Mr. Yudelson, a neighborhood elder who allays her worries by surmising that Dale is a stage name masking her Jewish one. The ending tacked onto the movie shows Jack's mother kvelling at his Broadway premier and Mary standing in the wings admiring his talent. The happy ending implies that the mother won't object to Jack marrying Mary.[54]

The heyday of the Irish-Jewish romance ceased with the onset of the Great Depression. High unemployment exacerbated ethnic, racial, and social tensions. To stall moves for the imposition of federal censorship laws, the MPPDA promulgated a more comprehensive and strict Production Code in 1930 to suppress the glorification of crime, sex, and other vices, as well as derogatory portrayals of ethnic and religious groups. Four years lapsed between the formulation of the code and the appointment of Joseph Breen of the Catholic Legion of Decency to head the Production Code Administration (PCA) to enforce its criteria for permissible movie content. During the interlude the studios pushed the limits of what was deemed taboo in a film. Some of them burrowed into the seamier side of American life emblematized by the country's ethnic, racial, and socioeconomic fault lines.[55]

Movies about the immigrant populations of big cities unmasked the biases and conflicts that tore at the social fabric of their neighborhoods. King Vidor's 1931 adaptation of the play *Street Scene* (1931) by Elmer

Rice, who penned the script, falls into this genre.[56] Inculcated in his Jewish grandfather's atheism and socialism, Rice never received a Jewish education and suffused his plays with politically and socially relevant themes.[57] Staged entirely in front of a Hell's Kitchen tenement, *Street Scene* portrays the overtly cordial but covertly hostile interactions of the ethnically diverse residents of the building. One of these subplots concerns Sam Kaplan's infatuation with Rose Maurrant. Modeled on Rice's grandfather, Sam's father sticks his head out of a window reading a Yiddish newspaper and pontificating to his neighbors about class conflict. Sam has almost completed college and intends to go to law school. Sam's mother frets that he will marry Rose whose abusive and alcoholic father is a "nothing" in her eyes. Worried that Sam's love for Rose will derail his legal studies, Sam's sister nips whatever romantic attraction exists between Sam and Rose by advising Rose to leave her brother. A tough Irish hooligan flirts with Rose and mocks Sam for lacking the physical prowess to defend himself. Rose follows the sister's recommendation. The class and ethnic differences are placed in stark relief by juxtaposing the intellectuality and passivity of Sam with the bullying of the Irishman and the drunkenness and violent predisposition of Rose's father who ultimately shoots and kills her mother for having an affair.[58]

Several factors diminished the prominence of Jewish characters in the Hollywood movies produced under Breen's stewardship of the PCA after 1934. Breen privately harbored defamatory sentiments about the Jewish studio owners, but in his official capacity he demanded redactions or shelving of scripts whose treatment of Jewish characters or themes might provide grist for anti-Semitic demagogues who denounced Hollywood for promoting Jewish causes—or scripts that criticized Nazi anti-Semitism because Germany threatened to bar all of a studio's productions from distribution if one of them offended the country's reputation. In effect this relegated the on-screen presence of Jews to minor roles or eliminated them from the casts of characters altogether.[59] The Irish-Jewish symbiosis reappeared in innocuous forms like the Jewish pawnbroker Dave Morris, who contributes money to Father Flanagan to keep Boys Town financially afloat in the eponymous movie (1938) about the famed orphanage.[60]

During World War II, the Office of War Information and its Bureau of Motion Pictures sought to align movie content with government propaganda. One of its guidelines stipulated that the movie industry should "emphasize that this country is a melting pot, a nation of many races and creeds, who have demonstrated that they can live together and progress."[61] Even before the United States entered the conflict, *The Fighting 69th* (1940) included a subplot about a Jewish soldier who passed himself off as Irish to enlist in the largely Irish American infantry regiment that distinguished itself during World War I.[62] It preceded a cycle of wartime films about multiethnic platoons in which Irish, Jewish, and other ethnic GIs literally become comrades in arms in the struggle against a common enemy.[63]

The revelations about the Holocaust in the last year of the war alongside public opinion polls measuring high levels of American anti-Semitism heightened public sensitivities about how Jews should be depicted in movies. Hollywood films gingerly broached the subject of American anti-Semitism toward the end of the war and more forthrightly in its aftermath with motion pictures like *Pride of the Marines* (1945), *Crossfire*, and *Gentleman's Agreement* (1947).[64] The unfavorable critical reception of the remake of *Abie's Irish Rose* (1946) reflected this new awareness.[65] The film rehashed its namesake's premise, but updated it with Abie meeting and marrying Rose on VE Day in London where she was entertaining American troops. A Protestant army chaplain marries them. The couple predictably dupes their parochial fathers about their spouse's religious affiliation and consents to separate Jewish and Catholic weddings. When their cover story unravels, they are disowned. At Christmas the fathers relent in their disapproval of the marriage, mollified by their children conferring an Irish and a Jewish name on their newborns. An Irish policeman lulls the babies to sleep by singing an Irish and then a Jewish lullaby. The trite plotline sparked more consternation than laughs. One film reviewer opined, "What may have been comical to the public in years gone by is no longer funny in these critical days. Having just emerged from a world conflict that was sparked by racial intolerance, the public is in no mood to find comedy in situations or characterizations that tend to degrade peoples."[66]

From 1945 until the 1960s, most films about relationships between Irish and Jewish characters eschewed controversy by soft-pedaling romantic entanglements between them in preference of less discordant affinities. *The Jolson Story* (1946) chronicles the show-business saga of its protagonist, but when it dramatizes his tempestuous marriage to the Irish American dancer Ruby Keeler, renamed Julie Benson in the film, it portrays her introduction to Jolson's family as amicable and omits any mention that her parents objected to her betrothal to Jolson until he bestowed a million dollars on her as a prenuptial gift.[67] *Crossfire* links anti-Irish and anti-Jewish bigotry in the United States when the Irish detective investigating the murder of a Jewish veteran perceives the killing of his grandfather at the hands of an anti-Irish mob and of the Jewish soldier as analogous hate crimes.[68] In the saccharine-sweet *Big City* (1948), a Protestant minister, a rabbi, and an Irish policeman jointly raise an abandoned orphan. They co-parent harmoniously until the policeman weds a nightclub singer whose lifestyle is unacceptable to the two clergymen. The three men resume caring for their daughter together when she delivers an ultimatum that she be placed in an orphanage if she can't stay with all of them.[69] The remake of *The Jazz Singer* (1951) alters the names of the lead Jewish singer and his presumably Gentile female lover and promoter. Audience expectations that an intermarriage might be in the offing are dashed when he brings her to his family's Seder and she remarks that she hasn't attended one since she moved away from home.[70]

By the 1960s the forces that had inhibited Hollywood from tackling more controversial issues or presenting alternatives to the melting-pot model of assimilation were waning. In 1952 the Supreme Court established the precedent that movies were a form of free speech. The retirement of Joseph Breen two years later further diminished the dwindling influence of the Production Code Administration, whose guidelines were replaced by an advisory rating system in 1968.[71] The studio system that empowered the film companies to exercise inordinate control over actors' careers, script content, and theatrical distribution was crumbling by the end of the 1950s owing to unfavorable judicial decisions and the deaths of the founding Jewish movie moguls, most of whom shunned making films that were too Jewish.[72] Finally, the antiwar, civil rights, and youth movements of the sixties inspired the grandchildren of immigrants to reclaim their ethnic, racial, or religious heritages in what evolved into the identity politics of the 1970s.[73] These developments encouraged Jewish filmmakers to spotlight their ethnic backgrounds in ways that previously would have been rejected by the PCA and the studios.[74]

This engendered a second wave of Gentile-Jewish romance movies in which the Jewish partner was visibly and verbally Jewish and the Gentile partner was an attractive Christian. Unlike in past films, however, these relationships were doomed because the cultural chasm between the couples could not be bridged. Elaine May's *The Heartbreak Kid* (1972), Sydney Pollock's *The Way We Were* (1973), and Woody Allen's *Annie Hall* (1977) exemplify this cycle of films in which distinctly Jewish leads ultimately realize that their Gentile lovers do not share their values.[75]

*The Heartbreak Kid* is the only one of these movies where the Christian mate is presumably Irish. Played by fashion model Cybill Shepherd, Kelly Corcoran possesses a cool demeanor, privileged upbringing, and stunning beauty in sharp contrast with Lenny's Jewish bride Lila's chubbiness, emotionality, and lack of refinement. The mystique Kelly cultivates motivates Lenny to ask Lila for a divorce during their honeymoon and to relocate to Minneapolis to win Kelly over despite her father's loathing for him. After prevailing in his quest, Lenny feels like an outsider at the church wedding whose formality stands in sharp contrast with the informality of the marriage ceremony held in the apartment of Lila's parents. He tries to mingle with Kelly's relatives and family friends, but obviously has little in common with them and finds himself isolated at the reception. Lester Friedman concludes that although Lenny "has captured the heart of the Irish princess, the golden *shiksa* goddess deemed the ultimate prize in previous intermarriage movies," he has lost "his family, friends, and heritage."[76] In an era of heightened ethnic sensitivities, the movie still occasioned criticism of its stereotype of Jewish women and conflation of the Irish rich with WASP elites.[77]

The sitcom *Bridget Loves Bernie*, broadcast during the 1972–73 television season, was a throwback to *Abie's Irish Rose*.[78] Bernie Steinberg, an aspiring playwright who drives a cab, lives with his parents above their kosher deli on the Lower East Side. Their modest means belied the remarkable upward mobility American Jewry had experienced in the postwar period. Conversely, Bridget Fitzgerald hails from a wealthy Irish family that resides on the Upper West Side. While much of the humor derives from the class differences between the two families, religious stereotyping renders both sets of parents comically awkward when it comes to accommodating the spouse their child has married. Bridget's brother Michael is a priest who carries on the tradition of clerical tolerance from prior Irish-Jewish love films and the interfaith understanding promulgated by the Second Vatican Council. The series updated the limited diversity of earlier Irish-Jewish films by casting an African American named Otis as Bernie's best friend and co-owner of his taxi. Jokes about what each group eats, the religious rituals they practice, Mrs. Steinberg's overprotectiveness, Mr. Steinberg's ethnocentrism, Mr. Fitzgerald's social snobbery, and Mrs. Fitzgerald's Gracie Allen–like ditziness pepper the dialogue and plotlines. A recurring motif is when Bridget or Bernie attempt to please the other's parents by immersing themselves in the other's religion.[79]

But some aspects of the show and its reception diverged from those of its cinematic predecessors. For example, a recurring plot device in the two *Abie's Irish Rose* movies was to bring the families together on Christmas Eve. In the episode "'Tis the Season," Bridget and Bernie confront the December dilemma of whether they should celebrate Hanukah with the Steinbergs or Christmas with the Fitzgeralds since both sets of parents have invited them to dinner on the same night. To avoid offending either, they arrange to go to a ski lodge on that date. In cahoots with the Fitzgeralds and the Steinbergs, Otis drives them back to their apartment where their parents surprise them by celebrating both holidays. Placing Hanukah, a minor Jewish festival, on equal footing with Christmas was novel for this genre of film. Striving to be more inclusive, the series privileged the ecumenical open-mindedness of the younger generation over the ethnocentrism of both sets of parents.[80]

*Bridget Loves Bernie* aired between the two trailblazing sitcoms *All in the Family* and *The Mary Tyler Moore Show*. Although it retained the majority of viewers who tuned in for *All in the Family* and ranked fifth in the Nielsen ratings, the show was canceled by CBS after one season because of protests emanating from a broad spectrum of Jewish groups from the liberal Reform movement to the right-wing Jewish Defense League. The ethnic and religious assertiveness that paved the way for CBS to greenlight *Bridget Loves Bernie* ironically contributed to its demise. When Jewish American intermarriage rates rose to over 30 percent during the 1970s, Jewish organizations feared that intermarriage posed an imminent danger to communal continuity. Cracks in the Black-Jewish alliance, concern about Israel's security, and the trauma of the Holocaust reinforced this anxiety. In comparison, Meredith Baxter, who played Bridget, does not recall an equivalent Catholic uproar over the series.[81]

Despite the fate of *Bridget Loves Bernie*, television sitcoms returned to the formulaic Irish-Jewish love story with varying degrees of success. Jackie Mason's series *Chicken Soup* (1989) featured an older Jewish man named Jackie courting a somewhat younger Irish Catholic woman named Maddie who lives in the same apartment building as he does. This sets up gags about the funny incongruities of their backgrounds and parental disapproval of their relationship.[82] What was different was that Mason bore no resemblance to the handsome and thoroughly Americanized Jewish boyfriends who populated earlier instances of this genre. Instead, his Jewish accent, appearance, and gestures rendered him an embarrassing stereotype to some Jewish organizations and viewers, as did the series's endorsement of an interfaith romantic relationship. A columnist for a Los Angeles Jewish newspaper denounced *Chicken Soup* as "a pathetic reminder of an era long ago … as inappropriate and offensive to Jews as *Amos and Andy* would be to blacks today." The high ratings the series attained did not compensate for the rancor it elicited, leading to its cancellation after eight episodes.[83] *Brooklyn Bridge*'s (1991–93) subplot about a Jewish teenage boy and his Irish teenage girlfriend preempted similar controversy by setting the story in the 1950s, treating their relationship as puppy love, and underscoring the multicultural diversity of their neighborhood.[84]

Within a decade, opportunities arose to infuse movies with more ethnic characters and plotlines. What made this development possible was the proliferation of Jewish American film festivals in the 1980s and of Irish American ones in the 1990s.[85] Moreover, the increased number of small theaters within multiplexes, subscription cable movie networks like HBO, and new technologies like VCRs, DVDs, and streaming services afforded independent and mainstream directors multiple venues for ethnically oriented film fare that in the past would have suffered from limited distribution or a tendency to crudely stereotype ethnic characters or universalize them by effacing their ethnic qualities to appeal to general audiences.[86]

Simultaneously, the multicultural paradigm competed if not displaced the melting-pot ideal in American cinema. Directors and writers have enlarged the repertoire of the roles, traits, and values of characters either coded or explicitly identified as belonging to a specific ethnic group. They have challenged the essentialism of ethnic politics in favor of hybrid identities that mirror the diversification of the American population.[87] A gauge of interfaith acceptance is the intermarriage rate, which currently stands at approximately 60 percent for Jewish Americans.[88] I have been unable to find comparable intermarriage statistics for Irish Americans, but research dating back to the 1970s pointed to "a gradual erosion of ethnic boundaries within the Catholic population."[89] The increasing frequency of intermarriage stems from the chronological and geographical distance of the third and fourth generations of hyphenated Americans from the immigrant experience of their ancestors and the ethnic enclaves where they had resided.

Let me conclude with recent examples of some multicultural depictions of Irish-Jewish romances. Director Edward Burns produced *The Brothers McMullen* (1995) on a shoestring budget by shooting it on 16 mm film.[90] Winning the Grand Jury Prize at the Sundance Film Festival secured it funding to transfer it to 35 mm stock and distribution by Twentieth Century Fox.[91] This film typified Burns's subsequent oeuvre in exploring how contemporary Irish American men evolve away from the detachment, inflexibility, machismo, and traditionalism of their fathers toward more diverse approaches to their Catholicism, emotions, masculinity, and relationships with women.[92] Patrick has been dating a Jewish woman named Susan whose inflections, materialism, and pushy personality identify her as an outsider among the McMullens. She tries to lure Patrick into marriage with her father's offers of a job in his company and payment for a shared apartment rent until they marry. Already doubting whether he loves her, Patrick declines, considering cohabitation out of wedlock sinful. She proposes that he convert to Judaism and discard his Catholic morality. When he goes to inform her that they should break up, she rebuffs him first because she is pregnant and plans to have an abortion, a decision she rightly assumes he will reject. Patrick recognizes their incompatibility and finds his soulmate in an Irish woman from his neighborhood. Placing his passion above his piety, he embarks on a cross-country road trip with her despite the fact that she has renounced Catholicism. This resolution does not preclude the possibility of successful mixed pairings since Patrick's brother Barry overcomes qualms about making a monogamous commitment to a woman whose complexion and eye shape signal viewers that she is definitely not Irish.

In *The Fitzgerald Family Christmas* (2012) Burns counterbalances his sexist denigration of Susan in *The Brothers McMullen* with an empathic Jewish husband.[93] Various dysfunctionalities like abandonment, abuse, divorce, and infidelity abound in the marriages and relationships the Fitzgerald siblings have with their partners. Sister Erin's marriage to a Jewish man constitutes the exception. To be sure, they disagree over whether they should spend the holidays with his parents or her family, but coping with a more substantive dilemma, he rises to the occasion. Erin's older brother and mother have been pressuring her to hold a baptism ceremony for her infant son ever since his birth. She demurs since both she and her husband are atheists. When the brother and mother persist, the husband capitulates in order to remove this bone of contention between his wife and her mother. He understands that the ritual will neither change what he and his wife believe nor how they will raise their child.[94]

Irish American actor Edward Norton and Jewish American screenwriter Stuart Blumberg fashioned their movie *Keeping the Faith* (2000) as a multicultural take on the Irish-Jewish romance.[95] The film illustrates how the identities of Americans constantly evolve as a syncretistic mixture of contemporary cultural and interpersonal influences and inherited ethnic, racial, and religious traditions. The film inverts the plotline of *The Jazz Singer* and the premise of overworked jokes about a rabbi and priest being friends. Jake Schram, Brian Finn, and Anna Riley were childhood buddies who dubbed themselves "two micks and a yid." After Anna moved away, the two boys resisted their parents' wishes to pursue lucrative careers and instead enrolled in seminaries to become a rabbi and a priest. As the assistant junior rabbi at a posh New York synagogue, Jake is the eligible bachelor every mother in his congregation wants her daughter to marry.[96] Brian is the assistant priest in a mixed-ethnic church. He belongs to a long line of Irish movie priests who compassionately minister to their parishioners, though his religiosity is far more progressive than that of his predecessors.[97] Both Brian and Jack endeavor to impart a modern spin to the doctrines and rituals of their faiths to render them relevant. They plan to open a community center with a karaoke bar for the diverse population of the neighborhood, or as they describe it, "a sort of a *Fiddler on the Roof* meets *Lord of the Dance* meets the *Buena Vista Social Club*." When Anna returns to New York as a successful corporate executive, she falls in love with Jake. Unaware of Jake and Anna's affair, Brian falls in love with her and wonders whether he should remain a celibate priest.

The film repeatedly subverts ethnic, racial, and religious stereotypes. Although the first woman Jake is fixed up with epitomizes a Jewish American princess, the second is a beautiful and sophisticated CNN correspondent. When Jake and Brian go shopping for a karaoke sound system, they encounter a Korean salesman whose accented English, high-pressure sales pitch, and stereotyped traits belie that he is actually an acculturated, low-key guy who acted in accordance with the preconceptions of Korean immigrants selling electronic equipment. In a reversal of *The Jazz Singer*'s blackface appropriation of jazz, Rabbi Jake chides his congregation for its lethargic rendition of a Jewish hymn and invites an African American gospel choir to perform it.

The most memorable ethnic character defying audience presumptions is the bartender Pauli Chopra. After it dawns on Brian that Anna loves Jake and not him, he goes on a drunken binge that ends up at an Irish pub owned by Pauli who sports a "Kiss Me I'm Irish" button. Brian relates the disappointment that reduced him to this inebriated state. Pauli responds by sharing his genealogy with Brain: "I'm a half Punjabi Sikh, one quarter Tamil separatist, my sister's married to a Jewish doctor from New Jersey, and our grandmother was an Irish nun, who left this bar to me, which is a very long story." Then he toasts Brian with an Irish "Slanté." Norton and Blumberg originally considered making the bartender Irish, but chose Indian actor Brian George to play the role to demonstrate how the occupational niches commonly associated with certain groups of immigrants change over time.[98] In the director's commentary on the DVD, Norton asserts that this casting demonstrated that "everybody in New York is a mutt."[99]

Deterred by angst that his mother and congregation will feel betrayed if he marries a Gentile, Jake breaks off the relationship with Anna. Though his mother had disowned his brother for marrying a Christian woman, she subsequently recognizes that she had been wrong and advises Jake to follow the dictates of his heart. Jake clearly regrets his decision to leave Anna and confides in his Yom Kippur sermon that he had failed to exhibit enough faith in the tolerance of his congregants. He conveys the film's multicultural message by declaring, "We live in a really complex world, a world where boundaries and differences are blurring and bleeding into each other in ways that I think challenge us not just as Jews, but as human beings." At the grand opening of the community center, Jake's mother and Anna arrive together. The senior rabbi from the synagogue greets Anna and inquires why she has missed his last few classes, implying she has been studying Judaism with the intention to convert. Jake is delighted that there is "so much interfaith dancing" at the event, and Brian interjects, "It's like the end of *West Side Story*."[100]

Jake is the only character whose ethnicity is fully developed. Anna may have referred to herself as a "mick" when she was growing up, but otherwise she evinces little of her Irish heritage. The movie characterizes her as a workaholic attracted to Jake's spirituality precisely because she lacks that quality in her life. Since her parents are absent from the film, the trope of both sets of parents opposing the mixed marriage of their children is absent too. Brian emerges as more Catholic than Irish as he struggles with celibacy and his sexual desire for Anna. Reform rabbis found the picture's treatment of interfaith marriage and innovative theology a refreshing departure from the typical cinematic depiction of Jewish parochialism; whereas Conservative ones castigated its flippant attitude toward Jewish continuity and tradition.[101] In her monograph on gender, class, and ethnicity in Irish American film, Alexandra Schein labels the intermarriage story "a minor plotline" and applauds how the film revived the figure of the Irish Catholic priest "by giving it a 'new spin' and salvaging it from its reputation of being antiquated and repressive."[102]

*Keeping the Faith*, however, may have been the swan song of the Irish-Jewish genre. The consternation over such pairings seems anachronistic in an era when the nationalities, races, and religions of immigrants to the United States have altered dramatically. As long as the United States beckons as a haven and home to immigrants and remains a diverse society, the complications arising from intermarriages will persist as a movie plotline, but who is marrying whom will adjust to the demographic composition of the population. The contemporary counterparts to Irish-Jewish love movies are films like *The Big Sick* (2017) about a Pakistani Muslim American marrying an American Christian.[103] When

Jewish characters become involved with Gentiles today, it is more likely that their partners will belong to an ethnic, racial, or religious group whose identity heightens the comedic incongruities or dramatic conflicts implicit in their relationships—as in *Peace after Marriage* (2013) about a Palestinian American marrying an Israeli woman to spare her from deportation.[104] For an increasingly diverse American population, Irish and Jewish characters falling in love or marrying will probably be perceived as just ordinary white couples.

8

Playing the Nation

*Constructing Cultural Revivals in the Irish and the Jewish Diaspora*

DAN LAINER-VOS

In the summer of 1904, Maurice Dowling informed the readers of the *Irish-American Advocate (IAA)* about the formation of a new organization, the Irish Counties Athletic Union (ICAU), an umbrella body that would organize and regulate Gaelic sports competitions in New York City. Dowling, the secretary of the new organization, explained that through the playing of Gaelic sport,

> men from the North will meet the South; men from the East will meet the West, and a fact ... will be set down in the history, reminding us of the glorious days when our gallant forefathers met in conference on the hill of Tara [the mythological home of the ancient kings of Ireland].... [The ICAU] is not organized merely for sporting purpose alone, but to bring more closely together the Irish people at this side of the Atlantic in order to defend and uphold that which is too often denied.[1]

Concerned about growing divisions among immigrants from different counties in Ireland, Dowling and his friends sought to spur Irish pride and unity by creating a place where their countrymen would engage each other and celebrate Irish culture.

Nearly forty years later, Shlomo Shulsinger, a Jewish American Zionist educator, expressed similar concerns. Jewish education in the United States, he complained, "endows the child with knowledge about the religion and culture of Israel ... [but fails to] materialize this knowledge in everyday life and fulfill the commandment *Vachai Bahem* [to live by the commandments]."[2]

Jewish schools in the United States, Shulsinger argued, were divided along denominational lines and focused on formal religious teaching. As a result, they failed to endow students with a sense of national belonging. To overcome this problem, Shulsinger and his colleagues sought to create a summer camp where campers would experience national belonging at first hand. Such a place, he argued, would "consolidate the spiritual possessions that do not find full expression in the Hebrew school . . . and give [campers] . . . a world of cultural wholeness and harmony."[3]

Differences notwithstanding, Dowling and Shulsinger were concerned with similar problems. In the United States, they suspected, attachments to the old homeland wither, and the tensions between immigrants from different counties in Ireland or Jews of various denominations become more pronounced. To overcome this problem and generate a sense of national belonging, these national entrepreneurs sought to create social spaces, a sports league in one case and a summer camp in another, where respective compatriots would mingle and celebrate their national cultures. They hoped that such places would generate the "deep, horizontal comradeship" that Benedict Anderson associated with national membership.[4]

Establishing such national spaces in the United States, however, proved to be a difficult challenge. Irish and Jewish national entrepreneurs had to create engaging events *and* contend with diverse constituencies, each with its interests and preferences. Sometimes they also had a distinct understanding of what membership in the nation meant. To enroll these heterogeneous groups, Dowling, Shulsinger, and their colleagues had to construct complex organizational mechanisms that allowed diverse groups to maintain their differences and yet cooperate and engage each other.

In the Irish case, the Gaelic Athletic Association of New York (the organization that succeeded the ICAU) created a two-tiered league structure that effectively regulated games between teams representing different counties in Ireland. This structure allowed different teams to engage each other in a spirit of friendly competition. Successful regulation of Irish sports provided the community with an institutional venue where immigrants from Ireland could interact with each other and do things Irish, thereby promoting a shared Irish diasporic identification.

In the Jewish case, Shulsinger's intense efforts created a simulation of Israel in a summer camp. Within this simulation, Jewish American campers negotiated their relationships to a faraway homeland. As in the Irish case, the simulation of Israel in the camp did not eliminate the differences between different groups of Jews, notably between Israeli counselors and the American Jewish campers, but it allowed them to engage each other and generate a sense of shared Jewish identification.

In a string of influential articles, Rogers Brubaker and his colleagues caution against groupism, that is, the tendency to treat ethnic groups as substantial entities with interests and agency. Ethnicity, they argue, "is fundamentally not a thing *in* the world, but a perspective *on* the world."[5] This cognitive turn focuses the researcher's attention on how and in what circumstances actors create ethnic categories and boundaries.[6] Missing from this perspective is an appreciation of the *organized* efforts involved in constructing national identification.[7] While ethnicity can be considered a perspective on the world, individuals negotiate a slew of competing identifications and categorizations (gender, class, family status, religious affiliation, etc.) in everyday life. For ethnicity to become a dominant frame with which individuals engage with the world and think about themselves, the ethnic category must be made relevant, and this is where organized efforts to increase the salience of ethnic categorization play a critical role.

In diasporic settings, the competition over one's identification is particularly intense. In addition to balancing between one's gender, family status, and so on, members of diaspora communities negotiate between competing demands for their ethnic or national affiliation. Scholars of diaspora communities sometimes emphasize the role of externally imposed stereotypes in the construction of diaspora identification.[8] For instance, immigrants from Ireland, so the argument goes, discover their Irishness because their neighbors label them as "Irish" and affix mostly negative meanings to this label. While labeling is without doubt important, the Irish and Jewish cases that I examine in this chapter suggest that diasporic identification is *also*, critically, a result of intense organizational work that regulates the relationships between putative members of the nation. This organizational work provides groups with institutional settings within which ethnic categorization becomes relevant to the lives of potential members of the group.

This chapter focuses on the organizational efforts of Irish and Jewish diaspora entrepreneurs. It delves into administrative minutiae that rarely find their place in studies of diaspora groups. This focus on seemingly technical detail is a crucial part of my argument. Rather than seeing diaspora identification as a result of external pressures or as a characteristic carried over from the past, this chapter demonstrates that diaspora identification is an extraordinary organizational accomplishment.

Examining the organization of Gaelic sports and a Jewish summer camp side by side is likely to raise objections. Indeed, Irish sports and Jewish camping are as different from one another as one can imagine. Yet, when properly understood, this side-by-side examination can be fruitful. The goal of this chapter is not to identify underlying causes of success or failure in diaspora building. Instead, I aim to identify common challenges in diaspora nation-building and chart some of the ways diaspora entrepreneurs accomplish their goals. Given this focus, the following sections examine the problems our diaspora entrepreneurs encountered and the solutions they devised. The discussion will attempt to put those narrative threads together and draw some conclusions about the diaspora nation-building process.

Engineering National Culture in the Diaspora

Making Irish or Jewish nationalism relevant in the United States required creating an exciting place where members of the respective diaspora communities could celebrate their distinct national cultures and engage each other. For Dowling and his friends at the ICAU, this meant establishing an organization that would regulate Gaelic sports in New York City. For Shulsinger and his colleagues, the secret sauce of Jewish belonging was speaking Hebrew and engaging in Jewish-Israeli practices. Therefore, they set out to create an Israel-centered Hebrew-speaking summer camp. The following subsections explore the difficulties these organizers encountered and the innovations they introduced to overcome them.

## Constructing an Irish American Sports League

Gaelic sports make up a critical part of Ireland's cultural revival. While evidence of the sports goes back centuries, they became a national pastime in the late nineteenth century when Michael Cusack established the Gaelic Athletic Association (GAA).[9] Concerned with soccer and rugby's rising popularity, the GAA sought to popularize distinctly Irish games like Gaelic football and hurling and cultivate Irish pride.[10]

In New York City, immigrants from Ireland played Gaelic football, hurling, and other sports since the late 1880s.[11] Different teams played in Celtic Park as part of annual picnics that were organized by county-based immigrant societies (from here on "date holders").[12] In 1904 Dowling and representatives of different city teams established the ICAU, hoping to set up an inclusive league dedicated to Irish games. The display of manly athleticism, they believed, would "vindicate our honor from the vile aspersions of those who would proclaim us a disunited people."[13]

The ICAU's call for unity is instructive. While immigrants from Ireland may have been identified as Irish by their neighbors, they did not always think of themselves in national terms. What they carried with them from Ireland was, in many cases, a county-level identification. These subnational attachments manifested in residential choices and occupational-concentration choices.[14] Immigrants from different counties settled in other parts of the city[15] and county-based organizations dominated communal life in the city.[16] To make these immigrants Irish, the ICAU had to engineer an organizational structure that could bring these groups together and celebrate a distinctly Irish pastime.

Scheduling games was the ICAU's first challenge. Following the GAA in Ireland, the ICAU limited participation to teams affiliated with county associations. Recognizing the popularity of Gaelic football, the ICAU's athletic committee scheduled two football matches and one hurling match every Sunday. Early in the season, teams were supposed to play at the provincial level, with winners moving up to compete at the interprovincial level and in championship games.[17] Responding to the new organization, existing county teams joined the ICAU, and new teams formed, representing previously unrepresented counties. In 1907 Patrick

Lennon, the ICAU's president, proudly reported that thirty teams (out of Ireland's thirty-two counties) had joined the league.[18]

Despite the successful launch, disputes and tensions soon became visible. Hoping to accommodate all teams, the ICAU's athletic committee scheduled two football games *before* the less popular hurling match. However, because of frequent delays, the organizers were often forced to end the hurling games early because of darkness. A minority within the ICAU, the hurling teams protested against their discrimination.[19] Scheduling the football games, too, proved difficult. Some teams, known as the "Big Four"—representing Kerry, Cork, Kildare, Kilkenny, and Tipperary (the exact composition changed over time) —enjoyed a large fan base and operated on a semiprofessional basis. Teams representing smaller counties, in comparison, were typically weaker and had fewer fans. The ICAU's schedules, following the league structure in Ireland, sometimes matched strong and weak teams or two weak teams. These games were relatively unattractive. Concerned with the turnout, the date holders who rented Celtic Park and paid the teams ignored the ICAU's schedules and hired the Big Four week after week. As a result, the weak teams were effectively excluded.[20] Even worse, Liam O'Shea, the *IAA* sports columnist, complained that scheduling the same four teams to play each week robbed the matches of the excitement.[21]

Regulating actual matches proved difficult as well. Sometimes the problem was related to the referees who, out of ignorance, bias, or error, accorded a point or a goal to the wrong team. On other occasions, the problems had to do with the shape of the goal cage in Celtic Park. The goal cages in Gaelic football and hurling have an H shape, like in rugby, but the space under the crossbar should be covered with a net, like in soccer. Passing the ball above the crossbar yields one point; passing the ball under the crossbar is a goal, equal to three points. In Celtic Park, however, goalposts were short and did not have a net. This physical layout, the *IAA* editor explained, create undue ambiguity about scoring: "The first thing that impresses the sportsman [in Celtic Park] is the loose scoring feature of either game. When he sees the balls soar high ... over the goal posts, the American flag waves a point scored."[22]

Sometimes disputes over refereeing or scoring deteriorated into brawls. Enraged by what they saw as cowardly behavior of the opposing team or an error of the referee, players or spectators would rush to the field and punch the offender. On occasions, these incidents turned into massive brawls. "In the second half, something besides football took place. A throw-in was the cause of a little unbilled commotion. The ball was driven out near the north goal, and when the lineman hurled it into the excited players, his action grated on the nerves of a gentleman outside the paling. Before one could say 'Jack Robinson,' this worthy ... planted a resounding right-hander in the neighborhood of the lineman's upper lip."[23]

Instead of friendly and exciting rivalry, frequent delays, disputes, and sometimes even brawls resulted in tensions and bitter disappointment.

From the ICAU leadership's perspective, the root of the problem was the Irish American Athletic Club (IAAC), the organization that owned Celtic Park. Regardless of the ICAU's requests, the IAAC rented the park to the highest bidders, including noncounty associations such as the Old Order of Hibernians. Furthermore, the IAAC refused to impose the ICAU's championship schedule. In October 1906 the ICAU purchased land in Wakefield on the Bronx's Yonkers side to overcome this problem. On a field of their own, the ICAU leaders planned to impose their championship schedule and bring order to the games.[24] However, plans aside, the date holders and many teams refused to relocate to the remote field, plunging the ICAU into a severe economic and leadership crisis.

With the championship schedule in disarray, in early 1908 the football teams of Kerry and Clare counties withdrew from the ICAU and created a rivaling governing body, the USGAA. The USGAA's president further declared that the ICAU was no longer affiliated with the GAA in Ireland.[25] Hoping to attract other teams, the USGAA invited all teams, regardless of county affiliation, to join its ranks.[26] In the following seasons, the two governing bodies competed for date holders and teams.

In the absence of one legitimate governing body, regulating the games became even more difficult. Knowing that they could always switch sides, individual players, teams, and date holders ignored the ICAU and USGAA schedules and rules.[27] Hoping to attract invitations to play, different teams ignored the GAA principle of amateurism and hired star players for specific games. In the short term, "picking" resulted in invitations to play, but the practice had a stifling effect over the long term. "No matter how bad a player may be, he thinks he is fairly good. . . . By culling him [to make place] for an outsider, you drive him out of the club, so that in the end you won't have enough [players] to form a team unless you pick."²⁸

For their part, date holders insisted on hiring the same Big Four teams week after week, effectively excluding weak teams and eventually creating repetitive matches. Reflecting on the state of the game, Liam O'Shea noted that the lack of interest displayed by some was becoming painfully clear and that another noticeable feature was "the disappearance of several junior football teams who occupied prominent positions . . . a few seasons ago."²⁹

O'Shea and others realized that declining participation in the games was not a matter of sport alone. Each player lost, whether because of picking or the collapse of weak teams, O'Shea lamented, "became lost entirely to the GAA, if not to Ireland."³⁰ An enraged spectator further protested: "Is there a young Irishman or woman worthy of same name, who can stand in Celtic Park and watch the manner in which our games are murdered—cruelly murdered and defiled—and our recognized Catholicity made pray for profanity; is there such a person, in whose heart is kindled the slightest spark of patriotism, who can look and not blush with the shame and indignation for his country?"³¹

Instead of unity and pride, at this point at least, it looked as if the ICAU and USGAA sparked enmity between different teams and reinforced anti-Irish stereotypes.

### Developing a Two-Tiered League System

Ever since the ICAU broke up, the *IAA* columnists had urged the formation of a unified governing body. O'Shea repeatedly pleaded: "Assert yourself, boys, and do not let that petty differences prevent you from coming together. . . . Forget that you are Clare men or Cork men and think of yourself as Irishmen; work hand in hand as Irishmen to drop the detestable belief that your county comes first."³²

In 1914 representatives of two dozen mostly weak teams formed the Gaelic Athletic Association of New York (GAANY). Hoping to entice the Big Four teams into the organization, O'Shea offered a hierarchical structure: "[The GAANY] would . . . form senior and junior football leagues. . . . By taking Kerry, Kilkenny, Cork and Kildare [the Big Four] and two or four other teams [who performed well in the 1915 season,] a senior league could be formed easily."³³

The division between a junior and a senior league deviated markedly from Ireland's GAA league structure, but it assured that all teams would play each week. This division also prevented dull matches between radically unequal teams. Perhaps even more importantly, the hierarchical structure also justified differential compensation for teams. After some haggling, the representatives of the Big Four teams and the GAANY agreed on the following pricing: senior-league teams would receive $100 per match, junior-league teams would play for $50 per contest, and the hurling teams would get $75 per game.³⁴

To curtail disputes, which had previously resulted in cancellations or violence, the GAANY appointed a Board of Referees that excluded active players from its ranks. As a result, the referees inspired more trust.³⁵ The GAANY also invested in proper goalposts and placed nets behind bars. These nets "save[d] a lot of trouble, for fewer arguments would be heard. In either hurling or football the ball, after passing between the posts, rests there, being caught by the screen, consequently saving an amount of trouble."³⁶

The two-tiered league structure balanced the interests of the different forces governing Gaelic sports in the city. The junior teams benefited from spillover crowds and were motivated by the chance to advance to the senior league in the future. The hurlers had to acknowledge their inferior status, but they secured regular scheduling and improved compensation. The senior teams looked forward to participating in real championship games without compromising their income. On the other hand, the date holders took no part in the negotiations, and the GAANY now forced them to pay $450, not including the rent for the park. They also lost the ability to pick the teams they wanted. Dismayed, some date holders broke with the GAANY and invited soccer teams to their annual picnic.³⁷ But with the Big Four and small teams in the league, the GAANY now enjoyed a monopoly position. Date holders who sought to recruit Gaelic sports teams had no choice but to work with the GAANY. Disgruntled teams faced a similar situation. When the Kerry football team considered withdrawing from the GAANY, they discovered that local teams, all affiliated with the GAANY, refused to play them.

The organization of Gaelic games under a unified governing body was consequential. With a better schedule and improved regulation, teams showed up in time and played the games in their entirety. The smooth operation attracted new crowds. At the end of the 1916 season, O'Shea rejoiced: "Not since the invasion of the Gaels in '88 has hurling and football obtained such a strong hold 'neath Uncle Sam's starry banner. All that was ever needed of the teams was to give clean exhibitions . . . which would make decent Irishmen feel proud of their national pastime."[38]

In the following years, Sunday picnics' popularity in Gaelic Park increased. During the early 1920s, some picnics attracted a crowd of twenty thousand spectators.[39] The surge of interest allowed teams from Ireland to visit Celtic Park as well. On occasion, Irish American teams traveled back to Ireland to participate in the All-Ireland GAA championship games. The league's successful regulation allowed immigrants from Ireland to engage in friendly competition, making Irishness fun and exciting. It is difficult not to imagine that political events in Ireland, being closely followed and sometimes shaped by Irish America, were not also a contributing factor to the surge in popularity of the sports.[40] Yet, this surge was not inevitable and was made possible by the effective regulation of the sports.

*Constructing a Zionist Summer Camp*

Like the Irish sports enthusiasts, Shlomo Shulsinger and his colleagues in the Union of Hebrew Youth, a small organization dedicated to Hebrew cultural revival, sought to demonstrate Zionism's promise to American Jews. Instead of national sports, Shulsinger and his colleagues resolved to create a Zionist summer camp that would celebrate Hebrew culture and language. This camp, they argued, would "consolidate the spiritual possession that does not find full expression in the Hebrew school, [and] heal the fractures in the heart of the Jewish child."[41]

To turn this idea into a reality, in the summer of 1941 Shulsinger and his friends opened Massad (literally "foundation"), a nondenominational Hebrew-speaking camp. A strong proponent of experiential education, Shulsinger shaped Massad as a *Yisrael Bi'Zeir Anpin*, that is, a miniature enactment of Israel in the United States.[42] The expectation was that unmediated exposure to Hebrew and Zionist ideals would instantly turn the campers into ardent Zionists.

The camp's educational plan rested on three pillars: using Hebrew in everyday life, modeling the camp after Israeli geography, and crafting ceremonies that fused Jewish and Israeli culture.[43] To entice campers to speak Hebrew, Massad educators couched American themes in Hebrew. Hebrew lyrics, for instance, were inserted into American popular songs. In the dining room, Shulsinger hung American popular commercials translated into Hebrew. Shulsinger also handed out weekly awards to campers who excelled in Hebrew speaking. To bring Hebrew to the playing field, he instructed counselors to subtract points or call a technical foul on teams that spoke English during games.[44]

Shulsinger also gave the bunks, the halls, and even the camp's lake and surrounding hills names that he borrowed from Israel's geography.[45] For instance, the camp's pond was "Kinneret" after the Sea of Galilee, and the "Emek" (Jezreel Valley) designated the girls' bunks area. This layout helped concretize Israel in the camp. Massad educators also created a vegetable garden where campers enacted the Zionist ideal of productivization.[46] Finally, Massad educators infused traditional religious practices with Zionist themes. The Kabalat Shabbat and the Havdalah, for instance, were augmented with Israeli dancing. The Ninth of Av, on the other hand, commemorated not only the destruction of the Temples but the Jewish Holocaust as well.[47] Massad's creative curriculum and its staff's boundless energies fostered a unique Hebrew atmosphere that campers and staff alike referred to as a "mini-Israel" in the heart of Pennsylvania's Pocono Mountains.

The creative curriculum and the staunch commitment to Hebrew speaking evoked strong reactions from campers and counselors alike. In a short story published in the camp's journal, two young campers described their time in Massad as an enchanting experience: "Sarah sits, listens, prays, and thinks. She thinks about the first week in camp and about a new feeling that entered her heart. . . . It is not the feeling she experienced before. Sarah is confident in that. . . . How sacred and beautiful is the Oneg Shabbat in the camp."

While not necessarily representative, similar sentiments are echoed in many writings and can be heard from alumni years later. Attesting to its success, Massad attracted a growing cohort of loyal campers during its first three decades. To meet demand, in 1948 the Massad board opened a second camp, and the third one in 1968. During the late 1960s, Massad camps hosted almost a thousand campers and counselors for action-packed, meaningful summers.

Despite these accomplishments, sustaining an enchanting Hebrew environment in Massad proved difficult. Every summer, at the end of the season, Shulsinger identified external disruptions that frustrated his plans. In response, he attempted to isolate and shield the camp through a never-ending sequence of adjustments. In its first season, in 1941, Massad operated as a day camp in Far Rockaway, Queens. At the end of the season, "the associates and friends still had the impression that the project was nothing but an abstract idea.... The proposal to continue as a day camp won no support due to the limited educational possibilities. We were left with the other option, to continue fundraising to purchase a base camp."[48] Proximity to an English-speaking environment or the campers' families, it seems, hindered the ability to experience unadulterated national membership.

Determined to operate as a full-board camp, in 1942 Massad rented the facilities of Machanaim, an Orthodox Jewish camp in New York State's Catskill Mountains. Yet, even there, Shulsinger found the surrounding environment disruptive: "Our position amid a camp that held cultural values . . . that are opposed to all our aspirations hampered our efforts to create a Hebrew environment. Therefore, we forced ourselves into segregation and isolation in all our activities, a type of voluntary ghetto. We saw that our campers and counselors would refrain from contacting *Machanaim*'s campers in games and amusement. We held our meals, swimming sessions, and sports activities right after our neighbors . . . evacuated the area."[49]

Massad was not a secular camp, but something in the Orthodox lifestyle of Machanaim threatened Shulsinger's plans. Therefore, the Union of Hebrew Youth determined to purchase a base of operations and leased a camp in the Poconos.

From 1943 onward Massad operated as a completely independent camp, but even then Shulsinger and his team continued to identify disruptions, this time from within the counselors' ranks. From its inception, Massad faced difficulties in recruiting counselors. Jewish American counselors often lacked Hebrew-speaking skills. On the other hand, Israeli emigrants, derogatorily known as *yordim* (literally "those who descend"), were suspected of lack of commitment to Zionism. Looking for a solution, in 1951 Massad launched a counselors-in-training program.[50] But even then, enforcing Hebrew continued to be complicated. Believing that English-speaking waiters prevented Hebrew from penetrating the dining room, Shulsinger set up a new division for the 15-year-old Hebrew-speaking campers who served as waiters. During the 1960s Yeshiva University students replaced the kitchen staff, enabling an entirely Jewish and Hebrew-speaking environment.[51]

Even in their own camp, Massad educators kept looking for ways to intensify the experience of "mini-Israel." Eventually, during the 1960s, Massad began to import counselors from Israel. Shulsinger's wife Rivka saw the recruitment of Israeli counselors as more than a solution to a chronic staffing problem. The Israelis, she argued, added "a Jewish-Israeli atmosphere that is original and authentic. This atmosphere that is the result of cooperation between the founders, the educational staff, and the counselors from Israel penetrates the camper's bones, and he needs it like air for breathing as he grows."[52]

Yet, even in their own space and in an exclusively Hebrew-speaking environment, Shulsinger continued to be concerned about disruptions of the campers' experience that threatened his educational vision. Nowhere was this threat more evident than in the use of Hebrew and the relationships between Americans and Israelis in Massad.

While many campers identified with Massad's Hebrew mission, Shulsinger's zeal provoked a backlash. Recalling his days in the camp, Hillel Halkin explained: "The English language, once outlawed, was given a new taste, that until then I noticed only in cursing. Even better, more joyous was the comradeship shared by all those who spoke English secretively. . . . Isn't that the comradeship of equals that I had dreamt about when I dreamt of Zion?"[53]

We should not interpret Halkin's sarcasm as a sign of failure. After all, decades after leaving the camp, he—like many other campers—wrote about Massad with extraordinarily deep affection. But the sarcasm suggests that the enactment of a mini-Israel in Massad was fraught with difficulties. The use of Hebrew, which was supposed to serve as the potion that generates a deep sense of national belonging, entailed a constant struggle.

The absorption of Israelis into the camp proved tricky as well. Despite their alleged devotion to Zionism, Massad offered them a first opportunity to see America. As a result, they wasted "a significant portion of the working time ... in planning the after-work tour, or in overexploiting vacation days."[54] Even when they were present, the visitors from Israel sometimes failed "to understand the principle of 'live Hebrew' that governs Massad. They are prepared [Shulsinger complained], too quickly, to avoid the obstacles this principle poses in order to establish a connection with a camper."[55]

The Israeli counselors used Hebrew pragmatically to communicate.[56] They had to be informed about the special significance of the language. Hoping to overcome these difficulties, Shulsinger decided to fly to Israel and choose the appropriate counselors himself.[57]

The never-ending modifications of the camp's educational program, the tensions surrounding Hebrew speaking, and the difficulties in absorbing the Israelis into the camp are not indications of its failure. Instead, as with the Irish sports league, these challenges suggest that engineering a place where national ideals are manifested and members experience "deep, horizontal comradeship"[58] is an extraordinary organizational accomplishment.

Despite the unique educational program, during the 1970s Massad camps experienced a severe crisis, rooted in broader changes in Jewish education in the United States. In 1948 the Jewish Conservative movement opened its own array of Ramah camps. The Reform movement followed suit in 1951 by establishing Reform-affiliated camps. As a result, Massad's enrollment plummeted. Perhaps even more significantly, when significant numbers of Conservative and Reform campers switched to denominational camps, Massad's clientele became increasingly Orthodox, which resulted in tensions over religious adherence. Moreover, during the 1970s cheap international flights meant that more campers left Massad in favor of a family trip abroad, sometimes to Israel. Facing increasing financial difficulties and the Shulsingers' retirement, in 1974 and 1979 Massad's governing board sold two camps, and eventually in 1981 it closed the last camp permanently.

## Organizing Diaspora Identification

The previous sections explored the construction of an Irish American sports league and a Jewish American Zionist summer camp. In both cases, the diaspora entrepreneurs who engineered these places attempted to foster a sense of pride and unity among their compatriots. They designed sites or events where belonging to a faraway nation would make intuitive, experiential sense. Dowling and his friends hoped that, by playing Gaelic sports in a spirit of friendly competition, Irish Americans would overcome their subnational county-level loyalties and develop lasting connections with their brethren in New York. Similarly, Shulsinger and his colleagues crafted a miniature version of Israel in the Pocono Mountains, hoping that by acting as if they were indeed in Israel, campers would engage Jews of other denominations and embrace Zionism. In both projects, the point was not to educate potential members about the nation as an abstract imagined community but to usher them into a world where they would viscerally experience diasporic national belonging.

Tracing the multiple challenges that Dowling, Shulsinger, and their colleagues confronted and the solutions they devised to overcome them demonstrates that diaspora nation-building is a unique organizational accomplishment. In the absence of geographic boundaries or a unified government that served to define membership from above, diaspora entrepreneurs had to operate at the meso-level and construct organizational practices that would sufficiently appeal to diverse groups of potential compatriots. Neither group of entrepreneurs could take such putative members for granted. They had to create enjoyable, exciting, and meaningful spaces and compete with alternative activities and loyalties. Catering to diverse groups of potential members of the nation—members of *different* county associations or Jewish religious denominations—meant that these national entrepreneurs had to regulate the relationships between different groups so as to bring these groups closer together and avoid tensions. Crafting enjoyable, meaningful spaces where diverse groups collaboratively interact is the crucial challenge of diaspora nation-building.

The link between organizational practices and identification is direct. As Howard Lune suggests, organizations actively shape the "meaning-making exchanges that occur in that field."[59] For instance, when immigrants from Ireland joined Gaelic football teams, their social ties and the stories they told themselves about who they were changed as well; they became more Irish. Similarly, Massad campers developed social relations with people who, like themselves, had already been to Israel, in a way, and who shared a deep connection to that place. They became, not Israeli perhaps, but more Zionist. In other words, if ethnic or diaspora nationalism are not things in the world but, fundamentally, ways of seeing and interpreting the world and our position in it,[60] these ways of seeing the world happen within specific social and organizational contexts.

The specific organizational mechanisms used to create diaspora identifications in the cases we examined were different. In the Irish case, the critical mechanism the ICAU and later the GAANY developed was competition, powered by a two-tiered league system. The idea that competition can sometimes strengthen social ties is not new. In *Conflict and the Web of Social Affiliation*,[61] Georg Simmel argues that unlike other forms of conflict, the conflict in competition is indirect. The coveted prize, be it the trophy or recognition and praise, is in the hand of a third party (the governing body or the spectators). Thus, competition brings the adversaries into close contact, but the indirect nature of the struggle diffuses part of the antagonism inherent in the encounter. Clifford Geertz's famous analysis of Balinese cockfights makes a similar point; the reenactment of village rivalries in a play form, he explains, turns real and potentially dangerous animosities into manageable feuds.[62] Both Simmel and Geertz overlook the complexities of organizing exciting real-life competitions; the repeated outbreaks of brawls in Celtic Park attest to the magnitude of this challenge. The general point they make, however, is valuable. By bringing teams representing different counties to engage in friendly competitions, the ICAU and later the GAANY formed an organizational scaffolding within which Irish belonging made sense even in New York at a critical moment in the nation-building endeavor in the homeland.

In the Jewish case, Massad educators developed a "mini-Israel" or simulation of Israel. This simulation served as a mechanism to enroll campers to Zionism. Simulations are scenarios or activities that participants designate as an approximation or imitation of some other, more real situation. Steve Hoffman argues that simulations direct participants to explore the distinctions "between what is real and what is not real, existence and nonexistence, in everyday context."[63] By continually referring to the camp as a miniature version of Israel, Massad educators enticed the campers to reflect on the differences between their lives and others' lives in the Jewish state. The purpose of this comparison was not to persuade campers that they were in Israel or that there was no difference between themselves and Israelis, but rather to persuade them that things that happened in Israel were relevant to their lives.

In both cases, the successful organization of diasporic attachment was a delicate organizational accomplishment. In the Irish case, a small glitch in regulating games, or in the structure of incentives that kept teams and date holders affiliated with the ICUA or the GAANY, resulted in disorder or disengagement of teams, date holders, or spectators. In Massad's case, failure to maintain a balance between English and Hebrew, or between the different campers' religious preferences, resulted in disengagement and drift toward Orthodoxy that further alienated campers.

Finally, the successful organization of diasporic attachment rested on regulating the relationships between the various groups that made up the nation. To successfully enroll Irish Americans in their diasporic project, the leaders of the ICAU and the GAANY did not eliminate the distinctions between immigrants from different counties in Ireland; instead, they harnessed these distinctions to create exciting, friendly competitions. When successful, these subnational identifications became part of a broader sense of shared Irish belonging. Similarly, Israel's simulation in Massad did not eradicate the distinction between Jewish Americans and Israeli Jews or between Jews of different religious denominations. Still, it allowed campers to develop an experiential sense of those differences as relative differences subsumed by a broader, religious-national, Jewish-Zionist identification.

In *Imagined Communities*, Anderson links the emergence and spread of nationalism to print capitalism and the possibilities of imaginary homogenization that print capitalism offers. The nation, he argues, "is imagined as a community because regardless of the actual inequality that may occur in each, the nation is always conceived as a deep, horizontal comradeship."[64] The thrust of Anderson's argument is toward homogenization. Following Anderson, scholars of nationalism and diaspora nationalism treat internal heterogeneity as an obstacle that national or diaspora entrepreneurs must somehow overcome or render irrelevant. In *Ethnic Groups and Boundaries*, Frederick Barth advances similar claims.[65] The cases examined here suggest an alternative to this approach. Rather than merely treating internal differences as an obstacle, the diaspora entrepreneurs we discussed—Dowling, Shulsinger, and their colleagues—used the differences and tensions between different groups as a resource to generate exciting and meaningful engagement with the nation. The challenge they confronted was not one of homogenization, real or imagined, but one of bringing the diversity of the groups that made up the nation into a productive tension.

In these American, asynchronic examples, we see how Irish and Jewish diasporic identifications were cultivated and played out in convergent ways. Individuals in the United States responded to events and trends in the homelands and applied organizational infrastructure to suit the local landscape. These historical examples provide context to today's immigrant communities who often respond to diasporic movement in similar ways, raising interesting questions about how ethnoreligious communities attempt to coalesce "diverse" stakeholders in their new settings.

# 9

## The Irish, the Jews, and Wilson's "Self-Determination"

MARION R. CASEY

William Orpen, the well-known Irish artist who had just spent World War I embedded with the British army in France, was commissioned by London's Imperial War Museum to document the postwar treaty negotiations in Paris. *A Peace Conference at the Quai d'Orsay* depicts January 18, 1919, and conveniently serves as a portal through which to begin a comparison of Jewish and Irish aspirations for self-determination.[1] Underneath a statuary representation of Victory in the clock room of the French Foreign Ministry, surrounded by the Council of Ten, Woodrow Wilson sits enthroned on a red velvet gilded chair, almost as if Orpen anticipated the historian Erez Manela's phrase "the Wilsonian moment."[2] There are no Jewish or Irish representatives in this august gathering, even though Ireland and Palestine were among the thorniest geopolitical issues of the day, and even though both groups had intense interests in the peace conference that were known to all the men depicted in the painting.

At that time, discourses swirling around the Irish and the Jews in Europe and the Middle East were often characterized as "the Irish question" or "the Jewish problem." Those nouns speak volumes because both peoples had historical relationships with specific places that had been usurped politically and militarily over many centuries. President Wilson claimed that at the Paris Peace Conference "all well-defined national aspirations shall be accorded the utmost satisfaction that can be accorded them without introducing new or perpetuating old elements of discord and antagonism that would be likely in time to break the peace of Europe and consequently of the world."[3] But how did that claim resonate with the Jews and the Irish, and to what extent were their hopes indeed satisfied? This chapter seeks to answer those questions by bringing key milestones in Irish nationalism and Jewish Zionism into dialogue with each other as well as with a condensed history of British and American high politics at this critical moment in world history. It suggests that Wilson's inspirational rhetoric was meaningless for both the Irish and the Jews because the British methodically preempted "self-determination" for them.

## Jewish and Irish Diaspora Nationalism, 1914–17

In 1914 the majority of the world's Jews did not live in or near what we know today as Israel. Most lived in Central and Eastern Europe or in the United States; in other words, they were not a self-governing nation. An estimated fifty-nine thousand Jews lived in what was then Ottoman Syria, in a Muslim-majority territory under Turkish rule. The Jewish settlements there, especially at the end of the nineteenth century, were thought of as Palestine and were almost totally dependent upon financial contributions from their religious brethren around the world.[4]

Likewise, the majority of the world's Irish did not live in Ireland. Most lived abroad, principally in the United States where they were among the largest of its foreign-born groups. Approximately four million on the island of Ireland were part of the British Empire, where a very old legacy of conquest meant no self-government and religious discrimination. In other words, political power was in the hands of a Protestant minority loyal to the crown. For Catholics, remittances from the diaspora were critical not only for personal economic needs but also to sustain aspirations for Irish independence.

Statelessness, exile, and aspirations for liberation, Judah Bernstein has argued, ultimately gave the Irish and Jewish diasporas much in common and, for both groups in the United States, dual loyalty was not perceived as inconsistent with American patriotism prior to World War I.[5] Organizations such as the United Irish League of America and the Federation of American Zionists, to name just two, reflected Jewish and Irish movements that were transnational or international, each with its own discrete political complexity and key players. For some, the corrective to the "Jewish problem" was Zionism, a movement that envisioned a "national homeland" for Jews and encouraged emigration to Palestine.[6] Not all Jews were Zionists; many were wary of equating Jewishness with "peoplehood" or a "distinct race" when settlements in places like Germany, England, and the United States had proved advantageous, or when distinctiveness had made them vulnerable to violence as in Russia. World War I, however, soon converted many Jews to Zionism.[7] For the "Irish question," the answer historically was either breaking or at least tempering the colonial connection with Great Britain. By 1914, after decades of political wrangling and setbacks, constitutional nationalists succeeded in passing legislation known as "Home Rule" that would have made Ireland a semi-independent dominion like Canada and Australia. There was, however, strong opposition to Home Rule from militant nationalists who desired an Irish Republic, as well as from unionists in Ulster who wanted to remain part of the Kingdom of Great Britain and Ireland. The prospect of a civil war on the island loomed so large that British prime minister Herbert Asquith is said to have sighed with relief when World War I distracted everybody and the implementation of Home Rule could be postponed.[8]

Between August 1914, when hostilities began, and April 1917, when the United States declared war on Germany, American neutrality created space for the exercise of diaspora nationalism on an unprecedented scale. Irish and Jewish American activism was pro-German. This was most inconvenient for the British, who were losing battles, under financial strain, and anxious for American intervention as time went on and casualties mounted. Great Britain was the traditional enemy of Irish nationalism and there were those among the Irish in America who saw opportunity for Ireland in supporting Germany, which had expressed interest in aiding an Irish rebellion as early as 1914.[9] Many American Jews also had sympathy with the Central Powers because they had granted civil and religious rights to minorities before the war.[10] In addition, Jewish immigration to the United States was mostly made up of German Jews with cultural ties to their former homeland, and Eastern European Jews whose persecution under the czar made them anti-Russian and hence anti-Allies. German propaganda in a neutral United States recognized and played upon these sympathetic leanings so that "Jewish, German, and Irish elements were attracted to [Germany's] claims that the Fatherland was fighting a war of self-defense" against Russian and British forces.[11] Yiddish and Irish newspapers in America tended to be strongly pro-German at this time, pointing to the hypocrisy of, for example, outrage at the violation of Belgian neutrality when Jewish massacres in Russia and historical oppression in Ireland including famine and evictions were conveniently ignored. As the British ambassador to the United States said despairingly in January 1916, "All the enemies of England have been marshaled against us [here] and the Irish have lent their unequaled power of political organization to Jews, Catholics and Germans."[12]

Although freedoms inherent in American democracy allowed both groups to advocate for Irish independence and for a Jewish homeland in Palestine, their approaches were compounded by domestic politics. In 1912 New York State Supreme Court Justice Daniel F. Cohalan, a second-generation Irish American big-city machine politician and a prominent Irish nationalist, opposed Woodrow Wilson's nomination for the presidency at the Democratic National Convention. Four years later he opposed Wilson's reelection, stirring up Irish discontent by pointing to Wilson's official recognition of a new revolutionary government in Mexico that suppressed the Catholic Church.[13] Wilson's antipathy toward "hyphenated Americans" was seen by many Irish Americans as un-American, anti-Irish, and even worse, pro-British.[14] At one point Irish resistance so annoyed Wilson that he famously cabled antiwar journalist Jeremiah O'Leary, "I would feel deeply mortified to have you or anybody like you vote for me. Since you have access to many disloyal Americans and I have not, I will ask you to convey this message to them."[15] In contrast, the leading American Zionist at the time was Louis Brandeis, a second-generation Boston Jew known as the "people's lawyer." He vigorously campaigned for Wilson in 1912, became a key adviser to the new administration, and broached Zionism with Wilson as early as 1914.[16] Wilson chose Brandeis for the US Supreme Court in June 1916—making him its first Jewish justice—even though his advocacy for many progressive social reforms including corporate regulation was politically risky for Democrats.[17]

It is against this backdrop that a comparison of Jewish and Irish American nationalism is instructive. From March 1916, a new lobbying organization called the Friends of Irish Freedom established a nationwide network of branches to raise awareness about Irish ambitions to be an independent republic. The British ambassador to Washington, Cecil Spring Rice, believed such Irish American pressure was "of very great political importance." On April 13, 1917, he wrote, "The President is by descent an Orangeman and by education a Presbyterian [i.e., an Ulster Protestant]. But he is the leader of the Democratic Party in which the [Catholic] Irish play a prominent part, and he is bound in every way to give consideration to their demands."[18] A good illustration of the political muscle that the Friends could mobilize occurred when America declared war on Germany that month. The speaker of the House of Representatives and 136 of its members sent a telegram to Lloyd George, the new British prime minister, reiterating "Wilson's position on the rights of small nations and emphasizing the importance of Irish independence to the American people."[19] Thomas Gallagher (D-IL), William Cary (R-WI), William Mason (R-IL), and Jeannette Rankin (D-MT) introduced four separate congressional resolutions that would have made Irish independence "a condition of any agreement to end the war."[20] These were conveniently pigeonholed "in the ample filing cabinets" of the House Committee on Foreign Affairs, while letters to Wilson on the "Irish question" were simply acknowledged as received and then ignored.[21] In fact, the White House used Wilson's Irish American private secretary, Joseph Tumulty, to stonewall or deflect almost all appeals.[22]

Undeterred, in June 1917 the Irish Friends of Liberty seized the opportunity of President Wilson's presence at the unveiling of a bronze statue of the 1798 Irish patriot Robert Emmet for the new Smithsonian Museum to drive home their message. Cohalan's New York State Supreme Court colleague Judge Victor Dowling said, "It is peculiarly appropriate that this statue should be unveiled when the land from which Emmet took his inspiration and in whose freedom he gloried, has taken up arms to vindicate the rights of all nations and to make the world safe for democracy." Irish flattery knew no bounds as Wilson, like Emmet, was called "the finished product of the highest education and an unselfish and genuine lover of human freedom."[23] Dowling ended by laying down the gauntlet: "Shall Ireland alone be left the last surviving victim of archaic despotism?"[24] While the "Irish question" continued to be politically troublesome for Wilson, no official statement of support for Irish independence—be it in the form of Home Rule or a republic—was ever coaxed from the president. On the contrary, by the autumn of 1917 the press revealed that the Wilson administration had used dirt obtained from the British embassy in Washington to smear Judge Cohalan and silence other prominent Irish nationalists over their pro-German activities with the militant secret organization Clan na Gael during the neutrality period.[25] Even though Wilson reluctantly agreed to meet a thirty-six-member Irish delegation in January 1918, he had no interest in their petition, which requested consideration of "our claims as a small nation governed without consent."[26] Stories about this particular meeting in the Irish American press led to Espionage Act warnings as well as to the ban of the January 18 edition of the *Irish World* from the mail.[27] As far as Wilson was concerned, by February 1918 he had already decided that "he would not allow Ireland to be dragged into a Peace Conference."[28]

The Jews did not need statues, petitions, or congressional resolutions to get their message across; in marked contrast to the Irish, "they eschewed noisy, hostile, and aggressive public demonstrations."[29] As the war sidelined the European-based World Zionist Organization, much of its advocacy and humanitarian relief work was taken up by prominent and politically well-connected American Jews. Unlike Judge Cohalan, Justice Brandeis carefully kept American Zionists neutral and the Jewish press endorsed Wilson for reelection in 1916, encouraged by the campaign slogan "He kept us out of war."[30] Simultaneously, Zionism grew among Jewish American labor activists who began to see Palestine in economic and political terms. When the United States declared war in April 1917, the newly formed Jewish League of American Patriots cooperated with the Wilson administration that spring to wear down any radical Jewish opposition by disseminating pamphlets and press releases in Yiddish that emphasized Zionism.[31] It has been argued that this confluence of interests—"essentially the ideological expression of the middle strata" of Jewish Americans—elevated Zionism with the Wilson administration.[32] Additionally, Brandeis never abused his access to the president even as he held important influence over him.[33] In May 1917 it was Brandeis who alerted the State Department to proposals being developed by the British that would recognize Palestine "as the Jewish National Home." The following month Wilson privately assured Brandeis and the Reform rabbi Stephen Wise that the Jews were "certain to be reborn after the war."[34]

The restoration of Palestine to the Jews fit neatly with Wilson's idealism about his new role on the international stage. His Presbyterianism may have also been a factor; it is said that "on more than one occasion he described his feelings for the Bible as fundamental to his attraction to Zionism."[35] When the Balfour Declaration, the official British statement on a Jewish homeland in Palestine, was announced in early November 1917, he received the worldwide adulation of Jews; according to the historian Frank Manuel, "Scores of telegrams of thanks poured into Wilson from all parts of the world, almost as if he had issued the Declaration."[36] There was so much Jewish American confidence that the Provisional Executive Committee for General Zionist Affairs, led by Brandeis, launched a million-dollar fundraising campaign for Palestine that December.[37]

### British Strategies for Ireland and Palestine, 1918

Shortly thereafter, in an address to Congress on February 11, 1918, President Wilson declared, "National aspirations must be respected; people may now be dominated and governed only by their own consent. 'Self-determination' is not a mere phrase; it is an imperative principle of action, which statesmen will henceforth ignore at their peril." This was explicit language that had not been in his Fourteen Points war-aims speech just a few weeks earlier.[38] Was Wilson's rhetoric—not only "self-determination" but loaded phrases he repeatedly liked to use thereafter, such as "peace without victory" and "to make the world safe for democracy"—made of promises that could, in fact, be kept? They reflected the left-of-center social and political ideals current among American progressive internationalists—like Jane Addams, Max Eastman, John Reed, and Mother Jones—who supported Wilson's reelection bid in 1916.[39] Such sentiments were certainly not understood in the same way by European leaders. Britain, for example, preferred the phrase "historical connection" rather than "self-determination."[40] In general, the Allies "declined to endorse or comment on Wilson's progressive war aims" and he didn't understand the significance of their silence until it was too late.[41] Even before the end of 1918, Robert Lansing, the US secretary of state, lamented that self-determination "is simply loaded with dynamite. It will raise hopes which can never be realized. . . . What a calamity that the phrase was ever uttered! What misery it will cause!"[42] Indeed, Irish nationalists and Jewish Zionists both understood Wilson's advocacy in literal terms and, as we have seen, the Jews had already had greater success with Wilson than the Irish in 1917 and early 1918.[43] Their diverging trajectories were not simply because Wilson preferred one group over the other but, rather, because Great Britain was anticipating a very specific endgame.

In Orpen's painting, *A Peace Conference at the Quai d'Orsay*, President Wilson sits at Georges Clemenceau's right hand. Even taking into consideration that the artist was working on commission, it is still striking that nine of the nineteen figures at the table represent the British Empire. At the margins are those watching the birth of a new world order: Italy, Belgium, Greece, Poland, Japan, and, for the purpose of reflections on Irish and Jewish self-determination, the pan-Arab nationalist Emir Faisal I. It is perhaps not an accident that Arthur Balfour, whose role must now be considered, is placed so far away him.[44]

As mentioned earlier, in the years when the United States was neutral, Irish and Jewish pro-German activism posed the greatest obstacle to American support for the Allies. This was a major headache for Great Britain that was subsequently exacerbated by a republican uprising in Ireland at Easter in 1916 (which required the diversion of troops from the European front) and two revolutions in Russia in 1917 (which revealed a secret treaty the British had signed with the French about the future disposition of Turkish territory). These unforeseen developments created new political situations for the Irish in Ireland and the Jews in Europe and the Middle East. Britain solved its dilemma in two different ways, both of which reverberated in the United States. First, on Balfour's hard-line advice, it executed the leaders of the Irish rebellion, imprisoned thousands, and imposed martial law on Ireland from May 1916.[45] Second, it made support for a national home for the Jewish people in Palestine an official wartime policy. This came in the form of a November 1917 letter from Balfour to Lord Rothschild, a retired member of parliament and prominent British Zionist, which read in part: "His Majesty's Government view with favour the establishment in Palestine of a national home for the Jewish people, and will use their best endeavours to facilitate the achievement of this object." The irony is that Balfour's foreign policy career began three decades earlier, in Ireland where he was chief secretary from 1887 to 1891. There he vigorously opposed efforts for Irish self-government, developed close friendships with extreme unionists, and earned the nickname "Bloody Balfour" for his ruthless suppression of agitation during an Irish nationalist campaign for reform of land ownership.[46] From 1911 until the start of World War I, he again concentrated on Ireland, publishing *Nationality and Home Rule* in 1913 in which he argued that the Irish would use "any limited measure of self-government . . . to obtain complete separation."[47] As one of his biographers observed, Balfour considered Ireland to be "the testing ground of imperial resolve, to be held at all costs."[48] After December 1916 Balfour, a former British prime minister now the new foreign secretary, was back in power to ensure that resolve.

Again, chronology is illuminating. Turkey was barely in the war when Great Britain began to consider its interests in the region, especially the Suez Canal and access to its colony in India. It declared Egypt a British protectorate on November 5, 1914, and quickly began to see "the question of Zionism" as politically expedient, reasoning that France already had vested interests with Arab Muslims and Russia with Syrian Christians.[49] In December, Balfour told Chaim Weizmann, the English Zionist leader, that a Jewish homeland in Palestine was "not a dream, it is a great cause and I understand it."[50] Another phrase, the "future of Palestine," was discussed by the British Cabinet as early as January 1915 and continued to be throughout that summer. The diplomat Mark Sykes was sent to Cairo to set up an intelligence command post that became the center of a vast network of informants stretching from Iraq to Washington. Late that year, the brand-new British Secret Intelligence Service set up a section in New York known as MI6 under cover of the so-called "American and Transport Department of the Ministry of Munitions."[51] Led by thirty-year-old William Wiseman, it proceeded to gather information on German, Irish, and Indian separatists through a network of informants and agents not unlike what the British had set up to monitor the Arabs and Turks. Britain became convinced that "a strong Jewish settlement in Palestine" was key to minimizing French influence in the Middle East as well as to sweeping "the whole of American Jewry into enthusiastic allegiance to their cause."[52] Two seminal documents toward achieving those ends—the secret Sykes-Picot Agreement of May 1916 and the Balfour Declaration of November 1917—made befriending Zionists in England and the United States essential, as was consulting President Wilson in advance about the declaration.[53]

Balfour personally traveled to Washington to meet with Wilson about Anglo-American cooperation in April 1917. Just prior to his visit he had a conversation with Walter Hines Page, the American ambassador in London. Page was under instructions from Washington to raise the Irish question with Lloyd George since Wilson was concerned that, in the recent congressional debates about American entry into the war, Ireland had come up even in the speeches of those "who were not themselves Irishmen or representatives of constituencies in which Irish voters were influential."[54] Page recalled that Balfour had said, "It's sad to me, that we are so unpopular, so much more unpopular than the French, in your country. Why is it? The old schoolbooks?" "It is the organized Irish," Page told him. "It's the effect of the very fact that the Irish question is not settled. You've had that problem at your very door for 300 years. What's the matter that you don't solve it?" Balfour sighed, "Yes, yes." Page thought, "The plaintive tone of such a man asking such a question was significant and interesting and—sad."[55] This exchange actually echoes Wiseman's intelligence memos that included observations about American attitudes, especially regarding British-American relations. "They have been taught in their schools, and by recent German propaganda," he wrote, "to regard the British as a nation of Imperialists, who want to boss the whole world. It is safe to say that 90 per cent of the American people regard our treatment of Ireland with disapproval. The more friendly look upon it as a grave political blunder; the majority regard it as a blot on civilization."[56]

A small group of moderate Irish American nationalists met with Balfour on May 3, 1917. Their intention was not to embarrass him but to "try to impress upon him the fact that the way to take the wind out of the sails of the irreconcilables, the way to put them out of business, [was] to have home rule given to an undivided Ireland." By "irreconcilables" they meant Judge Cohalan and the Friends of Irish Freedom who, in any event, considered the 1914 Home Rule legislation a "pitiful travesty upon self-government" because it included a clause that would permit Ulster to opt out. Balfour, who had no intention of dealing with the Irish at all, simply replied that he had "no authority to speak for the British Cabinet."[57] On this same trip to Washington, Balfour contacted Louis Brandeis whom he was apparently anxious to meet because of his influence on Wilson. Balfour thought Brandeis was "the most remarkable man he had met on his visit to the United States." His secretary also arranged to see Brandeis and dropped the hint that, in the event of European jealousies, perhaps an American protectorate for the Jews in Palestine was the best way forward. Although it was agreed that spring that "the time was not ripe for an open declaration about Palestine by either the United States or Great Britain," thereafter Anglo-American consensus on the "Jewish problem" moved forward so rapidly, despite US State Department opposition, that the Balfour Declaration was announced on November 2, 1917.[58]

This was possible because William Wiseman was "the single most important intelligence operative Britain employed in the U.S. during the war."[59] He set up a communication back channel between the American president and the British foreign secretary, Balfour, by befriending Wilson's closest personal adviser, Edward M. House, a retiring Texan with big diplomatic ambitions, sometimes referred to as "Wilson's silent partner" or as his "right hand," and with House's son-in-law, Gordon Auchincloss, a lawyer at the State Department.[60] Just how close is revealed in an entry in House's diary for February 28, 1918: "When I am awakened this morning I heard Sir William in the next room taking down a message from Balfour which was being repeated to him from my apartment in New York over the private telephone which now runs through the State Department and to Gordon's house [in Washington]." Wiseman had arrived before 7 a.m. to get the message without the knowledge of the British and American ambassadors or Secretary of State Lansing.[61] Wiseman's successful covert efforts to influence Wilson are illustrated by the conversation over dinner in the White House that very night: how "one stumbled over [the Jews] at every move and they were so persistent that it was impossible to avoid them." House remembered being surprised since "there were so few in the world. This brought on an argument as to how many there were." He continued:

> I thought not more than fifteen million—twenty million at the outside. Mrs. Wilson guessed fifty million and the President one hundred million. To settle it he sent the butler for a World's Almanac and was greatly surprised to find that in Europe there were less than ten million, in Asia about a half million and in this country about three million. He could not believe it even after he saw the figures.[62]

With his new American friends House and Auchincloss, Wiseman spent five days golfing and dining with President Wilson in Magnolia, Massachusetts, from August 15 to 19, 1918.[63] Both Wiseman and House recorded the president's comments on the Irish during this vacation. In a discussion about vacancies in the administration, Wilson told House that "he did not intend to appoint another Irishman to anything; that they were untrustworthy and uncertain."[64] Wiseman wrote to the British ambassador that he "was struck" when Wilson talked "one day at some length on the question of Anti-British feeling in America. He ascribes it, of course, chiefly to the Irish."[65] Neither Wiseman nor House mentions whether Jews, Zionism, or Palestine came up in discussion although House says he "took up many matters of international importance" with Wiseman on the 13th. It is surely not a coincidence that two days after returning to Washington from this same vacation, the president issued his first official statement on the Balfour Declaration on August 21. Timed to coincide with the Jewish New Year at the end of that month, Wilson said:

> I welcome an opportunity to express the satisfaction I have felt in the progress of the Zionist Movement in the United States and in the Allied countries since the declaration by Mr. Balfour on behalf of the British Government, of Great Britain's approval of the establishment in Palestine of a national home for the Jewish people, and his promise that the British Government would use its best endeavors to facilitate the achievement of that object, with the understanding that nothing would be done to prejudice the civil and religious rights of non-Jewish people in Palestine or the rights and political status enjoyed by Jews in other countries.[66]

This statement was not passed through Lansing or the State Department and thus actually carried no diplomatic weight. Nevertheless, Wilson swiftly became a hero; "in the glaring sun of messianic fervor which alone shone on Wilson in the fall of 1918," Selig Adler reflected, "the Jewish rays burned brightly."[67]

While the British agenda for Palestine moved forward with the Americans, discontent in Ireland escalated that same year. In calling for Ireland to become an independent republic, the new leader of the republican party, Sinn Féin, used Wilsonian rhetoric. "We say that if those who go about mouthing about self-determination do not take that interpretation of it, they are hypocrites," Éamon de Valera declared, "and we tell President Wilson, in view of the statements he has made, if he does not take that view of it, he is as big a hypocrite as Lloyd George."[68] Following the British attempt to extend compulsory conscription to Ireland in April 1918, there was almost unanimous opinion on both sides of the Atlantic that this would only exacerbate tensions and result in bloodshed.[69] To mute resistance, a sophisticated propaganda campaign was coordinated by the British Ministry of Information with the Committee on Public Information (CPI), an American public relations agency that Wilson had set up the previous year. It paid to plant stories in both nationalist and unionist newspapers published in Ireland that "praised Wilson, the U.S. war effort and 'Uncle Sam's Boys'" who were helping the Allies, essentially to convince the Irish not to focus on British imperialism but to take a "broader world view of the situation, and thus [make] them a bit ashamed to stand out of the show."[70] President Wilson took a personal interest in this kind of propaganda, holding fifty-six meetings with George Creel, head of the CPI, between April 1917 and November 1918. Bernadette Whelan has argued convincingly that, by emphasizing Irish American wartime loyalty, patriotism, and enlistments in units like the famous Fighting 69th between June and August 1918, the CPI persuaded nationalist readers in Ireland that "prompt progress" would be made "towards Irish independence in the post-war settlement."[71]

But Irish unionists feared that Irish Americans were going to use "self-determination" to trap Wilson. The House Committee on Foreign Affairs began hearing congressional testimony on the "Irish question" in December 1918, accompanied by rallies for "self-determination for Ireland" that were organized by the Friends of Irish Freedom from December 8 to 15, one of the largest of which drew over twenty-five thousand people in New York City. The *Belfast Telegraph*'s view was that "Uncle Sam's popularity in Ulster has undoubtedly waned with the growth in the United States of the tendency to tell us how to mind our own business."[72] The veteran Irish nationalist John Devoy soon astutely noted, "The term Self-Determination has caught [the American people], and holding it constantly up to [Wilson] is the best means of getting him to do something. Recognition of the Irish Republic he could very easily refuse, but making good his own oft-repeated words is something of a different kind. He promised Self-Determination to *all* peoples; why should he deny it to the Irish?"[73]

Paris, 1919

Woodrow Wilson insisted on leading the five-member American Commission to Negotiate Peace, with a support team that numbered more than a thousand.[74] Mark Sykes and William Wiseman emerged from the shadows of espionage to serve as secretaries to the British diplomats at the peace conference, Wiseman as "chief advisor to Arthur Balfour on American affairs."[75] How much power Wilson actually wielded once he sat down at the negotiating table has been the subject of much debate. Suffice it to say that there were many stakeholders in Paris and many small nations clamoring for attention that had bought into Wilsonian ideology. Because the literature is voluminous and the diplomatic intrigues of the conference so tangled, it is necessary to condense for the purposes of comparison and drawing some conclusions.

No representatives from Ireland—where elections in December 1918 had been a referendum on Irish independence and where a de facto republican government had been established—were ever allowed before this body of peacemakers, nor were Irish American delegates, led by the distinguished labor lawyer Frank Walsh, permitted to speak in their place.[76] The British used delaying tactics to get these delegates out of Paris on the pretext of exploring conditions in Ireland, where an intense military campaign was already underway, and then used the trip against them.[77] Under pressure from Joseph Tumulty, President Wilson finally agreed to meet a delegation led by Walsh and Judge Cohalan in New York City on March 4, 1919, but when asked to personally present Ireland's case to the peace conference, he "took an evasive and noncommittal stance, stating that the Irish question was a British domestic matter over which he had no control."[78] While it must be noted that the Irish were not the only ones rendered voiceless, especially when one considers the various minorities claiming rights from the European powers or the religious interests in Palestine of the Russian Orthodox Church, British determination vis-à-vis Ireland does underscore the prioritization of its Middle Eastern goals in the treaty negotiations as well as reveal the political impotence of the Americans.[79]

Wilson's idealism about self-determination for small nations was quickly abused in Paris. The British had made promises to the Arabs in return for help in defeating the Turks that ran counter to the promises they had made to Zionists. The Arabs reminded Wilson that "they had as much right to keep the Jews out of their country as the United States Congress had had to pass the Chinese Exclusion Act."[80] The British worried that Wilson's concept of national minorities "might encourage 'American negroes, Southern Irish, Flemings or Catalans' to 'appeal over the head of their own government'" to the proposed League of Nations.[81] But American Jews, as part of a very large European group of Zionists, presented their case to the peace conference on February 27, 1919. They had every expectation that it would endorse what the Balfour Declaration had already made explicit about a Jewish homeland in Palestine. Indeed, just three days later, President Wilson met with the American Jewish Congress in Chicago and then issued a statement: "I am ... persuaded that the Allied nations with the fullest concurrence of our own Government and people, are agreed that in Palestine shall be laid the foundations of a Jewish Commonwealth."[82]

William Orpen painted another canvas, *The Signing of Peace in the Hall of Mirrors*, set in the Palace of Versailles on June 28, 1919.[83] Now the Americans, especially Colonel House who had long been the administration's liaison to the European great powers, are relegated to left of center, with Greece, Portugal, Serbia, Yugoslavia, and Italy at the margins. Orpen portrays the Hall of Mirrors as if it were a House of Mirrors, reflecting the political distortions that had emerged over six months, painting Lloyd George, not Wilson, closest to Clemenceau. The new faces all have British interests: Maurice Hankey, the influential secretary of the Imperial War Cabinet; the exotic replacement for the emir, Major General Maharaja Sir Ganga Singh, who represented India in the Cabinet, behind whom stands the secretary of state for India, Edwin Montagu. Montagu was one of three English Jews in the Cabinet; the others were Rufus Isaacs, soon to be viceroy and governor general of India; and Montagu's cousin, Herbert Samuel, installed as the first High Commissioner for Palestine in 1920. Clearly missing is Faisal I who left Paris at the end of April, disillusioned that Britain's alliance with France regarding the Middle East left no room for Syrian Arabs. He was convinced that "Britain was not entirely the honest broker, let alone the unflinching ally" he had been led to believe.[84]

The Irish already knew this. "We were there at the time when all of Paris understood that the ideals for which we entered the war had been circumvented," Frank Walsh testified before Congress on the Treaty of Versailles in December 1919: "[All the small nations assembled there] called at the headquarters of the American commission, [to ask] why the 14 points were not being applied."[85] Even George Creel, who had so ably convinced Americans to support Wilson's war aims through the Committee on Public Information, questioned why Ireland was relegated to an English domestic problem. In *Ireland's Fight for Freedom* (1919), he argued:

> That magic formula, "self-determination," has marched armies and tumbled empires these last few years, playing too large a part in world-consciousness to be limited by any arbitrary discrimination in the hour of victory and adjustment.... In the United States there are over 15,000,000 people of Irish birth or descent, woven into the warp and woof of our national life by common aspirations and devotions. They stand implacably today between this country and England, crying out against any alliance, agreement, or even amity until the case of Ireland has been fairly considered and justly settled.... When the heart of humanity was never so sick of blood and injustice, what excuse can be offered, what excuse received, for continuing the chains that keep Ireland in the pit while other peoples climb from darkness to the light?[86]

Orpen's memoir of painting the Paris Peace Conference includes the observation that "President Wilson occasionally rose and spoke of love and forgiveness. Lloyd George just went on working, his secretaries constantly rushing up to him, whispering and departing, only to return for more whispers. Mr. Balfour, whose personality made all the other delegates look common, would quietly sleep."[87] For all intents and purposes, things Balfour had set in motion for Palestine and for Ireland five years earlier were about to be realized. The Union Jack would fly over Jerusalem from July 1, 1920, inaugurating the British Mandate period in Palestine, and over Belfast when the Government of Ireland Act created Northern Ireland on December 23, 1920. One year later, in December 1921, the Anglo-Irish Treaty made the "Irish Free State" a dominion of the British Commonwealth of Nations.

If this made perfect sense in the context of contemporary British imperialism, in hindsight, Balfour's sleepy contentment was its own tragic form of self-conceit and self-deception. In 1919 he may have ruthlessly hollowed out Wilson's concept of "self-determination," but he had neither solved the "Jewish problem" nor the vexing "Irish question." Despite their association with the League of Nations, neither Mandatory Palestine (after 1922) nor the Irish Free State (after 1923) were satisfactory solutions for Jewish and Irish diaspora nationalists. Indeed, strife over independence and borders would roil both Ireland and the Middle East for the rest of the twentieth century.

10

A Tradition of Acceptance

*Jews and Their Basketball Players at an Irish Catholic College*

JEFFREY S. GUROCK

During the period between the two world wars, the long-term relationships between New York City's Irish and Jews, often fraught with tensions, reached their nadir. Hibernians and Hebrews fought over jobs, housing, local politics, and even America's role in the world, making for a welter of disputes. Some contretemps led to street violence especially when the Irish perceived that the Jews were displacing them in the city's civil service—most notably in the public school teaching profession. These posts with their steady, secure incomes were especially coveted during the Great Depression.[1]

And yet, at the same time in a very different arena, Jews were accepted, and fit in comfortably, within an Irish midst. At St. John's College in downtown Brooklyn, aspiring Jewish students were admitted.[2] It is not known when the first Jews were enrolled.[3] And there are no statistics available quantifying the proportions of that minority group at the college. But by the 1920s they were a discernible, and frequently lauded, group within the campus community.[4]

To be sure, when these young men considered their college options, they had some weighty questions for themselves and their parents to ponder. The first issue was that there was a price to pay for a St. John's education. As of the mid-1920s, tuition and fees cost over $100 per semester—the equivalent of almost $1,500 today—making it financially off-limits to most Jewish families unless their young man qualified for a limited number of what we would call today "merit-based" scholarships. Given these dollars-and-cents realities, CCNY was the logical and extraordinarily popular alternative; that is, if these applicants had the grades to enter the tuition-free "Cheder [Jewish school] on the Hill" on

St. Nicholas Heights in Upper Manhattan. During that era close to 90 percent of that school's student body was Jewish.[5]

Second, presuming a student's family could fit the bill, there was then the question of whether the young man would be comfortable as a distinct religious minority at the Catholic school. Not until the early 1930s would there be any organized Jewish life on campus. At that point St. John's began to host a branch of Avukah, the American Student Zionist Federation. Perhaps more critically—for those who cared—the mission of the school was to raise "the cultured Catholic gentleman" who would be "good citizens of the state and a source of pride to the Church." Toward that end, "moral training and religious instruction" was deemed "a reason for the existence of the Catholic college." Would Jews have to endure religious indoctrination? And then there was the worry about fitting in socially among the Christian majority.[6]

Happily for Jews who gained admittance, the school's administration, without explicitly noting possible Jewish concerns, prescribed a subtle yet powerful accommodation that obviated the theology-courses question. Year after year from the 1920s to the mid-1930s, the college catalog decreed: "Religion is a required subject *for all Catholic* students." Moreover, the school ordained that "no year's work is complete . . . until the student, *if Catholic*, has passed his examination in the prescribed religion course, unless the student has already obtained the required eight semester" (emphasis added). In other words, Jews, and most definitely also the minority of Protestants at the college were exempt.[7]

The catalogs also noted a very different, but highly positive, aspect of a St. John's undergraduate education that proved attractive to Jewish students. The rule was that students who by their junior year had "shown marked ability in the course of their studies" were allowed, with the dean's permission, to "enter the School of Law" that opened in 1925. After one year of "satisfactory" study in that professional school, they would be awarded their baccalaureate degrees. All told, on the religious and academic side, a Jewish student whose family could afford tuition—or if the young man worked part-time to cover educational expenses—might take his prelaw courses and enter the law school after two years and without much difficulty. Assuming he stuck to his books, he would finish his education with two degrees. It has been estimated that as of 1930, five years after St. John's Law School opened, approximately 60 percent of the students were Jews. Upon graduation, he unfortunately would have to face the daunting task of securing a well-paying position as an attorney at a time when most upscale law firms would not hire Jews.[8]

On the social side, there is much evidence that day by day Jewish students integrated well among their non-Jewish classmates. There was very little nightlife on the small campus for informal gatherings—except perhaps attending the exciting winter basketball games. St. John's had no dormitories available for late-night bull sessions that would bring residents together. But in the lecture rooms and labs, Jews and Christians often became colleagues. Such was the case when, in 1928, Harry M. Liebowitz shared notes and test tubes with fellows named O'Leary and Lombardino in "investigating the secret of the early alchemists, thereby laying the foundation for his study of chemistry and physics." This troika was described favorably in the college yearbook as "the famous trio of the Irishman, the Italian and the Jew." Year by year, Jewish names were listed in that annual published compilation of those who participated in extracurricular activities. "Tireless, genial, loyal," Harold Cohen, class of '27, did his utmost to fit in through adopting the moniker "Hal Callahan." Praised for his school spirit as captain of the cheerleading squad, it was said in his graduation profile that this "most agile acrobat" possessed "muscles worthy of Ringling Brothers." Bringing fans out of their seats at football and basketball games was but one of his some twelve out-of-class activities. His exploits undoubtedly captured the attention of Ronald Bernstein, the assistant editor of the 1927 yearbook and a member of the staff of the school's student newspaper.[9]

Meanwhile, in 1930, the Upsilon chapter of the Sigma Omega Psi fraternity congratulated its "brother" Martin Levy on his nuptials and offered a mock-serious blessing—as college chums often do—to the couple hoping that "marital bliss [may] hold these two in each other's arms—until he gets his degree." "Brother" Herbie Neiman, fraternity scribe, may have authored that tidbit of sarcasm.[10]

Some Jewish students were not all-around fellows and focused solely on their schoolwork. Such was the case with Morton M. Jacobs, class of 1929. His behavior earned him the often-unflattering sobriquet of "class grind" in a class poll taken during his senior year. Yet, his yearbook biographer determined that "the world needs men of scientific exactness, and we feel that in the larger world 'Jake' will win laurels.... Precise, scientific and scholarly habits attained by painstaking application to exact work mark Jacob's striving toward the scientific ideal." Evidently, the bespectacled Mort was well-liked.[11]

Unquestionably, however, the Jews who received the warmest welcome on campus were a small group of Jewish athletes who were recruited to compete on St. John's basketball team. In fact, they became standard-bearers for this predominantly Irish institution, because the school's sports leaders believed—as did many fans and pundits in the 1920s and 1930s—that Jewish players were uniquely adept at roundball. The institution wanted to build up its reputation as a sports powerhouse. Once there, these athletes were commended as among St. John's best products. Even when, at the close of their sports careers on campus, questions were raised by media outsiders about a significant ethical flaw in their behavior, they were staunchly supported by fellow collegians who had long applauded their efforts on the court. The chosen young men bore the moniker of the "Wonder Five" and from 1928 to 1931 they proved the recruiters correct. Over those seasons, the four Jewish and one Catholic stars (the starting five) racked up a record of 67–4. In the 1929–30 campaign the club went 23–1. A year later their record was 21–1.[12]

During their arena apogees, the Wonder Five were the talk of the New York basketball world. One local Brooklyn scribe declared them "the greatest team this reporter has ever seen." In the decades to come, their successes would influence future generations of Jewish players to become "Redmen"—the school's sports nickname. Indeed, scant years after Max Kinsbrunner, Mac Posner, Allie Schuckman, and Jack "Rip" Gerson finished their college careers, Dan Parker, sports editor for the *New York Daily Mirror*, gushed: "The Litvak [Lithuanian Jewish] is all powerful even in such originally Celtic institutions as St. John's of Brooklyn, which year after year turns out almost 100 percent Yiddisher quintets that are among the best in the land." Notwithstanding Parker's hyperbole about the total presence of Jews in the school's lineup, and his geographical error about Kinsbrunner whose family hailed from Austria, Jewish "Johnnies"—another team moniker—would find their way to this Vincentian Catholic university into the 1960s. These athletes' careers highlight in bold relief a tradition of acceptance of Jews at St. John's. Along the way, their saga and the stories of those of their fellow Jewish sneakered successors on the Redmen's hardwood tell, in their own unique way, the history of that group's Jewish prominence, and ultimate decline, as stars in the "city game" of hoops.[13]

St. John's did quite well during its first two decades of basketball competition, suffering only five losing seasons between 1907 and 1927. Reportedly, their first win in 1907 was against Adelphi by the count of 18–17. Back then, long before the era of shot clocks, and even before ten-second midcourt lines were instituted, the scores were very low because once a tall center won the opening tap for his team, a skilled ball handler could keep the ball away from opponents for an indeterminate amount of time. And there were jump balls after every basket—not unlike a face-off in hockey—which meant that lesser-skilled and shorter foes might never secure the ball and "get on offense." The Wonder Five's success under these rules would be instrumental in the implementation of rules changes that involved speeding up contests and moving roundball toward the modern game it is presently. In any event, mentored by and the star player of Rev. James Chestnut, Teddy Jollon was the first marquee athlete described in the school newspaper as the "idol of colleagues and friends."[14]

In the 1910–11 season, the Redmen won all of their fourteen games under Claude Allen, who doubled as the track coach. A sportswriter for the local *Brooklyn Eagle* was fascinated by how "the St. John's boys chased the ball all over the floor and simply ran away from their opponents." The Helms Foundation of Los Angeles was even more impressed and designated the team as the "mythical," national college champions. But most likely students were even happier that from 1912 to 1918 the club, led for most of those years by star player Jim Mahoney and ably assisted by men named Farrell, Goette, Kelly, O'Brien, Schmidt, and Davidson, captured the Catholic championship of the Metropolitan District five times. Clearly, the squad did well against rivals from Manhattan and Cathedral Colleges but struggled versus Army, Yale, Columbia, Dartmouth, Lafayette, and most notably CCNY. Battles against the Lavender from St. Nicholas Heights would prove in the future to be the highlight of every campaign.[15]

The year 1919 was a down campaign for the club as Goette, O'Brien, Schmidt, Wells, Butler, and Lawler struggled to an 8–14 record. But the young men still garnered the admiration of their classmates. The yearbook summation of the basketball campaign concluded, "The varsity basketball team had made the name of St. John's respected in collegiate athletic circles. We look forward to the next year with the hope that the college quintet will occupy the position it formally held when it was one of the best teams in the country."[16]

The program was surely on the upswing during the 1924–25 campaign when it won 18 of its 24 contests and was praised as "the best team within the last five years." Kabat, Freeman, Reiher, Gallagher, Salz, McNearly, Feeney, and Conway—six of the eight were the school's own guys since they were "former St. John's Prep stars"—were proud of "the two defeats administered to Manhattan and the one to St. Francis [which] place St. John's on the same level with Fordham in regard to the Eastern Catholic College title."[17]

But Coach James "Buck" Freeman was out for bigger game. A standout on the 1926–27 squad during his senior year that went 15–10, he assumed the coaching reins of both the varsity and freshman hoops teams immediately upon graduation. He inherited from his predecessor John Crenny a solid nucleus of lettermen, including the "irrepressible" Jim "Rip" Collins. When he graduated in 1929, Collins was praised as the "ideal of the Catholic College athlete, ay, and the paragon of Red and Blue court stars." It was said that this Irish American athletic luminary of "resplendent character . . . engagingly modest and unassuming . . . was and will ever be our loudest cry and proudest boast." However, the ambitious Freeman also knew that to achieve his and his school's goal of national stature and perhaps supremacy, he had to surround Collins with a "conquering band" of teammates whom "lovers of the indoor pastime . . . countrywide" would acknowledge. He needed an "aggregation of perfect players" that would "burn the floors of eastern courts, standing out head and shoulders in the brand of basketball they exhibit." That goal motivated Freeman to seek out, and to bring onto the campus, the best ballplayers around. That meant recruiting Jews. These were teammates who would be even better than Collins, the alma mater's favorite son.[18]

Effectively, Freeman subscribed to the widely held opinion that Jews—based on their perceived background, training, and disposition—were the fellows to have on the team if a school wanted to win all the time. The positive albeit racially infused stereotype was that the Jewish immigrant quarters were "the crucible of basketball where more great lasting luminaries of America's most popular indoor game have been born and developed." It was widely said how "the characteristics inherent in the Jew and the nature of basketball have served as natural irresistible magnets." Indeed, in this sport, it was believed "the volatile Jew finds that imagination and subtlety, qualities inherent in him pay heaviest dividends." In other words, Jews had the "hair-trigger reaction which basketball demands." A Jew was "fast on the pick-up quick-witted" and "possesse[d] the required shiftiness."[19]

To be sure, Jewish predominance in basketball during Freeman's day was also read in decidedly negative racist terms. In other quarters, it was alleged that basketball "appeals to the Hebrew with his Oriental background [because] the game places a premium on an alert, scheming mind and flashy trickiness, artful dodging and general smartalecness." Freeman bought into the affirmative belief in Jewish abilities. As it would turn out, both views of Jews would be tested at St. John's at the close of the Wonder Five's careers.[20]

Jews had been members of the St. John's varsity before the arrival of the Wonder Five. In fact, during Freeman's senior campaign, he suited up with Harry Schulman and "Kleinman, former New Utrecht star." And a fellow named Weinbroun came up with Collins from the freshman squad. Apparently, Kleinman and Weinbraun were second-line players; Schulman was a starter. However, Freeman knew that there were even better Jewish players around. In the very months before he assumed the leadership of his club, he went on the road to find these athletes; and he did not have to travel too far.[21]

In the spring of 1927, sportswriter Arthur H. Wubnig of the *Brooklyn Times* announced his choices for the borough's all-scholastic teams. He allowed how "the material this year was more plentiful than it has been during the last five years." At least four of the five "A" squad honorees— including Schuckman and Kinsbrunner—were Jews. The "B" boasted at least six Jews; Mac Posnack, described as "the most competent schoolboy who has played ... for any length of time" was omitted from the list only because he had not played enough games to be considered. Freeman had targeted these three stars from nearby high schools. Schuckman and Posnack had attended Thomas Jefferson High School; Kinsbrunner was from New Utrecht. Freeman also had his eye on Gerson, another Brooklyn fellow who, two years earlier, had graduated from Commerce High School in Manhattan and had then studied at the Brooklyn College of Pharmacy.[22]

Identifying potential players was the easy part of Freeman's work; convincing these stars to come to St. John's was far more difficult. His growing reputation as a tactician, comparable, in the view of his fans, to the great Jewish hero Nat Holman who coached at CCNY, would go only so far. More critically, St. John's did not offer athletic scholarships as did many of the schools he was competing against for talent. Some stipends were delivered above the board; others below. Only one of the crew Freeman was looking at was a scholar-athlete who qualified for an academic grant; another apparently had parents who could pay his tuition. But how could Freeman spirit Kinsbrunner away from Syracuse where he was ticketed to attend? And then there was, of course, CCNY—the free school—that loomed with its esteemed coach and its growing reputation as a basketball powerhouse. Perhaps Freeman found ways to achieve his goals much as the others were doing, soliciting informal funding sources to bring the Wonder Five to his gym.[23]

In any event, as soon as Freeman's recruits arrived on campus, they immediately paid huge dividends on the hardwood. In the 1927–28 season, the team went 18–4. The most impressive win was, in fact, their first game when this "untried team—[with] a new coach" beat CCNY, reputed as "the strongest quintet in the Metropolitan district," by the score of 26–21. Redmen student scribes regaled their readers with how Kinsbrunner, Gerson, and Posnack combined with "the phenomenal playing" of Collins, along with another non-Jewish player (Schuckman not yet having joined the team), as a "fast, smooth-passing, much-cutting, close-guarding quintet of stars who were not individuals but a team." Soon thereafter, the Columbia Lions fell by a score of 43–14. Reportedly, "our . . . Big Red Quintet" got "the lion to eat out of its hand." For an excited fan base, the score was "truly an indication of the superiority of the Varsity" as they "display[ed] a dazzling brand of pass work and a mighty offense that slightly overshadowed an impregnable defense." The word around St. John's was that the 1927–28 squad "is not only a team, it is a great team."[24]

Meanwhile Jews, not only in New York but as far away as Minnesota, were taking note of—with a degree of pride—their fellows' athletic importance at St. John's. After the big win over CCNY, a writer for the *American Jewish World* out of Minneapolis reported that Holman's "all-Jewish team" had been defeated by a Catholic college [that] had three outstanding Jews" on its squad and that these players had rung up almost half of the Redmen's points.[25]

Prior to the 1928–29 campaign, Schuckman came up from the freshman squad and the Wonder Five in formation now had four Jewish contributors. In time, the team's supporters would judge Schuckman as even better than the iconic Collins as he fit in well in the "fast-moving and passing" offense that Freeman had installed. Redmen partisans were talking about national recognition for their heroes, who won 23 of their 25 games against opponents who were seen as "very likely the most formidable in the intercollegiate world." The leaders of the club were praised as "gargantuan in their playing deeds, masters of their positions, and above all, sportsmen to the core in a game in which sportsmanship is thoroughly tested." A highlighted match was against a "heralded" and fellow Vincentian institution, Niagara. These opponents were "bewildered by the Indian high-speed passing attack and disheartened by the brilliant Redmen defense." Kinsbrunner and Gerson were noted as the outstanding players as "the *Irish* guards" (emphasis added) of Brooklyn "scalped" the visitors by a score of 35–18.[26]

During the 1929–30 season, the Wonder Five filled out their lineup with the addition of freshman Marty Begovich from Hoboken, New Jersey. The "huge Yearling"—who was the one Christian starter—gave the group the one element they previously had lacked. Their new, very talented center stood six-feet-four. Remarkably, the four upperclassmen had done extremely well previously even though none of them was taller than five-feet-ten. Now, an undefeated season was in their reach. Losing on the road to Providence College, they came up short by only one game, earning a 23–1 record and getting crowned the "Champions of the East" (or "Metropolitan Basketball Champions"). For St. John's students "it was a title to be turned over in one's mind and relished, to be proclaimed from the housetops." Indeed, the demand for tickets was so great that several home games had to be moved off the campus to Brooklyn's Arcadia Hall, ordinarily a dance hall. And when CCNY came over from Manhattan, the police had to be called "to keep the multitudes unable to purchase tickets" out of the overcrowded venue. This game between what were then two undefeated teams was billed as a "strategic" battle between the city's two top coaches, Freeman and Holman. That evening, according to student reporters, "the cool, confident quintet from Brooklyn" outlasted the "nervous, tense" CCNY contingent by the score of 28–23. This season, "which brought fame to St. John's name in basketball," may have been capped off when an impressed sportswriter for a local newspaper named Jack Murray awarded them the title of "Mythical National College Court Champions."[27]

In the 1930–31 season, the club garnered real national attention on the road to a 21–1 record when they battled CCNY in the feature match of a triple-header in Madison Square Garden that brought together the half-dozen top college teams in the city. Fifteen thousand fans turned out for what was called a "basketball carnival" promoted to raise money for the unemployed of New York City. St. John's backers were delighted that their team won that night on the biggest indoor sports stage in the nation. For a Jewish journalist named Harry Glantz, reporting from as far away as Los Angeles, this was a victory of one Jewish team over another. He was quick to point out that the stars of the Catholic school were "our lads." However, many fans who sat through the game—not only disappointed Lavender rooters—along with members of the media left dissatisfied with the slow pace of the game. The final score was only 17–9 and in the second half CCNY scored but one basket. The CCNY Beavers simply could not get the ball away from dribbler extraordinaire Max Kinsbrunner and his similarly skilled teammates after Begovich won the opening tap. Those in the "gallery" could hardly get excited as the Johnnies "froze the ball the entire second half." Freeman and his fellows' style of play—fast and accurate passing but only limited shooting—did much to convince basketball officials, who hoped to grow their game as a spectator sport, to install that midcourt line and a ten-second rule to stop stalling.[28]

These tactical concerns did not bother the Redmen faithful who lauded Kinsbrunner with his "uncanny control of the ball" as "the most colorful court performer." Returning to Brooklyn several weeks later, seven thousand classmates and other hoops fans filled up the 102nd Regiment Armory and witnessed their team capture their second straight metropolitan championship, defeating Manhattan College by a tally of 30–14. "Class, that indescribable something," it was said, separated St.

John's men from their opponents. When the Wonder Five walked off the court for the final time, the throng "rose to its feet in tribute to the greatest team in the history of the sport."[29]

Two weeks later the team provided the school with "the greatest publicity stunt ever engineered" at St. John's when the team was the subject of a "short" produced by renowned sportscaster Ted Husing for the National Broadcasting Company. Now, "the representatives of the Red and White"—the school's colors—would be "immortalized on the Silver Screen in movie theatres all over the United States." Seemingly, the Redmen had become for basketball what the Fighting Irish of Notre Dame were for college football and Freeman could be compared to Knute Rockne. (Ironically, the legendary football mentor would die in a plane crash three weeks after St. John's finished its hoops season.) At that high moment, a New York Anglo-Jewish weekly was pleased to report that Posnack "was the unanimous selection of coaches and officials as the greatest star who stood out during the most successful season college basketball has ever known."[30]

Acclaim had, thus, been consistently lavished in grand terms from all quarters on the Wonder Five as they racked up their skein of victories. At school they had been cast as the true standard-bearers of their alma mater. They had been extolled as men of sterling character, as "sportsmen to the core," their feats to be "proclaimed from the housetops." If a Collins was described in heroic terms, so was a Schuckman. These Jews certainly were not seen as interlopers, as displacers, who had taken over the program. Rather, they had been lauded as mighty contributors to victories that everyone shared. For above and beyond the games the team had won, it had brought much positive, national recognition to the small Brooklyn school. While Jewish newspaper scribes noted the Jewish players' backgrounds as a source of great interest and pride, at St. John's, the school that had recruited them, welcomed them in, and benefited from their exploits, the team's religion and ethnicity was hardly in play. These "Indians" were not Jewish athletic outliers but esteemed members of the school's community.

However, just two weeks after their final conquest, the stars' reputation for rectitude was sullied when it was revealed that they had violated a cardinal principle of the code of amateurism. On March 20, 1931, St. John's athletic director Ray Lynch announced that the players "had been suspended from athletic competition pending an investigation that they had played professional basketball while representing St. John's in intercollegiate athletic competition" and they had been "barred ... from competing for the college." That was as far as the school's punishment would go. From a practical perspective, the ban affected only Kinsbrunner, Begovich, and Schuckman. Kinsbrunner, a five-letter man, would not be allowed to play baseball and run track during his last semester at the school. Schuckman lost his last year of basketball eligibility and Begovich would be kept off the basketball and baseball squads during his upcoming junior and senior years.[31]

When the investigation was publicized in the *New York Times*, all of the accused denied the charges. But when interviewed more extensively by the *Brooklyn Daily Eagle*, they told a somewhat different story. When queried whether he was still playing for a professional team, Gerson replied, "Not anymore ... there isn't enough money in it." As he saw the economics of the case, a real professional received $20 per match, while he was playing for $10–$20 a game. He also contended that St. John's players were far from the only ones moonlighting across the Hudson River in New Jersey to play against a YMHA squad or as far west as Carbondale, Pennsylvania. By his accounting, there were hundreds of stars from other college programs doing the same as he. Schuckman, for his part, denied outright that he had played "in Elizabeth, Newark or anywhere else" since he had "a scholarship and [didn't] need the money to risk [his] amateur standing." But he did indicate that some other teammates—like Mac Posnack—had played for pay and "they don't care who knows it." A subsequent investigation by Lynch would contradict Schuckman's apologia; the athletic director asserted that he had played under the assumed name of "Alberta." Finally, Begovich told the newspaper that he came from a family of some means and therefore had no reason to cross the line even though the newspaper said it was rumored that he had used the assumed name of "Stevens" when suiting up for a court appearance in Pennsylvania.

Amid these revelations about breaking with amateurism, an even more serious charge was leveled against Posnack and Gerson. It was alleged that during the triumphant season that had just ended, gamblers had offered them money to "lay down" during the crucial Manhattan College game. Coach Freeman was quick to defend his players against this assertion of profoundly egregious behavior, stating that the final score was proof enough that his Johnnies were not "crooked." He did not comment on the professionalism charge.[32] Athletic Director Lynch seemingly agreed that there was scant evidence of a fixing scandal. Arguably, had any of the Wonder Five truly consorted with gamblers in corrupting the games themselves, far more severe punishment would have been imposed.[33]

While the coach was silent on the issue of the players competing as pros, the Wonder Five's classmates had much to say about the amateurism issue and the school's response. The athletes were widely defended. Through all the turmoil, the predominantly Irish American student body continued to embrace these Jewish players as well as their Polish American teammate. If sports defined community, the Jewish players continued to be counted in. It is entirely possible that at a time when on the streets of Brooklyn and beyond all sorts of nasty things were being said about Jews, some students also may have thought of "sneaky" Jewish conspirators who had cynically surrendered their lofty amateur status for money, thereby besmirching St. John's reputation. But if those opinions were bandied about on campus, they were not in public view. Rather, editorial writers for school newspapers asked rhetorically: Why is an overheated media focusing their faux-righteous ire on our athletes when so many players elsewhere were acting similarly? The student's answer: "The St. John's team had compiled probably the greatest record considering their opposition of any college hardwood aggregation in three decades. . . . To expose them as alleged professionals would 'go big.' Consequently big-type headlines." Effectively taking Gerson's side, the advocate insisted how "professionalism in colleges means the bringing in of a finished athlete to an institution and returning to play on the school's teams." However, in these cases, it was contended that "because an athlete who comes directly from high school to a college where he is registered as a bona fide student plays a bit of outside ball does not make him a professional."[34]

Another supportive opinion argued similarly that when "each of these five boys [who] gave his best in every game played for the school . . . did play outside ball they did only what hundreds before had done and what in the basketball fraternity seemed to be legitimate." Moreover, our fellows were no different from "thousands of others who attended

St. John's" and faced financial difficulties amid the Great Depression. Readers were reminded how "these players did not come from wealthy families. It was necessary that each one of them work his way through college" while receiving "no subsidies because St. John's does not have the wealthy body of alumni possessed by some institutions." Along similar lines, a third writer intimated that the school had benefited largely from these standouts deciding to attend it since the college's inability to give players stipends threatened to render the athletic program unable "to cope with the keen competition that is constantly being presented on the intercollegiate stage."[35]

As far as the weighty allegation about Mac Posnack and gamblers was concerned, a columnist's riposte was that if the player had been offered "$3000 to 'throw' the Manhattan game by wagering this money at the prevailing odds of 5–1, Mac could have cleaned up some $18,000 on one contest. That's a tidy sum for a young college athlete to make in an evening. Especially when he is said to draw down a paltry eight dollars per evening in New Jersey." For this defender, the only "throwing" that took place that evening was when Posnack threw in "one-handed, two-pointers."[36]

Finally, the students were none too pleased with the administration's quick decision to bar the athletes from further representation of the school. In a sidebar piece, a month after the scandal broke, a reporter bemoaned that "it is really too bad that St. John's . . . should have been . . . so ready to expiate its 'sin,' suspending its entire team." Of course, only five players had been dismissed from intercollegiate sports. But the end result was that "now as the howl of the head-line wolves dies in the distance in pursuit of other prey, the Indian tribe mourns the wreckage of its team and ponders the validity of 'Honesty is the best policy.'" The writer called upon all loyal fans to "salute the Indian Wonder Five . . . who gave many a thrill . . . displayed the acme of basketball skill and then as a finale manfully bore the brunt of the recent interrogation with the stoicism typical of the Indian."[37]

Indeed, in the first years after the controversy blew over and the five players left the school, as the "five devout 'Catholic' basketballers"—as one Jewish journalist referred to them tongue in cheek—formed their own professional team called the Brooklyn or Brownsville Jewels (a play on words about their ethnicity, notwithstanding Begovich's Christian ancestry), they continued to be a welcome presence in campus gyms. For example, reportedly, before the 1931–32 season, "the boys were gracious enough to offer their services to Buck Freeman in aiding him to give this season's crew some workouts." Schuckman and Posner came back to scrimmage in subsequent seasons. With his reputation intact, in 1932 Jack Gerson—the most unrepentant of the play-for-pay athletes—was the subject of a laudatory retrospective "Flashbacks" column that reminded those who may have forgotten his exploits, or informed newcomers to campus who had not seen him play, what a "sportsman" he was. The spirit of the "Wonder Five" continued long-term as they went on with their professional basketball careers. Their legendary exploits influenced the next generation of Jewish basketball players of the 1930s to mid-1940s to come to St. John's.[38]

For example, Jack "Dutch" Garfinkel "idolized" Posnack whom he first watched from the stands when the Jewels played in Arcadia Hall. After graduating from Thomas Jefferson High School, he was recruited to play at George Washington University. But he chose St. John's because "there was team the Wonder Five, and they had a guard named Mac Posnack [who] was a great passer." He wanted to, and did, follow in his sneakered footsteps from 1938 to 1941.[39]

The year after Garfinkel graduated two other budding Jewish hoop stars—Hy Gotkin and Harry Boykoff—came together from Jefferson High, the consummate local feeder school. Gotkin felt his first connection to St. John's when he watched his cousin, Java Gotkin, play for Freeman. The University of Kentucky and its legendary coach Adolph Rupp offered Hy Gotkin an athletic scholarship but he was concerned that Rupp "did not like Jews." Besides which, Lexington, Kentucky, was seven hundred miles from New York's Lexington Avenue. Long Island University and its own stellar coach Clair Bee also showed up at the family's Brooklyn home with an offer, but Hy was ticketed for the Redmen. The diminutive Gotkin, who was only five-feet-eight, then combined with the six-feet-ten Boykoff—nicknamed "Big Hesh" and one of basketball's big men—in securing for the Johnnies the National Invitational Tournament (NIT) championship in 1943. After graduation Gotkin helped recruit Jewish players out of his old Brooklyn neighborhood and high school. In 1946 Max Zaslofsky came from Jefferson High to St. John's on his own and played one year on the varsity before competing in Chicago and for the New York Knicks in the fledgling new professional leagues.[40]

If these stars, and other Jewish players, harbored any latent apprehensions about the continuation of St. John's tradition of acceptance as an Irish Catholic institution, their concern would prove to be of no account with the arrival after the 1936 season of a new coach for the Redmen. In the years after the Wonder Five era, Freeman continued to put very competitive teams of Jews and Christians on the court. Indeed, in the 1931–32 campaign, men like Poliskin, Slott, Lazar, Brennan, and Smith contributed mightily to a very fine 22–4 record. However, none of his subsequent clubs earned national acclaim. After the 1935–36 campaign, having amassed a career record of 177–31 at the Brooklyn school, he took his estimable basketball skills to the University of Scranton, and Joe Lapchick was appointed in his stead.[41]

Lapchick had notable street credibility among Jews who followed the rise of hoops. After all, he had teamed up with the future CCNY coach Nat Holman on the "Original Celtics," a famous barnstorming team of the 1910s and 1920s. At St. John's, Lapchick established himself as a skilled tactician and a no-nonsense mentor. He also—most significantly—was tolerant of racial and religious minorities. Before his arrival at St. John's, as a Celtic, he had put himself on the line against segregationist mistreatment of the New York Rens, an all-black team out of Harlem. Later on in his life, he would be a prime, outspoken advocate for integration in sports. Seemingly, such egalitarians feelings also sat well in the athletic department and ultimately the larger school community. In 1939 African American Carl Fields was recruited out of Boys High School in Brooklyn and brought with him four other black athletes; together they upgraded the track program. The school wished to win in that athletic arena, too. But Fields—like the Jews who came before him—was not marginalized as an outlier. A fine scholar-athlete, he was elected to the Skull and Circle academic honor society, the first African American so recognized. In any event, as previously noted, on the hardwood under Lapchick's guidance, the Gotkin-Boykoff team helped the Johnnies recapture national basketball recognition when they won the NIT.[42]

After the 1946–47 season, Lapchick left St. John's to become the coach of the New York Knickerbockers and was replaced by St. John's alumnus Frank McGuire, class of 1936. (Lapchick would return for a second successful term at the college from 1956 to 1965.) During McGuire's five years at the helm, the Johnnies compiled a 102–36 record and his teams made it to the NIT four times. In the 1951–52 season, they almost captured the NCAA crown. However, when McGuire left to build a major program from scratch at the University of North Carolina, he did serious damage to the future of New York basketball through his creation of what would become known as the "underground railroad." With his connections in the city, he brought down to Tobacco Row a "raft of the city's high school stars"—Jews and Christians both—who immediately, and then consistently, made the Tar Heels a national power. One of his first great recruits was Bronx-born and Jewish Lenny Rosenbluth, who became an All-American and in 1957 was a major contributor on a team that would wrest the NCAA crown from the University of Kansas and its star Wilt Chamberlain. Rosenbluth and McGuire were a perfect match. The young man "wanted out of New York" after the point-shaving basketball scandal that befell CCNY and other top-notch metropolitan-area teams while Rosenbluth was still in high school. And McGuire knew of the player's potentialities from professional basketball experts like Arnold "Red" Auerbach of the Boston Celtics. Arguably, had McGuire stayed at St. John's and used his remarkable recruiting skills, Rosenbluth may well have led the Johnnies to additional national court recognition. Ironically, Harry Gotkin, Hy's cousin, helped McGuire spirit players away from the metropolis, starting with Rosenbluth. While McGuire searched for the best future stars, after getting heads-ups on talented prospects from Harry Gotkin, none other than the now elderly Buck Freeman served as an assistant coach and helped strategize games. In a sense, the University of North Carolina became "St. John's South."[43]

Alan Seiden was one fellow McGuire and his entourage could not grab. The last great Jewish Redmen player, Seiden led Jamaica High School to the public school basketball championship in 1955 before enrolling at St. John's. Lapchick and his assistant Lou Carnesecca had an easy time recruiting Seiden because he desired to stay around home. His brother Ron has recalled that "fifty schools were after him," including Ivy League universities that admired his basketball skills and high grade-point average. But Alan was a "local kid" whose family lived near the campus where, while still in high school, he had played informally with some of the school's best players. In addition, he liked the idea of playing at Madison Square Garden. Untouched by the destructive 1951 scandal, which caused CCNY to downgrade its program, the Redmen were one of the few high-quality local teams left that could fill up the Mecca of Basketball, much like the Wonder Five had done more than twenty years earlier. In 1959 Alan led the Johnnies to the NIT title before trying out unsuccessfully for the professional St. Louis Hawks of the NBA.[44]

In the years that followed, although an increasingly multicultural St. John's University continued to attract its share of Jewish students to its many graduate programs—and a few as undergraduates—and was praised, in 1962, as a Catholic college "run by Vincentians that has long welcomed low income Jews," the athletic department no longer sought out Jewish basketball players. By the mid- to late 1960s, few Jews were playing at the skill level worthy of the attention of St. John's coaches and recruiters. The few who could play big-time basketball were pursued not only by schools south of the Mason-Dixon line but by colleges all over the country. Most notably, Ernie Grunfeld, who played high school ball in Forest Hills, Queens, just a few miles from the Johnnies' Hillcrest, Queens, campus—one of the two Jews in the last half century to earn Division 1 All-American honors—teamed up with fellow New Yorker, African American Bernard King at the University of Tennessee. In contemporary times, basketball has become the African American sport. Instead of Jews, they now are assigned the positive and negative stereotypes that come with being heralded as the most proficient roundballers around. The long-past era of the Wonder Five is but a memory.[45]

ACKNOWLEDGMENTS

*Forged in America: How Irish-Jewish Encounters Shaped a Nation* originated from the celebration of a quarter century of New York University's Glucksman Ireland House. The community that surrounds Glucksman Ireland House is unique and its vision is oxygenated by inspiring faculty, dynamic students, and dedicated staff. But our enterprise in the conversations on the intersectionality of the Jewish and Irish experiences in the United States was also greatly enriched by the advisory board of Glucksman Ireland House. The enthusiasm with which initiatives have been greeted by the board is second to none. Gratitude must also be expressed to Ireland's Department of Foreign Affairs, specifically the team at the Consulate of Ireland (New York), and to the director of Glucksman Ireland House, Professor Kevin Kenny. New York University's Goldstein-Goren Center for American Jewish History provided wonderful support for the public programs connected to this initiative, for which we are thankful, and especially to Gavin Beinart-Smollan for his editorial support. We are very grateful to all the contributors, especially those who overcame research obstacles presented by the recent pandemic. We thank the team at NYU Press, including the reviewers and the production team, but especially Eric Zinner and Furqan Sayeed. The speaker series on the theme of the book was complemented by contributions from Abby Bender, James Carroll, Richard White, and our late colleague Mick Moloney. On the home fronts, we are so very appreciative of the support of Steve Diner and Eon Grey.

# NOTES

### INTRODUCTION
1 Malcolm Campbell, *Ireland's New Worlds: Immigrants, Politics, and Society in the United States and Australia, 1815–1922* (Madison: University of Wisconsin Press, 2008), vii.

### 1. A SINGULAR ENCOUNTER
1 A Jewish immigration from the Ottoman Empire commenced in the late nineteenth century. Small in number, little historical analysis has explored how their political and civic behaviors differed from the majority of Jews of European origins.
2 Alison Kibler, *Censoring Racial Ridicule: Irish, Jews, and African American Struggles over Race and Representation, 1890–1930* (Chapel Hill: University of North Carolina Press, 2015).
3 Jon Gjerde, *From Peasants to Farmers: The Migration from Balestrand, Norway to the Upper Middle West* (New York: Cambridge University Press, 1985).
4 A few exceptions include Jay Dolan, *The Immigrant Church: New York's Irish and German Catholics, 1815–1865* (Notre Dame, IN: Notre Dame University Press, 1975); Ronald Bayor, *Neighbors in Conflict: The Irish, Germans, Jews, and Italians of New York City, 1929–1941* (Baltimore: Johns Hopkins University Press, 1978); Gary Mormino, *The Immigrant World of Ybor City: Italians and Their Latin Neighbors in Tampa, 1885–1945* (Urbana: University of Illinois Press, 1987).
5 Works by Rudolf Glanz include "Jews and Chinese in America," *Jewish Social Studies*, no. 16 (July 1954): 219–34; *Jew and Mormon: Historic Group Relations and Religious Outlook* (New York: self-pub., 1963), *Jew and Irish: Historic Group Relations and Immigration* (New York: self-pub., 1968); *Jew and Italian: Historic Group Relations and the New Immigration (1881–1924)* (New York: self-pub., 1970).
6 Cormac O'Grada, *Jewish Ireland in the Age of Joyce: A Socioeconomic History* (Princeton, NJ: Princeton University Press, 2006).
7 David Sorkin, *Jewish Emancipation: A History across Five Centuries* (Princeton, NJ: Princeton University Press, 2019).
8 Ewa Morawska in her two volumes on Johnstown, Pennsylvania, shows how the Jews from Slavic lands and the Christian Slavic immigrants essentially recreated their Old World relationships with each other, with the former selling goods as

peddlers and shopkeepers to the latter who labored in the mines and steel mills. Ewa Morawska, *For Bread with Butter: The Life-Worlds of East Central Europeans in Johnstown, Pennsylvania, 1890–1940* (New York: Cambridge University Press, 1985); *Insecure Prosperity: Small-Town Jews in Industrial America, 1890–1940* (Princeton, NJ: Princeton University Press, 1996).

9 Robert Orsi, *The Madonna of 115th Street: Faith and Community in Italian Harlem, 1880–1950* (New Haven, CT: Yale University Press, 1985).

10 Hasia R. Diner, *Roads Taken: The Great Jewish Migrations to the New World and the Peddlers Who Forged the Way* (New Haven, CT: Yale University Press, 2015).

11 Gabriel Goldstein and Elizabeth Greenberg, *A Perfect Fit: The Garment Industry and American Jewry, 1860–1960* (New York: Yeshiva University Museum, 2012); Hadassah Kosak, *Cultures of Opposition: Jewish Immigrant Workers, New York City* (Albany: State University of New York Press, 2000).

12 Hasia R. Diner, *Erin's Daughters in America: Irish Immigrant Women in the Nineteenth Century* (Baltimore: Johns Hopkins University Press, 1985), 99–102. There is a history to be written about the employment of Irish women in the homes of affluent Jews.

13 Susan Glenn, *Daughters of the Shtetl: Life and Labor in the Immigrant Generation* (Ithaca, New York: Cornell University Press, 1990).

14 Diane Vecchio, *Merchants, Midwives, and Laboring Women: Italian Migrants in Urban America* (Urbana: University of Illinois Press, 2006).

15 Annelise Orleck, *Common Sense and a Little Fire: Working Class Women's Activism in the 20th Century United States* (Chapel Hill: University of North Carolina Press, 1995); Alice Kessler-Harris, "Where Are the Organized Women Workers?," *Feminist Studies* 3, no. 1–2 (Autumn 1975): 92–110.

16 Lara Vapnek, *Breadwinners: Working Women and Economic Independence* (Urbana: University of Illinois Press, 2009).

17 Leon Stein, *The Triangle Fire* (Philadelphia: Lippincott, 1962).

18 Stephen Brumberg, *Going to America, Going to School: The Jewish Immigrant Public School Encounter in Turn-of-Century New York City* (New York: Praeger, 1986).

19 Janet Nolan, *Servants of the Poor: Teachers and Mobility in Ireland and Irish America* (Notre Dame, IN: University of Notre Dame Press, 2004); Diner, *Erin's Daughters*, 96–99.

20 Joel Perlmann, *Ethnic Differences: Schooling and Social Structure among the Irish, Italians, Jews, and Blacks in an American City, 1880–1935* (Cambridge: Cambridge University Press, 2010).

21 Raymond A. Mohl, "Schools, Politics, and Riots: The Gary Plan in New York City, 1914–1917," *Paedagogica Historica* 15, no. 1 (1975): 39–72.

22 Irving Howe, *World of Our Fathers* (New York: Harcourt Brace Jovanovich, 1976), 271.

23 Myra Kelly, *Wards of Liberty* (New York: McClure's, 1907), xii.

24 Ruth J. Markowitz, *My Daughter the Teacher: Jewish Teachers in the New York City Schools* (New Brunswick, NJ: Rutgers University Press, 1993), 33.

25 Mark Wyman, *Round-Trip to America: The Immigrants Return to Europe, 1880–1930* (Ithaca, New York: Cornell University Press, 1993).
26 Simon Kuznets, "The Immigration of Russian Jews to the United States: Background and Structure," *Perspectives in American History*, no. 9 (1975): 35–124; Jonathan Sarna, "The Myth of No Return: Jewish Return Migration to Eastern Europe," *American Jewish History* 71, no. 2 (1981), 256–68; Kerby A. Miller, *Emigrants and Exiles: Ireland and the Irish Exodus to North America* (New York: Oxford University Press, 1985).
27 Steven P. Erie, *Rainbow's End: Irish-Americans and the Dilemma of Urban Machine Politics, 1840–1965* (Berkeley: University of California Press, 1988); Terry Golway, *Machine Made: Tammany Hall and the Creation of Modern American Politics* (New York: Liveright, 2014).
28 William Riordan, *Plunkitt of Tammany Hall: A Series of Very Plain Talks on Very Practical Politics, Delivered by Ex-Senator George Washington Plunkitt, the Tammany Philosopher, from His Rostrum—the New York County Court House Bootblack Stand* (New York: McClure, Phillips, 1905).
29 Joseph F. Dineen, *Ward Eight* (New York: Arno, 1976).
30 John A. Lucas, "Judge Jeremiah T. Mahoney, the Amateur Athletic Union, and the Berlin Olympics," *Journal of Sport History* 35, no. 3 (Fall 2008): 503–8: Robert Slayton, *Empire Statesman: The Rise and Redemption of Al Smith* (New York: Free Press, 2001); James Michael Curley, *I'd Do It Again: A Record of All My Uproarious Years* (Englewood Cliffs, NJ: Prentice-Hall, 1967).
31 Arthur Mann, *Yankee Reformers in the Urban Age: Social Reform in Boston, 1880–1900* (New York: Harper & Row, 1954).
32 Mary Boyle O'Reilly, "Mary Boyle O'Reilly, in Russia, Investigates 'Ritual' Murder," *The Day Book*, October 6, 1913, 1–5.
33 Charles P. Daly, *The Settlement of the Jews in North America* (New York: P. Cowen, 1893); Charles P. Daly, *The Jews of New York* (New York: American Hebrew, 1883); Max J. Kohler, *Charles P. Daly: A Tribute to His Memory* (New York: American Hebrew, 1899).
34 Edward H. Judge, *Easter in Kishinev* (New York: New York University Press, 1992); Steven Zipperstein, *Pogrom: Kishinev and the Tilt of History* (New York: W.W. Norton, 2018).
35 Michael Davitt, *Within the Pale: The True Story of the Anti-Semitic Persecutions in Russia* (Philadelphia: Jewish Publication Society of America, 1903).
36 Davitt, 107.
37 Davitt, 77.

## 2. THE RIGHT TO CHOOSE

1 Margaret Sanger to Lillian D. Wald, February 2, 1929, Subseries I, C04:0889, *Margaret Sanger Papers Microfilm Edition: Collected Documents*, ed. Esther Katz, Cathy Moran Hajo, and Peter C. Engelman (Bethesda, MD: University Publications of America, 1997).

2. Lillian D. Wald to Margaret Sanger, February 25, 1929, Subseries I, C04:0916, *Margaret Sanger Papers Microfilm Edition: Collected Documents*.
3. Marjorie Feld, *Lillian Wald: A Biography* (Chapel Hill: University of North Carolina Press, 2008), 21.
4. Jean Baker, *Margaret Sanger: A Life of Passion* (New York: Hill & Wang, 2012), 2–3, 20.
5. Feld, *Lillian Wald*, 9, 20–22.
6. Melissa R. Klapper, *Ballots, Babies, and Banners of Peace: American Jewish Women's Activism, 1890–1940* (New York: New York University Press, 2013), 4.
7. Gwendolyn Mink, *The Wages of Motherhood: Inequality in the Welfare State, 1917–1942* (Ithaca, New York: Cornell University Press, 1995), 8.
8. Lillian D. Wald, Application to New York Hospital Training School for Nurses, 1889, Box 2, Folder 1, Lillian D. Wald Papers 1889–1957, New York Public Library.
9. Lillian Faderman, *Odd Girls and Twilight Lovers: A History of Lesbian Life in America* (New York: Columbia University Press, 2012), 13–18.
10. Baker, *Margaret Sanger*, 45.
11. Baker.
12. Lillian D. Wald, Application to New York Hospital Training School for Nurses, May 27, 1889, Lillian D. Wald Papers 1889–1957, New York Public Library.
13. Feld, *Lillian Wald*, 7.
14. Feld, 42.
15. Feld, 58.
16. Joan I. Roberts and Thetis M. Group, *Feminism and Nursing: An Historical Perspective on Power, Status, and Political Activism in the Nursing Profession* (Westport, CT: Praeger, 1995), 73.
17. Lillian D. Wald, *The House on Henry Street* (New York: Henry Holt, 1915), v.
18. Wald, 1.
19. Feld, *Lillian Wald*, 33.
20. Wald, *House on Henry Street*, 7.
21. Wald, 7–8.
22. Wald, 6.
23. Wald, 60.
24. Lillian D. Wald, "The Treatment of Families in Which There Is Sickness," *American Journal of Nursing*, no. 4 (March–May 1904): 428.
25. Lillian D. Wald, "The Nurses' Settlement in New York," *American Journal of Nursing*, no. 2 (May 1902): 568.
26. Feld, *Lillian Wald*, 42.
27. Wald, *House on Henry Street*, 65.
28. Lillian D. Wald to Mr. Scherer, Syrian Protestant College, Beirut, Lebanon, July 10, 1908, Box 2, Folder 4, Lillian D. Wald Papers 1889–1957, New York Public Library.
29. Mink, *Wages*, 7.
30. New York Ladies' Health Protective Association, cited in Noralee Frankel and Nancy Schrom Dye, eds., *Gender, Class, Race, and Reform in the Progressive Era* (Lexington: University Press of Kentucky, 1988), 3.

31 Klapper, *Ballots*, 13.
32 Feld, *Lillian Wald*, 42.
33 Faderman, *Odd Girls*, 12–13.
34 Wald, *House on Henry Street*, 8–9.
35 Feld, *Lillian Wald*, 30.
36 Feld, 75–82.
37 Feld, 30.
38 Feld, 5–6.
39 Wald, "Nurses' Settlement," 572–73.
40 Maternity Appeal, Lillian D. Wald Papers 1895–1936, Columbia University Rare Book and Manuscript Library.
41 Darlene Clark Hine, *Black Women in White: Racial Conflict and Cooperation in the Nursing Profession, 1890–1950* (Bloomington: Indiana University Press, 1989), cited in Feld, *Lillian Wald*, 63.
42 Lillian D. Wald to Mr. Scherer, Lillian D. Wald Papers 1889–1957, New York Public Library.
43 On the NCJW, see Faith Rogow, *Gone to Another Meeting: The National Council of Jewish Women, 1893–1993* (Tuscaloosa: University of Alabama Press, 1993).
44 Feld, *Lillian Wald*, 50.
45 Wald, "Nurses' Settlement," 568.
46 Wald, *House on Henry Street*, 60.
47 Mina Carson, *Settlement Folk: Social Thought and the American Settlement Movement, 1885–1930* (Chicago: University of Chicago Press, 1990), 72.
48 Wald, *House on Henry Street*, 13.
49 Wald, "Nurses' Settlement," 568.
50 Mary Buell Sayers, "The Visiting Nurse and the Nurses' Settlement," October 1905, Box 87, Folder 1.10, Lillian D. Wald Papers 1895–1936, Columbia University Rare Book and Manuscript Library.
51 Wald, "Treatment of Families."
52 Wald, "Nurses' Settlement," 568.
53 Box 87, Folder 1, Lillian D. Wald Papers 1895–1936, Columbia University Rare Book and Manuscript Library.
54 Wald, *House on Henry Street*, 27.
55 Feld, *Lillian Wald*, 63.
56 "Discussion of Paper by LDW at Conference of Charities and Corrections," 1905, Lillian D. Wald Papers 1889–1957, New York Public Library.
57 Wald, *House on Henry Street*, 42.
58 Maternity Appeal, Box 87, Folder 1.8, Lillian D. Wald Papers 1895–1936, Columbia University Rare Book and Manuscript Library.
59 Wald, *House on Henry Street*, 42.
60 Wald, "Nurses' Settlement," 572.
61 Safe-milk stations provided pasteurized milk to prevent the spread of tuberculosis.
62 Baker, *Margaret Sanger*, 26.

63  Baker, 28.
64  Margaret Sanger to National Youth Administration, 1940, quoted in Baker, 22.
65  Ellen Chesler, *Woman of Valor: Margaret Sanger and the Birth Control Movement in America* (New York: Simon & Schuster, 1992); Margaret Sanger, *The Autobiography of Margaret Sanger* (Mineola, New York: Dover, 2004).
66  Chesler, 62.
67  Sanger, *Autobiography*, 86.
68  Sanger, 89.
69  Chesler, *Woman of Valor*, 13.
70  Andrea Tone, *Devices and Desires: A History of Contraception in America* (New York: Hill & Wang, 2001), 67–91.
71  Sanger, *Autobiography*, 89.
72  The sources refer to Sadie Sachs by her first name, so I have chosen to follow suit.
73  Sanger, *Autobiography*, 91.
74  Sanger.
75  Sanger, 92.
76  Chesler, *Woman of Valor*, 13.
77  Chesler.
78  Roberts and Group, *Feminism*, 69.
79  Chesler, *Woman of Valor*, 14.
80  Sanger, *Autobiography*, 93.
81  Chesler, *Woman of Valor*, 14.
82  Baker, *Margaret Sanger*, 77.
83  Baker, 70.
84  Baker, 58.
85  Sanger, *Autobiography*, 106.
86  Margaret Sanger, "Why the Woman Rebel?," *The Woman Rebel*, March 1914, in *The Selected Papers of Margaret Sanger*, vol. 1, *The Woman Rebel (1900–1928)*, ed. Esther Katz, Cathy Moran Hajo, and Peter C. Engelman (Urbana: University of Illinois Press, 2007), 71.
87  Sanger.
88  Sanger, *Autobiography*, 108.
89  Baker, *Margaret Sanger*, 75.
90  Sanger, *Autobiography*, 109.
91  Sanger.
92  Baker, *Margaret Sanger*, 44.
93  Baker, 58.
94  Baker, 79–82.
95  Margaret Sanger, "Should Women Know?," February 1915, Subseries IV, C16:0072, *Margaret Sanger Papers Microfilm Edition: Collected Documents*.
96  Margaret Sanger, "My Fight for America's First Birth-Control Clinic," February 1960, Subseries IV, C16:0496, *Margaret Sanger Papers Microfilm Edition: Collected Documents*.

97 Lillian D. Wald to Dr. Abraham Jacobi, May 27, 1915, Box 17, Folder 13, Lillian D. Wald Papers 1895–1936, Columbia University Rare Book and Manuscript Library.
98 Lillian D. Wald to Dr. S. Adolphus Knopf, September 22, 1916, Box 17, Folder 13, Lillian D. Wald Papers 1895–1936, Columbia University Rare Book and Manuscript Library.
99 Lillian D. Wald to A. G., December 3, 1921, Box 17, Folder 13, Lillian D. Wald Papers 1895–1938, Columbia University Rare Book and Manuscript Library.
100 Margaret Sanger to friends, January 26, 1916, Box 17, Folder 13, Lillian D. Wald Papers 1895–1938, Columbia University Rare Book and Manuscript Library.
101 See Lillian D. Wald to Executive Secretary of the American Birth Control League, November 29, 1921, Box 17, Folder 13, Lillian D. Wald Papers 1895–1938, Columbia University Rare Book and Manuscript Library; Lillian D. Wald to Mrs. Robertson Jones, February 21, 1929, Box 17, Folder 13, Lillian D. Wald Papers 1895–1936, Columbia University Rare Book and Manuscript Library; Lillian D. Wald to Margaret Sanger, October 2, 1931, Subseries I, C05:0253, *Margaret Sanger Papers Microfilm Edition: Collected Documents*.
102 Sanger, "My Fight."
103 Chesler, *Woman of Valor*, 209–10.
104 Esther Katz, "Margaret Sanger," *American National Biography Online*, February 2000, https://doi.org/10.1093/anb/9780198606697.article.1500598.
105 Chesler, *Woman of Valor*, 15.
106 Chesler, 211–13.
107 John Augustine Ryan, *Family Limitation and the Church and Birth Control* (New York: Paulist Press, 1921), 5.
108 Margaret Sanger to Lillian D. Wald, April 20, 1921, Box 9, Folder 1 to 7, Lillian D. Wald Papers 1895–1936, Columbia University Rare Book and Manuscript Library.
109 Baker, *Margaret Sanger*, 174; Chesler, *Woman of Valor*, 203.
110 Linda Gordon, *The Moral Property of Women: A History of Birth Control Politics in America* (Champaign: University of Illinois Press, 2007), 190–91.
111 Dorothy E. Roberts, *Killing the Black Body: Race, Reproduction, and the Meaning of Liberty* (New York: Vintage Books, 2017), 71.
112 Margaret Sanger to Lillian D. Wald, April 10, 1921, Box 9, Folder 1 to 7, Lillian D. Wald Papers 1895–1936, Columbia University Rare Book and Manuscript Library.
113 Julia Barrett Rublee to Lillian Wald, September 2, 1921, Box 17, Folder 14, Lillian D. Wald Papers 1895–1936, Columbia University Rare Book and Manuscript Library. It is unclear to what she is referring, since I have been unable to locate an American Health Association founded two hundred years previously.
114 "One Hundred Years of Birth Control: An Outline of Its History," *Birth Control Review*, November 1921, Box 17, Folder 13, Lillian D. Wald Papers 1895–1936, Columbia University Rare Book and Manuscript Library.
115 Gordon, *Moral Property*, 190–98.
116 "One Hundred Years of Birth Control."
117 "One Hundred Years of Birth Control."

118 "Birth Control Raid Made by Police on Archbishop's Order: Cat. Donohue's Only Instructions from Headquarters were to 'Look for Mgr. Dineen.' Suppressed Before Start. Policeman Testifies that Donohue Ordered Him to Get Mrs. Sanger off the Stage. The Two Prisoners Freed Evidence Lacking, Says Magistrate—Mgr. Dineen Explains Catholic Church's Attitude. Archbishop Hayes Invited. Archbishop Caused Birth Control Raid Told to See Mgr. Dineen. Evidence Submitted to Court Dismissal Recommended," *New York Times (1857–1922)*, November 15, 1921.
119 Chesler, *Woman of Valor*, 203.
120 Executive Secretary of the American Birth Control League to Lillian D. Wald, November 29, 1921, Box 17, Folder 13, Lillian D. Wald Papers 1895–1936, Columbia University Rare Book and Manuscript Library.
121 Margaret Sanger, "The Morality of Birth Control," November 18, 1921, Subseries IV, C16:0163, *Margaret Sanger Papers Microfilm Edition: Collected Documents*.
122 Sanger.
123 Chesler, *Woman of Valor*, 204.
124 Sanger, "Morality."
125 Sanger, 213.
126 Charles E. Curran, *Catholic Moral Theology in the United States: A History* (Washington, DC: Georgetown University Press, 2008), 47.
127 Margaret Sanger, "Birth Control Steps Out: A Note on the Senate Hearing," April 1931, Margaret Sanger Papers, Library of Congress, LCM S71:0220; Chesler, *Woman of Valor*, 335.
128 Lillian D. Wald to American Birth Control League, February 21, 1929, Box 17, Folder 13, Lillian D. Wald Papers, Columbia Rare Book and Manuscript Library.
129 Margaret Sanger to Lillian D. Wald, February 3, 1933, Subseries I, C05:0497, *Margaret Sanger Papers Microfilm Edition: Collected Documents*.
130 Chesler, *Woman of Valor*, 335.
131 Chesler, 344–47.
132 Chesler, 213.
133 Chesler, 15.
134 See Wald, "Nurses' Settlement" and Wald, *House on Henry Street*, 67.
135 Sanger, "Should Women Know?"
136 Wald, *House on Henry Street*, 66.
137 Sanger, "Why the Woman Rebel?," 72.

3. "TAMMANY'S CHOSEN PEOPLE"

1 The Deputies of Dáil Éireann, "Debate on the Treaty between Great Britain and Ireland, signed in London on the 6th December, 1921: Sessions 14 December 1921 to 10 January 1922," www.ucc.ie/celt/published/E900003-001/index.html, accessed through *CELT: Corpus of Electronic Texts Edition*, March 7, 2023.
2 Nathan Glazer and Daniel P. Moynihan, *Beyond the Melting Pot: The Negroes, Puerto Ricans, Jews, Italians, and Irish of New York City* (Cambridge, MA: MIT Press, 1970), 223.

3   Paul Ritterband, "Counting the Jews of New York, 1900–1991: An Essay in Substance and Method," www.pewresearch.org/wp-content/uploads/sites/7/2013/10/jewish-american-beliefs-attitudes-culture-survey-overview.pdf, accessed through the *Berman Jewish Policy Archive*, March 7, 2023.
4   For more on Whig and elite attitudes toward immigrants, see Terry Golway, *Machine Made: Tammany Hall and the Creation of Modern American Politics* (New York: Liveright, 2014).
5   Louis Eisenstein and Elliot Rosenberg, *A Stripe of Tammany's Tiger* (New York: Robert Speller & Sons, 1966), 15.
6   Ted Morgan, *FDR: A Biography* (New York: Simon & Schuster, 1986), 552.
7   *New York Times*, October 30, 1880; *New York Tribune*, October 27, 1880; October 24, 1880.
8   *New York Sun*, November 1, 1880.
9   *New York Sun*, November 1, 1880.
10  Sven Beckert, "Democracy and Its Discontents: Contesting Suffrage Rights in Gilded Age New York," *Past and Present* 174, no. 1 (2002): 137; *New York Tribune*, October 24, 1877.
11  Nancy Joan Weiss, *Charles Francis Murphy, 1858–1924: Respectability and Responsibility in Tammany Politics* (Northampton, MA: Smith College Press, 1968), 21.
12  Kilroe Tammany Collection, New-York Historical Society.
13  William L. Riordan, ed., *Plunkitt of Tammany Hall: A Series of Very Plain Talks on Very Practical Politics* (New York: Signet Classics, 1995), 48.
14  Eisenstein and Rosenberg, *Stripe of Tammany's Tiger*, 15.
15  For more on labor's demands after the Triangle fire, see Richard A. Greenwald, *The Triangle Fire, the Protocols of Peace, and Industrial Democracy in Progressive Era New York* (Philadelphia: Temple University Press, 2005).
16  An English version of the encyclical is available online: https://www.vatican.va/content/leo-xiii/en/encyclicals.html; The Reminiscences of Jeremiah T. Mahoney, Columbia University Oral History Project, 195.
17  Hasia R. Diner, "How the Irish Challenged American Identity: An Immigrant Group's History Lessons for Today," in Terry Golway, ed., *Being New York, Being Irish: Reflections on Twenty-Five Years of Irish America and New York University's Glucksman Ireland House* (Newbridge, Ireland: Irish Academic Press, 2018), 86.
18  Steven P. Erie, *Rainbow's End: Irish-Americans and the Dilemmas of Urban Machine Politics, 1840–1985* (Berkeley: University of California Press, 1988), 122.
19  A good minibiography of Smith and his alliances with Jews is contained within Robert Caro, *The Power Broker: Robert Moses and the Fall of New York* (New York: Vintage Books, 1975). See also Robert Slayton, *Empire Statesman: The Rise and Redemption of Al Smith* (New York: Free Press, 2001).
20  *New York Times*, October 2, 1917.
21  See Elisabeth Israels Perry, *Belle Moskowitz: Feminine Politics and the Exercise of Power in the Age of Alfred E. Smith* (New York: Oxford University Press, 1987).

22  Richard O'Connor, *The First Hurrah: A Biography of Alfred E. Smith* (New York: G. P. Putnam's Sons, 1970), 178.
23  Caro, *Power Broker*, 91.
24  For more on Murphy's desire for respectability, see Nancy Joan Weiss, *Charles Francis Murphy 1858–1924: Respectability and Responsibility in Tammany Politics* (Northampton, MA: Smith College Press, 1968).
25  For more on Flynn, see his memoir, *You're the Boss: The Practice of American Politics* (New York: Collier Books, 1962).
26  Edward J. Flynn to Eleanor Roosevelt, March 23, 1943, Franklin D. Roosevelt Presidential Library, President's Official File, 1892, Box 2.

## 4. JEWS, PAUL O'DWYER, AND A NEW YORK LIFE

1  Paul O'Dwyer, interviewed by Jill Levine, 1980, William Wiener Oral History of the American Jewish Committee, New York Public Library.
2  Paul O'Dwyer, *Counsel for the Defense: The Autobiography of Paul O'Dwyer* (New York: Simon & Schuster, 1979), 11–12.
3  O'Dwyer interview with Levine. On the Irish republicanism and skepticism about clerical authority that O'Dwyer absorbed in Bohola, see O'Dwyer, *Counsel for the Defense*, 19, 37–50.
4  O'Dwyer interview with Levine.
5  O'Dwyer, *Counsel for the Defense*, 59–61, 65.
6  O'Dwyer interview with Levine.
7  O'Dwyer, *Counsel for the Defense*, 65–66.
8  O'Dwyer, 67.
9  O'Dwyer, 67–71.
10  O'Dwyer interview with Levine.
11  O'Dwyer interview with Levine.
12  O'Dwyer, *Counsel for the Defense*, 74–76; William O'Dwyer, *Beyond the Golden Door* (New York: St. John's University, 1986), 114–18.
13  "Oscar Bernstien," *New York Times*, May 19, 1974, 59; "Rebecca Drucker Bernstien, 105," *New York Times*, January 2, 1996, C36; Oscar Bernstien, interviewed by John Kelly, July 1962, Oral History Research Office, Columbia University.
14  O'Dwyer, *Counsel for the Defense*, 86–87; Bernstien interview.
15  Ronald H. Bayor, *Neighbors in Conflict: The Irish, Germans, Jews and Italians of New York City, 1929–1941* (Baltimore: Johns Hopkins University Press, 1980); Stephen H. Norwood, "Marauding Youth and the Christian Front: Antisemitic Violence in Boston and New York during World War II," *American Jewish History* 91, no. 2 (June 2003): 238, 243, 260.
16  O'Dwyer, *Counsel for the Defense*, 96.
17  O'Dwyer, 96.
18  O'Dwyer, 100.
19  Robert D. Leiter, "The Fur Workers Union," *ILR Review* 3, no. 2 (January 1950): 163, 169–74, 186; Irving Howe, *World of Our Fathers: The Journey of the East*

*European Jews to America and the Life They Found and Made* (New York: Simon & Schuster, 1976), 338–41; David Yee, "SHTARKER: The Convergence of Organized Crime and Organized Labor in the New York Garment Industry" (master's thesis, City College, City University of New York, 2014), 38–48; Henry Foner interview with Daniel Soyer, ILGWU Heritage Project, *Cornell University ILR School*, https://ilgwu.ilr.cornell.edu, June 10, 2009; Philip S. Foner, *The Fur and Leather Workers Union: A Story of Dramatic Struggles and Achievements* (Newark, NJ: Nordan, 1950); Steve Fraser, *Labor Will Rule: Sidney Hillman and the Rise of American Labor* (Ithaca, New York: Cornell University Press, 1993).

20 For a summary of the trials, see, in the *New York Times*, hereafter *NYT*: "80 Indicted Here in Huge Fur 'Trust,'" *NYT*, November 7, 1933, 8; "Six Are Convicted in Fur Racket Case," *NYT*, December 17, 1937, 52; "Union Win Trust Case," *NYT*, December 20, 1938, 47; "U.S. Starts Fur Trial on Old Amen Charges," *NYT*, February 21, 1940, 3; "Gold and 10 Others Guilty in Fur Case," *NYT*, April 14, 1940, 14; "Fur Union Leaders Indicted by U.S.," *NYT*, May 15, 1940, 25; "Gold Is Acquitted in Jury Plot Trial," *NYT*, July 12, 1940, 34; "Convictions Voided in Fur Racket Case," *NYT*, November 5, 1940, 27. On Louis Boudin, see "Louis Boudin Dies; Labor Lawyer, 78," *NYT*, May 31, 1952, 72. Also see, on the American ORT, "History of American ORT," https://ort.org/en/about-ort/history/. On Samuel Leibowitz, see Dan T. Carter, *Scottsboro: A Tragedy of the American South* (Baton Rouge: Louisiana State University Press, 1969/2007); James Goodman, *Stories of Scottsboro* (New York: Pantheon, 1994). On Boudin, see "Boudin, Louis B.," in Mari Jo Buhle, Paul Buhle, and Dan Georgakas, eds., *Encyclopedia of the American Left* (New York: Oxford University Press, 1998).

21 On the furriers' trial and its legacy for O'Dwyer, see O'Dwyer, *Counsel for the Defense*, 96–97. On the founding of the National Lawyers Guild, see Jerold S. Auerbach, *Unequal Justice: Lawyers and Social Change* (New York: Oxford University Press, 1976), 198–211; Christopher H. Johnson, *Maurice Sugar: Law, Labor, and the Left in Detroit, 1912–1950* (Detroit: Wayne State University Press, 1988), 220–21, 249; *A History of the National Lawyers Guild, 1937–1987* (National Lawyers Guild Foundation, 1987), 7–14; Ann Fagan Ginger and Eugene M. Tobin, eds., *The National Lawyers Guild: From Roosevelt through Reagan* (Philadelphia: Temple University Press, 1988).

22 See Percival R. Bailey, "The Case of the National Lawyers Guild, 1939–1958," in Athan G. Theoharis, ed., *Beyond the Hiss Case: The FBI, Congress, and the Cold War* (Philadelphia: Temple University Press, 1982); Auerbach, *Unequal Justice*.

23 Maurice Isserman, "American Labor Party," in Kenneth T. Jackson, ed., *Encyclopedia of New York City*, 2nd ed.(New Haven, CT: Yale University Press, 2010), 35.

24 Chad Ludington, "Liberal Party," in Jackson, *Encyclopedia of New York City*, 736–37. Also see Daniel Soyer, *Left in the Center: The Liberal Party of New York and the Rise and Fall of American Social Democracy* (Ithaca, New York: Cornell University Press, 2021) and Soyer, "Executed Bundists, Soviet Delegates and the Wartime

Jewish Popular Front," *American Communist History* 15, no. 3 (2016): 293–97, 304–14, 326–27, 331–32.

25  O'Dwyer, *Counsel for the Defense*, 104–5, 113–15. Also see David Brundage, *Irish Nationalists in America: The Politics of Exile, 1798–1998* (New York: Oxford University Press), 184–85.

26  O'Dwyer, *Counsel for the Defense*, 150–54; Deborah Dash Moore, Jeffrey S. Gurock, Annie Polland, Howard B. Rock, and Daniel Soyer, *Jewish New York: The Remarkable Story of a City and People* (New York: New York University Press, 2017), 262–83; David S. Wyman, *The Abandonment of the Jews: America and the Holocaust, 1941–1945* (New York: New Press, 1998), 84–92; Adina Hoffman, *Ben Hecht: Fighting Words, Moving Pictures* (New Haven, CT: Yale University Press, 2019); Julien Gorbach, *The Notorious Ben Hecht: Iconoclastic Writer and Militant Zionist* (West Lafayette, IN: Purdue University Press, 2019).

27  O'Dwyer interview with Levine; Alexander Feinberg, "10,000 Protest on Palestine Here," *New York Times*, March 12, 1948, 8. On progressive American attitudes toward the founding of Israel and the lack of concern with Palestinians, see Amy Kaplan, *Our American Israel: The Story of an Entangled Alliance* (Cambridge, MA: Harvard University Press, 2018), 39–57. I also thank Paul Scham and Marjorie Feld for sharing their thoughts on this question.

28  O'Dwyer, *Counsel for the Defense*, 152–54, 164–65.

29  O'Dwyer, 160–64; Rafael Medoff, *Militant Zionism in America: The Rise and Impact of the Jabotinsky Movement in the United States, 1926–1948* (Tuscaloosa: University of Alabama Press, 2002), 201–11.

30  O'Dwyer, *Counsel for the Defense*, 165–67.

31  O'Dwyer, 133–41; Jacob K. Javits and Rafael Steinberg, *Javits: The Autobiography of a Public Man* (New York: Houghton Mifflin Harcourt, 1981), 107–12.

32  Javits and Steinberg, *Javits*, 107. Also see Robert W. Snyder, *Crossing Broadway: Washington Heights and the Promise of New York* (Ithaca, New York: Cornell University Press, 2015), 29–33.

33  O'Dwyer, *Counsel for the Defense*, 137–38.

34  O'Dwyer, 138–39; in *Aufbau*, see "Der Kampf um Washington Heights: Interview mit Paul O'Dwyer," October 8, 1948, 2, and "Der Kampf um Washington Heights, II: Interview mit Jacob Javits," October 15, 1948, 6; and in the *New York Times*, Kenneth Campbell, "Javits, O'Dwyer Seen in Close Race," October 15, 1948, 16, and "Javits, Paul O'Dwyer in a Spirited Debate," October 26, 1948, 38. My thanks to Peter Wortsman for translating O'Dwyer's interview in *Aufbau* from the original German.

35  O'Dwyer, *Counsel for the Defense*, 141; Javits and Steinberg, *Javits*, 113; Warren Moscow, "Marcantonio Wins by a Narrow Margin," *New York Times*, November 3, 1948, 1.

36  O'Dwyer, *Counsel for the Defense*, 177, 180–82.

37  On O'Dwyer, the National Lawyers Guild, and the Slansky trial, see Paul O'Dwyer's interview with Jane Conlon Muller (1990), Archives of Irish America,

NYU Tamiment Library, AIA.012, CD 12. I thank Rob Polner for sharing with me his notes on this interview. Also see Sidney E. Zion, "Says Paul O'Dwyer: 'The Times Seem to Have Caught Up With Me,'" *New York Times*, August 11, 1968, SM11. On the Slansky trial, see Michal Frankl, "Slansky Trial," *YIVO Encyclopedia of Jews in Eastern Europe* (2010), https://yivoencyclopedia.org, accessed March 10, 2023; Helaine Blumenthal, "Communism on Trial: The Slansky Affair and Anti-Semitism in Post-World War II Europe," *UC Berkeley Recent Work*, https://escholarship.org, 2009.

38 O'Dwyer, *Counsel for the Defense*, 141–50, 169–77, 180–85; on O'Dwyer's political trajectory, see Zion, "Says Paul O'Dwyer." On the Liberal Party, see Soyer, *Left in the Center*.

39 O'Dwyer, *Counsel for the Defense*, 122–23; also see, in the *New York Times*, "2 Balky Witnesses Cited by the House," September 4, 1959, 24, and "Lawyer Is Convicted," May 5, 1961, 12.

40 For Martin Popper's short essay, see *History of the National Lawyers Guild*, 11. On Popper's affection for O'Dwyer, see author interview with Dr. Laura Popper, September 2020.

41 On his encounter with young radicals in the 1960s, see O'Dwyer in his interview with Muller.

42 O'Dwyer, *Counsel for the Defense*, 184–85.

43 Wallace Sayre and Herbert Kaufman, *Governing New York City: Politics in the Metropolis* (New York: Russell Sage Foundation, 1960), 726–38. On Wagner, see Fred J. Cook and Gene Gleason, "Wagner: The Man Out Front" in "The Shame of New York," a special issue of *The Nation*, October 31, 1959, 274–78.

44 On O'Dwyer's style, see author telephone interview with Daniel Czitrom, September 2020. I learned much from Sarah and Victor Kovner, friends of Paul O'Dwyer and veterans of the reform Democratic movement, in a telephone interview conducted September 11, 2020. For a good discussion of reformers and regulars, framed through an analysis of the Village Independent Democrats, see Jonathan Soffer, *Ed Koch and the Rebuilding of New York City* (New York: Columbia University Press, 2010), 30–37, 40–52. There are useful ideas on the culture of reformers and regulars in Daniel Patrick Moynihan, "Bosses and Reformers: A Profile of the New York Democrats," *Commentary*, June 1961, 1–18 passim.

45 See Kovner interview and "Statement by Mayor Wagner on the Candidacy of Paul O'Dwyer," October 10, 1963, Box 060012W, Folder 14, Robert F. Wagner Documents Collection, LaGuardia Community College.

46 For summaries of O'Dwyer's races, see the following in the *New York Times*: "Truman Plurality 138,558 in County," November 21, 1948, 56; "Democrats Name Dudley," September 19, 1962, 1; "Vote Light Here," November 6, 1963, 1; "Javits Assisted by Liberal Voting," November 7, 1968, 40; "O'Dwyer Finishes Second on Strong City Showing," June 24, 1970, 1; "A Landslide Here," November 7, 1973, 1; "Voter Turnout Light," September 15, 1976, 93; "Koch and Cuomo Seek Support," September 10, 1977, 53; "News Summary," September 20, 1977, 86; "Carol Bellamy

'Proud' of Her Independence," September 20, 1977, 17. For an appreciative account of O'Dwyer's career, see Anna Quindlen, "Paul O'Dwyer Elects to Leave His Old Sod, Politics, and Is Moving On to New Ground," *New York Times*, September 21, 1977, 21.

47  Kovner interview; telephone interview with Lowry Hemphill, September 22, 2020; Zion, "Says Paul O'Dwyer"; Quindlen, "Paul O'Dwyer."

48  Zion, "Says Paul O'Dwyer"; James Clarity, "Javits-O'Dwyer-Buckley Race for Senate Just Plods Along," *New York Times*, October 31, 1968, 41; Seven V. Roberts, "O'Dwyer Pursues 'Old Politics' of Seeking Ethnic Group Votes," *New York Times*, September 30, 1968, 42; Sydney H. Schanberg, "Javits Assisted by Liberal Wing," *New York Times*, November 7, 1968, 40.

49  Edward I. Koch interview, Columbia University Oral History Research Office (1976), Interview I, Session 11, 354–57, 360; Lucinda Franks, "Council Presidency Getting New Look under O'Dwyer," *New York Times*, April 8, 1974, 76; Molly Ivins, "O'Dwyer: Figurehead or a Major Political Force?," *New York Times*, November 10, 1976, 30.

50  O'Dwyer interview with Levine; Robert Shelton, "Folk Performers Play for O'Dwyer," *New York Times*, October 10, 1968, 58; Jonathan Zalman, "Theodore Bikel, an Entertainment Giant, Dies at 91," *Tablet*, July 21, 1915. www.tabletmag.com.

51  On Charlie Keith, see "Charles Keith, Managed O'Dwyer's Race in 1973," *New York Times*, February 17, 1978, D12; for his biography, see "Keith, Charles Lawrence," *Abraham Lincoln Brigade Archives*, www.alba-valb.org/volunteers/charles-lawrence-keith, accessed March 7, 2023; "A Noble Itinerant," reprinted from *Newsday*, February 18, 1978, in Murray Kempton, *Rebellions, Perversities, and Main Events* (New York: Random House, 1994), 41–43.

52  On the 1976 primary, see "Voting in Primaries for U.S. House and State Legislature," *New York Times*, September 16, 1976, 34; Leandra Ruth Zarnow, *Battling Bella: The Protest Politics of Bella Abzug* (Cambridge, MA: Harvard University Press, 2019), 231–32. On O'Dwyer and Bellamy's contest in 1977, see, in the *New York Times*: "Koch and Cuomo Seek Support," September 10, 1977, 53; "O'Dwyer and Senator Bellamy Girding for Runoff," September 10, 1977, 17; "Carol Bellamy Won" in "News Summary," September 20, 1977, 86; "Carol Bellamy 'Proud' of Her Independence," September 20, 1977, 46; Quindlen, "Paul O'Dwyer."

53  O'Dwyer, *Counsel for the Defense*, 280–81; Eric Lichtblau, *The Nazis Next Door: How America Became a Safe Haven for Hitler's Men* (New York: Houghton Mifflin Harcourt, 2014), 134–35; Rachelle G. Saidel, *The Outraged Conscience: Seekers of Justice for Nazi War Criminals in America* (Albany: State University of New York Press, 1984), 79–86; "Remembering David Horowitz" at https://unitedisraelworldunion.com/category/remembering-david-horowitz/.

54  Suzanne Daley, "Manhattan's History to Have New Guardian," *New York Times*, July 23, 1986, B3; "Dinkins Drops a Plum into Paul O'Dwyer's Hands," *New York Times*, March 17, 1990, 32; Steven Lee Myers, "Former New York Battler Now a

Peacemaker at U.N.," *New York Times*, August 30, 1991, B1; "Dinkins Appoints Nadine B. Hack as Commissioner to U.N.," *New York Times*, December 13, 1991, B10.

55  See Brundage, *Irish Nationalists*, 198, 205, 210; also Francis X. Clines, "Paul O'Dwyer, New York's Liberal Battler for Underdogs and Outsiders, Dies at 90," *New York Times*, June 25, 1998, B9; Colin Miner, "How Two from N.Y. Aided Peace in Ireland," *NY Sun*, April 12, 2007, at www.odblaw.com/blog/how-two-from-n-y-aided-peace-in-ireland/; James O'Shea, "The Irish and the Clintons: A Love Affair," *Irish Central*, www.irishcentral.com/news/politics/the-irish-and-the-clintons-a-love-affair, January 20, 2014; Eamon Phoenix, "British Tried to Stop Clinton's Plan for Peace Envoy to the North," *Irish Times*, August 24, 2018, www.irishtimes.com.

56  Mike Allen, "Political Elite Out in Force to Mourn Democrat O'Dwyer," *New York Times*, June 28, 1998, 29.

57  Joshua B. Freeman, *In Transit: The Transport Workers Union in New York City, 1933–1966* (New York: Oxford University Press, 1989); Shirley Quill, *Mike Quill-Himself: A Memoir* (Greenwich, CT: Devin-Adair, 1985).

58  Allen, "Political Elite."

## 5. DEFENDING LITERARY GENIUS

1  Malcolm Cowley to Bennett Cerf, May 6, 1932, doc. 30, p. 12, in Michael Moscato and Leslie LeBlanc, *The United States of America v. One Book Entitled "Ulysses" by James Joyce* (Frederick, MD: University Publications of America, 1984).

2  Lindey to Ernst, August 6, 1931, doc. 1, p. 77, printed in Moscato and Leblanc, *United States*.

3  Alexander Lindey, Ernst's junior associate in their Greenbaum, Wolff & Ernst law firm, deserves recognition for his management of the case, including working closely with their client, the US attorneys, researching and writing their extensive legal memoranda, and filing a key challenge to a 1928 customs-court ruling. Two graduate student assistants and I have had a difficult time finding biographical information about Alexander Lindey. An immigrant from Hungary, he graduated from City College in New York City, then New York Law School in 1925, and joined the Greenbaum, Wolff & Ernst firm. After leaving the firm following World War II, he concentrated on entertainment law and wrote a book entitled *Plagiarism and Originality* (1952). He died in 1981. He is mentioned briefly in a history of the firm written in 1960, but had departed it by that time and was given short shrift. "Greenbaum, Wolff & Ernst: A brief history of the firm prepared for the occasion of its 40th Anniversary and a postscript thereto following its 45 Anniversary on May 15, 1960" (1960). Morris L. Ernst Papers, Harry Ransom Center, University of Texas, Austin, Box 846 (old filing system). Hereafter referred to as MLE Papers, HRC.

4  Morris Ernst, "Foreword" to James Joyce, *Ulysses* (New York: Random House, 1934), vii, 1946 ed.

5   Edmund Wilson, "James Joyce," originally published in *The New Republic*, December 18, 1929; in Moscato and LeBlanc, *United States*, doc. 4, pp. 79–98.
6   Paul Vanderham, *James Joyce and Censorship: The Trials of Ulysses* (New York: New York University Press, 1998), 7–8.
7   An extensive literature on Anthony Comstock describes his far reach into American culture and law. See especially Amy Werbel, *Lust on Trial: Censorship and the Rise of American Obscenity in the Age of Anthony Comstock* (New York: Columbia University Press, 2018); Nicola Beisel, *Imperiled Innocents: Anthony Comstock and Family Reproduction in Victorian America* (Princeton, NJ: Princeton University Press, 1997); Paul S. Boyer, *Purity in Print: Book Censorship in America from the Gilded Age to the Computer Age* (1968; 2nd ed., Madison: University of Wisconsin Press, 2002); Marjorie Heins, *Not in Front of the Children: Indecency, Censorship, and the Innocence of Youth* (New York: Hill & Wang, 2001); Helen Lefkowitz Horowitz, *Rereading Sex: Battles over Sexual Knowledge and Suppression in Nineteenth-Century America* (New York: Knopf, 2002); Geoffrey R. Stone, *Sex and the Constitution: Sex, Religion, and Law from America's Origins to the Twenty-First Century* (New York: Liveright, 2017). For a more contemporary view, see Heywood Broun and Margaret Leech, *Anthony Comstock: Roundsman of the Lord* (New York: Boni, 1927).

   For a history of contraceptive devices in the United States, see Andrea Tone, *Devices and Desires: A History of Contraceptives in America* (New York: Hill & Wang, 2001); Andrea Tone, ed., *Controlling Reproduction: An American History* (Wilmington, DE: SR Books, 1997); Peter C. Engleman, *A History of the Birth Control Movement in America* (Santa Barbara, CA: Praeger, 2011).
8   In early August 1931, Alexander Lindey wrote Ernst the first of many memos about Joyce's *Ulysses*, revealing that they had already begun planning a defense and were ready to move ahead on this project. Lindey told Ernst he had "stocked in a few copies of the book" for their preparations, and asked what he should do next. (Lindey memo to Ernst, August 6, 1931, doc. 1, p. 77, printed in Moscato and Leblanc, *United States*.) Ernst quickly replied, "Tell Mrs. Denis that I want to see her" when he returned to New York City from his vacation house on Nantucket. He confidently noted, "I am sure I can get a good publisher." Ernst, handwritten note on Lindey memo, Moscato and Leblanc, doc. 1, p. 78.
9   Morris L. Ernst and William Seagle, *To the Pure: A Study of Obscenity and the Censor* (New York: Viking, 1928; New York: Kaus Reprint Company, 1969).
10  In 1940 Ernst and Lindey cowrote a book chronicling their key victories to that point, entitled *The Censor Marches On: Recent Milestones in the Administration of the Obscenity Law in the United States* (New York: Doubleday, Doran, 1940). For cursory treatment of the firm's work in censorship cases, see "Greenbaum, Wolff & Ernst: A brief history"; the MLE Papers at HRC contain the bound volumes of documents surrounding these cases, with vols. 90–95 providing much of the documentation.
11  Ernst, "Foreword."

12 *United States v. Dennett*, Circuit Court of Appeals, Second Circuit, 39 F.2d 564 (1930); *United States v. One Obscene Book Entitled "Married Love,"* 48 F.2d 821; *US v. One Book, Entitled "Contraception" by Marie C. Stopes*, District Court, S.D. New York, 51 F.2d 525; 1931 U.S. Dist., July 16, 1931.
13 The literature on obscenity law and censorship is extensive. Some of the key works include: Jay A. Gertzman, *Bookleggers and Smuthounds: The Trade in Erotica, 1920–1940* (Philadelphia: University of Pennsylvania Press, 1999); Andrea Friedman, *Prurient Interests: Gender, Democracy, and Obscenity in New York City, 1909–1945* (New York: Columbia University Press, 2000); Felice Flannery Lewis, *Literature, Obscenity & Law* (Carbondale: Southern Illinois University Press, 1976); Heins, *Not in Front*.
14 Legal historian Roger K. Newman called Ernst the "most important civil libertarian in the first half of the 20th century" and also invoked Ernst's peripatetic energy and skill. Roger K. Newman, entry on "Morris Leopold Ernst," *Dictionary of American Biography* (New York: Charles Scribner's Sons 1995). Available online at http://galenet.galegroup.com/servlet/HistRC/.
15 Marquis James, "Morris L. Ernst," *Scribner's Magazine*, July 1938, 7–11, 57–58; Fred Rodell, "Morris Ernst: New York's Unlawyerlike Liberal Lawyer Is the Censor's Enemy, the President's Friend," *LIFE*, February 21, 1944, 96–107.
16 Rodell, "Morris Ernst."
17 Quote from James, "Morris L. Ernst," 9.
18 James, 9.
19 Quotes from Rodell, "Morris Ernst," 97. Ernst is quoted by Rodell, 97.
20 Michael Chabon, "'Ulysses' on Trial," *New York Review of Books*, September 26, 2019.
21 Ernst's recollections of this background pepper various documents and family histories. He discusses his father as a "peddler, like all immigrants" in a 1973 oral interview with Mary Batten. Mary Batten interview with Morris Ernst, September 13, 1973; MLE Papers, HRC, audio files. Ernst's papers also include various family-history documents, including one entitled "Unpublished Family History." See "Morris L. Family History (1961)," MLE Papers, HRC, Box 877 (old file system).
22 Quotes from Ernst oral interview with Mary Batten, September 1973, MLE Papers, HRC, audio files.
23 The most detailed study of Ernst's life and work is Joel Matthew Silverman, "Pursuing Celebrity, Ensuing Masculinity: Morris Ernst, Obscenity, and the Search for Recognition" (PhD diss., University of Texas at Austin, 2006); quotes from Silverman, 18, 28.
24 Ernst quotes from oral interview with Mary Batten, September 1973, MLE Papers, HRC, audio files.
25 Jerold S. Auerbach, "From Rags to Robes: The Legal Profession, Social Mobility and the American Jewish Experience," *American Jewish Historical Quarterly* 76, no. 2 (December 1976): 249–84.
26 See "Greenbaum, Wolff & Ernst: A brief history."

27 Ernst was the ACLU's co-general counsel and an Executive Board member. His junior associate Alexander Lindey was key legal strategist/analyst for the ACLU-affiliated National Committee for Freedom from Censorship (NCFC), and later Harriet Pilpel had a long affiliation with the ACLU, especially in reproductive-rights issues.

28 The literature on the ACLU is considerable. Leigh Ann Wheeler, *How Sex Became a Civil Liberty* (New York: Oxford University Press, 2014), is the best work on the ACLU and sexuality as a civil liberty; the classic history is Samuel Walker, *In Defense of American Liberty: A History of the ACLU* (New York: Oxford University Press, 1990); other excellent studies include Judy Kutulas, *The American Civil Liberties Union & the Making of Modern Liberalism, 1930–1960* (Chapel Hill: University of North Carolina Press, 2006); and Robert C. Cottrell, *Roger Nash Baldwin and the American Civil Liberties Union* (New York: Columbia University Press, 2000).

29 For treatment of the development of the free speech tradition following the war, see David Rabban, "Emergence of the Modern First Amendment Doctrine," *University of Chicago Law Review* 50, no. 4 (1983): article 2; David Rabban, "The Free Speech League, the ACLU, and the Changing Conceptions of Free Speech in American History," *Stanford Law Review*, no. 45 (November 1992): 47–114; David Rabban, *Free Speech in Its Forgotten Years* (Cambridge: Cambridge University Press, 1997); Fred D. Ragan, "Justice Oliver Wendell Holmes, Jr., and Zechariah Chafee, Jr.," *Journal of American History*, no. 58 (June 1971): 24–45; Richard Polenberg, *Fighting Faiths: The Abrams Case, the Supreme Court, and Free Speech* (New York: Viking, 1987); Geoffrey R. Stone, *Perilous Times: Free Speech in Wartime from the Sedition Act of 1798 to the War on Terrorism* (New York: W. W. Norton, 2004); Samuel Walker, *In Defense of American Liberty: A History of the ACLU* (New York: Oxford University Press, 1990).

30 See Wheeler, *How Sex Became a Civil Liberty*, for the most detailed and authoritative account of the ACLU's long history dedicated to expanding rights of sexual expression and practice, and protecting those rights legislatively and in the courts. See also Laura Weinrib, "The Sex Side of Civil Liberties: *United States v. Dennett* and the Changing Face of Free Speech" (Public Law & Legal Theory Working Paper No. 385, University of Chicago, 2012).

31 Ernst had many commitments besides his work in obscenity-law matters, many of which were directly related to his concerns about the marketplace and its constrictions. For his fullest articulation of his Brandeisian anti-oligopoly arguments, see Morris Ernst, *Too Big* (Boston: Little, Brown, 1940). He was counsel to the American Newspaper Guild, the Dramatists Guild, and the burlesque theater industry, and fought many battles with the commissioner of licenses in New York City over closings of both "legitimate" and burlesque theaters.

32 Ernst was prolific and wrote or cowrote many books, most of them addressing his anticensorship arguments in conjunction with his anti-oligopoly positions. See Ernst and Seagle, *To the Pure*; Ernst and Lindey, *Censor Marches On*; Morris L. Ernst, *The First Freedom* (New York: Macmillan, 1946); and Morris L. Ernst

and Alan U. Schwartz, *Censorship: The Search for the Obscene* (New York: Macmillan, 1964).
33  In US v. Harmon, 1892, the Comstock Act was challenged on constitutional grounds, namely that it interfered with First Amendment rights. But the federal court held that it was obvious that the First Amendment did not protect that which "outrages the common sense of decency, or endangers public safety." On Harmon, see Heins, *Not in Front*; and Frederick F. Schauer, *The Law of Obscenity* (Washington, DC: Bureau of National Affairs, 1976).
34  On Ernst's strategies on behalf of Radclyffe Hall's novel, see Leslie Taylor, "'I Made Up My Mind to Get It': The American Trial of *The Well of Loneliness*, New York City, 1928–1929," *Journal of the History of Sexuality* 10, no. 2 (April 2001): 250–86; Silverman, "Pursuing Celebrity," provides a rich treatment in his chapter 3, 100–134. On Schnitzler, see Magistrate Gottlieb decision, *Sumner v. Simon and Schuster*, re: "Casanova's Homecoming," vol. 90, MLE Papers, HRC.
35  Vanderham, *James Joyce*, 15. See also Kevin Birmingham, *The Most Dangerous Book: The Battle for James Joyce's "Ulysses"* (New York: Random House, 2014) for discussions of Joyce's intentional provocations.
36  Vanderham, *James Joyce*, 7–8.
37  Vanderham, 2.
38  The lawyer wrote a note to the Manhattan district attorney, Edward Swann. "Dear Sir," it said, "Surely there must be some way of keeping such 'literature' out of the homes of people who don't want it . . ." (quoted in Gillers, 252). For a fuller treatment of the 1921 trial, see Stephen Gillers, "A Tendency to Deprave and Corrupt: The Transformation of American Obscenity Law from Hicklin to *Ulysses* II," 85 *Washington University Law Review* 215 (2007).
39  Gillers, 251–52.
40  Vanderham, *James Joyce*, 39.
41  Quoted in Gillers, "Tendency," 252–53.
42  Gillers quotes from Quinn's explanation to Joyce about his strategy, revealing Quinn's condescension toward the judges whom he needed to persuade: "'I took the only tack that could be taken with the three stupid judges, and that was that no one could understand what the thing was about. I nearly got away with it'" (Gillers, "Tendency," 260).
43  The preliminary hearing in the Jefferson Market Courthouse before Magistrate Joseph E. Corrigan was, Vanderham recounts, "precisely the sort of spectacle that Quinn had hoped to avoid, for he disliked Joyce's writing being associated with Greenwich Village bohemia, and he did not want the connection bandied about in the press" (Vanderham, *James Joyce*, 43). Quinn's flippant letters to Ezra Pound reveal his disdain for his clients, Anderson and Heap, as well as the judges (see Vanderham, 43).
44  Gillers, "Tendency," 252–53.
45  It appears Cerf initially deferred to Viking to try and work out a deal to publish the book. Ernst and Huebsch met in mid-October 1931, and Ernst followed with

a detailed explanation of the legal challenge and its potential costs. Ernst's letter to Huebsch (October 21, 1931, doc. 5, pp. 98–100, in Moscato and LeBlanc, *United States*) clearly made no effort to seduce Huebsch and Viking.

46  See Cerf's letter to Ernst, March 23, 1932, about the "legal end of this matter" (doc. 11, p. 108, in Moscato and LeBlanc) and Lindey to Cerf, March 24, 1932 (doc. 12, p. 109, in Moscato and LeBlanc) clarifies the conditions of the contract. It is clear that Ernst and Lindey were key architects of the entire plan, although Cerf's versions are slightly different. See Gillers, "Tendency," 275–76.

47  Because Random House would bear the financial costs of the battle, Lindey tried to reassure Cerf that the overall costs (especially the $50 per diem on trial days) would probably not amount to much. He was partly correct in predicting that a trial wasn't likely, since "the United States Attorney would relish spending three weeks in court reading *Ulysses* no more than ourselves." Lindey to Cerf, March 24, 1932, doc. 12, p. 109, in Moscato and Leblanc, *United States*.

48  Cerf to Leon, April 19, 1932, doc. 23, p. 119, in Moscato and Leblanc.

49  Lindey to Cerf, March 29, 1932, doc. 15, pp. 111–12, in Moscato and Leblanc.

50  Dreiser to Cerf, May 13, 1932, doc. 30, p. 127, in Moscato and Leblanc.

51  Fitzgerald to Cerf, August 29, 1932, doc. 30, p. 128, in Moscato and Leblanc.

52  Cerf to Lindey, March 28, 1932, in Moscato and LeBlanc, *United States*, 110.

53  Lindey to Ernst, March 13, 1931, doc. 3, p. 78, in Moscato and Leblanc; he enclosed Wilson's essay, "James Joyce," reprinted as doc. 4, from the December 18, 1929 *New Republic*, 79–99, in Moscato and Leblanc.

54  Wilson, "James Joyce," doc. 4, pp. 80–81, in Moscato and Leblanc.

55  Lindey to Collector of Customs, May 2, 1932, doc. 39, pp. 133–34, in Moscato and Leblanc. The cases included: *US v. Mary Ware Dennett*, 39 Fed. (2d) 564; *US v. Married Love*, 48 Fed. (2d) 821; *US v. Contraception*, 51 Fed. (2d) 525; *Youngs, etc. v. Lee, etc.*, 45 Fed. (2d) 103; *People v. Rendling*, 258 NY 461.

56  Stewart to Lindey, May 13, 1932, doc. 52, p. 142, in Moscato and Leblanc.

57  Lindey memo to Ernst, June 14, 1932, doc. 69, p. 154, in Moscato and Leblanc.

58  Lindey memo to Ernst, July 30, 1932, reported his conversation with Coleman about leaving the final decision up to Medalie, doc. 75, p. 157, in Moscato and Leblanc.

59  Lindey memo to Ernst, August 12, 1932, doc. 76, p. 158, in Moscato and Leblanc.

60  Ernst memo re: Ulysses, September 27, 1932, doc. 80, in Moscato and Leblanc; see Vanderham, *James Joyce*, 90, and his fn. 19.

61  Ernst memo re: Ulysses, September 27, 1932, doc. 80, p. 160, in Moscato and Leblanc, *United States*. Ernst recorded that Medalie told him he was "not at all worried about the children," and was also interested in seeing all the expert opinion and "everything that comes from libraries and particularly from colleges." Ernst told Lindey they ought to get Medalie more pieces "particularly [from] those who can write." The slow process irritated Cerf, especially because he was hearing rumors from booksellers that another edition of *Ulysses* was to be published by a "notorious pirate" by the name of Joseph Meyers, whose company Illustrated Edi-

tions published cheap knockoffs of classics. Because Cerf's firm had no effective copyright claim on the book, he was powerless to stop the black-market piracy of his investment. Leon to Cerf, September 27, 1932, doc. 82, p. 161; Lindey memo on urgency of piracy matter, October 19, 1932, doc. 84, p. 162; Cerf to Ernst on Meyers piracy, October 20, 1932, doc. 85, pp. 6–163, all in Moscato and Leblanc.

62  Ernst had worked closely with Senator Bronson Cutting of New Mexico to insert this provision into the revised Tariff Act, aware it would aid the anticensorship cause.

63  Lindey to Collector of Customs, May 5, 1933, doc. 107, p. 177, in Moscato and Leblanc, *United States*.

64  H. C. Stewart to Lindey, May 10, 1933, doc. 108; Lindey to Stewart, May 13, 1933, doc. 109, pp. 178–79, in Moscato and Leblanc.

65  Lindey, "Petition for Release and Admission of Book," doc. 119, pp. 186–89, in Moscato and Leblanc.

66  Lindey.

67  Frank Dow, Acting Commissioner of Customs to NYC Collector of Customs, June 16, 1933, doc. 124, pp. 203–4, in Moscato and Leblanc, *United States*. Lindey had heard from the Division of Appeals and Protests in Washington on June 16 that his petition had been favorably passed upon, but was still awaiting official confirmation from H. C. Stewart, Collector of Customs in New York City, who held the book. Lindey to Collector of Customs, June 22, 1933, doc. 126, p. 205, in Moscato and Leblanc.

68  *New York Times* article "Ban upon 'Ulysses' to Be Fought Again," June 24, 1933, reprinted as doc. 127, pp. 205–6, in Moscato and Leblanc:

For eleven years, *Ulysses*, by James Joyce, has had wide recognition as a modern classic, but only bootleg sales in English speaking countries, where some of the words and situations in the book have been considered obscene. Now Bennett Cerf, head of Random House and The Modern Library, wants to publish the book here. It was learned yesterday that he [sic; it was Lindey] had won a preliminary victory by obtaining the admittance of one copy of the book. This was made possible by an exception in the 1930 Tariff Act, presumably made for the benefit of such collectors as J. P. Morgan and the great libraries.

69  Lindey to Ernst, June 30, 1933, doc. 129, p. 207, in Moscato and Leblanc.

70  Vanderham, *James Joyce*, 107.

71  Lindey to Ernst, July 25, 1933, doc. 137, pp. 212–13, in Moscato and Leblanc, *United States*.

72  Lindey to Ernst, August 9, 1933, doc. 141, pp. 216–17, in Moscato and Leblanc.

73  Ernst to Shapiro, August 15, 1933, doc. 142, p. 217, in Moscato and Leblanc

74  As Vanderham (*James Joyce*, 93) describes the above scenario:

Shortly after the US Attorney's office had made clear it intended to proceed against Joyce's novel, Woolsey announced that he would hear argument without briefs and that briefs should not be submitted unless he called for them. This arrangement accorded with the wishes of the government, but not with those of Random House and its legal counsel. Cerf was convinced that all material gathered in defense of *Ulysses* should be turned over to Woolsey "before he has a chance to complete his reading of the book." Lindey and Ernst were of the same mind. Thus, early in September, Lindey ignored Woolsey's directive, sending him a copy of the "Claimant's Preliminary Memorandum" (containing the material presented in Lindey's petition) and two critical books on Ulysses. Due to a number of delays, Woolsey would not hear argument until 25 November 1933. He would have plenty of time to familiarize himself with the material of which Ernst and Lindey hoped he would take "judicial notice."

75 Claimants Memorandum to Dismiss Libel, submitted October 14, 1933, doc. 164, pp. 235–72, 239, in Moscato and Leblanc, *United States*.
76 Claimants Memorandum to Dismiss Libel, p. 239.
77 Claimants Memorandum to Dismiss Libel, p. 239.
78 Claimants Memorandum to Dismiss Libel, p. 41.
79 Claimants Memorandum to Dismiss Libel, p. 242.
80 All quotes from Claimants Memorandum to Dismiss Libel, p. 245.
81 Claimants Memorandum to Dismiss Libel, p. 246.
82 Claimants Memorandum to Dismiss Libel, p. 248.
83 Claimants Memorandum to Dismiss Libel, p. 257.
84 Vanderham, *James Joyce*, 103.
85 Claimants Memorandum to Dismiss Libel, 266; see Vanderham's treatment of their argument, 96–97.
86 Claimants Memorandum to Dismiss Libel, 267.
87 Vanderham writes that Atlas's memorandum and use of documents provided by Lindey and Ernst "was motivated by his desire to argue the government's case against *Ulysses* in a manner that would make it clear that the government was not whole-hearted in its ostensible desire to censor Joyce's novel" (Vanderham, *James Joyce*, 106).
88 Vanderham, 106.
89 Atlas, "James Joyce," doc. 184, p. 295, in Moscato and Leblanc, *United States*.
90 Atlas, "James Joyce," doc. 184, p. 297, in Moscato and Leblanc.
91 The courtroom coverage by the *New York Herald Tribune*: "Ulysses Case Reaches Court After 10 Years" subtitled: "Woolsey Upset because He Fears He Understands Debatably Lewd Soliloquy" (*New York Herald Tribune*, November 26, 1933, doc. 79, p. 284, in Moscato and Leblanc).
92 *New York Herald Tribune*, November 26, 1933, doc. 79, p. 286, in Moscato and Leblanc, *United States*. The core "problem" of the book's possible obscenity was its revelation of female lust, both young Gerty McDowell's own lack of purity and her knowledge that Leopold Bloom was masturbating while watching her and Molly Bloom's ruminations on her lifetime of robust and eager sexual appetites. Both were serious transgressions against codes of female sexual reticence.
93 *New York Herald Tribune*, November 26, 1933, doc. 79, p. 286, in Moscato and Leblanc.

94  Woolsey decision, *US v. One Book Called "Ulysses,"* 5 F.Supp. 182. District Court, S. D. New York. December 6, 1933.
95  Woolsey decision, *US v. One Book Called "Ulysses,"* 5 F.Supp. 182. District Court, S. D. New York. December 6, 1933.
96  Woolsey decision, *US v. One Book Called "Ulysses,"* 5 F.Supp. 182. District Court, S. D. New York. December 6, 1933.
97  He accepted the body of law they cited, which included several decisions he had made in previous cases: Dunlop v. United States, 165 U. S. 486, 501, 17 S. Ct. 375, 41 L. Ed. 799; United States v. One Obscene Book Entitled "Married Love" (D. C.) 48 F.(2d) 821, 824; United States v. One Book, Entitled "Contraception" (D. C.) 51 F.(2d) 525, 528; and compare Dysart v. United States, 272 U. S. 655, 657, 47 S. Ct. 234, 71 L. Ed. 461; Swearingen v. United States, 161 U. S. 446, 450, 16 S. Ct. 562, 40 L. Ed. 765; United States v. Dennett, 39 F. (2d) 564, 568, 76 A. L. R. 1092 (C. C. A. 2); People v. Wendling, 258 N. Y. 451, 453, 180 N. E. 169, 81 A. L. R. 799.
98  Woolsey decision, *US v. One Book Called "Ulysses,"* 5 F.Supp. 182. District Court, S. D. New York. December 6, 1933.
99  It is useful to think of the aphrodisiac test as the "whether it 'induced masturbation' test." This gave the judges a way out: they could honestly acknowledge that it was dirty in parts, even revoltingly so, that it offended all kinds of sensibilities, but that its overall effect was not the production of lust = masturbation and thence shame, so it couldn't be "obscene."
100  Ernst, "Foreword."
101  *US v. One Book Called Ulysses* By James Joyce, Circuit Court of Appeals, Second Circuit, 72 F.2d 705, August 7, 1934.
102  *US v. One Book Called Ulysses* By James Joyce, Circuit Court of Appeals, Second Circuit, 72 F.2d 705, August 7, 1934.
103  Lindey to Ernst, August 6, 1931, doc. 1, 77, printed in Moscato and Leblanc, *United States of America v. One Book Entitled "Ulysses" by James Joyce.*

6. LAUGHTER AND LOVE BETWEEN THE IRISH AND THE JEWS
Excerpts from *The Irish Way: Becoming American in the Multiethnic City* by James R. Barrett, copyright © 2012 by James R. Barrett. Used by permission of Penguin Press, an imprint of Penguin Publishing Group, a division of Penguin Random House LLC. All rights reserved.
This essay is dedicated in love and thanks to Jenny Barrett.
  1  Louis Hyman, *The Jews of Ireland from Earliest Times to 1910* (Shannon: Irish University Press, 1972), 213; Ray Rivlin, *Shalom Ireland: A Social History of Jews in Modern Ireland* (Dublin: Gill & Macmillan, 2003), 29–34; Cormac O'Grada, *Jewish Ireland in the Age of Joyce: A Socioeconomic History* (Princeton, NJ: Princeton University Press, 2006), 14–16, 118, 179–181.
  2  Frederic Thrasher, *The Gang: A Study of 1,313 Gangs in Chicago* (Chicago: University of Chicago Press, 1927), 137, quote, 212; "The Wickedest District in the World," *Chicago Tribune*, February 6, 1910, H7.

3 Abraham Bisno, *Abraham Bisno, Union Pioneer* (Madison: University of Wisconsin Press, 1967), quote, 55. For similar problems in New York City, see Harry Golden, *The Right Time: An Autobiography* (New York: G. P. Putnam's Sons, 1969), 49; Thomas Jesse Jones, *The Sociology of a New York Block* (New York: Columbia University Press, 1904), 99, 123.

4 Judah Bernstein, "'The Two Finest Nations in the World': American Zionists and Irish Nationalism, 1897–1922," *Journal of American Ethnic History* 36, no. 3 (Spring 2017): 5–37; Hasia R. Diner, *The Jews of the United States, 1654–2000* (Berkeley: University of California Press, 2006), 92; Gil Ribak, "'Beaten to Death by Irish Murderers': The Death of Sadie Dellon (1918) and Jewish Images of the Irish," *Journal of American Ethnic History* 32, no. 4 (Summer 2013): 41–74.

5 James R. Barrett, *The Irish Way: Becoming American in the Multiethnic City* (New York: Penguin Books, 2012), 195–97; William V. Shannon, *The American Irish* (New York: Macmillan, 1963), quote, 139–40.

6 Barrett, *Irish Way*, 212–13; William L. Riordan, *Plunkitt of Tammany Hall: A Series of Very Plain Talks on Very Practical Subjects*, ed. Terrence McDonald (Boston: Bedford Books, 1994), quote, 75; Louis Eisenstein and Elliot Rosenberg, *A Stripe of Tammany's Tiger* (New York: Robert Speller & Sons, 1966), 10–17.

7 Steven Erie, *Rainbow's End: Irish-Americans and the Dilemmas of Urban Machine Politics, 1840–1945* (Berkeley: University of California Press, 1988), 101; David Hammack, *Power and Society: Greater New York at the Turn of the Century* (New York: Russell Sage Foundation, 1982), 89.

8 Barrett, *Irish Way*, 220–29; John R. McKivigan and Thomas J. Robertson, "The Irish American Worker in Transition, 1877–1914: New York City as a Test Case," in Ronald Bayor and Timothy Meagher, eds., *The New York Irish* (Baltimore: Johns Hopkins University Press, 1996), 313. On the importance of patronage jobs and social welfare policies in maintaining Irish control during the early twentieth century, see Erie, *Rainbow's End*.

9 Barrett, *Irish Way*, 229–31; Ronald H. Bayor, *Neighbors in Conflict: The Irish, Germans, Jews, and Italians of New York City, 1929–1941* (Baltimore: Johns Hopkins University Press, 1978), 87–108, 152–56; John F. Stack Jr., *International Conflict in an American City: Boston's Irish, Italians, and Jews, 1935–1944* (Westport, CT: Greenwood, 1984), 22–23, 55–56, 92, 94, 130, 134–39; Steven Fraser, *Labor Will Rule: Sidney Hillman and the Rise of American Labor* (New York: Free Press, 1991), 338, 356, 366, 367, 417, 424; Alan Brinkley, *Voices of Protest: Huey Long, Father Coughlin, and the Great Depression* (New York: Knopf, 1982), 128–33; David J. O'Brien, *American Catholics and Social Reform: The New Deal Years* (New York: Oxford University Press, 1968); Neil Betten, *Catholic Activism and the Industrial Worker* (Gainesville: University of Florida Press, 1976).

10 Jones, *Sociology*, 12, 15; John J. Appel, "*Betzemer*: A Nineteenth-Century Cognomen for the Irish," *American Speech*, no. 38 (1963): 307–8.

11 Robert W. Snyder, "The Irish and Vaudeville," in Joe Lee and Marion Casey, eds., *Making the Irish American* (New York: New York University Press, 2006), 406.

12  Gavin Rogers, *Strange Talk: The Politics of Dialect Literature in Gilded Age America* (Berkeley: University of California Press, 1999), 173–77; Mick Moloney, "Irish American Music," in Lee and Casey, *Making the Irish American*, quote, 387.
13  Moloney, "Irish American Music," 387.
14  Paul Antoine Distler, "Ethnic Comedy in Vaudeville and Burlesque," in Myron Matlaw, *American Popular Entertainment* (Westport, CT: Greenwood, 1979), 38. The "ethnic cross-dressing concept is Michael Rogin's." See Michael Paul Rogin, *Blackface, White Noise: Jewish Immigrants in the Hollywood Melting Pot* (Berkeley: University of California Press, 1996), 53.
15  Joyce Flynn, "Melting Plots: Patterns of Ethnic and Racial Amalgamation in American Drama before Eugene O'Neill," *American Quarterly* 38, no. 3 (1986): 426, quote, 429.
16  James H. Dormon, "European Immigrant/Ethnic Theatre in Gilded Age New York: Reflections and Projections of Mentalities," in William Pencak, Selma Berrol, and Randall M. Miller, eds., *Immigration to New York* (Philadelphia: Balch Institute, 1991), 148–55, quote, 149; see also Matthew Frye Jacobson, *Special Sorrows: The Diasporic Imagination of Irish, Polish, and Jewish Immigrants* (Berkeley: University of California Press, 2002), 82–93.
17  Dormon, "European Immigrant/Ethnic Theatre," 156–66; Moses Rischin, *The Promised City: New York's Jews, 1870–1914* (New York: Harper & Row, 1962), 265–66.
18  Hartley Davis, "In Vaudeville," *Everyone's*, no. 24 (August 1905): 238, quoted in Dormon, "European Immigrant/Ethnic Theatre," 165.
19  Snyder, "Irish and Vaudeville," 407; Distler, "Ethnic Comedy," 36. See also Sabina Haenni, *The Immigrant Scene: Ethnic Amusements in New York, 1880–1920* (Minneapolis: University of Minnesota Press, 2008), 14–16.
20  Armond Fields and L. Marc Fields, *From the Bowery to Broadway: Lew Fields and the Roots of American Popular Theatre* (New York: Oxford University Press, 1993), 32–33, quote, 35; Peter Murdock, ed., *Studies in the Science of Society* (Freeport, NY: Books for Libraries Press, 1969), 21; Krystyn R. Moon, *Yellow Face: Creating the Chinese in American Music and Performance, 1850s–1920s* (New Brunswick, NJ: Rutgers University Press, 2005), 148–50; David Nasaw, *Going Out: The Rise and Fall of Public Amusements* (New York: Basic Books, 1993), 52–53.
21  Rogin, *Blackface*, 56–58, quote, 56.
22  Eric Goldstein, *The Price of Whiteness: Jews, Race, and American Identity* (Princeton, NJ: Princeton University Press, 2006).
23  Quoted in Daniel J. Murphy, "The Reception of Synge's *Playboy* in Ireland and America, 1907–1912," *Bulletin of the New York Public Library*, no. 64 (1960): 526–27. On the Ancient Order of Hibernians' protests and others, see *Chicago Tribune*, May 7, 1902, 1; Kathleen Donovan, "Good Old Pat: An Irish American Stereotype in Decline," *Éire-Ireland*, no. 15 (1980): 13; John P. Harrington, *The Irish Play on the New York Stage, 1874–1966* (Lexington: University of Kentucky Press, 1997), 61.

24 On the Irish American theater riots, see "Hissed off the Stage by Angry Irishmen," *New York Times*, January 25, 1907, 3; "Egg Russell Brothers in Brooklyn Theatre," *New York Times*, February 1, 1907, 1; M. Alison Kibler, "The Stage Irishwoman," *Journal of American Ethnic History* 24, no. 3 (Spring 2005): 5–7; James R. Barrett, "Irish Americanization on Stage: How Irish American Playwrights, Musicians, and Writers Created a New Urban American Culture," *Journal of History for the Public*, no. 10 (2013): 62–65; "Riot in Theatre Over an Irish Play," *New York Times*, November 28, 1911, 1, 3. On the New York City licensing bill, see "McKee Warns City to Censor Movies," *New York Times*, October 12, 1927, 1; "Film Absent at Film Hearing," *New York Times*, October 15, 1927, quote, 21.

25 Managers' Report Book, p. 297, Boston, April 27, 1903, Keith/Albee Collection, Special Collections, University of Iowa Library. My thanks to Alison Kibler for this reference.

26 *New York Times*, July 15, 1923, E6; "To Boycott the Stage Jew," *New York Times*, April 25, 1913, 3; "All Races to War on Play Ridicule," *Chicago Tribune*, April 25, 1913, 5; "Anti-Defamation League Becomes Nationwide," *Chicago Tribune*, November 14, 1913, quote, 14; *Chicago Tribune*, September 21, 1903, 4. See also Matthew Frye Jacobson, *Whiteness of a Different Color: European Immigrants and the Alchemy of Race* (Cambridge, MA: Harvard University Press, 1999), 183; Nasaw, *Going Out*, 53.

27 Lyrics in Mick Moloney, *Far from the Shamrock Shore: The Story of Irish-American Immigration through Song* (New York: Crown, 2002), 34.

28 William H. A. Williams, *"'Twas Only an Irishman's Dream'": The Image of Ireland and the Irish in American Popular Song Lyrics, 1800–1920* (Urbana: University of Illinois Press, 1996), 181–99, song lyrics quoted, 196. See also Moloney, "Irish-American Popular Music," 393–96; Moloney, *Far from the Shamrock Shore*, 36–37.

29 "Comedies for All," *New York Times*, August 29, 1926, X1; Ann Nichols, *Abie's Irish Rose: A Novel* (New York: Grosset & Dunlap, 1927), 75–79, 95–98, 101–6; Riv-Ellen Prell, *Fighting to Become Americans: Jews, Gender, and the Anxiety of Assimilation* (Boston: Beacon, 1999), 72–77; Rudolf Glanz, *Jew and Irish: Historic Group Relations and Immigration* (New York: Waldon, 1966), 105–6; Joseph M. Curran, *Hibernian Green on the Silver Screen: The Irish and American Movies* (New York: Greenwood, 1989), 36; Ted Merwin, "The Performance of Jewish Identity in Anne Nichols's 'Abie's Irish Rose,'" *Journal of American Ethnic History*, no. 20 (Winter 2001): 3–37; Rogin, *Blackface*, 104. See also Mari Kathleen Fielder, "Fatal Attraction: Irish-Jewish Romance in Early Film and Drama," *Éire-Ireland: A Journal of Irish Studies* no. 3 (Fall 1985): 6–18; Lester D. Friedman, *Unspeakable Images: Ethnicity and American Cinema* (Urbana: University of Illinois Press, 1991), 58–61; Goldstein, *Price of Whiteness*, 134, 135.

30 *New York Times*, August 29, 1926, X1; Nichols, *Abie's Irish Rose*, 75–79, 95–98, 101–6; Riv-Prell, *Fighting to Become Americans*, 72–77; Glanz, *Jew and Irish*, 105–6; Curran, *Hibernian Green on the Silver Screen*, 36; Merwin, "The Performance of

Jewish Identity: 3–37; Rogin, *Blackface*, 104. See also Fielder, "Fatal Attraction," 6–18; Goldstein, *Price of Whiteness*, 134, 135.
31 *Chicago Tribune*, April 15, 1928, A3. On the affinity of the Irish and the Jews and its relationship to American popular culture, see also Rogin, *Blackface*, 58.
32 Prell, *Fighting to Become Americans*, 77.
33 Julius Drachsler, *Intermarriage in New York City: A Statistical Survey of the Amalgamation of European Peoples* (PhD diss., Columbia University, 1921), especially 56; Bronwen Walter, *Outsiders Inside: Whiteness, Place, and Irish Women* (New York: Routledge, 2000), 34–35; Thomas J. Archdeacon, *Becoming American: An Ethnic History* (New York: Free Press, 1983), 139–40; William Z. Ripley, "Races in the United States," *Atlantic Monthly*, December 1908, 745–59. On nineteenth-century Irish intermarriage, see Hasia R. Diner, *Erin's Daughters: Irish Immigrant Women in the Nineteenth Century* (Baltimore: Johns Hopkins University Press, 1983), xiv, 8–9, 30–34, 51; Graham Hodges, "Desirable Companions and Lovers: Irish and African Americans in the Sixth Ward," in Bayor and Meagher, *New York Irish*, 107–24; Tyler Anbinder, *Five Points: The Nineteenth-Century New York City Neighborhood That Invented Tap Dance, Stole Elections, and Became the World's Most Notorious Slum* (New York: Free Press, 1991), 263, 314, 320, 389–90; on Irish intermarriage with later ethnic groups, Joel Perlmann, "The Romance of Assimilation? Studying the Demographic Outcomes of Ethnic Intermarriage in American History" (Working Paper No. 230, Jerome Levy Economics Institute, Bard College, 1988), especially table 9; Joel Perlmann, "Demographic Outcomes of Ethnic Intermarriage in American History: Italian Americans through Four Generations" (Working Paper No. 372, Jerome Levy Economics Institute, 2000), especially table 13; and on intermarriage in the third generation and beyond along religious lines, see Will Herberg, *Protestant, Catholic, Jew: An Essay on American Religious Sociology* (Chicago: University of Chicago Press, 1955); Harold Abramson, *Ethnic Diversity in Catholic America* (New York: Wiley, 1973), 51–99; Stephen Steinberg, *The Ethnic Myth: Race, Ethnicity, and Class in America* (Boston: Beacon, 1989), 68; and R. J. R. Kennedy, "Single or Triple Melting Pot? Intermarriage Trends in New Haven, 1870–1940," *American Journal of Sociology* 49, no. 4 (January 1944): 331–39.
34 Bruce M. Stave and John F. Sutherland with Aldo Salerno, eds., *From the Old Country: An Oral History of European Migration to America* (New York: Twayne, 1994), 185–87, 190; Fielder, "Fatal Attraction," 12, 13. The question of whether mixed marriages involving the Irish led to a relatively greater number of Irish-identified offspring has yielded differing answers. See Richard Alba, *Ethnic Identity: The Transformation of White America* (New Haven, CT: Yale University Press, 1990), 59–61. For the view that Irish identity claims approximate "actual" ancestry, cf. Michael Hout and Joshua R. Goldstein, "How 4.5 Million Irish Immigrants Became 40 Million Irish Americans: Demographic and Subjective Aspects of the

Ethnic Composition of White Americans," *American Sociological Review*, no. 59 (February 1994): 64–82. Thanks to Gill Stevens for this reference.

## 7. IRISH-JEWISH COUPLES IN AMERICAN FILM AND TELEVISION

This chapter is dedicated to my favorite Irish-Jewish couple: Bridget Kerrigan of County Galway, Ireland, and Michael Rubin of Cook County, Illinois.

1. *Becky Gets a Husband* (1912; Philadelphia: Lubin Manufacturing Company); Patricia Erens, *The Jew in American Cinema* (Bloomington: Indiana University Press, 1985), 38.
2. Kevin Brownlow, *Behind the Mask of Innocence* (New York: Knopf, 1990), 301–423; Thomas Cripps, "The Movie Jew as the Image of Assimilation," *Journal of Popular Film* 4, no. 3 (1975): 190–203.
3. Joshua Louis Moss, *Why Harry Met Sally: Subversive Jewishness, Anglo-Christian Power, and the Rhetoric of Modern Love* (Austin: University of Texas Press, 2017), 1–17; Stephen Sharot, *Love and Marriage across Social Classes in American Cinema* (London: Palgrave Macmillan, 2017), 148–56.
4. Kerby A. Miller, *Emigrants and Exiles: Ireland and the Irish Exodus to North America* (New York: Oxford University Press, 1985).
5. Avraham Barkai, *Branching Out: German Jewish Immigration to the United States, 1820–1914* (New York: Holmes & Meier, 1994); Hasia R. Diner, *A Time for Gathering: The Second Migration, 1820–1880* (Baltimore: Johns Hopkins University Press, 1995).
6. Ronald Sanders, *Shores of Refuge: A Hundred Years of Jewish Immigration* (New York: Henry Holt, 1988); Tara Zahra, *The Great Departure: Mass Migration from Eastern Europe and the Making of the Free World* (New York: W. W. Norton, 2016).
7. Hasia R. Diner, "Irish and Jewish American Intersections," Glucksman Ireland House of New York University, 1:13:32, February 1, 2018, www.youtube.com/watch?v=3JovNGwLPWs.
8. James R. Barrett, *The Irish Way: Becoming American in the Multiethnic City* (New York: Penguin Books, 2012), 165–81.
9. Barrett, 175–81; Mick Moloney, "If It Wasn't for the Irish and the Jews," Glucksman Ireland House of New York University, 1:27:10, March 1, 2018, www.youtube.com/watch?v=WAfnQAj_KTA.
10. Roger Daniels, *Guarding the Golden Door: American Immigration Policy and Immigrants since 1882* (New York: Hill & Wang, 2005); Katie Oxx, *The Nativist Movement in America: Religious Conflict in the Nineteenth Century* (New York: Routledge, 2013); Peter Schrag, *Not Fit for Our Society: Immigration and Nativism in America* (Berkeley: University of California Press, 2010).
11. Erens, *Jew in American Cinema*, 33–51; Miriam Hansen, *Babel and Babylon: Spectatorship in American Silent Film* (Cambridge, MA: Harvard University Press, 1991), 68–89.
12. Mari Kathleen Fielder, "Fatal Attraction: Irish-Jewish Romance in Early Film and Drama," *Éire-Ireland* no. 3 (Fall 1985): 8–9.

13  *For the Love of Mike and Rosie* (1916; Culver City, CA: L-Ko Kompany); "For the Love of Mike and Rosie," *Moving Picture World*, April 1, 1916, 108; Lester Friedman, *The Jewish Image of American Life: 70 Years of Hollywood's Vision of Jewish Characters and Themes* (Secaucus, NJ: Citadel, 1987), 27.
14  Charles E. Davenport, dir., *Broken Barriers* aka *Khavah* (1919; New York: Zion Films); J. Hoberman, *Bridge of Light: Yiddish Film between Two Worlds* (Philadelphia: Temple University Press, 1995), 53–54.
15  Oliver D. Bailey, dir., *The Melting Pot* (1915; Bayonne, NJ: Centaur Film Company Studios); Moss, *Why Harry Met Sally*, 87–89.
16  Riv-Ellen Prell, *Fighting to Become Americans: Assimilation and the Trouble between Jewish Women and Jewish Men* (Boston: Beacon, 1999), 72.
17  Tino Balio, *The American Film Industry* (Madison: University of Wisconsin Press, 1985), 103–6; Kia Afra, *The Hollywood Trust: Trade Associations and the Rise of the Studio System* (Lanham, MD: Rowman & Littlefield, 2016), 1–32.
18  M. Alison Kibler, *Censoring Racial Prejudice: Irish, Jewish, and African American Struggles over Race and Representation, 1890–1930* (Chapel Hill: University of North Carolina Press, 2015), 149–51.
19  Sheri Chinen Biesen, *Film Censorship: Regulating America's Screen* (New York: Wallflower, 2018), 7–10; Laura Wittern-Keller, *Freedom of the Screen: Legal Challenges to State Film Censorship, 1915–1981* (Lexington: University of Kentucky Press, 2008), 40–47.
20  Daniels, *Guarding*, 27–58; Schrag, *Not Fit for Our Society*, 139–62.
21  Cripps, "Movie Jew," 199.
22  Steven Alan Carr, *Hollywood and Anti-Semitism: A Cultural History up to World War II* (New York: Cambridge University Press, 2001), 60–93.
23  Afra, *Hollywood Trust*, 159–202; Brownlow, *Behind the Mask*, 13–25.
24  As its title indicates, the Kibler book cited in n. 18 examines the lobbying of Irish, Jewish, and African American organizations for the establishment of censorship bodies to monitor the film and stage portrayals of their respective nationality, religion, or race.
25  Larry May, *The Big Tomorrow: Hollywood and the Politics of the American Way* (Chicago: University of Chicago Press, 2000), 57–65.
26  Prell, *Fighting to Become Americans*, 67–69.
27  Barrett, *Irish Way*, 180–81; Hasia R. Diner, *Erin's Daughters in America: Irish Immigrant Women in the Nineteenth Century* (Baltimore: Johns Hopkins University Press, 1983), 50–51.
28  Stephen Birmingham, *Real Lace: America's Irish Rich* (Guilford, CT: Lyons, 2016); Jay P. Dolan, *The Irish Americans: A History* (New York: Bloomsbury, 2008), 209–28.
29  Cormac Ó Gráda, *Jewish Ireland in the Age of Joyce: A Socioeconomic History* (Princeton, NJ: Princeton University Press, 2006), 179–92; R. M. Douglas, "'Not So Different after All': Irish and Continental European Antisemitism in Comparative Perspective," in *Irish Questions and Jewish Questions: Crossovers in Culture*,

ed. Aidan Beatty and Dan O'Brien (Syracuse, NY: Syracuse University Press, 2019), 31–46.
30. George Bornstein, *The Colors of Zion: Blacks, Jews, and Irish from 1845 to 1945* (Cambridge, MA: Harvard University Press, 2011), 24–204; Mathew Frye Jacobson, *Special Sorrows: The Diasporic Imagination of Irish, Jewish, and Polish Immigrants in the United States* (Berkeley: University of California Press, 2002).
31. Barrett, *Irish Way*, 22–25; Rudolf Glanz, *Jews and Irish: Historic Group Relations and Immigration* (New York: Alexander Kohut Memorial Foundation, 1966); Gil Ribak, *Gentile New York: The Images of Non-Jews among Jewish Immigrants* (New Brunswick, NJ: Rutgers University Press, 2012), 64–70.
32. Timothy Meagher, "Abie's Irish Enemy: Irish and Jews, Social and Political Realities and Media Representations," in *Screening Irish-America: Representing Irish-America in Film and Television*, ed. Ruth Barton (Dublin: Irish Academic Press, 2009), 48–49.
33. Ted Merwin, "The Performance of Jewish Ethnicity in Anne Nichols' 'Abie's Irish Rose,'" *Journal of American Ethnic History*, no. 20 (Winter 2001): 3–4.
34. Anne Nichols, *Abie's Irish Rose* (New York: Harper & Brothers, 1927).
35. Victor Fleming, dir., *Abie's Irish Rose* (1928; Los Angeles: Paramount Famous Lasky Corporation).
36. Brownlow, *Behind the Mask*, 422.
37. Erens, *Jew in American Cinema*, 106–7.
38. The film is not extant; the Library of Congress houses only several reels from it. Scripts of it survive; see "Abie's Irish Rose—Script," November 7, 1927, Folder A-15, 71489571, Paramount Pictures Scripts, Margaret Herrick Library-American Academy of Motion Picture Arts and Sciences, Beverly Hills, CA.
39. Fielder, "Fatal Attraction," 14.
40. Phillips Smalley and Lois Weber, dirs., *The Jew's Christmas* (1913; New York: Rex Motion Picture Company); Erens, *Jew in American Cinema*, 46–47.
41. Brownlow, *Behind the Mask*, 423.
42. Merwin, "Performance," 26.
43. Prell, *Fighting to Become Americans*, 10–14.
44. Prell, 76–77.
45. Fielder, "Fatal Attraction," 13.
46. Moss, *Why Harry Met Sally*, 69–80.
47. Christopher Shannon, *Bowery to Broadway: The American Irish in Classic Hollywood Cinema* (Scranton, PA: University of Scranton Press, 2010), 65–85; Marshall Neilan, dir., *Amarilly of Clothes-Line Alley* (1918; Los Angeles: Mary Pickford Company); Alfred E. Green, dir., *Irene* (1926; Burbank: First National Pictures).
48. Harry A. Pollard, dir., *The Cohens and the Kellys* (1926; Universal City, CA: Universal Pictures).
49. "Nichols v. Universal Pictures Corporation," *Casetext: Smarter Legal Research*, casetext.com, November 10, 1930.
50. Edward Sloman, dir., *His People* (1925; Universal City, CA: Universal Pictures).

51 Lawrence Baron, "Empty Hearts and Full Wallets: Poverty and Wealth in American Jewish Film, 1921–1932," in *Wealth and Poverty in the Jewish Tradition*, ed. Leonard J. Greenspoon (West Lafayette, IN: Purdue University Press, 2015), 232–37; Lester D. Friedman, "A Forgotten Masterpiece: Edward Sloman's *His People*," in *Hollywood's Chosen People: The Jewish Experience in American Cinema*, ed. Daniel Bernardi, Murry Pomerance, and Hava Tirosh-Samuelson (Detroit: Wayne State University Press, 2013), 19–34.
52 Alan Crosland, dir., *The Jazz Singer* (1927; Burbank, CA: Warner Brothers).
53 Samson Raphaelson, "The Day of Atonement," in *The Jazz Singer*, ed. Robert L. Carringer (Madison: University of Wisconsin Press, 1979), 152–54.
54 Raphaelson, 156–62.
55 Thomas Doherty, *Pre-Code Hollywood: Sex, Immorality, and Insurrection in American Cinema 1930–1934* (New York: Columbia University Press, 1999), 1–67; May, *Big Tomorrow*, 55–99.
56 King Vidor, dir., *Street Scene* (1931; Culver City, CA: Feature Productions).
57 Anthony F. R. Palmieri, *Elmer Rice: A Playwright's Vision of America* (Rutherford, NJ: Farleigh Dickinson University Press, 1980).
58 Erens, *Jew in American Cinema*, 142–43.
59 Thomas Doherty, *Hollywood's Censor: Joseph I. Breen and the Production Code Administration* (New York: Columbia University Press, 2007), 199–214.
60 Norman Taurog, dir., *Boy's Town* (1938; Culver City, CA: Metro-Goldwyn-Mayer). The character of Dave Morris is based on the Jewish activist and philanthropist Henry Monsky. See Hugh Reilly and Kevin Warneke, *Father Flanagan of Boy's Town: A Man of Vision* (Boys Town, NE: Boys Town Press, 2008), 45–46.
61 "The Issues: Why We Fight: What Kind of Peace Will Follow Victory," *Government Information Manual for the Motion Picture Industry* (Washington, DC: Office of War Information, 1942), 12, bl-libg-doghill.ads.iu.edu/gpd-web/historical/gimmpi/gimmpii.pdf.
62 William Keighley, dir., *The Fighting 69th* (1940; Burbank, CA: Warner Brothers); Shannon, *Bowery to Broadway*, 124–34.
63 Erens, *Jew in American Cinema*, 170–73. For an overview of how these platoon movies advanced the message of a pluralistic America, see Richard Slotkin, "Unit Pride: Ethnic Platoons and the Myths of National Unity," *American Literary History* 13, no. 3 (Autumn 2001): 478–87.
64 Vincent Sherman, dir., *Mr. Skeffington* (1944; Burbank, CA: Warner Brothers Studio); Delmer Daves, dir., *Pride of the Marines* (1945; Burbank, CA: Warner Brothers Studio); Elia Kazan, dir., *Gentleman's Agreement* (1947; Los Angeles: Twentieth Century Fox); Edward Dmytryk, dir., *Crossfire* (1947; Los Angeles: RKO Studios); Lawrence Baron, "Picturing Prejudice in Hollywood's First Films about Anti-Semitism," in *American Judaism in Popular Culture*, ed. Leonard J. Greenspoon and Ronald A. Simkims (Omaha, NE: Creighton University Press, 2006), 23–30; Joseph M. Curran, *Hibernian Green on the Silver Screen: The Irish and American Movies* (New York: Greenwood, 1989), 104–5.

65 A. Edward Sutherland, dir., *Abie's Irish Rose* (1946; Los Angeles: Bing Crosby Productions).
66 Pete Harrison quoted in Doherty, *Hollywood's Censor*, 219.
67 Alfred E. Green, dir., *The Jolson Story* (1946; Culver City, CA: Columbia Pictures); Michael Freedland, *Jolson: The Story of Al Jolson* (Portland, OR: Vallentine Mitchell, 2007), 136–63.
68 Erens, *Jew in American Cinema*, 173–77.
69 Norman Taurog, dir., *Big City* (1948; Culver City, CA: Metro-Goldwyn-Mayer).
70 Michael Curtiz, dir., *The Jazz Singer* (1952; Burbank, CA: Warner Brothers Studio); Vincent Brook, "The Four Jazz Singers: Mapping the Jewish Assimilation Narrative," *Journal of Modern Jewish Studies* 10, no. 3 (2011): 401–20.
71 Biesen, *Film Censorship*, 94–119; Wittern-Keller, *Freedom*, 107–48, 247–72.
72 Douglas Gomery, *The Hollywood Studio System: A History* (London: British Film Institute, 2006); Neil Gabler, *An Empire of Their Own: How the Jews Invented Hollywood* (New York: Anchor Books, 1988).
73 Mathew Frye Jacobson, *Roots Too: White Ethnic Revival in Post-Civil Rights America* (Cambridge, MA: Harvard University Press, 2008), 11–71.
74 Jacobson, 72–129.
75 Elaine May, dir., *The Heartbreak Kid* (1972; Los Angeles: Palomar Pictures International); Sydney Pollack, dir., *The Way We Were* (1973; Culver City, CA: Columbia Pictures and Rastar Productions); Woody Allen, dir., *Annie Hall* (1977; New York: Jack Rollins-Charles H. Joffe Productions); Moss, *Why Harry Met Sally*, 157–69.
76 Friedman, *Jewish Image*, 200–201; Joseph Greenblum, "Does Hollywood Still Glorify Jewish Intermarriage? The Case of *The Jazz Singer*," *American Jewish History* 83, no. 4 (December 1995): 447.
77 Lester Friedman, *Hollywood's Image of the Jew* (New York: Frederick Ungar, 1982), 253–56; Barbara Quart, *Women Directors: The Emergence of a New Cinema* (New York: Praeger, 1988), 42–43.
78 Bernard Slade, creator, *Bridget Loves Bernie*, performed by David Baxter and Meredith Baxter (1972–1973; Culver City, CA: Douglas S. Cramer Company, Thornhill Productions, and Screen Gems: CBS, television).
79 David Zurawik, *The Jews of PrimeTime* (Waltham, MA: Brandeis University Press, 2003), 78–96.
80 *Bridget Loves Bernie*, Season 1, Episode 14, "Tis' the Season," directed by Bernard Slade (December 16, 1972, CBS); Jonathan Pearl and Judith Pearl, *The Chosen Image: Television's Portrayal of Jewish Themes and Characters* (Jefferson, NC: McFarland, 1999), 209–10.
81 Vincent Brook, *Something Ain't Kosher Here: The Rise of the "Jewish Sitcom"* (New Brunswick, NJ: Rutgers University Press, 2003), 48–52; Zurawik, *Jews of PrimeTime*, 93–99.
82 Bernie Orenstein and Saul Turteltaub, creators, *Chicken Soup* (1989; Los Angeles: Carsey-Werner Company: ABC, television).

83 Brook, *Something*, 68–73.
84 Gary David Goldberg, dir., *Brooklyn Bridge* (1991–93; Los Angeles: Paramount Studios, television); Brook, *Something*, 84–89.
85 Skadi Loist, "The Film Festival Circuit: Networks, Hierarchies, Circulation," in *Film Festivals: History, Theory, Method, Practice*, ed. Marijke de Valck, Brendan Kredell, and Skadi Loist (New York: Routledge, 2016), 57–58.
86 Charles R. Acland, *Screen Traffic: Movies, Multiplexes, and Global Culture* (Durham, NC: Duke University Press, 2003); Barbara Klinger, *Beyond the Multiplex: Cinema, New Technologies, and the Home* (Berkeley: University of California Press, 2006); Derek Johnson, *From Networks to Netflix: A Guide to Changing Channels* (New York: Routledge, 2018); Dina Iordanova, *Digital Disruption: Cinema Moves On-line* (Edinburgh: St. Andrew Press, 2012).
87 Michael M. J. Fischer, "Film as Ethnography and Cultural Critique in the Late Twentieth Century," in *Shared Differences: Multicultural Media and Practical Pedagogy*, ed. Diane Carlson and Lester D. Friedman (Urbana: University of Illinois Press, 1995), 29–51; Vivian Sobchack, "Postmodern Modes of Ethnicity," in *Unspeakable Images: Ethnicity and the American Cinema*, ed. Lester D. Friedman (Urbana: University of Illinois Press, 1991), 329–50; Nathan Abrams, *The New Jew in Film: Exploring Jewishness and Judaism in Contemporary Cinema* (New Brunswick, NJ: Rutgers University Press, 2012); Maria Pramaggiore, *Irish and African American Cinema: Identifying Others and Performing Identity 1980–2000* (Albany: State University Press of New York, 2007).
88 "Jewish Americans in 2020," Pew Research Center, https://www.pewresearch.org/religion/2021/05/11/marriage-families-and-children, May 11, 2021.
89 Richard D. Alba and Ronald C. Kessler, "Patterns of Interethnic Marriage among American Catholics," *Social Forces* 57, no. 4 (June 1979): 1137–38.
90 Edward Burns, dir., *The Brothers McMullen* (1995; New York: Good Machine).
91 Edward Burns and Todd Gold, *Independent Ed: Inside a Career of Big Dreams, Little Movies, and the Twelve Best Days of My Life* (New York: Avery, 2015), 23–50.
92 Alexandra Schein, *The Charm of Unchanging Identities: Negotiating Gender, Class, and Ethnicity in Irish-American-Themed Film and Television* (Leipzig: Leipziger Universitätsverlag, 2016), 197–98.
93 Edward Burns, dir., *The Fitzgerald Family Christmas* (2012; Santa Monica, CA: Marlboro Road Gang Productions).
94 Burns and Gold, *Independent Ed*, 211–22.
95 Edward Norton, dir., *Keeping the Faith* (2000; Burbank, CA, and Los Angeles: Touchstone Pictures, Spyglass Entertainment, and Triple Threat Talent).
96 Lawrence Baron, "*Keeping the Faith*: A Multicultural *Jazz Singer*," in *The Modern Jewish Experience in World Cinema*, ed. Lawrence Baron (Waltham, MA: Brandeis University Press, 2011), 412–14.
97 Schein, *Charm of Unchanging Identities*, 194–97; Lawrence J. McCaffrey, "*Going My Way* and Irish American Catholicism: Myth and Reality," in *Screening Irish-America: Representing Irish-America in Film and Television*, ed. Ruth Barton

(Dublin: Irish Academic Press, 2009), 180–90; Shannon, *Bowery to Broadway*, 101–52.
98   Baron, "*Keeping the Faith*," 415–16.
99   "Audio Commentary," *Keeping the Faith*, directed by Edward Norton (2000; Burbank: Buena Vista Entertainment, DVD).
100  Baron, "*Keeping the Faith*," 416–18.
101  Stephen Silver, "'Keeping the Faith' is 20 years old. Rabbis and priests look back at the interfaith romcom that was ahead of its time," *Jewish Telegraphic Agency*, www.jta.org, April 29, 2020.
102  Schein, *Charm of Unchanging Identities*, 195–97.
103  Michael Showalter, *The Big Sick* (2017; Los Angeles: Apatow Productions and New York: Film Nation).
104  Bandar Albuliwi and Ghazi Albuliwi, dirs., *Peace after Marriage* (2013; Los Angeles: Falafel Entertainment and Paris: Good Lap Production).

## 8. PLAYING THE NATION

1  *IAA*, July 2, 1904.
2  Shlomo Shulsinger-Shear Yashuv, "The Story of Massad," in *Kovetz Massad: Pirkey Sifrut ve'Hagut*, vol. 1, ed. Meir Havazelet (New York: Mahanot Massad, 1978), 274. [Hebrew]
3  Hebrew Union of America, "Instructions for Couselors" (Massad Camps, 1950), F51/37, CZA.
4  Benedict Anderson, *Imagined Communities* (London: Verso Books, 2016), 19
5  Rogers Brubaker, Mara Loveman, and Peter Stamatov, "Ethnicity as Cognition," *Theory and Society* 33, no. 1 (February 2004): 32; see also Rogers Brubaker and Frederick Cooper, "Beyond 'Identity,'" *Theory and Society* 29, no. 1 (February 2000): 1–47; Rogers Brubaker, "The 'Diaspora' Diaspora," *Ethnic and Racial Studies* 28, no. 1 (2005): 1–19.
6  See also Fredrik Barth, *Ethnic Groups and Boundaries: The Social Organization of Culture Difference* (Prospect Heights, IL: Waveland, 1998).
7  See Howard Lune, *Transnational Nationalism and Collective Identity among the American Irish* (Philadelphia: Temple University Press, 2020).
8  Matthew Frye Jacobson, *Special Sorrows: The Diasporic Imagination of Irish, Polish, and Jewish Immigrants in the United States* (Cambridge, MA: Harvard University Press, 1995).
9  Marcus De Búrca, *The GAA: A History* (Dublin: Gill & Macmillan, 1980); William F. Mandle, *The Gaelic Athletic Association & Irish Nationalist Politics, 1884–1924* (Dublin: Helm, 1987).
10 For outsiders, Gaelic football looks like a combination of soccer and rugby. Teams of fifteen players compete on a rectangular grass pitch that is slightly larger than a soccer field. Players advance the ball with a combination of carrying, *soloing* (dropping and toe-kicking the ball back into hands), kicking, and passing. The goalposts in Gaelic football have an H shape. Players can earn a point by passing

the ball above the crossbar, like in American football, or score a goal, which is worth three points, by passing the ball under the crossbar. Hurling teams play on the same field but the shape of the ball and the technique for advancing it are different. In hurling, players advance a ball that is slightly larger than a baseball, called a *sliotar*, using an ax-shaped wooden stick called a hurley or *camán*. Handling the hurley demands extraordinary skill and therefore the game is less popular than Gaelic football.

11  Paul Darby, "Gaelic Games, Ethnic Identity and Irish Nationalism in New York City c.1880–1917 [1]," *Sport in Society* 10, no. 3 (2007): 347–67; Paul Darby, *Gaelic Games, Nationalism and the Irish Diaspora in the United States* (Dublin: University College Dublin Press, 2009); Hanna Fergus, "The Gaelic Athletic Association," in *The Encyclopedia of the Irish in America*, ed. Michael Glazier (Notre Dame, IN: Notre Dame University Press, 1999), 352–56.

12  John T. Ridge, "Irish County Societies in New York, 1880–1914," in *The New York Irish*, ed. Ronald H. Bayor and Timothy Meagher (Baltimore: Johns Hopkins University Press, 1997), 275–300.

13  *IAA*, February 18, 1905. Almost all of the data on Irish sports comes from the sports section of the *Irish-American Advocate (IAA)*, a New York weekly published between 1893 and 1911 (stored in the special collection of the New York Public Library).

14  Miriam Nyhan, "Comparing Irish Immigrant and County Associations in New York and London: A Cross Cultural Analysis of Migrant Experiences and Associational Behavior circa 1945–1965" (PhD diss., European University Institute, 2008).

15  Ridge, "Irish County Societies," 276.

16  Nyhan, "Comparing," 114–17.

17  *IAA*, June 9, 1906.

18  *IAA*, May 11, 1907.

19  Pilkington, *IAA*, July 3, 1909.

20  *IAA*, November 28, 1908. During 1905 a successful picnic could yield $650, a sum that no date holders could forfeit. Bad weather or an unattractive match, however, could result in a loss. *IAA*, September 9, 1905.

21  *IAA*, May 1, 1909.

22  *IAA*, August 3, 1907; see also Liam O'Shea, *IAA*, June 12, 1909. In Ireland, a white flag denotes a point and a green flag denotes a goal. In Celtic Park, apparently, the American flag signaled a point and the Irish flag marked a goal.

23  Liam O'Shea, *IAA*, September 10, 1910; see also Sheridan, *IAA*, February 19, 1910; April 13, 1907.

24  *IAA*, October 20, 1906; June 6, 1909.

25  *IAA*, June 6, 1908.

26  *IAA*, June 13, 1908.

27  "GAA Notes," *IAA*, August 8, 1908; Pilkington, *IAA*, November 6, 1909; February 26, 1910.

28  *IAA*, June 22, 1912.
29  *IAA*, November 30, 1912.
30  *IAA*, May 27, 1911.
31  *IAA*, April 3, 1915.
32  *IAA*, December 17, 1910.
33  *IAA*, September 18, 1915; see also June 12, 1915.
34  *IAA*, March 18, 1916.
35  Liam O'Shea, *IAA*, April 24, 1915; Touchline (pen name), *IAA*, August 7, 1915.
36  O'Shea, *IAA*, June 12, 1912.
37  *IAA*, April 22, 1916.
38  *IAA*, October 14, 1916.
39  Sara Brady, "Irish Sport and Culture at New York's Gaelic Park" (PhD diss., New York University, 2005); Darby, *Gaelic Games*; Fergus, "Gaelic Athletic Association"; Ridge, "Irish County Societies."
40  John T. Ridge, "Irish County Associations in New York and the Easter Rising," in *Ireland's Allies: America and the 1916 Easter Rising*, ed. Miriam Nyhan Grey (Dublin: University College Dublin Press, 2016), 257–67.
41  Hebrew Union of America, "Instructions for Counselors," Massad Camps, 1950, F51/37, CZA. [Hebrew]
42  Meir Moskowitz, "From the Treasure House of My Memories," in *Kovetz Massad*, ed. Shlomo Shulsinger-Shear Yashuv and Rivka Shulsinger-Shear Yashuv (Jerusalem: Irgun Mahanot Masad be-Yisrael, 1989), 302–7. [Hebrew]
43  Hebrew Union of America, "Instructions for Couselors."
44  Yaakov Kabakov, "The Cultural Program of Massad," in *Kovetz Massad: Pirkey Sifrut ve'Hagut*, vol. 1, ed. Meir Havazelet (New York: Mahanot Massad, 1978), 277–80. [Hebrew]
45  Shlomo Shulsinger-Shear Yashuv and Rivka Shulsinger-Shear Yashuv, eds., *Kovetz Massad: A Pictorial History*, vol. 3 (Jerusalem: Irgun Mahanot Masad be-Yisrael, 1991). [Hebrew]
46  A central tenet of Zionism, "productivization" meant that in Israel Jews would not be concentrated in white-collar jobs but would work with their hands, ideally in agriculture.
47  Ira Spodeck, "Massad—I Shall Never Forget You," in *Kovetz Massad*, ed. Shlomo Shulsinger-Shear Yashuv and Rivka Shulsinger-Shear Yashuv (Jerusalem: Irgun Mahanot Masad be-Yisrael, 1989), 292. [Hebrew]
48  Shulsinger-Shear Yashuv, "Story of Massad," 62.
49  Shulsinger-Shear Yashuv, 266.
50  Meir Moskowitz, "The 'Machon'—Aims and Objectives," in *Kovetz Massad: Pirkey Sifrut ve'Hagut*, vol. 1, ed. Meir Havazelet (New York: Mahanot Massad, 1978), 281–88. [Hebrew]
51  Ira Spodeck, "Summer Camp as an Educational Experience: The History of Camp Massad" (master's thesis, Yeshiva University, 1974).

52  Rivka Shulsinger-Shear Yashuv, "The Israeli Emissaries in Jewish American Camps," in *Kovetz Massad: Pirkey Sifrut ve'Hagut*, vol. 1, ed. Meir Havazelet (New York: Mahanot Massad, 1978), 291.
53  Hillel Halkin, "Massad: A Personal Memoir," in *Kovetz Massad: Mahanaut Ivrit*, vol. 2, ed. Shlomo Shulsinger-Shear Yashuv (Jerusalem: Irgun Mahanot Masad be-Yisrael: Igud Bogrei Masad be-Artsot ha-Berit, 1989), 274–75.
54  Shulsinger-Shear Yashuv, "Israeli Emissaries," 295.
55  Shulsinger-Shear Yashuv, 296.
56  On Hebrew in Jewish summer camps, see Sarah Bunin Benor, Jonathan Krasner, and Sharon Avni, *Hebrew Infusion: Language and Community at American Jewish Summer Camps* (New Brunswick, NJ: Rutgers University Press, 2020).
57  Spodeck, "Summer Camp," 97.
58  Anderson, *Imagined Communities*, 19.
59  Lune, *Transnational Nationalism*, 5.
60  Brubaker, Loveman, and Stamatov, "Ethnicity."
61  Georg Simmel, *Conflict and the Web of Group Affiliations* (New York: Free Press, 1964).
62  Clifford Geertz, *The Interpretation of Cultures: Selected Essays* (New York: Basic Books, 1973).
63  Steve Hoffman, "How to Punch Someone and Stay Friends: An Inductive Theory of Simulation," *Sociological Theory* 24, no. 2 (June 2006): 170–93.
64  Anderson, *Imagined Communities*, 19.
65  Barth, *Ethnic Groups*.

## 9. THE IRISH, THE JEWS, AND WILSON'S "SELF-DETERMINATION"

1  William Orpen, *A Peace Conference at the Quai d'Orsay* (1919), Imperial War Museums, London, Art.IWM ART 2855, www.iwm.org.uk/collections/item/object/20779, accessed October 13, 2018.
2  Erez Manela, *The Wilsonian Moment: Self-Determination and the International Origins of Anticolonial Nationalism* (Oxford: Oxford University Press, 2007). In 1914 George Bernard Shaw predicted that the end of the war would require "a world conference with the President of the United States in the chair." Shaw to Irish American journalist Mary Boyle O'Reilly, October 1, 1914, quoted in Thomas H. Dickinson, "Bernard Shaw and Woodrow Wilson," *Virginia Quarterly Review* 7, no. 1 (January 1931): 13. See also Ed Mulhall, "'Common Sense' and the War: George Bernard Shaw in 1914," *Century Ireland*, www.rte.ie/centuryireland, accessed November 21, 2018.
3  *Address of the President of the United States, Delivered at a Joint Session of the Two Houses of Congress, February 11, 1918* (Washington, DC: Government Printing Office, 1918), 7.
4  Justin McCarthy, *The Population of Palestine: Population History and Statistics of the Late Ottoman Period and the Mandate* (New York: Columbia University Press,

1990), 30; Hasia R. Diner, "A Century of Jewish Politics 1820–1920," in *The Jews of the United States 1654–2000*, ed. Hasia R. Diner (Berkeley: University of California Press, 2006), 181; Gudrun Krämer, *A History of Palestine: From the Ottoman Conquest to the Founding of the State of Israel* (Princeton, NJ: Princeton University Press, 2008), 104.

5   Judah Bernstein, "'The Two Finest Nations in the World': American Zionists and Irish Nationalism, 1897–1922," *Journal of American Ethnic History* 36, no. 3 (Spring 2017): 6, 11, 16; Mark A. Raider, *The Emergence of American Zionism* (New York: New York University Press, 1998), 26; Ronald Sanders, *The High Walls of Jerusalem: A History of the Balfour Declaration and the Birth of the British Mandate for Palestine* (New York: Holt, Rinehart & Winston, 1983), 323–24.

6   Frank E. Manuel, *The Realities of American-Palestine Relations* (Washington, DC: Public Affairs Press, 1949), 3; Diner, "Century of Jewish Politics," 164, 176.

7   Diner, "Century of Jewish Politics," 17.

8   D. G. Boyce, "'That party politics should divide our tents': Nationalism, Unionism and the First World War," in *Ireland and the Great War: "A War to Unite Us All"?*, ed. Adrian Gregory and Senia Pašeta (Manchester: Manchester University Press, 2002), 192.

9   Michael Doorley, "Judge Cohalan and American Involvement in the Easter Rising," in *Ireland's Allies: America and the 1916 Easter Rising*, ed. Miriam Nyhan Grey (Dublin: University College Dublin Press, 2016), 158.

10  "In its broader aspects, the Jewish rights movement was anti-Russian in orientation, as most American Jews believed that a Russian victory would be a deathblow for the emancipation of Jewish communities." Joseph Rappaport, "Jewish Immigrants and World War I: A Study of American Yiddish Press Reactions" (PhD dissertation, Columbia University, 1951), 75, 120.

11  Rappaport, 104–5; Sanders, *High Walls of Jerusalem*, 320–22.

12  Sanders, *High Walls of Jerusalem*, 331.

13  Wilson D. Miscamble, "Catholics and American Foreign Policy from McKinley to McCarthy: A Historiographical Survey," *Diplomatic History* 4, no. 3 (July 1980): 227; William M. Leary, Jr., "Woodrow Wilson, Irish Americans, and the Election of 1916," *Journal of American History* 54, no. 1 (June 1967): 57, 62.

14  John French, "Irish-American Identity, Memory, and Americanism during the Eras of the Civil War and First World War" (PhD diss., Marquette University, 2012), 247–53.

15  *New York Times*, September 30, 1916, as quoted in Leary, "Woodrow Wilson," 64; Joseph P. Tumulty, *Woodrow Wilson as I Know Him* (New York: Doubleday, Page, 1921), 214.

16  Rappaport, "Jewish Immigrants," 77.

17  Diner, "Century of Jewish Politics," 158; Bruce Allen Murphy, *The Brandeis/Frankfurter Connection: The Secret Political Activities of Two Supreme Court Justices* (New York: Anchor Books, 1983), 27–28.

18  Sir Cecil Spring-Rice to Lord Robert Cecil, April 13, 1917, quoted in Charles Callan Tansill, *America and the Fight for Irish Freedom: 1866–1922* (New York: Devin-Adair, 1957), 226. The fact that President Wilson's paternal grandparents emigrated from Ulster was irrelevant in the context of World War I high politics and power. Wilson was only vaguely aware of his Irish connection; see Erick Montgomery, "Reconsidering the Immigration Story of President Woodrow Wilson's Paternal Grandparents," *National Genealogical Society Quarterly*, no. 102 (March 2014): 25–44. For two varying accounts of Wilson referencing his ancestry in January 1918, see Leah Levenson and Jerry H. Natterstad, *Hanna Sheehy-Skeffington: Irish Feminist* (Syracuse, NY: Syracuse University Press, 1986), 106–7, and Tansill, *America*, 240–41.
19  "Rising Up in the House—Part II: The House Debates the 'Irish Question,'" *History, Art & Archives, United States House of Representatives* (July 13, 2016), https://history.house.gov, accessed October 20, 2018.
20  "Rising Up in the House—Part II."
21  Tansill, *America*, 221, 227, n. 31.
22  Tumulty said Wilson had a "keen interest" in the Irish question but this is at odds with Irish nationalists like Tansill, *America*, 227–28, 230, 273, and Sean Cronin, *The McGarrity Papers* (Tralee, Co. Kerry, Ireland: Anvil Books, 1972), 69. Wilson asked for Tumulty's resignation in 1916 then changed his mind: "Tumulty remained for Wilson's second term, but under what must have been humiliating circumstances, for the President neither sought nor accepted to any considerable extent Tumulty's advice." Donald McDonald, review of *Joe Tumulty and the Wilson Era*, by John Morton Blum, *Commonweal* 54, no. 19 (August 17, 1951): 460.
23  "Wilson Will Pay Honor to Emmet," *Washington Post*, June 27, 1917.
24  "Honor Irish Patriot," *Washington Post*, June 29, 1917.
25  Tansill, *America*, 234–40; Michael Doorley, *Justice Daniel Cohalan, 1865–1946: American Patriot and Irish-American Nationalist* (Cork, Ireland: Cork University Press, 2019), 100–4; Doorley, "Judge Cohalan,"160.
26  Levenson and Natterstad, *Hanna Sheehy-Skeffington*, 106–7; Doorley, *Justice Daniel Cohalan*, 106.
27  Mick Mulcrone, "'Those miserable little hounds': World War I Postal Censorship of the Irish World," *Journalism History* 20, No. 1 (Spring 1994): 15–24. The *Irish World* was later suspended again "for hoping that Palestine never became a Jewish Kingdom," according to French, "Irish-American Identity," 254.
28  Wiseman to Drummond and Balfour, February 4, 1918, quoted in W. B. Fowler, *British-American Relations 1917–1918: The Role of Sir William Wiseman*, supplementary volume to the papers of Woodrow Wilson (Princeton, NJ: Princeton University Press, 1969), 262.
29  This was a strategy also favored by other American Jews seeking "redress from the American government" in the wake of human rights violations in Eastern Europe from the 1890s to the 1920s. Diner, "Century of Jewish Politics," 182–83.

30  Sanders, *High Walls of Jerusalem*, 322; Melvin I. Urofsky, *American Zionism from Herzl to the Holocaust* (Lincoln: University of Nebraska Press, 1995), 186; Joseph Rappaport, *Hands across the Sea: Jewish Immigrants and World War I* (Lanham, MD: Hamilton Books, 2005), 62, 68–69.
31  Rappaport, *Hands across the Sea*, 131–32.
32  Raider, *Emergence of American Zionism*, 27–28; Manuel, *Realities*, 163.
33  Hisham H. Ahmed, "From the Balfour Declaration to World War II: The U.S. Stand on Palestinian Self-Determination," *Arab Studies Quarterly* 12, no. 1/2 (Winter/Spring 1990): 15–16.
34  This was a "facile" promise according to Manuel, *Realities*, 165; Urofsky, *American Zionism*, 228.
35  Manuel, *Realities*, 165.
36  Manuel, 171; Selig Adler, "The Palestine Question in the Wilson Era," *Jewish Social Studies* 10, no. 4 (October 1948): 303–34.
37  Rappaport, *Hands across the Sea*, 149.
38  *Address of the President of the United States Delivered at a Joint Session of the Two Houses of Congress, February 11, 1918*, Office of the Historian, Papers Relating to the Foreign Relations of the United States, 1918, Supplement 1, The World War, Volume I, https://history.state.gov, accessed December 26, 2019.
39  Thomas J. Knock, "Wilsonian Concepts and International Realities at the End of the War," in *The Treaty of Versailles: A Reassessment after 75 Years*, ed. Manfred F. Boemeke, Gerald D. Feldman, and Elisabeth Gläser (Cambridge: Cambridge University Press, 1998), 112–13.
40  John T. McTague, Jr., "Zionist-British Negotiations over the Draft Mandate for Palestine, 1920," *Jewish Social Studies* 42, no. 3/4 (Summer-Autumn 1980): 288–89.
41  Knock, "Wilsonian Concepts," 115. One historian argues that Wilson actually meant "the civil right of self-*government*," not "the national right of self-*determination*," and that any other interpretation was a "relic of the mid-twentieth century, when the vogue was to blame Wilson and his counterparts in Paris for the toxic nationalism that ignited World War II." Trygve Throntveit, "The Fable of the Fourteen Points: Woodrow Wilson and National Self-Determination," *Diplomatic History* 35, 3 (June 2011): 446–47.
42  Robert Lansing, *The Peace Negotiations, a Personal Narrative* (Boston: Houghton Mifflin, 1921), 97–98.
43  Bernstein, "'Two Finest Nations,'" 19–20.
44  William Orpen, *A Peace Conference at the Quai d'Orsay* (1919), Imperial War Museums, London, Art.IWM ART 2855, www.iwm.org.uk/collections/item/object/20779, accessed October 13, 2018. Seated, from left to right: Vittorio Emanuele Orlando (Italy), Robert Lansing (USA), Woodrow Wilson (USA), Georges Clemenceau (France), David Lloyd George (Great Britain), Bonar Law (Great Britain), Arthur Balfour (Great Britain). Standing behind, from left to right: Paul Hymans (Belgium), Eleftherios Venizelos (Greece), Emir Feisal (Syria), William Massey (New Zealand), Jan Smuts (South Africa), Edward House (USA), Louis

Botha (South Africa), Saionji Kinmochi (Japan), Billy Hughes (Australia), Robert Borden (Canada), George Nicoll Barnes (Great Britain), Ignace Paderewski (Poland).
45 Catherine B. Shannon, *Arthur J. Balfour and Ireland, 1874–1922* (Washington, DC: Catholic University of America Press, 1988), 213.
46 Shannon, 1–81; Sanders, *High Walls of Jerusalem*, 114; Andrew Hillier, review of *Balfour's World: Aristocracy and Political Culture at the Fin de Siècle*, by Nancy W. Ellenberger, *Reviews in History*, www.history.ac.uk/reviews/review/2026, accessed October 13, 2018.
47 James Quinn, "Balfour, Arthur James 1st Earl of Balfour," *Dictionary of Irish Biography*, ed. James McGuire and James Quinn (Cambridge: Cambridge University Press, 2009), https://dib.cambridge.org, accessed October 13, 2018.
48 Quinn, "Balfour." In June 1916 Balfour, uncharacteristically and only then very briefly, suggested that the British consider an Irish Home Rule settlement as a "wartime expedience," but this idea was abandoned altogether when unionists in Ulster argued that it was nothing short of "a concession to [the Easter] rebellion." Shannon, *Arthur J. Balfour*, 223.
49 Mayir Vereté, "The Balfour Declaration and Its Makers," *Middle Eastern Studies* 6, no. 1 (January 1970): 55.
50 Sanders, *High Walls of Jerusalem*, 121.
51 Fowler, *British-American Relations*, 18.
52 Lucien Wolf, although an anti-Zionist British Jew, wrote a key memorandum in December 1915 that first made this case forcibly. Sanders, *High Walls of Jerusalem*, 330; Cecil Bloom, "Sir Mark Sykes: British Diplomat and a Convert to Zionism," *Jewish Historical Studies*, no. 43 (2011): 142, 145–47; Cecil Bloom, "Aaron Aaronsohn: Forgotten Man of History?," *Jewish Historical Studies*, no. 40 (2005): 182.
53 Sanders, *High Walls of Jerusalem*, 330, 334–35, 542.
54 Tansill, *America*, 230.
55 Memorandum, March 27, 1917, reproduced in chapter 22, "The Balfour Mission to the United States," Burton Hendrick, *The Life and Letters of Walter H. Page* (Garden City, NY: Doubleday, Page, 1923), 251.
56 Fowler, *British-American Relations*, 292. Such specificity came through Wiseman's informants, unofficial British envoys like Shane Leslie who was cultivating President Wilson's innermost circle to block any movement on the "Irish question." Tansill, *America*, 241–42. Leslie was a "Home Rule" Irish nationalist based in the United States at this time; his goal was to "neutralise Irish opposition to the entry of America into the war" and "to stem the defection of the Irish Americans" toward support for an independent Irish Republic. Charles Lysaght, "Leslie, John Randolph ('Shane')," *Dictionary of Irish Biography*, ed. James McGuire and James Quinn (Cambridge: Cambridge University Press, 2009), https://dib.cambridge.org, accessed October 13, 2018.
57 Tansill, *America*, 226–28.
58 Sanders, *High Walls of Jerusalem*, 537–39.

59 Richard Spence, "Englishmen in New York: The SIS American Station, 1915–21," *Intelligence and National Security* 19, no. 3 (2004): 513; Fowler, *British-American Relations*, 93–95.

60 Fowler, *British-American Relations*, 93. See also Charles E. Neu, *Colonel House: A Biography of Woodrow Wilson's Silent Partner* (Oxford: Oxford University Press, 2014) and Godfrey Hodgson, *Woodrow Wilson's Right Hand: The Life of Colonel Edward M. House* (New Haven, CT: Yale University Press, 2008).

61 "MS 466, Edward Mandell House Papers, Series II, Diaries, Volume 6: House Diaries," 77, Yale University Library, http://digital.library.yale.edu/cdm/ref/collection/1004_6/id/5010, accessed November 24, 2018.

62 "MS 466, Edward Mandell House Papers, Series II, Diaries, Volume 6: House Diaries," 80, Yale University Library, http://digital.library.yale.edu/cdm/ref/collection/1004_6/id/5010, accessed November 24, 2018.

63 Although Wiseman reported that the Wilsons had arrived "quite unexpectedly, having only decided upon the trip the day before," House had known about it since mid-July, had arranged for the loan of a nearby cottage for the president, and had had the Secret Service up to assess security in Magnolia. "MS 466, Edward Mandell House Papers, Series II, Diaries, Volume 6: House Diaries," 201, 203, Yale University Library, http://digital.library.yale.edu/cdm/ref/collection/1004_6/id/5010, accessed November 24, 2018; Fowler, *British-American Relations*, 281.

64 "He thought Tumulty [Wilson's secretary] was the only one he had come in contact with who was [trustworthy]. It is curious he should pick him as an exception to the rule. Dudley Malone and some others have brought him to this frame of mind and he does the Irish an injustice." "MS 466, Edward Mandell House Papers, Series II, Diaries, Volume 6: House Diaries," 208, Yale University Library, http://digital.library.yale.edu/cdm/ref/collection/1004_6/id/5010, accessed November 24, 2018. Colonel House refers to the activist Irish American lawyer Dudley Field Malone, once an ardent Wilson supporter who had broken with him the previous summer "in a dramatic protest of the administration's failure to endorse women's suffrage and its arrest of militant suffragists picketing in Washington." David Brundage, "The Easter Rising and New York's Anticolonial Nationalists," in *Ireland's Allies: America and the 1916 Easter Rising*, ed. Miriam Nyhan Grey (Dublin: University College Dublin Press, 2016), 357.

65 Wiseman to Arthur C. Murray, August 30, 1918, reprinted in Fowler, *British-American Relations*, 280–82.

66 As Frank Manuel wrote in 1949, "The problem remains whether the President makes foreign policy every time he utters a sentence about it." Manuel, *Realities*, 176; Rappaport, *Hands across the Sea*, 151–52.

67 Adler, "Palestine Question," 314.

68 Tansill, *America*, 241.

69 Tansill, 246–47.

70 Bernadette Whelan, "American Propaganda and Ireland during World War One: The Work of the Committee on Public Information," *Irish Studies Review* 25, no. 2 (2017): 144, 150–54; J. C. Walsh, "Ireland at the Peace Conference," *Studies: An Irish Quarterly Review* 8, no. 30 (June 1919): 180; Elmer E. Cornwell Jr., "Wilson, Creel, and the Presidency," *Public Opinion Quarterly* 23, no. 2 (Summer 1959): 197–98.

71 Whelan, "American Propaganda," 153. These were louder voices than those minority anti-British Irish in America who were easily targeted and silenced under the Espionage Act, such as Judge Cohalan and John Devoy, publisher of the *Gaelic American*.

72 Whelan, "American Propaganda," 158; Doorley, *Justice Daniel Cohalan*, 112–13. See also United States Congress, House Committee on Foreign Affairs, *The Irish Question: Hearings Before the Committee On Foreign Affairs, House of Representatives, Sixty-fifth Congress—third Session On H. J. Res. 357, Requesting the Commissioners Plenipotentiary of the United States of America to the International Peace Conference to Present to the Said Conference the Right of Ireland to Freedom, Independence, And Self-determination. December 12, 1918* (Washington, DC: Government Printing Office, 1919).

73 John Devoy to Dr. Patrick McCartan, April 21, 1919, Box 4, Folder 4, Daniel F. Cohalan Papers, American Irish Historical Society, New York, New York.

74 Lawrence R. Gelfand, "The American Mission to Negotiate Peace: An Historian Looks Back," in *The Treaty of Versailles: A Reassessment after 75 Years*, ed. Manfred F. Boemeke, Gerald D. Feldman, and Elisabeth Gläser (Cambridge: Cambridge University Press, 1998), 257.

75 "Sir William Wiseman Dies at 77; British Diplomat Was Financier; Head of Intelligence in U.S. in World War I—Partner of Kuhn, Loeb & Co. Here [sic] Wartime Liaison Man Had Impaired Eyesight in Bankers' Group," *New York Times*, June 18, 1962, 25; "Sir William Wiseman, 77; Wilson's 'Mystery Man,'" *Newsday*, June 18, 1962, 1; "World War I's Mystery Man in U.S. Is Dead: Wiseman, a Briton, Held Wilson's Ear," *Chicago Daily Tribune*, June 18, 1962, B8.

76 Three delegates were named by the third Irish Race Convention, held in Philadelphia in March 1919: Frank Walsh, Edward F. Dunne, and Michael J. Ryan. Doorley notes that Wilson told the US State Department not to issue a passport to Judge Cohalan if he was chosen as a delegate. Doorley, *Justice Daniel Cohalan*, 120, 247, n. 44.

77 David Brundage, *Irish Nationalists in America: The Politics of Exile, 1798–1998* (Oxford: Oxford University Press, 2016), 155. This is covered in more detail by Francis M. Carroll, "The American Commission on Irish Independence and the Paris Peace Conference of 1919," *Irish Studies in International Affairs* 2, no. 1 (1985): 103–18.

78 Doorley, *Justice Daniel Cohalan*, 117.

79 Carole Fink, "Louis Marshall: An American Jewish Diplomat in Paris, 1919," *American Jewish History* 94, no. 1/2 (March–June 2008): 30–31; Oleg Budnitskiĭ,

"Battling Balfour: White Diplomacy, the Russian Orthodox Church, and the Problem of the Establishment of the Jewish State in Palestine," in Oleg Budnitskiĭ, *Russian Jews between the Reds and the Whites, 1917–1920*, trans. Timothy J. Portice (Philadelphia: University of Pennsylvania Press, 2012), 339, 344–46.

80  Adler, "Palestine Question," 321

81  Carole Fink, "The Minorities Question at the Paris Peace Conference: The Polish Minority Treaty, June 28, 1919," in *The Treaty of Versailles: A Reassessment after 75 Years*, ed. Manfred F. Boemeke, Gerald D. Feldman, and Elisabeth Gläser (Cambridge: Cambridge University Press, 1998), 257.

82  Manuel, *Realities*, 233–34; Mark Levene, "Nationalism and Its Alternatives in the International Arena: The Jewish Question at Paris, 1919," *Journal of Contemporary History* 28, no. 3 (July 1993): 512; Fink, "Minorities Question," 254.

83  William Orpen, *Signing the Peace Treaty in the Hall of Mirrors* (1919), Imperial War Museums, London, Art.IWM ART 2856, www.iwm.org.uk/collections/item/object/20780, accessed October 13, 2018.

84  Ali A. Allawi, *Faisal I of Iraq* (New Haven, CT: Yale University Press, 2014), 222–23. The British eventually made Faisal King of Iraq in 1921.

85  Statement of Frank P. Walsh, August 30, 1919, United States Congress, Senate, Committee on Foreign Relations, *Treaty of Peace With Germany: Hearings Before the Committee On Foreign Relations, United States Senate, Sixty-sixth Congress, First Session On the Treaty of Peace With Germany, Signed At Versailles On June 28, 1919, And Submitted to the Senate On July 10, 1919, by the President of the United States* (Washington, DC: Government Printing Office, 1919), 840, 847.

86  George Creel, *Ireland's Fight for Freedom: Setting Forth the High Lights of Irish History* (New York: Harper & Brothers, 1919), xi–xii, 199.

87  William Orpen, "Ch. XIV The Peace Conference," in Sir William Orpen, *An Onlooker in France 1917–1919* (London: Williams & Norgate, 1921), 100. According to Gelfand, "American Mission," 189, 195–96: "At least thirty American diaries, most unpublished . . . lie extant in libraries and archives across the United States [in addition to letters from the hundreds of members of the American Commission]. . . . Toward the end of May 1919, [Adolf] Berle stated in a letter . . . 'The general feeling in the delegation is that they have been duped. They resent keenly the manner in which the peace has been framed; the secrecy, the autocratic methods of the Big Four, the refusal to listen to criticism; the contemptuous flouting of the will of the people.'"

## 10. A TRADITION OF ACCEPTANCE

1  On tensions between Jews and the Irish in the 1920s and 1930s, see Ronald Bayor, *Neighbors in Conflict: The Irish, Germans, Jews, and Italians of New York City, 1929–1941* (Baltimore: Johns Hopkins University Press, 1978).

2  Although St. John's University has admitted, from its very start, students of varying ethnicities, during much of its 150-year history it possessed a discernible Irish American tenor. Certainly that is true of its academic leadership.

For example, from its inception in 1870 at least thirteen of the seventeen presidents of the school had Irish surnames. Year by year, most of its other administrators and many of its faculty were of similar descent. For instance, in 1929 the five administrators pictured in the student yearbook were named Cloonan, Reilly, Walsh, Ryan, and O'Grady. That same year a Father Corrigan, speaking at a student pep rally, suggested tongue in cheek, but indicatively, that "the genealogy of the Indians"—the mascot was a "Redman" since the athletes wore red uniforms—could be "trac[ed] back to the Irish." It is not possible to exactly determine what proportion of the student body, year by year, was Irish. Still, a look at the names of the members of the graduating classes of the school of liberal arts from 1929 to 1931, the years of the ascendancy of the "Wonder Five," shows that 67 of 169 graduates seem to have been Irish. The second-largest cohort seems to have been Italian. In all cases ethnicity was determined by surnames. The school does not have student-body records or surveys that indicate ethnicity or religion. For yearbook information, see *The Vincentian* (1929–31), published by the College of Liberal Arts and Sciences of St. John's College.

3   Identifying students and student athletes as Jews is a difficult challenge and has its limitations because only rarely were students identified by their religion or ethnicity in the school's literature of the time. In many cases I have designated individuals as Jews primarily through their last names, with the understanding that sometimes a German or Eastern European first- or second-generation American Christian might carry a "Jewish" surname. Often first names—which could suggest religion or ethnicity—were omitted from accounts. Of course, the Wonder Five's "Jewishness" was noted in many contemporary reports in the general and Jewish press and in all historical treatments of that era's teams.

4   Early in St. John's history, a newspaper report noted that it was a school open to students who were not Catholics. But the report does not specify whether non-Catholics included Jews. See "St. John's College," *Brooklyn Daily Eagle*, August 28, 1873. The question of admitting Jews and Protestants was discussed in 1906 or 1907 by leaders of the college governing board; it was determined that Protestants were acceptable and Jews were not. (See Minutes of the Domestic Council, May 16, 1906 or 1907 [most likely 1907], 13T.1, Box 6, St. John's University Domestic Council Minutes 1879–1945, Board of Trustees, 1874–1932, St. John's Diocesan Seminary, 1899–1927 Correspondence, Ducournau Archives. I am grateful to Professor Susie Pak for alerting me to these sources.) However, it is impossible to determine to what extent that exclusion was enforced in the school's early years. Clearly Jews were noted on campus in the 1920s in the college yearbook; regrettably the yearbook is not extant from before 1918.

5   For tuition charges as of 1926–27, see the *Annual Catalog of St. John's College, September–June 1927–28* 6, no. 2 (hereafter *Catalog*). For an example of the lists of scholarships, see *Catalog, 1926–27*: 72–75.

6   On the religious goals of the school, see *Catalog*, 16–17, 1927–28.

7 *Catalog, 1926-27*, 26. The wording of that exemption remained in effect until the 1936-37 catalog where the wording was changed slightly to a vague statement about the obligations incumbent on Catholic men. See, for example, *Catalog, 1936-37*. That wording was not changed until the 1946-47 catalog, which discussed the "definitely Catholic atmosphere" at the school; the catalogs for 1944-45 omits any statement about religious atmospheres. See *Catalog, 1946-47*. In 1963 the wording was changed again and spoke of enabling men and by then women "to develop in learning and culture according to the philosophical and theological principles of the Roman Catholic Church." See *Catalog, 1963*, 7.
8 *Catalog, 1926-27*, 21. On the problems Jews had with placement in law firms, see Henry L. Feingold, *A Time for Searching: Entering the Mainstream, 1920-1945* (Baltimore: Johns Hopkins University Press, 1992), 140-41. I am again grateful to Professor Susie Pak for this item, providing me with the estimates of the percentage of Jewish students in St. John's Law School.
9 *The Vincentian* (1927): 4, 49; (1928): 35, 65.
10 "Fraternities," *St. John's Analyst*, March 1930, 6.
11 *The Vincentian* (1929): 30.
12 On the team's record and list of game results, see *The Vincentian* (1928-31).
13 The quote from an unnamed writer for the *Brooklyn Standard Union* is derived from Arieh Sclar, "'A Sport at Which Jews Excel': Jewish Basketball in American Society, 1900-1951" (PhD diss., Stony Brook University, 2008), 144, n. 10. For Parker's statement, see "Sports Slants," *Jewish Telegraphic Agency Daily Bulletin*, January 21, 1935.
14 Jim O'Connell, *100 Years of St. John's Basketball* (New York: St. John's Department of Athletics, n.d.), probably published in 2007. It should be noted that early statistics on the team are often inaccurate except for the names and scores that appear in *The Vincentian*. The numbers offered by sportsreference.com, for example, should be used with caution.
15 O'Connell, *100 Years*, 102. For the names of players and the teams St. John's played in 1918, see *The Vincentian* (1918): 118-22. The Helms Foundation was not really a foundation; it was the brainchild of Bill Schroeder and Paul Helms of Los Angeles who from 1901 chose what they believed was currently the best college basketball team. Still, their discussions engendered pride and discussions among honorees and fans. On its history, see "The Facts," www.bigbluehistory.net/bb/helms.html, accessed March 9, 2023.
16 *The Vincentian* (1919): 112-15.
17 *The Vincentian* (1925): 89-93.
18 On Freeman's appointment, see O'Connell, *100 Years*, 8. For the tributes to Collins and the lofty expectations for St. John's basketball, see "The Conquering Band," *The Vincentian* (1929): 127.
19 These statements about Jews were derived from Stanley Frank, *The Jew in Sports* (New York: Miles, 1936), 52-55. In his important analysis of this apologetic work,

Sclar notes that "Frank . . . used public perceptions of 'the Jew' in his construction of Jewish basketball." See Sclar, "'Sport at Which Jews Excel,'" 167.

20 This statement by newspaperman Paul Gallico in the 1930s is the most often quoted statement about anti-Semitic imagery connected to Jewish abilities in basketball. For a most recent assessment of Gallico, see Jeffrey Goldberg, "Scheming Oriental Hebrew Basketball Players," *The Atlantic*, January 22, 2010, online edition.

21 It is possible that Davidson, who played on the 1918 squad, was—based on his name—a Jew. On the composition of the 1926–27 squad, see *The Vincentian* (1927): 118.

22 The source for the Wubnig piece is an undated article entitled "The Brooklyn Times All-Scholastic Basketball Teams, 1926–27" that was saved in Allie Schuckman's scrapbook. I am grateful to Linda Schuckman Yori for providing me with this and other sources. On Gerson's road to St. John's, see Charley Rosen, *The Chosen Game: A Jewish Basketball History* (Lincoln: University of Nebraska Press, 2017), 36.

23 The answer to how Freeman was able to attract the Wonder Five to St. John's is shrouded in mystery. It is definitely known that in the 1920s, despite efforts among the incipient national collegiate governing group over athletics—the NCAA—and within many conferences to eliminate athletic scholarships, many schools continued that practice, which was very common at the turn of the twentieth century. Beyond what institutions did, many coaches went outside the lines with emoluments to potential players. It is entirely possible, but not verifiable, that an ambitious coach like Freeman may have followed suit. In 1929 a national report detailed many of these problematic practices. See Howard J. Savage, *American College Athletics* (New York: Carnegie Foundation, 1929). For the best analysis of the problem, see Ronald Austin Smith, *The Myth of the Amateur: A History of College Athletic Scholarships* (Austin: University of Texas Press, 2021). I thank Professor Smith for his assistance. As far as the individual recruitments are concerned, there is lack of agreement over what transpired from the limited sources available. The Kinsbrunner family's lore has it that Max attended Syracuse and "transferred" to St. John's; yet *The Vincentian* (1928) has him as a freshman at their school, seemingly right out of high school. Indeed, he played on the varsity as a freshman; back then schools played fast and loose with the freshman-ineligibility rule. The Schuckman family has their ancestor, Allie, playing at Adelphi before coming to St. John's; again, *The Vincentian* (1929) has him as having played on the school's freshman team. And significantly in 1925, Adelphi became an all-women's college and remained as such until the 1940s. As alluded to in n. 22, Rosen in *Chosen Game* has Gerson coming from the Brooklyn School of Pharmacy seemingly with some advanced credit. There is no extant information on the recruitment saga as it applies to Begovich or Posner. Finally, on the question of why the four Jews did not enroll at CCNY, it is possible that with the exception of Schuckman, who merited an academic scholarship, none of his teammates had the grades to be ad-

mitted to "Jewish Harvard." One of Schuckman's brothers preceded him at CCNY, complicating the saga of his decision-making. Another brother attended St John's. See interviews with Donna Kinsbruner, December 5, 2020, and Linda Schuckman Yori, November 30, 2020.

24 *The Vincentian* (1928): 108–10. There were other Jewish players on the 1927–28 squad, incumbents named Kleinman and Schulman and perhaps a fellow named "Red" Wolf.

25 "Jewish Sports Notes," *American Jewish World*, May 13, 1932, first noted in Sclar, "'Sport at Which Jews Excel,'" 143.

26 *The Vincentian* (1929): 126–31. On the possibility that Schuckman was better than Collins, see an undated article seemingly from 1929 in Schuckman's scrapbook, courtesy of Linda Schuckman Yori.

27 *The Vincentian* (1930): 138–42. Murray's tribute to the Wonder Five was in an undated article entitled "Mythical National College Court Champions: St. John's Quintet of 1929–30 Greatest in School History" in Allie Schuckman's scrapbook, again courtesy of Linda Schuckman Yori.

28 "15,000 See St. John's, Columbia and Manhattan Quintets," *New York Times*, January 20, 1931, 30. For Glanz's comment that appeared in the *B'nai B'rith Messenger*, see Peter Levine, *Ellis Island to Ebbets Field: Sport and the American Jewish Experience* (New York: Oxford University Press, 992), 77. On the rules changes attributed to the slowdown style of basketball, see Arieh Sclar, "From Wonder Five to CCNY, 1931–1934," jewishbasketball.wordpress.com, February 23, 2018.

29 "St. John's Defeats Manhattan, 30–16," *The Torch*, March 11, 1931, 1, 8.

30 "Redmen to Be Immortalized on Silver Screen," *The Torch*, March 11, 1931, 8; "Max Posnack,"*American Hebrew*, March 13, 1931, 438. I am grateful to Alexander Wildes for researching this item from the Anglo-Jewish press.

31 Arthur J. Daley, "Barred at N.Y.U. as Basketball Pros," *New York Times*, March 21, 1931, online edition. Four NYU players were also implicated in this scandal. See also Jack Farrel, "Manhattan's Ok—But Take Slant at This!" *New York Daily News*, March 24, 1931. Sclar, "Sport at Which Jews Excel," has the players "suspended" from the school; they were, in fact, suspended from playing sports, p. 140. For the sake of completeness, it should be noted that a search of the very incomplete registrar's records from the 1920s and 1930s suggests the unlikely scenario that the five players were not enrolled at the school during their tenure as players, notwithstanding all the sources that have them as the highest-of-profile students at St. John's. For example, it is noted that "Kinsbrunner entered in February 1931" and "Gerson left in September, 1930" at a time when newspaper sources within and without the institution portray them as student-athletes at the height of their storied careers on campus. Additionally, Kinsbrunner and Schuckman family lore has their ancestors graduating from St. John's. It also should be noted that Kinsbrunner's picture as a graduating senior appears in the 1931 *Vincentian*. My thanks go to St. John's archivist Alyse Henig for her assistance in searching for these records.

32 On the allegation that Shuckman played under an assumed name, see "Indians of Court Barred from Future Encounters," *The Torch*, April 1, 1931, 7. The following articles in the *Brooklyn Eagle* cover the story of professionalism at St. John's: "Gerson Denies Charge That He Played Pro," April 4, 1930; "Everything in the Name of College Sports, Lynch Satisfied," April 7, 1930. "Bars St. John's Five from Games Pending Quiz on Pro Charge," March 20, 1931; "St. John's Five under Probe," March 20, 1931; "St. John's Man Returned $3,000 to Throw Game," March 21, 1931; "Team Was Warned by A. D. Lynch," March 21, 1931; "St. John's Men Admit Charge," March 22, 1931. I am grateful to Clark Whitfield for sharing these important sources with me derived from his unpublished paper "St. John's University: The Wonder Five" (December 5, 2018), written for Professor Konrad Tuchscherer. I am also thankful to Professor Tuchscherer for his assistance in this project.

33 Twenty years later, the involvement of players with gamblers not in fixing games but in corrupting the point spread that was established by bookies to encourage betting in games between stronger and weaker teams—the basis for most illegal wagering—was the predicate for the great 1951 CCNY basketball scandal that led to the arrest of players involved and their dismissal from the school. See on this subject Matthew Goodman, *The City Game: Triumph, Scandal, and a Legendary Basketball Team* (New York: Ballantine Books, 2019).

34 "Cui Boni," *The Torch*, March 25, 1931, 2.

35 "Editorial," *St. John's Analyst*, April 31, 1931, 4. Similar sentiments were articulated by Herbert J. Haberle, "The Observation Tower," *The Torch*, March 25, 1931.

36 John E. Freeze, Jr., "$18,000 or $8," *The Torch*, March 25, 1931, 7.

37 Freeze, "Virtue Its Own Reward," *The Torch*, April 1, 1931, 6.

38 "Varsity Quintet Opposes Jewels," *The Torch*, November 25, 1931, 6; "Varsity Cage Practice Featured by Scrimmage," *The Torch*, November 11, 1933, 6; "Flashbacks," *The Torch*, October 15, 1932, 5; "Basketball Dribbles," *Jewish Telegraphic Agency*, March 12, 1934.

39 Douglas Stark, *When Basketball Was Jewish: Voices of Those Who Played the Game* (Lincoln: University of Nebraska Press, 2017), 151.

40 Frank Litsky, "Hy Gotkin, 81, Guard in 40s for St. John's N.I.T. Winner," *New York Times*, April 15, 2004, online edition; on Gotkin's early interest in St. John's, see Gus Alfieri, *Lapchick: The Life of a Legendary Player and Coach in the Glory Days of Basketball* (n.p.: All-American Sports Press, www.gusalfieri.com, 2016), 70–71; Frank Litsky, "Harry Boykoff, 78, St. John's Star in the 1940's, Dies," *New York Times*, April 15, 2001. See Levine, *Ellis Island*, 45, for an account of Zaslofsky at St. John's.

41 For the names of players on the 1931–32 squad, see "St. John's Cagers in Early Practice," *The Torch*, November 18, 1931, 6. For Freeman's statistics and those of subsequent coaches and teams, see "Traditions: St. John's Athletics," *We Are New York's Team*, https://redstormsports.com/sports/2018/6/12/trads-stjo-trads-html.aspx, accessed March 9, 2023.

42  Lapchick had a close personal relationship with Holman in addition to a sports connection. They were each other's best men at their respective weddings. See Richard Lapchick to Gurock, December 15, 2020, in Alfieri, *Lapchick*, 17–19, 152, 156. On Carl Fields, see an article on him at *Blacks at Princeton*, www.blacksatprinceton.com/eastward, accessed March 9, 2023.

43  On Lapchick as coach of the Knicks, see Alfieri, *Lapchick*, 132–46; Sam Goldaper, "Frank McGuire, 80, Basketball Coach, Dies," *New York Times*, October 12, 1994, B8; interview with Lenny Rosenbluth, December 16, 2020. On Harry Gotkin and Buck Freeman at North Carolina, see interview with Gus Alfieri, December 8, 2020, and interview with Mark Gotkin, December 17, 2020.

44  George Vecsey, "A Fallen Star of the City Game," *New York Times*, May 6, 2008, D3; interview with Lou Carnesecca, December 3, 2020; interview with Ronald Seiden, December 16, 2020.

45  "Best Catholic Colleges" *Time Magazine*, February 9, 1962, 53. On the past and present status of Jewish basketball players, see Jeffrey S. Gurock, "Boys from the City: New York's Jewish Basketball Stars," in *City Game: Basketball in New York*, ed. William C. Rhoden (New York: Rizzoli, 2020), 31–36.

ABOUT THE EDITORS

HASIA R. DINER is the Paul and Sylvia Steinberg Professor of American Jewish History at New York University, with joint appointment in the Department of History and the Skirball Department of Hebrew and Judaic Studies. She is also Director of the Goldstein-Goren Center for American Jewish History. She has built her scholarly career around the study of American Jewish history, American immigration and ethnic history, and the history of American women. She has written about the ways in which American Jews in the early twentieth century reacted to the issue of race and the suffering of African Americans, and the process by which American Jews came to invest deep meaning in New York's Lower East Side. She is the author of *We Remember with Reverence and Love: American Jews and the Myth of Silence after the Holocaust* (2009), winner of a National Jewish Book Award and the American Jewish Historical Society's Saul Viener Prize, and *Roads Taken: The Great Jewish Migration to the New World and the Peddlers Who Led the Way* (2015), a global history of Jewish peddling and Jewish migrations. She is a coeditor of *1929: Mapping the Jewish World* (2013), winner of a National Jewish Book Award for anthologies. A Guggenheim Fellow, Diner has also written about other immigrant groups and the contours of their migration and settlement, including a study of Irish immigrant women and of Irish, Italian, and Eastern European Jewish foodways.

MIRIAM NYHAN GREY has taught history at New York University's Glucksman Ireland House since 2009, where she has also served as Director of Graduate Studies, Associate Director, and NYU's Global Coordinator for Irish Studies. She is the founder of the Black, Brown and Green Voices Project, a documentation strategy and public humanities initiative that seeks to amplify diversity in the Irish diasporic experience. She sits on the board of the African American Irish Diaspora Network. She is the author of a monograph on Ford Motor

Company's only Irish plant and she is editor of *Ireland's Allies: America and the 1916 Easter Rising* (2016). She was the inaugural Associate Editor of the NYU Press Glucksman Irish Diaspora Series and is a coeditor of the *American Journal of Irish Studies*. In 2018, during Professor Diner's tenure as Interim Director of Glucksman Ireland House, Dr. Grey cocurated a series of public lectures on the Jewish and Irish experience in the United States.

ABOUT THE CONTRIBUTORS

LAWRENCE BARON is Professor Emeritus of Modern Jewish History at San Diego State University. He has authored/edited four books including *The Modern Jewish Experience in World Cinema* (Brandeis University Press, 2011) and has lectured on various topics related to Jewish cinema.

JAMES R. BARRETT is Professor Emeritus of History and African American Studies at the University of Illinois at Urbana-Champaign and a Scholar in Residence at the Newberry Library in Chicago. He is the author of *The Irish Way: Becoming American in the Multiethnic City* (Penguin Books, 2012) and *History from the Bottom Up and the Inside Out: Ethnicity, Race, and Identity in Working-Class History* (Duke University Press, 2017). With Jenny Barrett, he is working on *Chicago: A Peoples' History*.

MARION R. CASEY teaches at NYU where she is a Clinical Professor of Irish Studies, Glucksman Ireland House, and Affiliated Faculty, Department of History.

BRETT GARY's research takes a historical approach to media, culture, and politics. He is Associate Professor at NYU Steinhardt. His first book focused on the role of propaganda in American political life, and he is now completing a biography of the civil liberties lawyer Morris Ernst and his advocacy for James Joyce.

TERRY GOLWAY is a senior editor at POLITICO States, responsible for New York State political coverage out of Albany. He was a member of the *New York Times*'s editorial board and was city editor of the *New York Observer*. He is the author of several works dealing with Tammany Hall, the most powerful force in New York City politics.

JEFFREY S. GUROCK is the Libby M. Klaperman Professor of Jewish History at Yeshiva University. He is the author or editor of over twenty books and over one hundred scholarly articles and reviews. A leader among American Jewish historians, he served for twenty years as an editor of *American Jewish History*.

KEVIN KENNY is Professor of History, Glucksman Professor in Irish Studies, and Director of Glucksman Ireland House at NYU. He received his PhD from Columbia University in 1994, where his dissertation won the Bancroft Award. He is the author of seven books.

DAN LAINER-VOS's research examines the formation of national attachments among Irish Americans and Jewish Americans. He looks at concrete instances where national entrepreneurs try to mobilize diaspora groups in order to identify the mechanisms developed in the process of nation-building.

ROBERT W. SNYDER is Professor Emeritus of Journalism and American Studies at Rutgers University-Newark and Manhattan Borough Historian. He has written five books on the history of New York City.

HANNAH ZAVES-GREENE is an academic writer, editor, and researcher who is pursuing her PhD in Hebrew and Judaic Studies at NYU, focusing on American Jewish history and literature.

# INDEX

*Abie's Irish Rose* (Nichols), 123–26, 133–34, 139, 141–42
Abraham Lincoln Brigade, 73
Abramowitz, Bessie, 17
Abzug, Bella, 86
ACLU. *See* American Civil Liberties Union
Adams, Gerry, 87
Addams, Jane, 173
Adelphi, 188
Adler, Selig, 178
Ahearn, John, 60, 117
Aleichem, Sholem, 130
Aliens Act of 1905, 30
Allen, Claude, 188
Allen, Woody, 141
*All in the Family*, 142
*Amarilly of Clothes-Line Alley*, 135
American Bar Association, 75
American Birth Control League, 50, 52
American Civil Liberties Union (ACLU), 96; Ernst and, 222n27; on sexual expression, 222n30
American Commission to Negotiate Peace, 180
American Health Association, 50
*American Hebrew*, 27–28
Americanization, 120–21, 131
American Jewish Congress, 181
American Jewish Historical Society, 26
American Labor Party, 67, 76–77, 81
American League for a Free Palestine, 77, 78, 80
American Organization for Rehabilitation through Training, 75

American Student Zionist Federation, 185–86
Ancient Order of Hibernians, 121; O'Dwyer, P., in, 73–74
Anderson, Benedict, 165–66
Anderson, Margaret, 99
Anglo-Irish Treaty, 56, 182
*Annie Hall*, 141
anti-Catholicism, 31
Anti-Defamation League, 122
anti-Semitism, xv, 22, 69, 131; Irish immigrant opposition to, 25–26; PCA and, 138
Asquith, Herbert, 169
Atlas, Nicholas, 105, 106
Auchincloss, Gordon, 177, 178
Auerbach, Arnold "Red," 200
Auerbach, Jerold, 95–96
*Aufbau*, 80

Balfour, Arthur, 174–75, 176, 180, 245n48
Balfour Declaration, 173, 174, 178, 181
Baron, Lawrence, xv
Barrett, James, x, xiv
Barry, Leonora, 17
Barth, Frederick, 166
Batten, Mary, 221n21
Beach, Sylvia, 100
*Becky Gets a Husband*, 123–24, 127, 128
Bee, Clair, 198
Begin, Menachem, 79
Begovich, Marty, 192–93, 195, 197–98
Beilis, Mendel, 26
Beilis Affair, 26

259

Bellamy, Carol, 86
Bellevue Hospital, 34
Bergson, Peter, xiii, 77–78
Bergson Group, xiii
Bernstein, Judah, 168
Bernstien, Oscar, 72–73
*Big City*, 140
*The Big Sick*, 147–48
Bikel, Theodore, 85
Birmingham, Kevin, 99
birth control, 33, 43, 47–48; Catholicism on, 51–53; history of, 45; Sanger on, 44–46, 50–51; Wald on, 48–49
Birth Control and Research Clinic, 32
*Birth Control Review*, 53
Bisno, Abraham, 116
Black Americans, 3
B'nai B'rith lodges, 24
Bohola, 68–69
Boland, Harry, 56
Boston, 24–25
Boudin, Louis, 75
Boykoff, Harry, 198
Brahmin elites, 26
Brandeis, Louis, 97, 170, 176–77; and President Wilson, 172
Breen, Joseph, 137–38, 140
*Bridget Loves Bernie*, 141
Briscoe, Robert, 78–79
*Broken Barriers*, 130
Bronstein, Irwin, 71
*Brooklyn Daily Eagle*, 195
Brooklyn's Bridge, 143
*Brooklyn Times*, 190
*The Brothers McMullen*, 144
Broun, Heywood, 72
Brubaker, Rogers, 151
Burns, Edward, 144

Cahn, Emanuel, 60
capitalism, 165
Cardozo, Albert, 59, 72
Cardozo, Benjamin, 59

Carnesecca, Lou, 200–201
Caro, Robert, 64
Cary, William, 171
*Casanova's Homecoming* (Schnitzler), 99
Casey, Pat, 127
*Casti connubii* proclamation, 53
Catholic Charities Appeal, 49
Catholic Legion of Decency, 137
Catholics and Catholicism, xii, 3–4, 15, 25, 32; on birth control, 51–53; persecution of, 128; Sanger on, 43, 49–50, 51–53; at St. John's University, 249n4, 250n7; at Tammany Hall, 57–58
Celtic Park, 154
*The Censor Marches On* (Ernst & Lindey), 220n10
censorship, xiv, 46, 93; Ernst on, 96–97; film, 130–31; *Ulysses* and, 112–13
Cerf, Bennett, 93, 102, 104, 105, 223n45, 224n47, 225n68, 226n74
Chabon, Michael, 93
Chamberlain, Wilt, 200
Chesler, Ellen, 44
Chestnut, James, 188
Chicago Federation of Labor, 18
*Chicken Soup*, 143
children, Jewish immigrants as, 19–20
Chinese Exclusion Act, 11, 181
Chinese immigrants, 11
Christian Front, 73, 80
Christianity, 13
Christian Mobilizers, 73, 80
Church of Ireland, 14
citizenship, of Jewish immigrants, 23
Claessens, Gus, 61
Clan na Gael, 121, 172
Clinton, Bill, 87
Cohalan, Daniel F., 170
Cohen, Becky, 127
Cohen, Fania, 17
Cohen, Harry, 186
*The Cohens and the Kellys*, 135–36
Cold War, 77

Coleman, Samuel C., 104–5
Collins, Jim "Rip," 189, 191
Collins, Michael, 56
Columbia University, 20–21
Committee for the Relief of Ireland, 27–28
Committee on Public Information (CPI), 179
Comstock, Anthony, 90
Comstock Act, 43–44, 46, 47–49, 90, 92; First Amendment and, 223n33; legal challenges to, 223n33
*Conflict and the Web of Social Affiliation*, 164
*Contraception* (Stopes), 98, 105
Corrigan, Joseph E., 223n43
Coughlin, Charles, x, 73
Council of Catholic Women, 54
*Counsel for the Defense*, 81
Cowan, Philip, 27, 31
Cowley, Malcolm, 89
CPI. *See* Committee on Public Information
Creel, George, 179, 182
Cripps, Thomas, 130–31
Croker, Richard, 57
*Crossfire*, 139
cultural appropriation, xiv
cultural pluralism, 24, 31; of immigrants, xi
Curley, James Michael, 25
Cutting, Bronson, 225n62
Czarist Russia: Jewish people fleeing, 129–30

Daly, Charles P., 31; on Jewish immigrants, 27–28
Davitt, Michael, 28–31
Democratic National Committee, 65
Democratic National Convention, 170
Democratic Reform Movement, 82
Dennett, Mary Ware, 91–92, 98
diaspora, 6, 151; Irish, 168–73; Jewish, 62–63, 168–73; national culture in, 152–62; organization of identification, 163–66
Dinkins, David, 86
Dowling, Maurice, 149, 150, 152, 163
Dowling, Victor, 171
Dreiser, Theodore, 102
Drucker, Rebecca, 72–73
Dublin, 20–21
Dunne, Edward F., 247n76

Eastman, Max, 173
Edison, Thomas, 130
Egypt, 175
Eisenstein, Louis, 57, 60–61
Ellis Island, xi
Emmet, Robert, 171
entrepreneurs, 151–52
Erie, Steven, 62
Ernst, Morris Leopold, xiv, 89–91, 101, 102, 220n10; ACLU and, 222n27; on censorship, 96–97; fame of, 114; family background, 94–95, 221n21; legal commitments of, 222n31; in legal defense, 107–9; legal education of, 95–96; magazine profiles of, 92–93; Medalie and, 224n61; on rational sex laws, 91–92
Espionage Act, 172, 247n7
ethnic animosity, xv
ethnic diversity: Irish immigrant exposure to, 13–14; Jewish-Irish encounters and, 14–15; in vaudeville, 119–21
*Ethnic Groups and Boundaries*, 166
eugenics, Sanger on, 50–51

Fahy, Jack, 73
Faisal I, 181
*Family Limitation*, 47
Federation of American Zionists, 168
feminism, 47
Fielder, Mari Kathleen, 129, 134
Fields, Carl, 199
*The Fighting 69th*, 139

First Amendment, 97; Comstock Act and, 223n33
First American Birth Control Conference, 50
Fitzgerald, F. Scott, 103
Fitzgerald, John "Honey," 25
*The Fitzgerald Family Christmas*, 145
Flynn, Edward J., 65
Flynn, Joyce, 119
Ford, Henry, 131
Fordham, 70
*For the Love of Mike and Rosie*, 129
Freeman, James "Buck," 189–90, 193, 195–96, 198
free speech, 92–93
Free Synagogue, 39
Friends of Irish Freedom, 170–71

GAA. *See* Gaelic Athletic Association
GAANY. *See* Gaelic Athletic Association of New York
Gaelic Athletic Association (GAA), xv–xvi, 150–51, 153
Gaelic Athletic Association of New York (GAANY): two-tiered league system of, 156–58
Gaelic football, 153–54, 238n10
Gallagher, Thomas, 171
Gallico, Paul, 251n20
Garfinkel, Jack "Dutch," 198
garment industry, 15–19
Gary Plan, 20
Geertz, Clifford, 164
gender: Jewish-Irish encounters and, 16–17; nursing and, 34–36. *See also* Irish women; Jewish women; maternalism
Genoa, 15
*Gentleman's Agreement*, 139
George, Lloyd, 176, 181
Gerson, Jack "Rip," 187, 191, 195, 196, 198
Gillers, Stephen, 99, 223n42
Glantz, Harry, 193
Glanz, Rudolf, 10–11

Glucksman, Lew, ix, 5, 6
Glucksman, Loretta Brennan, ix, 5, 6
Glucksman Gallery, 5
Glucksman Ireland House, ix, xviii; anniversary of, 6–7; founding of, 4–5; influence of, 5–6
Glucksman Map Library, 5
Gold, Ben, 74, 78
Goldfinger, Rosie, 129
Goldfogle, Henry, 61
Golding, Louis, 107–8
Goldsmith, Milton, 60
Golway, Terry, xiii
Gotkin, Hy, 198
Gotkin, Java, 198
*Governing New York City* (Wallace & Sayre), 82–83
Government of Ireland Act, 182
Grace, William Russell, 58–59
Grant, Ulysses S., 58
Great Britain: Ireland and, 173–83; Palestine and, 173–83
Great Depression, 71–72, 73, 83, 118, 184, 197; Jewish-Irish romance after, 137–38
Great Famine, x, xii, 6, 32
Greenbaum, Eddie, 91, 96
Greenbaum, Laurence, 91, 96
Greenbaum, Wolff & Ernst, 219n3
Grunfield, Ernie, 201
Gurock, Jeffrey S., xvii
gynecology, 43–44

Habimah Theater, 85
Haganah, 78–79
Halkin, Hillel, 161
Hall, Radclyffe, 98
Hand, Augustus, 113
Hand, Learned, 113
Hankey, Maurice, 181
Harburger, Leopold, 60
Harnischfeger, Philip, 60
Havdalah, 159
Hayes, Patrick, 51–52

Hays, Arthur Garfield, 96
healthcare: Sanger on, 43–44; Wald on, 42–43
Heap, Jane, 99
*The Heartbreak Kid*, 141
Hecht, Ben, 77
Helms, Paul, 250n15
Helms Foundation, 250n15
Hemphill, Lowry, 84
Henry Street Settlement House, 39–40, 44
*Heymoolen* case, 100, 104–6
Hillman, Sidney, 18
Hillquit, Morris, 61
Hirsch, Emil, 122
historical connection, 173
Hitler-Stalin Pact of 1939, 76–77
Hoffman, Steve, 164–65
Holman, Nat, 191, 193, 199, 254n42
Holmes, Frank, 74
Holmes & Bernstien, 72
Holocaust, xiii, 138–39
Homer, 104
Home Rule, 169, 171, 176, 245n48, 245n56
homogenization, 165
Horowitz, David, 86
House, Edward M., 177
*House on Henry Street* (Wald), 36
Howe, Irving, 20
Huebsch, Ben, 101
Husing, Ted, 194
Hylan, John, 61, 63

IAA. See *Irish-American Advocate*
IAAC. See Irish American Athletic Club
ICAU. See Irish Counties Athletic Union
identity formation, xv
"If It Wasn't for the Irish and the Jews," 123
*Illustrated Hebrew Almanac for the Year 5641*, 25
*Imagined Communities* (Anderson), 165–66
immigrants: cultural pluralism of, xi; in London, 3; in New York City, 3; in the United States, 10; in urban history, 1–2. See also specific topics
Immigration Act of 1882, 27
Immigration Act of 1903, 30
intermarriage, 231n34; Jewish-Irish encounters and, xv, 123–26, 131–33
International Federation of Catholic Alumni, 54
International Fur and Leather Workers, 74
International Ladies' Garment Workers Union, 117
IRA. See Irish Republican Army
Ireland: Great Britain and, 173–83; Jewish immigrants in, 11, 115–16; Northern Ireland, 182; religion in, 13–14
*Ireland's Fight for Freedom* (Creel), 182
Irgun Zvai Leumi, 77, 78, 79, 80
*Irish-American Advocate* (IAA), 149, 154
Irish American Athletic Club (IAAC), 155
Irish Americans, ix–x; film depictions of, 134–35; identity of, 151; on self-determination, 179–80; at St. John's University, 248n2; at Tammany Hall, 56–57, 59, 116; Tin Pan Alley and, 122–23; in vaudeville, 120–21
Irish Counties Athletic Union (ICAU), 149; breakup of, 156; challenges of, 153–54; establishment of, 153; schedules, 153–54
Irish Free State, 183
Irish Friends of Liberty, 171
Irish gangs, 116
Irish immigrants, x–xi; anti-Semitism opposed by, 25–26; economic sectors of, 15–16; ethnic diversity exposure of, 13–14; first wave of, 3–4, 10, 132; group defense of, 9–10; history of, 3; in municipal politics, 22–25; nationalism of, 116, 179–80, 245n56
Irish-Jewish encounters. See Jewish-Irish encounters
Irish question, xvi, 167; Wilson, W., on, 176, 243n22

Irish Race Convention, 247n76
Irish Republican Army (IRA), 67, 69, 79, 85
Irish Studies, 4
Irish women, 125; employment of, 16–17; in public school teaching, 18–22
Isaacs, Rufus, 181
Israel, 158–59; O'Dwyer, P., on, 78–79
Italian immigrants, xiii, 11
"It's Tough When Izzy Rosenstein Loves Genevieve Malone," 123, 128–29

Jacobs, Morton M., 186
Javits, Jacob, xiv, 68, 84; O'Dwyer, P., and, 79
*The Jazz Singer*, 137, 140, 145
Jerome and Schwartz, 123–24
"Jew and Chinese in America" (Glanz), 10–11
*Jew and Irish* (Glanz), 10–11
*Jew and Italian* (Glanz), 10–11
*Jew and Mormon* (Glanz), 10–11
Jewish Americans: film depictions of, 134–35; identity of, 151; O'Dwyer and, 68–70; on self-determination, 181; in sports, 187–88, 189–91; at St. John's University, 185–88, 197–98, 201, 249n4; Tammany Hall and, ix–x, 24, 60; Tin Pan Alley and, 122–23; in vaudeville, 121–22
Jewish Conservative movement, 162
Jewish Defense League, 142
Jewish diaspora, 62–63; nationalism and, 168–73
Jewish immigrants, xi; children, 19–20; citizenship of, 23–24; from Czarist Russia, 129–30; Daly on, 27–28; economic sectors of, 15–16; first wave of, 10, 18, 132; German, 169–70; group defense of, 9–10; history of, 2; in Ireland, 11, 115–16; as permanent immigrants, 22–23; persecution of, 13

Jewish-Irish encounters, ix–xi, 2–3; characterizing, 115; ethnic diversity and, 14–15; films about, 130–31, 133–47; gender and, 16–17; history of, 9–10, 12–13; hostility in, 132; intermarriage and, xv, 123–26, 131–33; in New York City, 3, 116–17; at New York University, 4; romantic, and Great Depression, 137–38; in Tin Pan Alley, 123–24; in United States, 115–18; in vaudeville, 118–23
"Jewish Lion," 129
Jewish problem, xvi, 167; Zionism as answer to, 168–69
Jewish Publication Society of America, 29, 31
Jewish Reform Democrats, xiii
Jewish women: employment of, 16–17; in public school teaching, 22
*The Jew's Christmas*, 134
*The Jews of New York* (Daly), 27
John F. Ahearn Association, 57, 60
Johnson-Reed Act, 127
Johnstown, Pennsylvania, 205n8
Jollon, Teddy, 188
*The Jolson Story*, 139–40
Jones, Mother, 173
Joyce, James, xiv, 4–5, 89–90, 106, 109, 223n42
Judaism: Wald on, 32, 35, 37–39

Kabalat Shabbat, 159
Kaplan, Benjamin, 91
Kaufman, Herbert, 82–83
Keating, Sean, 79
*Keeping the Faith*, 145
Keith, Charlie, 73, 85
Kelly, "Honest John," xii
Kelly, Myra, 20–22
"The Kellys," 122–23
Kempton, Murray, 86
Kennedy, Patrick, 25
Kenny, Kevin, 6

Kinsbrunner, Max, 187, 190–91, 193, 195; family background of, 251n23, 252n31
Kishinev, 28–29, 30
Kleinfeld, Philip, 72
Klopfer, Donald, 102
Knesset, 85
Knights of Columbus, 54
Knights of Labor, 17
Know Nothings, 58
Koch, Ed, 85
Kohler, Max, 28
Kook, Hillel. *See* Bergson, Peter
Koreh, Ferenc, 86
Kovner, Sarah, 217n44
Kovner, Victor, 83–84, 217n44

labor unions, 71, 74
Labor Zionists, 79
La Guardia, Fiorello, xiii, 65, 73, 76, 117
Lainer-Vos, Dan, xv–xvi
Lansing, Robert, 17, 173
Lapchick, Joe, 199–200, 254n42
League of Nations, 181, 183
Leibowitz, Samuel, 75
Lennon, Patrick, 153–54
Leon, Paul, 106
Leo XIII, 62
Levy, Aaron, 57
Levy, Abraham, 125
Levy, Martin, 186
Levy, Newsome, 91
Lewis, John L., 73
Liberal Party, 77, 81, 84–85
Liebowitz, Harry M., 186
*Life*, 92–93
Lindey, Alexander, 89–91, 93–94, 101, 102, 105, 220n10, 224n47; at Greenbaum, Wolff & Ernst, 219n3; in legal defense, 107–9, 219n3
*Little Aliens* (Kelly, M.), 21
*Little Citizens* (Kelly, M.), 21
*The Little Review*, 99–101

Lomasney, Martin, 24–25
London: immigrants in, 3
Lower East Side, 116–17
Lune, Howard, 163–64

*Machanaim*, 160
*The Madonna of 115th Street* (Orsi), 15
Mahoney, Jeremiah, 25, 62
Mahoney, Jim, 188
Malone, Dudley, 246n64
Manela, Erez, 167
Manton, Thomas, 113
Manuel, Frank, 172
*Married Love* (Stopes), 98, 105
Marx, Karl, 75
*The Mary Tyler Moore Show*, 142
Mason, William, 171
Massad, xv–xvi, 158–60, 164–65
maternalism, 34, 38, 45–46
Maxwell Training School, 22
May, Elaine, 141
McCarran, Pat, 54
McCarthy, Eugene, 84
*McClure's*, 21
McDowell, Gerty, 100
McGuire, Frank, 200
McIntyre and Heath, 120
Meagher, Timothy, 132
Medalie, George M., 105; Ernst and, 224n61
*The Melting Pot* (Zangwill), 130
melting pot narrative, 130–31
Merwin, Ted, 134
Meyers, Joseph, 224n61
Mitchel, John Purroy, 63
Moloney, Mick, 119
Montagu, Edwin, 181
Morawska, Ewa, 205n8
Morgan, J. P., 225n68
Moses, Robert, xiii, 63, 64
Moskowitz, Belle, xiii, 63
Moss, Joshua Louis, 135
Mother's Bill of Rights, 53–54

Motion Picture Producers and Distributors of America (MPPDA), 131, 137
Moynihan, Daniel Patrick, 56, 86
MPPDA. *See* Motion Picture Producers and Distributors of America
Mullaney, Kate, 17
municipal politics: Irish immigrants in, 22–25
Murphy, Charles Francis, 56–57, 59, 65
Murphy, Rosemary, 125
"My Yiddisha Colleen," 123, 128–29

National Catholic Welfare Conference (NCWC), 49–50, 53–54
National Committee for Freedom from Censorship (NCFC), 222n27
National Council of Jewish Women, 40
National Invitational Tournament (NIT), 198
nationalism, 165–66; Irish diaspora and, 168–73; of Irish immigrants, 116, 179–80, 245n56; Jewish diaspora and, 168–73
National Lawyers Guild: O'Dwyer, P., at, 75–76, 81
National Maritime Union, 85–86
nativism, 130–31
NCFC. *See* National Committee for Freedom from Censorship
NCWC. *See* National Catholic Welfare Conference
Neiman, Herbie, 186
Nestor, Agnes, 17
New Deal, 50, 61, 73, 75, 81–82
Newman, John, 58
Newman, Pauline, 17
*The New Republic*, 103
New York City: ethnic factions in, 87–88; immigrants in, 3; Jewish-Irish encounters in, 3, 116–17; Lower East Side, 116–17
New York Court of Special Sessions, 100
New York Juvenile Asylum, Wald working at, 36–37

*New York Times*, 195
New York University, Jewish-Irish encounters at, 4
Nichols, Anne, 123–26, 133–34, 136
NIT. *See* National Invitational Tournament
Northern Ireland, 182
nursing: gender and, 34–36; Wald on, 34–35, 42–43. *See also* public health nursing

obscenity laws, xiv, 101–2; enforcement of, 91; *Ulysses* and, 90–91, 103
O'Dwyer, Bill, 70, 72, 73, 77, 79
O'Dwyer, Kathleen, 74
O'Dwyer, Paul, xiii, 67, 217n44; in Ancient Order of Hibernians, 73–74; education of, 70–71; funeral of, 88; on Israel, 78–79; Javits and, 79–80; Jewish people and, 68–70; at National Lawyers Guild, 75–76, 81; Sutton on, 87; Wagner and, 83–84
O'Dwyer & Bernstien, 74
*Odyssey* (Homer), 104
Office of War Information, 138–39
O'Leary, Jeremiah, 170
Oneg Shabbat, 159
*One Hundred Years of Birth Control*, 50
O'Reilly, John Boyle, 25–26, 31
O'Reilly, Leonora, 17
Orpen, William, 167, 174, 181
Orr, Louis, 61
Orsi, Robert, 15
O'Shea, Liam, 154, 156
O'Sullivan, Mary Kenny, 17
Ottoman Empire, 205n1

Page, Walter Hines, 176
Palestine, 170; Great Britain and, 173–83
Paris Peace Conference, xvi, 181–82
PCA. *See* Production Code Administration
*Peace after Marriage*, 148
Peace Conference, 172

*A Peace Conference at the Quai d'Orsay*, 167, 174
*The Pilot*, 25
Pilpel, Harriet, 91, 222n27
Pius XI, 53
*Plagiarism and Originality* (Lindey), 219n3
*Playboy of the Western World* (Synge), 121
Plunkitt, George Washington, 60, 117
Pocono Mountains, 159
pogroms, 29, 30
Poland, 13
Pollock, Sydney, 141
Popper, Marin, 81–82
Popular Front, 75, 77
Posnack, Mac, 195, 197, 198
Posner, Mac, 187, 191
Pound, Ezra, 223n43
poverty, 37
Prell, Riv-Ellen, 134–35
*Pride of the Marines*, 139
Production Code Administration (PCA), 137, 140; anti-Semitism and, 138
productivization, 240n46
Progressive Era, 38, 40–41
Proskauer, Joseph, xiii, 63, 64
Protestantism, 13–14, 15
public health nursing, xii, 41–42
public school teaching: Irish women in, 18–22; Jewish women in, 22

Quill, Mike, 73, 76
Quinn, John, 100, 223n42, 223n43

racial and ethnic stereotypes: in vaudeville, 120–22
Random House, 107, 112, 224n47
Rankin, Jeannette, 171
rational sex laws, 91–92
Redmen, 187–88, 193–94, 198, 201
Reed, John, 72, 173
religion: in Ireland, 13–14
reproductive rights, xii
*Rerum Novarum*, 62

Revisionist Zionists, 78, 79
Rice, Cecil Spring, 170
Robinson, Mary, 6
Roche, Jeffrey, 25–26, 31
Rodell, Fred, 93
Rogin, Michael, 120–21
Roman Catholicism, 13–14
Roosevelt, Eleanor, 65, 82
Roosevelt, Franklin Delano, 50, 54, 58, 65, 72, 75
Roosevelt, Theodore, 21
Root, Elihu, 58
Rosen, Julius, 60
Rosenbluth, Lenny, 200
Rupp, Adolph, 198
Russian Orthodox Church, 180
Ryan, John, 50
Ryan, Michael J., 247n76

Sacco and Vanzetti case, 71
Sachs, Sadie, 45
Samuel, Herbert, 181
Samuels, Margaret, 95
Sanger, Margaret, xii; arrest of, 47–49; on birth control, 44–46, 50–51; on Catholicism, 43, 49–50, 51–53; on eugenics, 50–51; on healthcare, 43–44; legacy of, 54–55; Wald and, 32–33, 54–55
Savarese, Joan O'Dwyer, 88
Sayre, Wallace, 82–83
Scally, Robert, 6
Schiff, Jacob, 39
Schindler, Solomon, 25
Schneiderman, Rose, xiii, 17, 61
Schnitzler, Arthur, 99
Schroeder, Bill, 250n15
Schuckman, Allie, 187, 190–91, 194–95, 198; family background of, 251n23, 252n31
Schulman, Harry, 190
Schur, Samuel, 91
Scottsboro Boys, 75
*Scribner's*, 92
Seiden, Alan, 200–201

self-determination, 167, 173, 244n42; Irish Americans on, 179–80; Jewish Americans on, 181; Wilson, W., on, 179–81, 183
*The Settlement of Jews in North America* (Daly), 27
*The Sex Side of Life* (Dennett), 98
Shakespeare & Co., 100
Shannon, William V., 117
Shaw, George Bernard, 241n2
Sherman Anti-Trust Act, 74, 75
Shulsinger, Rivka, 161, 163
Shulsinger, Shlomo, 15–159, 160
Sigma Omega Psi, 186
*The Signing of Peace in the Hall of Mirrors*, 181
Silverman, Matthew, 95
Simmel, Georg, 164
Singh, Ganga, 181
Sinn Fein, 69, 87, 178–79
Skirball Department of Hebrew and Judaic Studies, 6
Slavic immigrants, 205n8
Smith, Alfred E., xiii, 25, 61; advisers of, 62–64
Smith, Goldwin, 28
Social Gospel, 37
socialism, 45–46; Tammany Hall and, 60–62
Solomon, Charles, 61
Spanish Civil War, 73, 85
sports, 149; Jewish Americans in, 187–88, 189–91. *See also* Irish Counties Athletic Union
Stewart, H. C., 104
St. John's University, xiii, xvii, 70; Catholics at, 249n4, 250n7; Irish Americans at, 248n2; Jewish people at, 185–89, 197–98, 201, 249n4; student demographics at, 248n2
Stopes, Marie, 91–92, 98, 105
St. Patrick's Society, 27
*Street Scene* (Rice), 137–38
Suez Canal, 175

suffrage, 60
Sugar, Maurice, 75
Sullivan, Big Tim, 116–17
Sumner, John Saxton, 97, 98
Sutton, Percy, 85; on O'Dwyer, P., 87
Swann, Edward, 223n38
Sykes, Mark, 175, 180
Sykes-Picot Agreement, 175
Synge, John M., 121

Tammany Hall, xii, 20; Catholics at, 57–58; decline of, 117–18; Irish Americans at, 56–57, 59, 116; Jewish people and, ix–x, 24, 60; scandals around, 64–65; socialism and, 60–62
Tarbell, Ida, 72
Tariff Act, 104, 106
theater riots, 121
Thrasher, Frederic, 116
Tin Pan Alley, xv; Irish Americans and, 122–23; Jewish Americans and, 122–23; Jewish-Irish encounters in, 123–24
Tolk, Moritz, 60
Transport Workers Union, 73
Treaty of Versailles, 181–82
Triangle Shirtwaist Factory fire, xiii, 61
Trinity College, 5
Truman, Harry, 65
tuberculosis, 43
Tumulty, Joseph, 180
Turkey, 175

*Ulysses* (Joyce), xiv, 89; American publication of, 101–4; banning of, 90, 100; censorship and, 112–13; as classic, 105–7; customs' seizure, 104–5; early legal travails of, 99–101; expert testimonials, 101–4; formal elements of, 103; government case against, 109–10; illegal distribution of, 100–101; legal defense of, 91–92, 107–9; obscenity laws and, 90–91, 103; *Odyssey* and, 104; serial publication of, 99–100; Woolsey on, 110–13

United Irish League of America, 168
United Irish Societies, 121
United Mine Workers, 73
United States: growth of Zionism in, 172; immigrants in, 10; Jewish-Irish encounters in, 115–18
*United States v. One Book Called "Ulysses,"* 112–13
universalism, 43
University College Cork, 5
University of Limerick, 5
Untermeyer, Joseph, 79
Uprising of 1909, 17
urban history, 1–2
USGAA, 155
*US v. Harmon*, 223n33

Valera, Éamon de, 179
Vanderham, Paul, 90, 99
vaudeville, 124–25; ethnic diversity in, 119–21; Irish Americans in, 120–21; Jewish Americans in, 121–22; Jewish-Irish encounters in, 118–23; racial and ethnic stereotypes in, 120–22
vaudeville theater, xiv
Vice Society, 98
Vidor, King, 137–38
Vietnam War, 84
Viking Press, 101
Visiting Nurse Service, 39–40

Wagner, Robert, xiii, 61, 63, 82; O'Dwyer, P., and, 83–84
Wald, Lillian, xii, 52; on birth control, 48–49; childhood of, 33–34; employment at New York Juvenile Asylum, 36–37; financial backers of, 39–41; on healthcare, 42–43; on Judaism, 32, 35, 37–39; legacy of, 54–55; on nursing, 34–35, 42–43; Sanger and, 32–33, 54–55
Waldman, Louis, 61
Walsh, Frank, 180, 182, 247n76
*Wards of Liberty* (Kelly, M.), 21

*The Way We Were*, 141
Weber and Fields, 120
Weizmann, Chaim, 175
*The Well of Loneliness* (Hall), 98
Weschler, Nancy, 91
Wheeler, Leigh Ann, 96
Whelan, Bernadette, 179
Williams College, 95–96
Wilson, Edmund, 90, 103, 109
Wilson, Woodrow, xvi, 167, 170, 171–72, 243n18; Brandeis and, 172; on Irish question, 176, 243n22; on self-determination, 179–81, 183; on Zionism, 178–79
Wise, Stephen, 39, 172, 177
Wiseman, William, 175, 178, 180, 246n56
*Within the Pale* (Davitt), 28–29
Wolff, Herbert, 91, 96
*The Woman Rebel* (Sanger), 46–47
Women's Trade Union League, 17
Wonder Five, xvii, 187–88, 192–96, 199, 248n2, 251n23
Woolsey, John M., 105, 107, 109, 225n74, 226n74; on *Ulysses*, 110–13
Woolsey, Theodore Dwight, 59
Workingman's Democratic Republic Association, 27
*World of Our Fathers* (Howe), 20
World Zionist Organization, 172

Yeats, William Butler, 4–5
"Yiddisha Luck and Irisha Love," 128–29
Yiddish theater, 119
*Yisrael Bi'Zeir Anpin*, 158–59
yordim, 161

Zangwill, Israel, 130
Zaslofsky, Max, 198–99
Zaves-Greene, Hannah, xii
Zionism, xvi, 30, 65, 116, 161–62, 164; as answer to Jewish problem, 168–69; growth of, in United States, 172; productivization in, 240n46; summer camp, 158–62; Wilson, W., on, 178–79

www.ingramcontent.com/pod-product-compliance
Lightning Source LLC
Chambersburg PA
CBHW020358080526
44584CB00014B/1079